The Development of Future-Oriented Processes

THE JOHN D. AND CATHERINE T. MACARTHUR FOUNDATION
Series on Mental Health and Development

THE
DEVELOPMENT
OF FUTURE-
ORIENTED
PROCESSES

MARSHALL M. HAITH,

JANETTE B. BENSON,

RALPH J. ROBERTS JR.,

AND

BRUCE F. PENNINGTON

THE UNIVERSITY OF CHICAGO PRESS
Chicago and London

At the University of Denver, Marshall M. Haith is professor of
psychology and author of *Rules That Babies Look By: The
Organization of Newborn Visual Activity*; JANETTE B.
BENSON is associate professor of psychology; RALPH J.
ROBERTS JR. is associate professor of psychology; and
BRUCE F. PENNINGTON is professor of psychology and
author of *Diagnosing Learning Disorders: A
Neuropsychological Framework*.

The University of Chicago Press, Chicago 60637
The University of Chicago Press, Ltd., London
© 1994 by The University of Chicago
All rights reserved. Published 1994
Printed in the United States of America

03 02 01 00 99 98 97 96 95 94   1 2 3 4 5

ISBN: 0-226-31306-9 (cloth)

The University of Chicago Press gratefully acknowledges a
subvention from the John D. and Catherine T. MacArthur
Foundation in partial support of the costs of production of this
volume.

Library of Congress Cataloging-in-Publication Data

The Development of future-oriented processes / Marshall M.
    Haith . . . [et al.].
        p.   cm. — (The John D. and Catherine T.
    MacArthur Foundation series on mental health and
    development)
      Rev. proceedings of a conference of the MacArthur
    Foundation held in Apr. 1992.
      Includes bibliographical references and index.
      1. Expectation (Psychology)—Congresses.   2. Expectation
    (Psychology) in children—Congresses.   3. Expectation
    (Psychology)—Physiological aspects—Congresses.   I.
    Haith, Marshall M., 1937–   . II. John D. and Catherine T.
    MacArthur Foundation.   III. Series.
    BF323.E8D48   1994
    155.4'13—dc20   94-12390
                                                              CIP

Contents

Introduction

Marshall M. Haith, Janette B. Benson,
Ralph J. Roberts Jr., and Bruce F. Pennington

This book was conceived for a very specific purpose—to generate an interest in how people, especially children, come to organize their behavior around the future and how they develop an understanding of the future. Our motivation was to launch systematic inquiry into this fascinating domain by raising sensitivity to the general issues, asking some important questions, and presenting the most relevant methodologies and research programs available. At the same time, the papers in this book can only be considered an initial foray; emphasis on this topic is so new that one could hardly expect more. That fact alone is curious.

Our society is obsessed with the future. The United States government, for example, is consumed with predicting the military actions of other countries, population trends and economic activity in our own country, the impact of changes in the interest rate, educational and health programs, and so on. Corporations devote a great deal of energy to developing strategic plans, mission and goals statements, and implementation strategies for ensuring competitive positioning. All of these institutional efforts reflect a strong orientation to the future. A consideration of the psychological world of individuals reveals little difference. We are constantly thinking through such issues as what to wear today, whom we should invite for lunch, how best to organize a presentation, and which investment strategy will yield the best return for retirement.

I

In a recent study, young women were asked how much time they spent thinking about the past, the present, and the future; they reported spending most of their time thinking about the future and the least time thinking about the past (Jason, Schade, Furo, Reichler, & Brickman, 1989). More formal documentation comes from mothers' reports of what they talk about to their offspring, as described by Benson in this volume.

But even for the individual, a preoccupation with the future extends beyond the exclusively personal. Witness the popularity of science fiction and such "future world" attractions as Epcot Center near Orlando, Florida. Of course there are many examples for which personal issues are the driving force, as when some of us appeal to fortune-tellers, astrologists, and biorhythm charts for a hint about what awaits us.

In the light of all of these indications of how much mental time and effort we devote to the future, it is surprising that no systematic conceptual framework exists for talking about psychological representations of the future, nor is there a critical mass of literature for developing such a conception. The situation is even worse when one attempts to approach developmental questions about this domain. Why?

Historians will differ in the story they tell. We have three hypotheses to offer, and they are strongly influenced by the enormous amount of attention that has been paid to memory—the processes and content that deal with the past—in comparison with considerably less concern for the processes and content that deal with the future. The field of memory enjoys a sophisticated taxonomy, a treasure of methods, and no dearth of theories and concepts. Not so for the future.

The first hypothesis concerns psychology's favoritism for the concrete and the specifiable. This claim is not difficult to document through the phases of operationalism and behaviorism in the field. Notwithstanding the enlightenment of current researchers for whom mental constructs are employed with ease, we are all products of our intellectual history. Memory fits these historical dispositions more easily than do future-oriented processes. The past is certain, concrete, and specifiable. It is not difficult for us to think of changes in the brain, be they neural or biochemical, by which experience can be represented. But the future is uncertain, ephemeral, and nonexistent. (It hasn't happened yet!) How do we talk about a nonevent? How can we think about brain processes that represent events that have not yet occurred?

A second hypothesis concerns the discomfort of scientists, in general, in dealing with reverse causality—the dreaded problem of teleology. The future seems to work backward in time, controlling what we do in the present. How can something that will occur later affect what is happening now? We have no good way of dealing with that problem except to invoke explanations, based on nervous system organization, that "make it appear" that the future is controlling current behavior when in fact it is not. Examples include "purposeful" web spinning of spiders to trap insects, the dance of the honey bee to communicate the source of food to members of the hive, and the burial of piñon nuts by the Sierra Nevada nutcracker bird in late fall to stave off hunger in the forthcoming winter. We shrug off these examples in terms of "in the gene" controls or adaptive tropisms. Such explanations are less comfortable when we try to accommodate the behavior of humans who do very diverse and sometimes brand-new things that are oriented toward future purpose. Here we turn to explanations that lean on mental representations of the future that control current behavior, but no one would claim that we have anything close to a satisfactory scheme to account for any kind of future-directed activity that is even mildly complex.

A third hypothesis is that psychologists have not seen future-oriented processes as an integrated set in the same way that past-oriented, or memory, processes have been seen to be interrelated. By using the term "future-oriented processes" we mean to embrace such concepts as intentionality, goal setting, prediction, set, expectation, preparation, anticipation, planning, and feedforward computation. In fact such topics have been researched, even developmentally, but in isolation. For example, Piaget devoted considerable discussion to the development of means-ends relations in early childhood, which involves some notion of a goal. The cognitive revolution opened the horizons of psychologists by demonstrating the value of mental constructs for conceptualizing human thought; many of these constructs are relevant to our topic. And planning in children has received some attention. These examples and the very fact that future orientation is so immanent in behavior and thought, as we argued earlier, imply that psychologists have certainly studied phenomena that involve future-oriented processes. However, no attempt has been made to consider these processes as manageable under the same umbrella, as has been the case for "past-oriented processes," generally treated under the rubric of memory. A good analogy to the current state of affairs is the history of the relation between learning and memory. Memory is clearly related to learning, but research on learning continued apace for many years without deep consideration of memory. The focus of investigators' attention on memory as an interesting process per se had revolutionary effects on the study of human cognition. In the same way that refocusing attention on past-oriented processes (memory) produced immense advances in our knowledge, it may be that turning the spotlight on future-oriented processes will also yield rich dividends.

At the invitation of Robert Emde in 1988, several of the chapter authors organized as an interest area under the Network on Early Transitions that he headed within the Health Science Program of the MacArthur Foundation. We called ourselves the Interest Area on the Development of Future-Oriented Processes and met approximately twice each year to discuss various issues raised by our mandate and to plan research. A key task for us was to examine whether the concepts we have described above do indeed form a meaningful set. Would the beginnings of a conceptual formulation emerge that could satisfactorily integrate these various concepts, and would research in the separate areas under consideration be enriched by this broader perspective? Near the end of the five years that we met, in April 1992, we held a conference in Breckenridge, Colorado, to gather together ourselves and relevant outside people to focus on the topic of the development of future-oriented processes per se. The enthusiasm and encouragement of this group reinforced our sense that we were on a productive path. This book is a product of that conference. The experiment has been too brief to decide whether the domain of "future-oriented processes" will survive as a viable and productive category for study, but the early indications are that it is a worthy endeavor to pursue.

An issue that monopolized much of our discussion was the role of memory in future-oriented processes. An extreme view was that future orientation is just memory replayed. Does one's representation of the future simply represent the past pushed forward? In some cases, the answer is probably yes, but in others it most assuredly is no. Some conceptions of the future can be seen as projections of a repeating past or of past trends, but others seem to be explainable more in terms of construction from analogy and from knowledge.

The future as projection of a repeating past. Examples that fit this portrayal are easy to generate. We hear a dripping faucet, and soon we form an expectation that the next drip will occur at a particular moment. More complex examples among subhuman animals that might fit this category are nicely documented in Gallistel's recent book (1990). Animals come to anticipate feeding times that are tied to the 24-hour diurnal cycle; one could account for this behavior by arguing that animals come to forecast that the past will serve as a guide to the future and form expectations on this basis. This type of future orientation seems to be at play in the chapters by Haith and Reznick. Even though Haith's chapter explores infant expectations in the very early months based on varying rules and cues, basically the baby's expectations for what comes next depend on a repeat of what came before. Reznick, studying older infants, shows that such expectations can become strong enough to result in anticipatory activity that overcomes infants' very strong tendency to respond to the here and now. These may be the very earliest forms of future-oriented processes, tied to fairly concrete recent experience.

One can think of far more sophisticated examples of related processes. For example, predictions (often erroneous) of earthquakes, volcanic eruptions, and solar flares often depend on a cyclicity that has been discovered from past records. Here the boundary of this category gets a bit fuzzy, because "memory" is often not personal but cultural. Even so, this is hardly the whole story.

The future as projection of past trends. The formulations of the future by human adults most certainly go beyond simple replays of past experience. Consider the focus of several scientific disciplines that model a future that is not a replay of the past. Rather, they use trends in the past to project forward. Examples include predictions of future populations in various countries, the spread of AIDS, the effects of tropical deforestation and the decline in biodiversity, and what automobiles will look like in the future. The events in question have never happened before; they are an extrapolation of what is happening now and the trend line leading to the current state of affairs. Predictions of whether the universe will expand forever or collapse for another big bang might also fit this rubric.

The future as construction from analogy. At some age children begin to represent their own future, but it seems highly unlikely that such a representation is based on a trend line. And there can be no question whether it is based on memory. Rather, a child may identify with the same-sex parent or older youngsters and think about the personal self at a comparable later stage of life. Ironically, such analogizing may lead some children to place little faith in any future at all—for example, inner-city children who live in ghettos where violence and death are routine (Kotlowitz, 1991). Here the construction of a future depends on an analogy or a comparison with others. Another example is planning for one's death. Most of us believe our personal death is not an event that has occurred before. Rather, we plan for death based upon what we know has happened to others and what we see around us.

The future as construction from knowledge. One of the most sophisticated organizations of the future seems to involve events that are completely novel and do not depend in any direct way on historical trends. Consider the state of affairs in 1961 when John Kennedy announced that we would put humans on the moon by the end of the decade. Scientists planned and worked toward this goal for years, employing knowledge and experimentation to accomplish a task that had never been attempted before and did not depend in any meaningful way on a projection of historical trends. Other examples include preparation for the emergency program to repair the Hubble telescope, the attempts by biochemists to achieve rational drug design, or for many of us, the plan to test new hypotheses in our laboratories. And we need not limit ourselves to science. Here we are talking about imagination, equally the province of authors, painters, sculptors, and composers—even the sentence-generating child.

These categories prompt speculation both about phylogeny and about development. Whereas the past is certain and concrete, the future is abstract and uncertain—but in degrees, as represented by these categories. It is easy for us to imagine that the lowest-level category is applicable to the cognition and actions of subhuman animals and infants, but few of us would make such a claim for the final category. Perhaps here we have the beginning of a sketch of the stages that children go through in their development of future-oriented processes. Separately, is it uniquely human to imagine what has never happened before? The future at this level is based on knowledge about what can happen—perhaps on how knowledge can be created—not on memory.

At the same time that we can differentiate future-oriented processes (FOPs) from memory, we wonder if the conceptual and empirical advances in this field can provide a springboard for conceptualizing future-oriented processes. For example, is it worthwhile to distinguish short-, intermediate-, and long-term FOPs? Can we distinguish between implicit and explicit FOPs or between central and incidental FOPs? Are some FOPs semantic and others episodic? The answer to at least some of these questions appears to be yes, which suggests that memorial distinctions reflect something meaningful not only about memory but about the general operation of the human mind. Thus the pursuit of these ideas may enrich not only the domain of FOPs but also that of memory and of cognition in general.

What we try to establish here is a foundation and provocation for the study of future-oriented processes. The reader will find amazing diversity, tied together by common problems and concepts. The chapters by Hofsten and by Roberts and Ondrejko illustrate how pervasive is the need for prospective processes even in perceptually driven motor control and how one must represent the future state of things for efficient, dynamic skilled action. Rumbaugh and his coauthors demonstrate that these processes are not the exclusive privilege of the human species. Bidell and Fischer, and also Klahr, carry these ideas forward into problem-solving contexts where children have time for thought rather than having to respond to ever-changing events.

Working memory and the role that the prefrontal area of the brain plays in executive processes are fields of strong interest to current researchers. However, there has been little discussion of how these topics relate to future-oriented processes. In fact the use of the term "memory" in the phrase "working memory" seems to obscure just how future oriented executive processes are. Nevertheless, both Weinberger and his colleagues and Pennington address the role of working memory and the prefrontal area in future-oriented activity in both children and adults.

The remaining chapters consider the development of future orientation in a social and linguistic context. While Bates and her coauthors consider the role of language in communicating and representing the future relative to the present and the past, Trabasso and Stein illustrate how inferences about the future orientation of others are crucial to a child's understanding of their behavior.

Finally, Rogoff and her colleagues, Benson, and Stein and Trabasso move beyond the laboratory to discuss future-oriented processes in the everyday social world of children.

The book closes with an epilogue by Robert Emde, who congratulates us on opening the door while showing us how far there is to travel.

We close this section by expressing our deep gratitude to the MacArthur Foundation for funding our meetings and research, and also to Robert Emde for taking a chance on something new and different. It goes without saying that the trip we undertook could not have begun without the exploratory spirit of both these sources of inspiration.

Finally, we would like to acknowledge the Colorado Lottery for helping us to decide on the order of the editors for this book (with the exception of the first editor). Also, we appreciate several sources of support that aided the preparation of this book: National Institute of Mental Health Research Scientist Award MH00367 and National Institutes of Health research grant HD20026 to Haith, a MacArthur Foundation grant to Benson, National Science Foundation grant BNS86108043 and National Aeronautics and Space Administration grant R91091 to Roberts, and NIMH Research Scientist Development Award MH00419, NIMH research grants MH38870 and MH45916, and National Institutes of Child Health and Human Development center grant HD27802 to Pennington.

REFERENCES

Gallistel, C. R. (1990). *The organization of learning.* Cambridge: MIT Press.

Jason, L. A., Schade, J., Furo, L., Reichler, A., & Brickman, C. (1989). Time orientation: Past, present, and future perceptions. *Psychological Reports,. 64,* 1199–1205.

Kotlowitz, A. (1991). *There are no children here: The story of two boys growing up in the other America.* New York: Doubleday.

EARLY EXPECTATIONS

Chapter One

Visual Expectations as the First Step toward the Development of Future-Oriented Processes

Marshall M. Haith

INTRODUCTION

Our actions and thoughts are almost always organized around the future. Whether we get up from our desks and walk down the hall to toss a letter onto the mail stack, or try to figure out what minor tasks we can accomplish in the ten minutes before lunch, or check our schedule for our next appointment, our orientation is not to the here and now or to the past, but to the future. Such an orientation is adaptive. Nothing can be done about the past. The present becomes the past too quickly for us to react efficiently on an exclusively ad hoc basis. So the future must be expected for optimally adaptive action. Shakespeare's Hamlet put it cogently when he noted that "readiness is all."

In light of the pervasive importance of future orientation in organisms, it is puzzling that so little attention has been paid to future-oriented processes in the psychological literature. Part of the reason is that psy-

This research was supported by research grants to me from the National Institute of Mental Health (MH23412) and the National Institute of Child Health and Human Development (HD20026) and was carried out while I was supported by an NIMH Research Scientist Award (MH00367). Several people participated in collection and analysis of data for the studies reported here, including Denise Arehart, Joan Bihun, Roberta Hood, Beth Lanthier, and Michael McCarty.

chology has focused so heavily on how organisms deal with events that happen to them—how they respond to this stimulus or that and how they remember the stimulus or event. Of course the experimenter can manipulate such stimuli, which makes them amenable to experimental inquiry. But one consequence is that, despite the pervasive influence of the future on the behavior of intelligent organisms, psychology has focused mainly on present and past influences on behavior.

In principle, one could study future-oriented processes in situations that involve discrete events "happening" to the individual, as I will demonstrate later. However, when one tries to account for self-initiated activity as opposed to reactive activity, the *necessity* of incorporating future processes into a conceptualization of mental activity becomes even clearer. It seems impossible to account for such self-initiated actions as rising from one's desk to walk down the hall, figuring out what to do in the next 10 minutes, or organizing a schedule without incorporating notions about the future.

In addition to the field's investment in experimentally controllable events, there has been an overwhelming preoccupation with two concepts that have limited theorizing about how knowledge is acquired and, relatedly, how people form an understanding of the future, especially during infancy. These concepts are control and contingency. Even in this post–reinforcement theory era, our models of how people acquire knowledge depend heavily on standard notions of learning. And even if we cast aside traditional reinforcement notions, there is still a pervasive belief that babies learn through controlling events in their environment and by events' being contingent on their actions. These beliefs have conspired with investigators' preference for experimentally controllable stimuli to limit their interest to events that are currently available to the infant or to events that have occurred in the past.

Yet it is amazingly obvious that people acquire an extraordinary amount of knowledge about events in their world even when they have no control over those events and when they are not contingent on their behavior. Examples include the knowledge that objects fall to the ground when they are not supported, that they make a sound when they strike hard surfaces, that an approaching bank of clouds means rain is likely in the near future, and that night follows day. Examples out of the domain of nature's imperatives include one's awareness that the house on the corner of the block is green (perhaps reaching the level of consciousness only when the owners decide to paint it red), that a sign with a bent arrow on the side of the highway means a curve lies ahead, and so on. This type of knowledge, certainly based on learning, involves no control or contingent relation between an individual's actions and the event in question.

Basically, people (and animals) routinely accumulate information about the world, constantly processing the "ambient" sources of energy that impinge on their receptors. An argument I will make here is that because the information they collect takes place in time, a natural consequence of this "ambient" processing is the automatic formation of expectations about what comes next as well as about what the future portends.

There are at least two ways of looking at why people form expectations for future events. I have suggested elsewhere that people may form expectations for upcoming information because these expectations ease the processing load; on-line processing is difficult and inefficient in the absence of constraints on what can happen (Haith, 1993). This principle holds both for internal processes, such as reading and decision making, and more obviously for overt motor activity. As David Lee pointed out (1989), without future-oriented or "prospective" processes, our feet would smash into the risers as we ascend stairways, we would step into puddles before realizing the consequences, and we would steer our automobiles into the curb while negotiating a turn. To some extent these consequences reflect the sheer delays inherent in nerve impulse propagation and in moving body (or automobile) mass. The future time window varies depending on the mass in question; the captain of the *Queen Mary* needs more time to steer around an obstacle than the driver of a motorboat.

Thus, one might claim that people form expectations for the future because efficient functioning requires it. As we shall see, however, babies form expectations even when efficient functioning, at least in an instrumental sense, is not required. Perhaps individuals form expectations for upcoming events because ad hoc processing is too slow and impedes acquisition of knowledge. This possibility emphasizes the ongoing, natural learning that occurs, whether or not the individual controls the events involved, and this perspective provides a context for considering why the motorically incompetent baby might accommodate to future events in its world.

RATIONALE FOR THE CURRENT APPROACH

We have been interested in the earliest roots of future-oriented processes, as early as the first two months of life. Such exotic processes as planning seem to be well beyond the cognitive pale for infants at this age, and current theorizing notwithstanding, babies at this age control a very small fraction of the events that occur around them. However, if infants process the noncontrolled "ambient" flow of events in their environment, and if they acquire knowledge about that information, they might also come to know something about the future course of those events, perhaps initially in the form of expectations for their occurrence. Logically this seems to be the earliest stage for the development of FOPs. This was our beginning assumption.

The Constituents of Expectations, and Eye Movements as an Index of Future-Oriented Processes

By definition, expectations involve a time element, although the time window can be very broad. Additionally, expectations involve a content element, in that the expectations one forms are expectations for something. Perhaps a less obligatory element is a spatial component, that an expectation for something to occur must involve a place for the happening. In any case, because we planned to use eye movement as an indicator of an expectation, it became necessary for us to manipulate spatial location in our studies. Thus time, event content, and space have constituted important elements for our studies of expectations.

Why eye movement as an indicator of expectation? Of course, verbal indicators are not an option in infancy. And as I mentioned earlier, babies control very little of their perceptual world; one reason is that their motor control is generally poor in the early months of life, so their motor options are limited also. Two exceptions to this general rule are sucking and head turning. Sucking is quite well coordinated, often even at birth. But sucking bears no natural relation to perceptual systems that are likely to be of interest over a reasonable age range, and sucking changes drastically with development, which creates problems for comparing performance across age. Head turning gradually improves over the early months, but it is a rather slow and cumbersome system.

Eye movements, on the other hand, are under control at birth and are very fast. Thus the visual system can keep up with events that occur in close order, which makes it possible to place minimal demands on memory or the infant's patience. In addition, eye movements can be recorded easily, and they change their properties very little over the life span. They can also be measured in animals. Eye movements are obviously closely tied to the visual perceptual system, and they can be easily exploited to study auditory expectations when a spatial component is involved.

Finally, the eye-movement system connects closely to the current goals and functioning of the brain—in essence, what is currently at the "top of the mental stack." Although the human adult can devote central attention to visual events that are not fixated (Posner & Presti, 1987), this mode of functioning is unusual, and it seems very unlikely for young infants.

The logic of our approach is to create a flow of events that obey a predictable course and to examine whether, after some experience, the baby forms expectations for forthcoming events as indicated by visual activity. For example, the baby watches a TV screen on which attractive small pictures appear to the left and right of visual center. These pictures appear in sequence, in alternating left-right locations, separated by an interstimulus interval (ISI). Evidence for the formation of expectations consists of anticipatory fixations to the location of the forthcoming picture before it occurs, or a faster reaction to it than if the picture appears in an unpredictable location. Control conditions use the same paradigm, stimuli, and measures, but the picture sequences are unpredictable with respect to the duration of each ISI and the spatial location of each picture.

A specific example study will help to ground these ideas.

The Prototypic Study

The first study we carried out (Haith, Hazan, & Goodman, 1988) used the simplest sequence of time/space events that we could construct. Babies watched a screen on which small pictures appreared to the left (L) and right (R) of visual center while an infrared TV camera recorded the image of one eye. The pictures were red, green, yellow, black, and white images of schematic faces, bull's-eyes, checkerboards, diagonal stripes, and diamond shapes displayed by slides in this study, but by computer animation on a TV screen in later studies (see Figure 1.1) One picture at a time appeared for 700 ms and engaged in one down/up cycle of motion at the rate of 4.4°/s, to increase the baby's interest.

The pictures appeared in two sequences. An alternating sequence consisted of an L-R series of 30 pictures, separated by intervals of 1,100 ms, and an irregular sequence consisted also of 30 pictures, but the order of L and R appearances was randomly determined (but balanced), and the ISIs were also, varying among the values of 900, 1,100, and 1,300 ms. Each of the twelve 3.5-month-olds in the study saw both sequences, counterbalanced for order. The whole experiment lasted 106.9 s.

The picture sequences were designed to examine whether babies naturally formed expectations for pictures in the regular alternating sequence. If so, we hoped to find evidence of anticipatory fixations to the side on which a picture was forthcoming, during the ISI following the preceding picture offset (or so quickly after onset that the brain command must have been generated before onset). Another possibility was that fixation reaction time (RT) to picture onset would be speeded through expectations, in the same way that a response to an event is quicker when one knows beforehand that the event is going to happen. The irregular sequence provided a control over the baseline likelihood of infants' shifting fixation to the opposite side after picture offset inde-

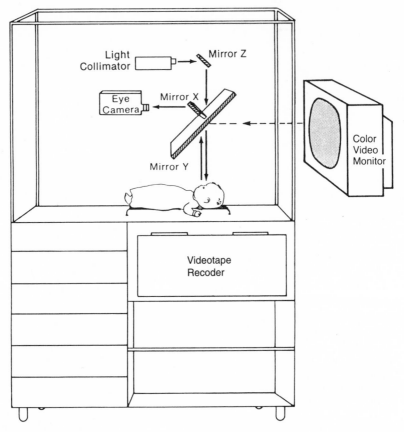

Figure 1.1   The recording and stimulus-presentation arrangement used in expectation studies. Stimuli were computer-animated pictures displayed on a color CRT. The infant viewed the CRT screen by reflection from mirror Y. An infrared collimator illuminated the infant's eye by reflection from mirror Z and transmission through mirror Y. The image of the infant's eye was recorded by the infrared TV camera after passing through mirror Y and reflecting from mirror X. (From Canfield & Haith, 1991; copyright 1991 by the American Psychological Association, reprinted by permission of the publisher.)

pendent of spatial regularity and also an estimate of RT to picture onsets that were unpredictable.

Babies did form expectations during the alternating sequence and did so surprisingly quickly. Figure 1.2 shows a typical fixation record for one baby. Overall, the percentage of fixation side shifts (anticipations for the alternating sequence) was almost twice as high during the alternating sequence as during the irregular sequence (22.0% vs. 11.1%). And the

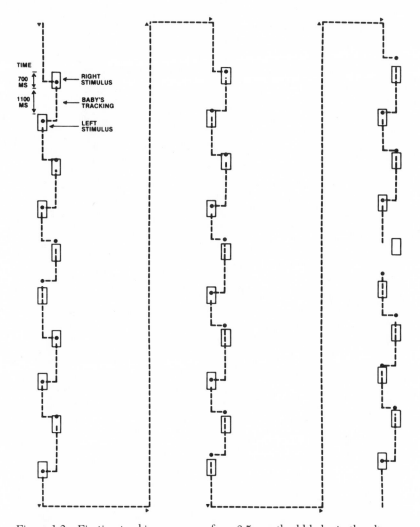

Figure 1.2   Fixation-tracking sequence for a 3.5-month-old baby in the alternating condition. Time flows from top to bottom for each block of 10 pictures and from left to right for successive blocks. The outlined boxes represent picture onsets on the left and right sides, and the space between successive boxes represents the ISI. The dashed line represents the position of the baby's fixations. Fixation at the location of the impending picture during the ISI or within 200 ms of its onset were counted as anticipations; these are particularly frequent in the present diagram for the second and third blocks of trials (columns 2 and 3). (From Haith, 1993; reprinted by permission of Lawrence Erlbaum Associates.)

median RTs were significantly faster in the alternating than in the irregular condition (391 ms vs. 462 ms, $p < .05$). For all babies who produced at least one anticipation, the first anticipation occurred, on average, after 16 s of exposure to the alternating sequence, after only five pictures on the relevant side.

This prototype study provides a basis for considering several questions I will pose and for understanding the studies that follow. Before proceeding, however, I want to be clear about how I use three key concepts in the description that follows. These concepts are *expectation, anticipation,* and *facilitation.* The term "expectation" will refer to a mental process of forecasting that has no direct observable behavioral equivalent. Rather, an expectation will be inferred from anticipation and facilitation. "Anticipation" refers to an observable behavioral act that is initiated before the event for which it is adaptive. "Facilitation" refers to the increased efficiency of an act that happens after an event occurs, by virtue of the forecasting of that event. In our situations, facilitation is measured by reduced RT in predictable conditions, compared with RT in less predictable conditions. These terms have broader meaning in the lay literature. "Anticipation" is often used interchangeably with "expectation." Both terms have found their way into discussions of consciousness and intentionality. The issue of consciousness is no easier to resolve for babies than for any other nonverbal animal (although see Reznick, this volume). For our purposes, however, it is important to be as clear as possible about the use of these terms. With definitions of these concepts in mind, we can move on to studies that constitute other facets of our research program.

ISSUES IN THE FORMATION OF EXPECTATIONS

The earlier discussion highlighted our interest in three components of events that are relevant to the formation of expectations—their timing, their spatial location, and their content. I will now describe studies we have carried out that address each of these issues in turn. Then I will describe studies that begin to address how limited or general these expectations are, whether they can be remembered, and whether they transfer to related events.

The Issue of Time

A question arises from the initial study concerning to what extent the expectations babies form may be limited to series that obey symmetry with respect to the onset and offset time of the repeating pictures. One might argue that the babies tune in to a fixed, balanced rhythm of picture presentations, or even that the rhythm we used entrained a natural biological rhythm. Such interpretations undermine the inference that babies were forming expectations for events before they occurred.

We asked about this issue by carrying out a study that closely paralleled the prototypic study we started with, the only change being that a different ISI duration occurred before the left picture appeared than before the right picture (or vice versa). If infants exploited an entrained biological rhythm in the earlier study, this rhythm should be thrown off when different ISIs are used on the two sides, thereby eliminating the performance differences between the control and experimental conditions. If babies were not simply synchronizing their looking with a biological rhythm, there are at least three other possibilities. Babies might govern their fixations by averaging the two ISIs, in which case more anticipations would occur for the longer ISI side. Or if they governed their fixations based on only one of the ISI values, we should find either no difference in performance for the two sides (if based on the shorter ISI) or more anticipations for the longer ISI side (if based on the longer ISI). If the baby was able to form expectations for the two different ISI values simultaneously, however, we might expect no difference in performance for the two sides, but anticipatory fixations would occur in different places in the ISI time window for each side. The data supported the last possibility, suggesting that babies can form expectations for two time values simultaneously.

Three-month-old babies ($N = 32$) saw an L-R alternating series of pictures that appeared for 700 ms. An ISI of 800 ms preceded the pictures that appeared on the left side, and an ISI of 1,200 ms preceded those that appeared on the right (or vice versa). Babies also saw a control series of pictures that obeyed the same timing parameters, but these appeared in an irregular spatial sequence. There were 30 pictures in both the alternating and the control series.

Babies were able to form expectations when the timing series was not symmetric. During the alternating series, they had a significantly higher percentage of anticipations than in the control series (16.0% vs. 9.5%, $p < .01$), and they had a significantly lower median RT (433 ms vs. 500 ms, $p < .01$). This same relation held whether the experiment was considered as a within-subject design (collapsing order conditions of alternating condition first or alternating condition second) or as a between-subjects design (i.e., considering only the first 30 pictures presented). The data are shown in Tables 1.1 and 1.2. Thus there is no reason to believe that the effect we uncovered is limited to a symmetric timing series or that we exploited a natural biological rhythm in the previous study.

There were several other interesting findings from this study. First, although the absolute percentage of anticipations was about the same as

TABLE 1.1 Percentage of Anticipations for Nonsymmetric Timing Study with Predictability as a within-Subject and between-Subjects Factor

	CONDITION	
Factor	Predictable	Unpredictable
Within-subject	16%$_b$	9.5%$_a$
Between-subjects	16.5%$_b$	8.4%$_a$

Note. Within a row, entries with different subscripts differ at $p < .01$.

TABLE 1.2 Reaction Times for Nonsymmetric Timing Study with Predictability as a within-Subject and between-Subjects Factor

	CONDITION	
Factor	Predictable	Unpredictable
Within-subject	433 ms$_b$	500 ms$_a$
Between-subjects	424 ms$_b$	502 ms$_a$

Note. Within a row, entries with different subscripts differ at $p < .05$.

we have obtained in other studies for the irregular condition (approximately 10%), the percentage was lower for the alternating condition (16% here as opposed to approximately 20%–25% in symmetric studies). Thus, in our first study babies may have generalized a single ISI time value across the two sides when the timing was symmetric, enhancing their formation of expectations. Second, we found no stable differences in performance for pictures on the side that followed the longer ISI than on the side that followed the shorter ISI. Although this lack of difference was not surprising for RT, it was surprising for percentage of anticipations; the longer ISI, with a 50% longer time window for a fixation to meet the anticipation criterion, might have been expected to yield a higher value. One interpretation is that babies formed differential temporal expectations for the two sides.

The third finding resulted from our further exploration of this possibility. If babies were forming different temporal expectations for the two sides, then one might find that when an anticipatory fixation did occur, it would occur later in the ISI when that ISI was longer than when it was shorter. One way to examine this possibility (without troubling artifacts) is to count the number of anticipations that occurred for either side before the end of the anticipation time window for the shorter side. Consider that the 800-ms ISI side had an upper limit of 1,000 ms following prior picture offset for a refixation to qualify as an anticipation (see

Haith, Hazan, & Goodman, 1988, for explanation). If babies were not adjusting the timing of their anticipations to the two sides, we would expect them to make an equal number of anticipations within this time window to each side, independent of whether a picture was preceded by a long or short ISI. However, 19 of 26 babies who showed a difference had more anticipations within this time window for the shorter than the longer ISI side ($p < .05$). Almost 2.5 times as many eye movements occurred under 1,000 ms for the shorter ISI side (the upper limit for anticipation on that side) than for the longer ISI side. Babies clearly adapted the timing of their anticipatory fixations to the duration of the different ISIs on each side.

Thus the findings from this experiment suggest both that babies form expectations for alternating events that are not time symmetric and that they can form expectations for two time intervals simultaneously.

Evidence from other quarters supports the notion that babies use time to support the formation of expectations (McCarty & Haith, 1989a). One group of babies saw the prototypic alternating sequence of pictures with a duration of 700 ms onset and ISI of 1,000 ms. Another group also saw pictures in an alternating sequence, but the ISI was unpredictable, varying randomly among the values of 700, 1,000, and 1,300 ms. Although the side of appearance was equally predictable for both groups, the babies who had a predictable ISI generated a significantly higher percentage of anticipations than those who had a variable ISI.

These studies indicate that babies' expectations at this age do involve a time element, and that they are capable of "keeping track" of at least two time values. At one level, these findings should not surprise us. Animals are exquisitely attuned to the timing of events, and they form expectations for these events, as has been well documented by Gallistel (1990). Certainly those creatures that must capture living, moving animals for food would quickly become extinct if they were unable to predict the timing of the movements of their prey.

On the other hand, the literature is silent with respect to how early such a capability is present, certainly for more than one time interval that governs the occurrence of events. Moreover, sensitivity to timing of events that have no consummatory consequences for the infant or that do not depend on the infant's actions have been ignored. What these findings imply is that babies can form expectations for the timing of multiple events that they simply observe. This type of temporal mapping may form the basis for the temporal expectations and planning they will employ later when more advanced motor skills permit them to mesh their own activity with the events they can only observe at this early age.

The question before us now is how well their skill in forming temporal expectations is integrated with their knowledge about the spatial location of events.

The Issue of Spatial Location

To some degree, our prototypic study indicated that babies must use spatial information in forming expectations, or they would not have exhibited anticipatory fixations to the location of a forthcoming picture. However, it is unclear from that study whether babies can do more than simply switch their fixation from one side to the other in a pendular sequence; if not, there is a question about how far their expectations truly involve a spatial component.

One way to ask this question is to break up the simple alternating series by increasing the complexity of the spatial sequence. Canfield and Haith (1991) carried out such a manipulation by presenting one of four series to each of four groups of infants, all with the same timing of 700 ms onset and 1,000 ms ISI. A 1/1 series matched our prototypic alternating condition. A 2/1 series repeated a two-pictures-left, one-picture-right sequence (L-L-R), or vice versa. A 3/1 series repeated a three-pictures-left, one-picture-right sequence (L-L-L-R), or vice versa. Finally, an irregular condition included 1/1, 2/1, and 3/1 episodes in an unpredictable sequence to provide a comparison for the likelihood of the baby's shifting fixation from one side to the other after one, two, or three pictures and also for the baby's RT for each of these conditions (see Figure 1.3).

Whereas both 2- and 3-month-old babies provided evidence that they formed expectations for the 1/1 series, only the 3-month-olds provided evidence that they formed expectations for events in the 2/1 series. The 3-month-olds were more likely to switch fixations from one side to the other after two pictures than after one (34% vs. 20%, $p < .01$), and they were more likely to shift after two pictures than babies in the 3/1 series (34% vs. 18%, $p < .05$). In addition, their RT decline from baseline was faster (for nonanticipations) than for the irregular comparison group (21% vs. -4%). The evidence that they were forming expectations came not only from the multiple-picture side but also from the single-picture side. Babies were more likely to switch fixations back to the multiple-picture side after one picture on the single-picture side than for comparable control condition comparisons. However, the evidence for the 3/1 series was less clear. Whereas 2-month-olds provided no positive evidence at all, the findings were ambiguous for 3-month-olds. No evidence was found in the RT data or in comparisons between the 3/1 and irregular groups for anticipation percentages. The 3/1 group did show a higher likelihood of shifting fixations after the third picture than after the second

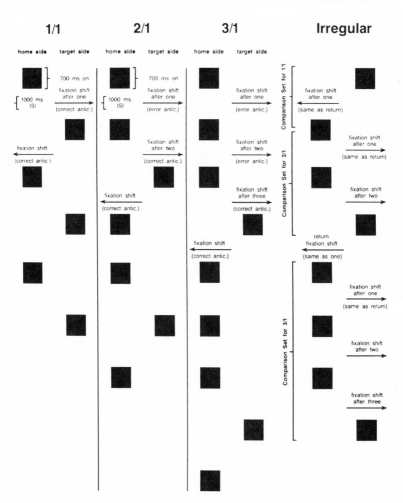

Figure 1.3 Locations of the series of pictures for the four groups in the Canfield and Haith (1991) study. Time flows from top to bottom, and each column represents the series for a different group. The solid boxes represent the picture onsets for each group. (From Canfield & Haith, 1991; copyright 1991 by the American Psychological Association, reprinted by permission of the publisher.)

or first picture, but it appeared that they were suppressing fixation shifts after pictures 1 and 2 rather than increasing fixation shifts after picture 3.

Several interesting conclusions emerge from this study. First, babies' formation of expectations does not depend on numeric or spatial symmetry any more than on temporal symmetry; their performance with the 2/1 series illustrates this point. Second, babies are able to adapt their expectations for at least two occurrences of an event in a particular place. Third, babies can simultaneously form expectations for one number of events in one place and a different number in another place. Finally, 2-month-olds do seem to form expectations in the simplest, alternating condition, but not in conditions that are any more spatially complex; thus these additional claims do not seem to hold for 2-month-olds.

An interesting question arises from this study for the 3-month-olds, given that they can clearly master the 2/1 series but provide only weak evidence of mastering the 3/1 series. Are memory limitations constraining the length of a series that will permit them to form expectations? Two variables differ between the 2/1 and 3/1 series: the total number of pictures in a repetition (three vs. four) and the maximum number of pictures on a side before a change occurs (two vs. three). Confounded with the difference in the number of total pictures is the time an episode lasts. What matters—the number of events in an episode, the duration of the episode, or the number of events that occur in a place before a change occurs?

We asked about these possibilities by presenting babies with a symmetric variant of the multiple-side appearance paradigm. Babies were shown a 2/2 series (double alternation; e.g., L-L-R-R) and an irregular series (counterbalanced for order) or a 3/3 series (triple alternation; e.g., L-L-L-R-R-R) and an irregular series (counterbalanced for order). The irregular series had 2/2 and 3/3 series embedded in an unpredictable sequence. The 2/2 series had as many events as the 3/1 series of the previous study and was of equal duration, but it had fewer events on one side before a change. However, events in episodes that are spatially symmetrical may be easier to form expectations for; the 3/3 series provided a symmetrical comparison for the 2/2 series but with more events on a side before a change. Thirty-one 3-month-old babies participated, and the picture duration was 700 ms with a 1,000-ms ISI. If the total number of pictures or the total duration of a repetition was at issue in the Canfield and Haith study, then babies should have provided weak evidence, if any, for expectations for the 2/2 series, equal in number of events and duration to the 3/1 series in the earlier study. However, if instead babies can form expectations only for so many events on a side before a change (perhaps a "counting" limitation), then they should be

TABLE 1.3 Proportion of Fixation Shifts for the Double- and Triple-Alternation Study, with Predictability as a within-Subject and between-Subjects Factor

	CONDITION			
Shift after	Double-alternating (2/2 series)	Irregular	Triple-alternating (3/3 series)	Irregular
	Predictability as a within-subject variable; collapsed across order			
One picture	14%$_a$	14%$_a$	11%$_a$	9.4%$_a$
Two pictures	24%$_c$	16%$_{ab}$	16%$_{ab}$	18%$_{bc}$
Three pictures	n/a	n/a	14%$_a$	14%$_{abc}$
	Predictability as a between-subjects variable; first series in each condition			
One picture	15%$_a$	14%$_a$	7.8%$_a$	13%$_a$
Two pictures	29%$_c$	13%$_{ab}$	13%$_{ab}$	20%$_{bc}$
Three pictures	n/a	14%$_a$	9.4%$_a$	15%$_{abc}$

Note. Under each subheading, entries with no overlapping subscripts differ at $p < .05$ (one-tail).

TABLE 1.4 Reaction Times for Double-Alternating Sequences

	SEQUENCE			
	Double-alternating-early		*Double-alternating-late*	
Reaction Time after	Predictable early	Irregular late	Predictable late	Irregular early
One picture	n/a	473 ms$_x$	n/a	426 ms$_x$
Two pictures	450 ms$_a$	427 ms$_{ab}$	474 ms$_{abc}$	536 ms$_{cd}$

Note. Within a row, entries with no overlapping subscripts differ at $p < .05$ (one-tail); within a column, entries with different subscripts differ at $p < .05$ (one-tail).

able to form expectations for the events in the 2/2 series but not for the 3/3 series. That is what happened.

The data are shown in Tables 1.3 and 1.4. While watching the 2/2 series, infants were more likely to shift sides after two pictures than one picture (24% vs. 14%, $p < .05$), whereas this was not true when they saw the unpredictable series (16% vs. 14%); the interaction between picture number and condition was significant ($p < .05$). Additionally, infants were more likely to shift after two pictures in the 2/2 condition than they were in the irregular condition (24% vs. 16%, $p < .05$). The same findings emerged even more strongly when only the first half of the experiment was considered, which reduced the design to a between-subjects comparison (29% vs. 13% for the double-alternation and irregular series, respectively). As opposed to the 3/1 condition in the earlier study, there was evidence that fixation shifts after two pictures in the

2/2 condition actually increased in probability, whereas for the earlier study there was evidence only in the 3/1 series that fixation shifts were suppressed after one or two pictures.

The RT data supported the anticipation findings, but the results were a bit more complex; there was an apparent carryover effect when the 2/2 sequence appeared first that affected performance on the following irregular sequence. For the irregular conditions considered alone, babies had a reliably lower RT after two pictures on a side when they saw the irregular condition after the 2/2 condition than when they saw the irregular condition first (427 ms vs. 536 ms, $p < .05$). When the design was treated as a between-subjects experiment, considering only the first condition presented, the median RTs for the 2/2 condition were reliably faster than for the irregular condition (450 ms vs. 536 ms, $p < .05$).

There was no indication at all that babies formed expectations for where the pictures in the 3/3 series would appear, either from visual anticipations or from RTs.

In all, the data from this experiment suggest that 3-month-old babies can form expectations for as many as four pictures in a series. Thus the findings from the Canfield and Haith experiment appear to reflect a limitation on babies' capacity at this age to master series that involve more than two occurrences of an event in the same place, and not a limitation based on the total number of items in a series or the duration of that series. This conclusion seems warranted from the findings that babies at this age form expectations for a 2/1 series, and that they provide only suppressive evidence for a 3/1 series, strong evidence for a 2/2 series, and no evidence for a 3/3 series. Although the 2/2 series included as many pictures as the 3/1 series and took just as long, at 3 months of age babies were able to form both enhancing and suppressive expectations for the former but not for the latter. Babies at 2 months of age were unable to form expectations for pictures in series that were any more complicated than the 1/1 series. Finally, there seems to be no particular advantage for a symmetric spatial series over a nonsymmetric series.

The temptation is to account for these data by appealing to counting limitations in early infancy. One interpretation is that babies cannot count beyond one at 2 months of age or beyond two at 3 months. Although this is a viable hypothesis, there are other possibilities. First, there was a confound in these studies between the number of times a picture appeared in a place before a side location shift and the amount of time that passed before a location shift occurred. Perhaps babies have a limit on how long a duration they can monitor. A study is being carried out that eliminates this confound. Second, even if the number of pictures appearing in a location is the operative variable, it may be that the numeric limitation is more severe when items appear in the same location than when they appear in different locations. This issue will be tougher to decide.

In any case, focusing on capacities rather than limitations, the ability of 3-month-olds to deal with double-alternation sequences reflects unknown capacities; that is, it is unclear exactly how the babies deal with this task. One possibility is that they base their expectations on a single rule: "two on a side, then shift." If this is the case, then babies must be able to extract a common principle that governs event occurrence on the two sides and to generalize the principle across the two locations, to support expectations. Another possibility is that they treat the two sides differently and detect no commonality for event occurrences across the two locations but are able to manage two rules for the two sides simultaneously. This latter interpretation accommodates the 2/1 performance of babies in the Canfield and Haith study, where a single rule was not applicable to the two sides. Regardless of which of these hypotheses is correct, babies' performance at this age is impressive.

Of course, events in the infant's world appear in more than two places, and it is usually true that places where things can potentially appear are marked, as opposed to the context we have used. In our context, when a picture is not present, the screen is blank. The only cue for a potential picture location is an "imagined" target relative to where the baby is currently fixating or relative to vague edges of the blank screen. In a separate study we asked whether infants use spatial markers to support expectations and whether they can form expectations for more than two locations (Arehart & Haith, 1992).

The study involved twenty-four 3-month-old infants who participated in one of three groups: (a) a group that saw a screen with four marked locations and saw pictures appear in these locations in a predictable clockwise or diagonal pattern—the *marked-predictable group;* (b) a group that saw the same patterns as in (a), but with unmarked locations—the *unmarked-predictable group;* and (c) a group that had marked locations but saw an unpredictable pattern of pictures—the *marked-irregular group.*

The potential picture locations were indicated, for the two "marked" groups, by a simple rectangular outline, creating four "windows" in which pictures could appear in a 2 × 2 array. Picture onsets were 700 ms, separated by a 1,000-ms interval. Before each four-picture cycle, a centered picture appeared to attract the infant's attention, following a paradigm used by Smith (1984). When the baby appeared to be looking at this centered picture, the picture went off, and then an ISI of less than 500 ms preceded the onset of the first picture in a cycle, followed by three other pictures in different locations in a sequence of 700 ms on, 1,000 ms off.

The marked-predictable group produced reliably more anticipations than the marked-irregular group whether the predictable pattern was clockwise or diagonal (20.0% vs. 12.7%, $p < .05$). Thus 3-month-old babies were able to form expectations for events in series that involved four separate locations. Although the RTs were in the right direction, the differences were only marginally stable, perhaps owing to the small number of subjects in the groups.

The second question concerned the facilitating value of marking the picture locations. Babies did perform better in the marked-predictable than in the unmarked-predictable group, producing a reliably higher percentage of anticipations whether in the clockwise- or diagonal-pattern subgroup (20.0% vs. 9.7%, $p < .05$). Again, although the marked subgroups had lower median RTs than the unmarked group, the differences were not significant.

Thus it appears that babies at this age can deal with more than two locations and that place markers for potential stimulus locations aid expectations. Perhaps babies use these markers to help constrain the possibilities for where an event can happen, so that they can devote more of their effort to predicting exactly where and when it will happen. Whether younger infants can deal with this larger number of locations with the aid of markers or whether their performance would even be improved by location marking are questions we have not yet addressed. However, a question we can address is whether babies form expectations for what they will see as well as when and where they will see it.

The Issue of Content

The foregoing studies asked questions about infants' expectations for time and spatial location. I have avoided the issue of exactly what the infants were expecting, other than a picture of some kind. In fact, babies in those studies were not given an opportunity to form an expectation for a particular picture, because picture content was unpredictable. We had guessed that the babies' interest would be maintained best if we changed the pictures from one presentation to the next, so the picture content was randomly determined from among a set of alternatives.

Can babies form expectations for picture content as opposed to simply forming an expectation that *something* will happen at a particular time and place? Wentworth and Haith (1992) asked this question by altering the standard paradigm so that the picture on one side (e.g., left) was always the same, whereas the picture on the other side changed from one appearance to the next, randomly selected from a set of seven. As

TABLE 1.5 Percentage of Anticipations and Median Reaction Times as a Function of Age and Changing or Unchanging Stimuli

	Age	STIMULUS		Difference
		Changing	Unchanging	
Anticipations	2 months	15.6%	25.2%	9.6%°
	3 months	16.8%	23.9%	7.1%°
Reaction time	2 months	572 ms	517 ms	−55 ms°
	3 months	490 ms	512 ms	22 ms

°$p < .05$.

usual, the pictures appeared in a L-R alternating sequence with a 700-ms duration and a 1,000-ms ISI.

Consider the possible outcomes of this manipulation. Here the comparison of interest is fairly subtle, simply the difference in the infants' performance between the left and right sides as a function of whether pictures on a side remain constant or change in content while both timing and location are predictable. There were three possible outcomes. The first would be no difference between sides, suggesting that whether picture content is constant or variable matters little and that content plays a minor role, if any, in infants' formation of visual expectations. The second derives from a habituation hypothesis. If babies do form expectations for content as well as time and location, then they might tire of the constant picture and display a higher percentage of anticipations and faster RTs to the side on which picture changes occur. Still a third possibility is that babies form expectations for picture content and that a predictable content augments the time/space information on which expectations are based, in which case a higher percentage of expectations and faster RTs would occur to the constant side. Although the third possibility was not our prediction, the data from three separate studies supported this alternative.

Both 2-month-olds and 3-month-olds participated in these studies. In the first study, the constant stimulus was a stationary solid white circle that alternated with pictures on the other side that were brightly colored and that spun, oscillated, or otherwise moved. In study 2, the constant stimulus was a revolving double-headed arrow that alternated with the spinning, oscillating, or otherwise moving pictures. In study 3 the constant stimulus was randomly chosen from a set of eight for each baby, and the remaining seven pictures appeared in random order on the unchanging side.

The combined data from the three studies are shown separately for the 2- and 3-month-olds in Table 1.5 for anticipations and for median

RT. For anticipations, there was a higher percentage for the constant side than for the changing side for both the 2- and 3-month-olds. Overall, 51.8% more anticipations occurred on the constant side than on the changing side (24.6% vs. 16.2%, $p < .001$).

The RT data were somewhat less striking. For the 3-month-olds, the RT difference between the constant and changing sides was small and unreliable (512 ms vs. 490 ms, respectively). For the 2-month-olds, however, the difference was larger and significant, with the RT to the constant side faster than to the changing side (517 ms vs. 572 ms, $p < .05$). For the side on which the picture was constant, the median RT of the 2-month-olds approximated that of the 3-month-olds.

These three studies, involving 80 infants, clearly support the notion that event content is a factor in infants' formation of expectations and that stability of content may be even more facilitating for 2-month-olds than for 3-month-olds. Thus babies seem to be able to form expectations not only for where and when something will appear but also for what it will be. We move along now to ask whether the expectations babies form are limited to the particular session in which they are formed and to the particular action used to perform them—the issue of generality.

The Issue of Generality

The expectations we have demonstrated, though impressive for infants in the first three months of life, have relatively limited applicability. The value of forming expectations is that an individual can prepare for what comes next and can respond more adaptively than if behavior is regulated strictly ad hoc. However, the expectations we have demonstrated seem applicable only at the current moment and for the situation at hand. This is a problem, because it is rare that two situations will be identical, and even if they are, expectations normally must be applied at different moments in time.

For an expectation to be carried forward in time in our paradigm, the baby would have to remember the "rule" that generated the time and space structure for the sequence of events and apply that rule at a later time. Of course "remembering the rule" need not be a conscious process and might be based on a procedural, nonsymbolic representation rather than a declarative, symbolic type of memory. In any case, we asked whether babies behave as though they carry forward the basis for forming an expectation over several days (Arehart & Haith, 1990a).

The strategy for our approach was to compare the performance of two groups of babies under identical conditions after they had received differential previous experience. The identical "test" condition was the standard alternating-picture sequence we used in our original study. The differential previous experience, several days earlier, consisted of exposure to the same sequence by one group and to an irregular sequence by the other group. This strategy ensured that any differences occurring on the second visit could not be attributed to stimulus or timing effects at test time and, given that babies saw the same pictures in the same paradigm for the first visit, that second-visit differences could also not be attributed to laboratory or stimulus familiarity.

Twenty-four 3-month-olds participated in two visits to the laboratory, separated by four to seven days. All babies saw 70 pictures (the typical combination) with a 700-ms duration and 1,000-ms ISI. On the second visit, all babies saw these pictures in a L-R alternating sequence, and the data analyses concentrated on performance during this visit. On the first visit, half of the infants saw the identical sequence they would also see on visit 2. The remaining infants saw an irregular sequence with the L-R location of each picture determined randomly (but balanced overall for position), and with ISIs that varied randomly among the three values, 750, 1,000, and 1,250 ms (also balanced overall). The overall duration of the 70-picture sequence on the first visit was the same for both groups.

A graph of the median RTs for the two groups over seven blocks of 10 trials is shown in Figure 1.4. Overall, the median RT for the rule-rule group remained within about 20 ms of 400 ms over the seven blocks of trials. On the other hand, the median RT for the irregular-rule group was 486.1 ms on Block 1 (almost 100 ms higher than for the rule-rule group) and gradually declined over blocks until it matched the low value for the rule-rule group on Block 4, presumably as the irregular-rule group detected the rule and gradually formed expectations based on it. The difference between groups on Block 1 was significant ($p < .01$), and the irregular-rule group had a significantly higher percentage of slow RTs (> 466 ms, $p < .01$).

A graph of the percentage of anticipations is shown in Figure 1.5. This graph shows that, for the rule-rule group, the percentage of anticipations remained within 3% of 22.0% over all seven blocks, starting out on Block 1 at 19.6%. In contrast, the percentage of anticipations on Block 1 for the irregular-rule group was 2.8%, and though the anticipation percentage increased through Block 4, it never matched the level of the rule-rule group. Overall, the difference in percentage of anticipations for the rule-rule and irregular-rule groups was significant (22.0% vs. 9.2%, $p < .01$).

This study demonstrated that babies can carry forward expectations over at least several days, and they appear to be able to remember a rule that constitutes the basis for forming expectations. These findings fill a gap in our research by showing that expectations can be applied at a different time from which they are originally acquired, a feature that seems necessary if expectations are to have adaptive value at this early age.

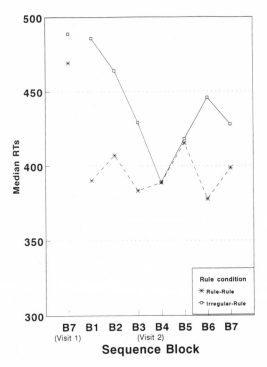

Figure 1.4 Median reaction times across blocks for the rule-rule and irregular-rule conditions for the last block of Visit 1 and the seven blocks of Visit 2.

There is another sense of the word "generalization" that is more traditional in psychology—the application of skill or knowledge acquired in one task or context to another task or context. In fact, it is very unusual that one situation would be identical to the next. The skill a batter acquires for extrapolating the trajectory of a pitch to a future location that will correspond to where his bat will be at a position and time of (hopeful) interception must have some generality. It will be rarely, if ever, that one will see two identical pitches with the same speed, curving path, height, and distance from the body. (Also, see Roberts, this volume.)

Is the young infant capable of forming expectations that have any generality, in the sense that they enhance performance in a related task? This turns out to be a fairly difficult question. All the advantages I cited for using eye movements as an indicator system of expectations make this system fairly unusual at this age. Thus it does not seem possible to find another system that would permit us to test generality of expecta-

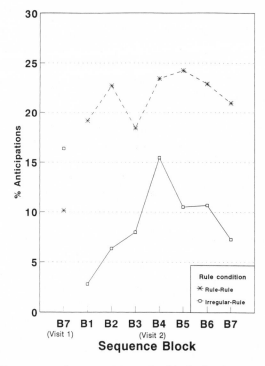

Figure 1.5 Percentage of anticipations across blocks for the rule-rule and irregular-rule conditions for the last block of Visit 1 and the seven blocks of Visit 2.

tions across a different response system. Given that we were constrained to work with the eye-movement system, it seemed to make the most sense to test the generality issue across eye movements that are as different as possible.

We decided that a test of generalizability across vertical and horizontal eye movements was the most viable alternative. Vertical and horizontal eye movements use different sets of extraocular muscles, and they are controlled by different brain areas (Alpern, 1969). It has long been known, for example, that horizontal eye movements can be produced by stimulating only one hemisphere of the brain, whereas vertical eye movements require stimulation of eye-movement areas in both hemispheres (Bender & Shanzer, 1964; Crosby, Foss, & Henderson, 1952; Wagman, 1964). Horizontal eye movements are much more prevalent in newborn babies than vertical eye movements, and horizontal tracking occurs earlier in development than vertical tracking (Haith, 1980; Jones, 1926). Vertical eye movements are more susceptible to the effects of fatigue and drugs than horizontal eye movements (Crosby et al., 1952; Stark, 1971). Thus, converging evidence supports the notion that vertical and horizontal eye movements are governed by different control systems.

The logic for the experiment was similar to that for the memory study just described. We assessed the performance of all infants on an identical task after they had received differential experience. The identical postexperience task was a sequence of pictures that alternated between locations above and below visual center (up-down, or U-D) of the CRT display. The preexperience task was a sequence of pictures that, as usual, appeared in the L-R locations, in an alternating pattern for some babies and in an irregular pattern for others. We predicted that the rule-rule babies would perform better on the postexperience U-D task than the irregular-rule babies.

A variant of this study had been carried out before with 3-month-old babies, and the results were encouraging but somewhat marginal (Arehart & Haith, 1990b; McCarty & Haith, 1989b). Rule-rule babies in the earlier study had reliably more anticipations in the second block of trials following the postexperience changeover than irregular-rule babies, but no other differences were stable. The present study was carried out with somewhat older babies (20-week-olds) in the hope of finding stronger results.

Thirty-seven 20-week-old infants participated in the study for a single visit (Bihun, Hanebuth, & Haith, 1993). All babies watched a sequence of 70 pictures that appeared for a duration of 700 ms, separated by a 1,000-ms ISI. The last 30 pictures appeared in an identical alternating U-D sequence. However, the sequence for the first 40 pictures differed among infants. For 17 babies these pictures appeared in an alternating L-R sequence; for the remaining 20 babies the pictures appeared in the L-R locations, but the sequence of appearance was random. The question, of course, was whether the rule-rule group could transfer the rule for forming expectations—in this case, simple alternation—from the L-R sequence to the U-D sequence, as would be evidenced by better anticipation or RT performance in the U-D condition.

The results were somewhat stronger than in the earlier study, especially for RTs. Over all three blocks of 10 trials for the U-D condition, the median RTs were lower for the rule-rule than for the irregular-rule group (overall medians were 409 ms vs. 448 ms, $p < .05$). However, there were no stable differences in the percentage of anticipations.

Note that this is a fairly subtle manipulation, so the consistency across two studies in the predicted direction is encouraging. The subtlety lies in our looking for performance differences in a task that neither group had seen before (U-D) after being exposed to sequences (L-R) that were identical with respect to the pictures presented, their duration, their

ISIs, and where they could occur and differed only in whether the pictures obeyed a strict alternation sequence of appearance.

Although we need more data on this issue, the rule-transfer studies support the notion that babies can apply a rule for expectations that they employ for one action set to a second action set. Thus expectations do not appear to be limited to the particular motor context in which they are acquired and do seem to generalize across different stimulus sets and motor acts.

SOME CLOSING THOUGHTS

What I have documented here is that very young babies use all the fundamental components of expectations. They appear to be able to detect the time, space, and content regularity of events that enables them to know what comes next and when and where, in a predictably unfolding scenario. In addition, there is at least some generality for these predictions, in the sense that they can be used at a different time than they are acquired and can be applied to related series in a different motor context. Of course this is unlikely to be true for all scenarios or all time values. But the basic ability to extract predictability from a dynamic series is present at an early age and no doubt is applied to more sophisticated episodes as the child matures.

It is important to realize that babies in these studies have demonstrated more than simply the ability to detect predictability in series of events. They could easily have detected the regularity in events but done nothing about their discovery; we might have, for example, been able to demonstrate such detectability only in a habituation experiment, in which more attention would be shown to a new series after habituation to an old series. After detecting regularity, the infants might also have formed expectations for each event in turn but not have used those expectations. Perhaps we might have been able to demonstrate such expectations only by a violation paradigm, measuring the infants' response by physiological parameters such as heart rate. An interesting feature of these studies is that, in fact, babies did appear to use their expectations to guide adaptive behavior, which leads me to conclude that they engaged in all three components: *detection, the formation of expectations,* and *the application of expectations to guide adaptive behavior* in the form of visual anticipations and facilitated reactions. Thus, infants use regularity not only to *know* what comes next but also to *do* something about it.

It is unclear how representative visual expectations are of expectations that form in other perceptual modes. The eyes are part of a wonderful perceptual-action system that dynamically reports on infants' momentary expectations and what they are trying to accomplish. Perhaps the eyes will serve as a model system for other types of expectations that involve different action systems and other perceptual modalities. Whether common principles for the formation of expectations will emerge across action and perceptual modes is yet to be resolved.

One of the functions of predicting the short-term future seems to be the more efficient processing of information as it arrives. Even if one only mentally constrains the possibilities rather than predicting the exact forthcoming event, information processing is enabled. I believe, in fact, that this is one benefit for infants of forming expectations. The benefit of facilitated processing is quite evident when manual actions must be performed in a dynamic, on-line context, as Roberts and Hofsten describe later in this volume. However, the babies in our setting were not required to perform manual motor actions to fulfill demands of the task. With infants as for adults, the formation of expectations probably enhances the ongoing mental processing of events even when instrumental action is not required.

Another question arises concerning action besides whether expectations are or are not useful only when action is required. That is, can expectations even be formed without the occurrence of motor activity in early infancy? Traditional developmental theory suggests they cannot, but the answer for expectations is unclear to me. One could argue that eye movements constituted the "action" component in our studies and that such action is necessary for expectation formation. But it is also possible that adaptive action is simply a by-product of expectation formation in our studies, which is in turn a by-product of the continuing processing of dynamic events, as I suggested in my opening comments. In this case we are simply lucky in having a motor activity—eye movement—that broadcasts internal mental activity. Still it may be, at least at this age, that action is *necessary* for forming expectations and even for detecting predictability of events in the types of series we used here. The studies we reported were not designed to answer this question, but the issue should be addressed, since it has a history in early cognitive development and the answer could have profound implications.

I want to stress that the expectations we were studying were formed by infants who were simply watching what was going on. The infants' visual activity had no effect on the events that unfolded; I have referred to the infants' expectations and learning in this manner as gratuitous, to emphasize that instrumental event control is not at issue (Haith, 1991). I believe this model of the infant's learning is much more characteristic of how knowledge is acquired in the early months than the standard contingency and control models that have characterized our field. The implication is that the predictability of the "ambient" environment is very important for the infant's acquisition of a knowledge base apart from the events a baby controls; the effects of such noncontingent learning have not been well studied or adequately discussed in the literature.

Future-oriented processes, of course, embrace a much broader set of phenomena than visual expectations. An open question is what role such expectations play in forming a platform for more complex expectations and for other future-oriented processes that will emerge later in life. It seems reasonable to argue, for example, that the type of short-term expectations we have observed form a basis for the development of longer-term expectations at an older age. Also, it seems reasonable to suggest that infants' mapping and prediction of events in the noncontrollable world will help them form expectations for events they will later control. For example, such expectations will be called into play for feedforward programming of motor activity when the baby has an interest in physical interaction with dynamic events in the environment that requires perception-action coordination. There is no question that even more sophisticated concepts of the future, and the ability to govern one's actions around forecasted events, must have a beginning.

Visual expectations, most likely, constitute the first step along the path to development of these crucial skills.

REFERENCES

Alpern, M. (1969). Part I: Movements of the eyes. In H. Davson (Ed.), *The eye* (Vol. 3). New York: Academic Press.

Arehart, D. M., & Haith, M. M. (1990a, April). *Memory for space-time rules in the infant visual expectation paradigm.* Poster presented at the International Conference on Infant Studies, Montreal.

Arehart, D. M., & Haith, M. M. (1990b, June). *Evidence for space-time rule transfer in 13-week-old infants.* Poster presented at the meetings of the Developmental Psychobiology Research Group, Estes Park, CO.

Arehart, D. M., & Haith, M. M. (1992, May). *Infants' use of visual landmarks in forming expectations for complex sequences.* Poster presented at the meetings of the International Conference on Infant Studies, Miami.

Bender, M. B., & Shanzer, S. (1964). Oculomotor pathways defined by electric stimulation and lesions in the brainstem of the monkey. In M. B. Bender (Ed.), *The oculomotor system.* New York: Harper and Row.

Bihun, J., Hanebuth, E., & Haith, M. M. (1993, March). *Evidence for rule transfer with 20-week-old infants in the visual expectation paradigm.* Paper presented at the meetings of the Society for Research in Child Development, New Orleans.

Canfield, R. L., & Haith, M. M. (1991). Active expectations in 2- and 3-month-old infants: Complex event sequences. *Developmental Psychology, 27,* 198–208.

Crosby, E. C., Foss, R. E., & Henderson, J. W. (1952). The mammalian midbrain and isthmus regions. *Journal of Comparative Neurology, 97,* 357–383.

Gallistel, R. (1990). *The organization of learning.* Cambridge: MIT Press.

Haith, M. M. (1980). *The rules that babies look by.* Hillsdale, NJ: Erlbaum.

Haith, M. M. (1991). Gratuity, perception-action integration, and future orientation in infant vision. In F. Kessel, M. Bornstein, & A. Sameroff (Eds.), *The past as prologue in developmental psychology: Essays in honor of William Kessen.* Hillsdale, NJ: Erlbaum.

Haith, M. M. (1993). The early development of visual expectations. In C. Granrud (Ed.), *Carnegie-Mellon symposium on cognition visual perception and cognition in infancy.* Hillsdale, NJ: Erlbaum.

Haith, M. M., Hazan, C., & Goodman, G. S. (1988). Expectation and anticipation of dynamic visual events by 3.5-month-old babies. *Child Development, 59,* 467–479.

Jones, M. C. (1926). The development of early behavior patterns in young children. *Pedagogical Seminary, 33,* 537–585.

Lee, D. (1989, April). *The use of dynamic information for the perception of direction.* Paper presented at the Center for Advanced Studies in the Behavioral Sciences, Palo Alto, CA.

McCarty, M. E., & Haith, M. M. (1989a, April). *Predictability and its effects on infant visual expectations.* Poster presented at the meetings of the Society for Research in Child Development, Kansas City, MO.

McCarty, M. E., & Haith, M. M. (1989b, April). *Rule transfer in the infant visual expectation paradigm.* Poster presented at the meetings of the Society for Research in Child Development, Kansas City, MO.

Posner, M., & Presti, D. (1987). Selective attention and cognitive control. *Trends in Neuroscience, 10,* 12–17.

Smith, P. H. (1984). Five-month-old infant recall and utilization of temporal organization. *Journal of Experimental Child Psychology, 38,* 400–414.

Stark, L. (1971). The control system for versional eye movements. In P. Bach-y-Rita & C. C. Collins (Eds.), *The control of eye movements.* New York: Academic Press.

Wagman, S. H. (1964). Eye movements induced by electric stimulation of cerebrum in monkeys and their relationship to bodily movement. In M. B. Bender (Ed.), *The oculomotor system.* New York: Harper and Row.

Wentworth, N., & Haith, M. M. (1992). Event-specific expectations of 2- and 3-month-old infants. *Developmental Psychology, 28,* 842–850.

Chapter Two

In Search of Infant Expectation

J. Steven Reznick

Future-oriented processing implies the capacity for predicting events or states before they occur and is related to many common notions in psychology, such as intentionality, goal setting, planning, preparation, set, anticipation, and expectation. The overarching construct is some form of prediction, but the timing of the process may be in milliseconds, minutes, weeks, or years, and the process may be posited to be either conscious or unconscious. The advantage of this generous definition is that it invites broad application, but the disadvantage is the distinct risk of including almost every behavior imaginable.

In this chapter I will describe some research I have conducted on one aspect of future-oriented processing—expectation in infants—and my efforts to constrain the commonsense definition of expectation so that

This research was supported financially by a grant from the John B. and Catherine T. MacArthur Network on Early Childhood Transitions and intellectually by Marshall Haith's Future-Oriented Processing working group within that network. My interest in this topic was also nurtured by meetings of Intentionali-Tea, held at Yale University in 1990–1992. I thank my colleagues in each of these groups for their wisdom and encouragement. I thank Evelyn Backa, Maura Hofstadter, Phil Zelazo, Suzanne Zeedyk, and Nina Sayer for their contributions to the present chapter and also acknowledge helpful suggestions from Janette Benson, Marshall Haith, Ralph Roberts, Bill Kessen, and Bruce Pennington. Finally, I appreciate the parents and infants who participated in these experiments and the Yale undergraduates who helped with the tedious coding of eye movements.

it has a more precise and useful meaning for developmental psychology. Specifically, I will attempt to restrict the term "expect" to references to an intentional state in the philosophical sense. Following the definition offered by John Searle (1983), intentional states are *directed at* or are *about* or are *of* objects and states of affairs in the world. The classic example is a belief, which has intentionality when it is a belief that such and such is the case (e.g., a belief that it will snow). Another example is a fear, which has intentionality when it is a fear of something or that something will occur (e.g., a fear of snakes). In parallel with these terms, I prefer to use "expect" in cases where the evidence suggests there is some more or less explicit object or state that is expected. For example, I *expect* that some readers will find this chapter interesting. Wittgenstein (1953), in *Philosophical Investigations*, states this boldly: "If someone could see the mental processes of expectation, he would necessarily be seeing what was being expected" (p. 132).[1]

INFANT INTENTIONALITY

The term "intentionality" is applied to an infant when an observer believes the infant's actions are done on purpose or have meaning. Obviously, the ontological status of infant intentionality is dubious at best. To quote Piaget (1952), "Unfortunately, nothing is more difficult to define than intention" (p. 147). Some theoretical accounts of infancy simply posit intentionality from birth. For example, Trevarthen (1977) claims that infants are born with an innate, rudimentary form of intentionality that becomes more controlled and elaborated over time, and Butterworth and Hopkins (1988) posit an innate endowment for goal-directed behavior. The intentionality-from-birth position is appealing, first, because babies seem to have the equipment to support intentionality (they do look like us) and, second, because positing intentionality helps us predict and understand their behavior (a position that Dennett, 1987, calls "the intentional stance"). Searle (1983) supports this acceptance of early intentionality with an ad hominem argument: "Only some-

---

1. One source of confusion about intentionality is a failure to recognize that there are two senses of the term "intentional" and that the philosophical sense is different from the more common usage in which intentional refers to means-ends behaviors (e.g., I intentionally left the door open to cool off the room). Intentionality in the latter sense has intentionality in the philosophical sense, because behavior that is called intentional generally has a more or less explicit goal. But there are many behaviors that are intentional in the philosophical sense yet do not necessarily result in goal-directed behavior—for example, to fear, to believe, to know. In the present chapter the term "intentional expectation" will be used to refer to a mental state that has an object, but the behavior resulting from an intentional expectation need not be goal directed.

one in the grip of a philosophical theory would deny that small babies can literally be said to want milk" (p. 5).

But from a more conservative perspective, and one more sensitive to the developmentalist's view of this question, maybe we *can* deny that small babies literally "want milk." At 11 months, my daughter seemed to be quite clear in her priorities regarding liquid beverage (sometimes apple juice just would not do), but it was not clear that she knew what she wanted at 4 months, and it was certainly questionable that she knew what she wanted during her first month. And pushing the argument further, why should the moment of birth confer a new potential for intentionality? Doesn't the same stance imply that the fetus captured in an ultrasound image with a thumb in her mouth wants her thumb? Thus I lean toward a second approach, which entails the search for principled criteria by which we can detect the emergence of intentional states (such as expectation) in the infant.

The most compelling evidence for intentional behavior is a verbal report indicating an intentional state (e.g., I tell you I am expecting it to snow), but even this evidence is fallible because I may be unwilling or unable to state my expectations or I may report my expectations falsely. One would certainly be reluctant to assume intentionality based on the parrot's statement, "Polly want a cracker." Moreover, adherence to the verbalization criterion ipso facto precludes the possibility of intentional states in infants (the word "infant" is from the Latin *in,* "not," and *fari,* "to speak") as well as in individuals who do not speak a language we understand (e.g., most nonhumans) and adult humans who are mute. For these reasons, I believe most psychologists will not accept verbal report as the criterion for intentionality. As Bruner (1973, p. 2) has stated, "Intention viewed abstractly may be at issue philosophically. But it is a necessity for the biology of complex behavior, by whatever label we wish to call it."

Another source of evidence suggesting intentionality is nonverbal behaviors that seem to imply intentional states. For example, by 2 months of age the smooth pursuit movement system allows infants to behave as if they are calculating a target's trajectory of movement (Shea & Aslin, 1990), and Hofsten (1979, 1980) has shown that 4.5-month-old infants capture a moving object through hand and arm movements based on the object's trajectory. In both of these situations the organism is responding to an ongoing, continuous stimulus, so it is not clear that infants are forming an expectation in the sense of a forecast that an event will occur before it actually happens. Instead, the behavior could be based on what Piaget (1952) calls the extension of an act of accommodation: muscular coordination that produces the continuation of an ongoing movement or the lack of a mechanism to inhibit ongoing activity. The modern instantiation of this explanation is the mechanism that Fodor (1983) labels an informationally encapsulated perceptual process, Searle (1990) calls a brute, blind neurophysiological process, and Posner (1978) denotes as a functional or isolable subsystem. This type of behavior could be accomplished by the nervous system without any accessible representation of or reflection on an explicit expectation or forecast. In other words, this system can be described *as if* expectations are present, but the actual mechanism involved has neither the capacity nor the need for mental content.

Other behaviors seem more compelling as evidence for intentionality, and there is a rich tradition in developmental psychology of linking intentionality to the onset of specific abilities. Bruner (1973) sees intentionality in the development of the skill to manipulate objects. Early instantiations of intentional behavior involve postural adjustment or effector movement relative to a desired target (described above as *as if* intentionality). These early reflexive or instinctual behaviors become truly intentional when infants have the opportunity to observe the results of their own acts. According to Bruner, intentional behaviors have several measurable features: anticipation of the outcome of an act, selection among appropriate means for achieving an end state, sustained direction of behavior during deployment of means, a stop order defined by an end state, and finally some form of substitution rule whereby alternative means can be deployed to correct deviation or fit idiosyncratic conditions.

Other theorists have focused on other aspects of intentional behavior. Piaget (1952) defines intention as the infant's consciousness of a desire or an outcome. The transition from elementary adaptations (*as if* intentionality) to intentional adaptations has various aspects, but Piaget seems most willing to posit intentionality when the infant is able to relinquish one object in order to grasp another. For example, at 8 months of age Laurent holds a toy lamb in his left hand and a rattle in his right. Piaget offers him a small bell, and he lets go of the rattle "in order to" grasp the bell (Piaget 1952, p. 221). In early observations Laurent attempted to grasp new objects without relinquishing items already in his hands. Finally, Olson (1988) suggests that the child's ability to use language to make statements, requests, and promises provides the cognitive machinery that allows intentional states. Thus Olson posits the emergence of intentionality late in the second year.

One strategy for mapping the onset of intentional states would be to note the onset dates of seemingly intentional behaviors such as skilled action, but this strategy is problematic. First, the onset of any particular behavior may reflect an emerging cognitive capacity, but it may also reflect the maturation of an output system that allows the capacity to be expressed (e.g., control of reaching) or a change in the infant's motivation to perform the behavior. Second, many of the very rich behaviors that suggest intentionality in individual infants occur rarely or in an idiosyncratic context, precluding their use in a systematic investigation. Third, unless the behavior can be tapped across a wide age range, it may not reveal the development of partial accomplishments toward intentionality.

A potentially more effective strategy for mapping the onset of intentional states is to note changes in some relatively simple behavior that implies intentionality but that can be observed in the laboratory across a wide age range. Specifically, the present chapter reports cross-age comparisons for infants' performance in the visual expectation paradigm (VExP) developed by Haith and his colleagues to study future-oriented behaviors. Infants in the VExP watch a repetitive pattern in which a stimulus appears at one location, disappears, then reappears at another location. For example, Haith, Hazan, and Goodman (1988) showed 3.5-month-old infants a sequence of pictures visible for 1 s followed by a 0.7 s intertrial interval. The pictures appeared to the left or right of visual center in either a random sequence or an alternating left-right sequence. Reaction time (RT) to direct gaze toward an ongoing stimulus was significantly faster for the left-right alternation than for the random sequence, suggesting that gaze shift was facilitated by expectations about stimulus occurrence. More important, infants shifted fixation to the side of a to-be-active event before the event's onset on significantly more trials with the left-right sequence than with the random sequence, suggesting the formation of an expectation about the upcoming event (for a review of this work see Haith, Wentworth, & Canfield, 1993).

The VExP can be contrasted with examples of visual behavior described above as *as if,* in that the event in the VExP is composed of spatially discontinuous components. Thus, anticipation seems to imply intentional expectation in the sense that infants may direct their gaze to the location where the next event will occur because they forecast or predict that an event will appear there.

To try to understand the meaning and significance of infants' behavior in the VExP and its relation to expectations, I have approached this question developmentally, in search of systematic changes in future-oriented behavior during the first year. The work by Haith and his colleagues indicates that 2- and 3-month-olds who see a left-right alternating pattern behave in ways that suggest they have begun to expect stimulus occurrences, but we know very little about how these behaviors change during the first year. Robinson, McCarty, and Haith (1988) explored this effect developmentally, comparing response to alternating versus irregular stimuli at 6, 9, and 15 weeks. There was evidence for anticipation to alternating stimuli at each age, but only the facilitation of RT to alternating stimuli increased with age. This finding suggests the possibility of developmental differences in infant expectations, but the age range tested by Robinson et al. was relatively narrow.

The VExP has also been used with older infants. Jacobson, et al. (1992) presented 6.5-month-old infants with videotaped geometric designs, schematic faces, and revolving or erupting designs. A baseline was established with an irregular left-right presentation, and then infants saw 60 events in a left-right alternating pattern. The median baseline RT was 0.34 s, which is 0.15 s faster than performance for the comparable condition at 3 months. Percentage of anticipations increased from 18.4% at 3 months to 28.1% at 6.5 months. DiLalla et al. (1990), and Benson, Cherny, Haith, and Fulker (1993) used the VExP with 8-month-olds, presenting the original Haith et al. (1988) stimuli in either random, left-right, or left-left-right patterns. Baseline RT to the initial alternating trials was 0.42 s and 0.36 s, respectively, and percentage of anticipation was 17% and 19.3%. The improvement in RT is comparable to the results reported by Jacobson et al. and suggests that infants become faster at directing their gaze toward a predictable stimulus. However, the percentage of anticipation in these two studies was markedly below scores reported by Jacobson et al. and comparable to results presented in previous work for 2–3-month-olds.

Our understanding of the development of expectations is limited by the lack of research affording a broad cross-age comparison. In the experiment described below, infants were tested at 4, 8, and 12 months. The youngest group abuts the previous research by Haith and his colleagues and thus anchors the present study in the existing literature. The 8-month group allows a comparison with the work reported by DiLalla et al. (1990) and Benson et al. (1993). The 12-month group represents an age where many developmental theorists assume that infants are capable of intentional action and thus are likely to have expectations about upcoming events (e.g., Bruner, 1973; Piaget, 1952; Willats, 1984). Further, the four-month interval between contiguous groups affords a rough estimate of the growth function for future-oriented abilities.

One strategy in a developmental assessment of expectations is to contrast encumbered and unencumbered gaze shifts. An encumbered gaze shift is a shift away from an ongoing event, and an unencumbered gaze shift takes place while there is no ongoing event. Stechler and Latz (1966) reported a phenomenon they labeled "obligatory attention," in which infants 2 months old and younger seemed unable to disengage from a visual stimulus, and Aslin and Salapatek (1975) found that 1- and 2-month-old infants had difficulty performing a saccadic eye movement toward a peripheral target during ongoing stimulation in the central visual field. The profound effects of encumbrance appear to weaken at

about 4 months. Harris (1973) found that 6-month-old infants shift attention from a central target to a novel adjacent stimulus more frequently
than do 3-month-old infants, and Hood and Atkinson (1990) reported
that 1-month-old infants exposed to a peripheral stimulus were more
disrupted by a competing central stimulus than were 3-month-old infants. Johnson, Posner, and Rothbart (1991) tested infants at 2, 3, and
4 months and found that only the 4-month-olds could consistently disengage their gaze from a central stimulus to orient toward a simultaneously
presented peripheral target. Johnson (1990) has suggested that maturation of cortical layers 2 and 3 during the third and fourth postnatal
months enables a frontal eye field pathway in the visual system that
allows infants to overcome obligatory attention and engage in temporal
sequencing of eye movements.

In the experiment reported below, I explored the effect of encumbrance on anticipations. That is, I attempted to determine the age at
which infants will shift their gaze away from an ongoing stimulus to
fixate on the location where an event will occur. Failure to make an
encumbered anticipation does not necessarily imply the lack of an expectation: the infant could be expecting the peripheral event but be unable
to disengage from the central stimulus to act on that expectation. This
situation is similar to the notion of covert attention shift suggested by
Posner and Rothbart (Posner & Rothbart, 1981; Rothbart, Posner, &
Boylan, 1990) in which one can attend to a target without actually looking
at it, which suggests the calculation of an explicit expectation regarding
target location before outward motor manifestations. However, it does
seem relevant to note the age when the infant's behavior suggests that
the expectation that an event will occur at a peripheral location may be
potent enough to disrupt attention to an ongoing event. Encumbered
anticipations could indicate a greater articulation of the expectation or
a more active influence of the expectation on behavior. In either case,
the development of encumbered anticipations should be relevant for a
developmental account of expectations.

METHOD

Subjects

To obtain a sample size of 36 infants (12 each at 4, 8, and 12 months),
41 infants were tested. Five infants would not participate due to fussiness
or an unwillingness to sit still. These included 1, 2, and 2 infants at 4,
8, and 12 months, respectively. There were 6 boys and 6 girls at each
age group in the final sample. Each infant was tested within one week
of his or her 4-, 8-, or 12-month birthday.

Infants were recruited through letters to parents listed in birth records published in the local newspaper. The sample was predominantly European American middle class but represented a range of education and occupation. All but one of the mothers had completed high school, and 53% had completed a four-year college. Their average age was 31.5 years, and 45% worked outside the home. Fathers were slightly older (33 years), and 50% had completed four years of college.

Stimuli and Apparatus

Two stimulus events were used. The first was an array of two panels, each containing red, green, and yellow light-emitting diodes (LEDs) arranged in circle. When the panel was activated, each LED blinked randomly, and a speaker directly behind the panel broadcast a pulsating audio signal. The circle of LEDs had a diameter of 6 in., and each circle contained 20 LEDs. The second stimulus event was two identical mechanical "cheerleading" bears, each housed in a separate Plexiglass-covered bay. When the event was activated, lights inside the bay made the bear visible, and the bear raised and lowered its arms, to which were attached colorful plastic pom-poms and small bells.

The apparatus contained four stimulus bays, but each presentation of stimulus events used a laterally adjacent pair of bays. The centers of the bays were 24 in. apart. The child sat on the parent's lap approximately 20 inches from the center of the apparatus and 23 inches from either stimulus. Each stimulus was approximately 6 in. square, so each subsumed a visual angle of 15°. The distance between the inner edges of the stimuli was 18 in., spanning a visual angle of approximately 50° and thus causing infants to attend to a single event at a time and make an obvious shift to attend to the alternative event.

A videocamera with a 12-mm lens at the center of the apparatus was used to monitor eye fixations. The parent watched the child's face in a small video monitor above and behind the apparatus, out of the child's line of sight, and oriented the child to keep the face in view. This procedure kept the child centered, provided a good video record, and prevented the parent from observing the event pattern. A computer operated the panels or mechanical toys in sequence and recorded trial number and the onset and offset of each event on the videotape to aid in subsequent frame-by-frame coding of direction of gaze.

Procedure

After the child had been acclimated to the laboratory and informed consent had been obtained from the parent, the child was seated on the parent's lap facing the apparatus. Each episode began with the activation of the left stimulus for 1 s, followed by a 1-s intertrial interval (ITI), and then the right stimulus was activated for 1 s followed by a 1-s ITI. The stimuli continued to alternate in this manner for 50 trials (i.e., for 100 s) or until the child lost interest.

Each set of 50 trials was considered a single episode, and each subject saw four such episodes: two episodes with panels and two with mechanical toys. Episodes were counterbalanced such that Episodes 1 and 2 were either panels then toys or toys then panels. Following a short break, Episodes 3 and 4 were administered, replicating the order of Episodes 1 and 2. To avoid incomplete blocks in the analysis below, Episodes 1 and 2 were categorized as prebreak and Episodes 3 and 4 were categorized as postbreak.

Laterally contiguous bays were used for each class of stimulus event. Half of the children saw the panels as the top two bays and the bears as the bottom two bays, and the other half saw the opposite configuration. The stimulus placement used on Episodes 1 and 2 was repeated on Episodes 3 and 4.

Data Reduction

An observer coded eye movements by scanning each frame of the videotape for gaze shifts and stimulus onsets. The exact time of gaze shift and stimulus onset as indicated on a stopwatch readout on the videotape were recorded by hand and subsequently stored on a computer. Each frame advance of the Panasonic AG-6300 videocassette recorder moved the stopwatch by 0.03 or 0.04 s, thus defining the upper limit on accuracy of coding.

Reaction time is generally defined as the delay between stimulus onset and the initiation of a response. Thus, previous research using the VExP has measured RT as the lag between stimulus onset and the initiation of an eye movement. This approach works particularly well in the traditional VExP apparatus, where the controlled environment gives the infant virtually no alternative but to shift gaze between the targets. In this situation, a shift away from one target is almost always a shift toward the other target. Unfortunately, I found that older infants who are not constrained within an apparatus often make gaze shifts away from one target that are not gaze shifts toward the other target. Instead, on some trials infants shift gaze toward some other feature of the apparatus or some other target such as their hands or feet and then eventually fixate the target. One alternative would have been to eliminate these trials, but the loss of data would have been excessive. Instead I opted for a nontraditional definition of RT, coded as the lag between stimulus onset and the time when the infant fixated the new target. This coding strategy introduced a more or less systematic increase in the timing of gaze onset, but it bolstered confidence that each gaze shift coded was indeed a shift to the target.

The reliability of video coding was established by having a second observer code 50 trials for six children, two at each age. Several indexes of reliability were calculated. The first was a correlation between the two coders' estimates of the latency to fixate a location. Separate correlations were calculated for each child across trials, and the average value was $r = .93$. Inspection of the raw data revealed that these correlations were deflated due to a few outlying trials. A more robust estimate of reliability was obtained by inspecting the distribution of absolute differences between the latencies recorded by the two coders. The median difference between the two coders averaged 0.01 s (less than one frame), and the third quartile of the distribution averaged 0.033 s (approximately one frame). Given that infants were seated on a parent's lap, this degree of reliability is impressive. Frame-by-frame coding of the videotapes was tedious but clearly supports a strong inference regarding the direction of the infant's gaze, at least for when gaze arrived at a particular target.

An anticipation was scored if the infant fixated the location of the to-be-active event during the 1 s ITI preceding the event or fixated that location within 0.25 s after its onset. The latter criterion was included because a fixation this quick must have been initiated before the event's onset (see Haith et al., 1988, for a defense of this claim).[2] The two coders agreed on the presence of an anticipation on 94% of the trials. Discrepancies arose when the fixation latency was close to the 0.25-s criterion.

RESULTS AND DISCUSSION

Missing Trials

Each infant had the opportunity to see four 50-trial episodes, but some trials were not available for analysis for various reasons. Trials were classified *no look* if the infant never looked at the side of the event within the boundaries of that trial. Some infants became cranky or refused to sit still before all trials were presented, resulting in trials' being *not*

2. Haith and colleagues use an offset value of 0.20 s to distinguish reactions that are initiated so soon after stimulus onset that they are likely to have been anticipatory. In the present experiment, reaction was defined as time of arrival at a new location rather than time of departure from an old location, so reaction times were systematically slower. Inspection of the data suggested that for most infants the transit time between stimuli averaged 0.05 s. Therefore the offset value to define reactions that were considered anticipations in the present experiment was increased to 0.25 s.

presented. Finally, infants sometimes developed a tendency to stare at just one side for portions of the presentation, resulting in a characteristic pattern of maximal anticipation of the preferred side alternating with nonlooking on the nonpreferred side. Runs of trials with this pattern were classified as reflecting *side bias.* An Age (4 versus 8 versus 12 months) × Event (bears versus panels) × Time (first two episodes versus second two episodes) analysis of variance (ANOVA) on the percentage of trials eliminated revealed significant main effects for event $F(1, 28) = 41.93, p < .01$, and time $F(1, 28) = 32.68, p < .01$. Fewer trials were eliminated for the bears ($M = 13\%, SD = 13$) than for the panels ($M = 29\%, SD = 17$), and for the first half of the session ($M = 14\%, SD = 12$) than for the second half ($M = 28\%, SD = 16$).

The percentage of trials eliminated was calculated for each child on each episode. All children lost some data, and a few had few data remaining after these exclusions. Inspection of the distribution of the percentage of usable trials suggested a discontinuity at approximately 30%, so any episode with less than 30% usable data was eliminated. At 4 months this eliminated one episode for one child and two episodes for two others. At 8 months and at 12 months, one episode was eliminated for one child.

Baseline Reaction Time

Reaction time was defined as the onset of gaze to the active event relative to the time the event became active. An estimate of baseline RT was calculated as the median response across the first five trials presented, presumably before the infant was affected by the predictability of the sequence.[3]

A baseline RT score was calculated for each child on the first episode presented, and an ANOVA was computed with age and event as between-subjects effects. This analysis revealed a main effect of age, $F(2, 30) = 15.25, p < .01$. Group means and standard deviations are listed in Table 2.1. Planned comparisons of contiguous ages using one degree of freedom F tests indicated a significant reduction of RT between 4 and 8 months but not between 8 and 12 months.

The main goal in the present experiment was to explore the development of visual expectation. The results for the baseline RT measure suggest that there is improvement in latency to fixate a peripheral stimu-

---

3. In previous work using the visual expectation procedure with 4-month-olds, baseline RT was calculated based on the first 10 trials (Haith & McCarty, 1990), but comparable work with 8-month-olds has used the first five trials (DiLalla et al., 1990) or eight trials (Benson et al., 1993), presumably because older infants should be affected sooner by the predictability of the sequence. Because the present study compared 4-, 8-, and 12-month-olds, the five-trial measurement of baseline RT was adopted.

TABLE 2.1 Means and Standard Deviations for Age Groups and Pattern of Mean Differences

Dependent variable	AGE (MONTHS)		
	4	8	12
Baseline RT	0.73 (0.28) >	0.43 (0.10) =	0.37 (0.07)
Response RT	0.54 (0.10) >	0.42 (0.07) =	0.40 (0.04)
Percentage of anticipation	19% (9) <	39% (14) <	49% (10)

Note. Mean (standard deviation).

lus between 4 and 8 months but not between 8 and 12 months. One interpretation is that latency to fixate a peripheral stimulus reaches an asymptote at about 8 months, at least within the levels of sensitivity possible here. To explore this further, I had three adult subjects view the stimulus presentation and instructed them to shift gaze when the peripheral stimulus appeared. Their median RT was 0.33 s, supporting the claim that older infants may be approaching asymptotic performance.

Despite the modifications of procedure, the present results were comparable to previous reports. Given that the coding procedure used here should add approximately 0.05 s to RT compared with the coding procedures used by Haith and his colleagues, the baseline RT of 0.43 s at 8 months observed here was remarkably close to the value of 0.42 s reported by DiLalla et al. (1990) and 0.36 s reported by Benson et al. (1993). Haith and McCarty (1990) report a baseline RT for 4-month-olds of 0.53 s, but in their analyses RT was based on a median across 10 trials. To allow a comparison with the present sample, a 10-trial baseline RT was calculated for 4-month-olds. The resulting value of 0.59 s was comparable to Haith and McCarty's value of 0.53 s given the expected 0.05 s offset due to differences in coding technique.

The baseline data reported thus far were for response to the first episode only. Initial responsiveness on any set of trials could have a different meaning when the child sees additional episodes in that the predictability of stimulus events should become more apparent. An analysis in which each infant contributed four baselines (a baseline from the first five trials of each of the four episodes) revealed an effect of age, $F(2, 28) = 20.48$, $p < .01$, with 8-month-olds significantly faster than 4-month-olds but not different from 12-month-olds, replicating the finding from the first baseline. Within-subject comparisons revealed a main effect of event, $F(1, 28) = 7.94$, $p < .01$, with slower RTs to panels ($M = 0.50$, $SD = 0.18$) versus bears ($M = 0.42$, $SD = 0.17$), which suggests that panels may have been less interesting to the infants. This hypothesis is compatible with the description of unusable data reported above, indicating that the panels produced more missing trials than the bears.

Response Reaction Time

Infants who detected the alternation pattern should fixate peripheral events faster. To assess this hypothesis, the median response latency was calculated across all postbaseline trials in which the infant fixated a stimulus event following its presentation. An ANOVA on these scores revealed a main effect of age, $F(2, 26) = 10.10$, $p < .01$. The means and standard deviations are presented in Table 2.1. Planned comparisons between contiguous ages revealed a significant reduction in RT between 4 and 8 months but no difference between 8 and 12 months. As suggested in the analysis of baseline RT, by 8 months infants reached an asymptote for latency to fixate a peripheral event. Also, as reported above, response was faster to bears ($M = 0.38$, $SD = 0.11$) than to panels ($M = 0.47$, $SD = 0.10$), $F(1, 26) = 31.06$, $p < .01$.[4]

Inspection of mean RT scores revealed that RT tended to decrease over repeated trials on an episode, but the pattern for individual children was haphazard. Many infants seemed to be sensitive to the pattern of stimulus onset across some period of the presentation, but this sensitivity never spanned the entire set of 50 trials (45 of them postbaseline). To measure optimal performance, median postbaseline RTs were calculated across smaller subsets of trials—specifically, sets of 10 trials—and the minimum RT value across subsets was used as an estimate of optimal RT. The pattern of results for optimal RT was identical to RT across all postbaseline trials, as reported above.

Baseline versus Postbaseline Performance

Given the similarity of results for baseline and postbaseline performance, it is relevant to determine whether RT to fixate peripheral stimuli changes as infants become familiar with the pattern of presentation. To assess this, an ANOVA was calculated in which the baseline versus postbaseline comparison was tested as a within-subject effect for just the first event and a second ANOVA compared baseline versus postbaseline across all four events. In both analyses, main effects were subsumed by a Change × Age interaction, $F(2, 25) = 6.18$, $p < .01$, in the former and $F(2, 26) = 6.22$, $p < .01$, in the latter. Post hoc analysis using Tukey's Studentized Range Test indicated that 4-month-olds reduced

---

4. Error *df* here and in subsequent repeated-measures analyses reflects casewise deletion of five subjects who were missing one or more episodes.

their RT from baseline to postbaseline, but 8- and 12-month-olds did not change over trials.

One component of visual expectation is facilitation—a reduction in RT to peripheral visual events as a function of the familiarity of their pattern of presentation. The present data suggest that this aspect of visual expectation is relevant for 4-month-olds: they do improve their RT over trials. But 8- and 12-month-olds quickly attain asymptomatic RTs for fixating peripheral visual stimuli, and development does not enhance their responsiveness.

Anticipation

Trials in which the infant fixated the correct location before (or less than 0.25 s after) stimulus onset were regarded as evidence of anticipation. The primary index of anticipation was the percentage of trials on which anticipation occurred. An ANOVA on this variable yielded main effects of age, $F(2, 28) = 17.07, p < .01$, and time, $F(1, 28) = 15.06, p < .01$. Planned comparisons indicated a significant increase in percentage of anticipation between 4 and 8 months and between 8 and 12 months. (Means and standard deviations are listed in Table 2.1.) The time effect was caused by an increase in the mean percentage of anticipation from 28% $(SD = 15)$ prebreak to 34% $(SD = 17)$ postbreak.

These results suggest that for a relatively coarse scale of measurement (increments of four months), infants show steady progress between 4 and 12 months in their ability to control eye movements to direct their gaze to anticipate the onset of a new stimulus. However, the specific values for anticipation reported here are somewhat discrepant from some anticipation scores observed in other laboratories. Haith and McCarty (1990) find that 4-month-olds anticipation on 17.4% of trials during a left-right alternating sequence, which is comparable to the 17% anticipation reported here. DiLalla et al. (1990) report only 17% anticipation, and Benson et al. (1993) report 19.3% anticipation for their sample of 8-month-olds, notably smaller than the 30% observed here.

It seems likely that older infants should improve in their ability to anticipate the onset of events in a left-right alternating sequence, so the results reported by DiLalla et al. and Benson et al. deserve closer scrutiny. One possible basis for their relatively low percentage of anticipation scores is the context in which the left-right alternation sequence occurs. Both DiLalla et al. and Benson et al. present left-right alternation trials interspersed with blocks of left-left-right or random presentation trials, which may have confused some infants and hampered their ability to notice and respond to the regularity in the left-right alternation. A second potential source of difference is that the three studies calculated percentage of anticipation over a different number of trials. DiLalla et al. used a denominator of 50 trials, and Benson et al. used a denominator of 28 trials, but in the present study percentage of anticipation was based on 200 trials. The extended experience with alternating trials may have given infants more opportunity to notice the pattern and respond by anticipating. Indeed, infants in this study had higher percentage of anticipation scores for their third and fourth episodes. Finally, the stimulus events used here, particularly the mechanical toys, may have been more engaging for older infants than the computer-generated stimuli used by DiLalla et al. and Benson et al. There was no effect of stimulus event on percentage of anticipation scores, but other aspects of the data indicate that infants who saw the mechanical toys were more engaged in the task.

Encumbered Anticipations

Anticipations can be divided into two types: those occurring while the opposite stimulus is still active, designated here as *encumbered,* and those occurring while no stimulus is active, designated here as *unencumbered.* An additional analysis was conducted to determine the percentage of anticipations that were encumbered. Inspection of the data revealed virtually no encumbered anticipations among the 4-month-olds. For the 43 usable episodes, 3 had one encumbered anticipation, and 1 had two encumbered anticipations. Thus, although 4-month-olds do anticipate, their anticipations always take place while the opposite stimulus is not active. Encumbered anticipations were frequent enough to analyze but still rare among 8- and 12-month-olds. An ANOVA revealed a main effect for age, $F(1, 19) = 10.04$, $p < .01$, and for stimulus, $F(1, 19) = 8.14$, $p < .01$, but both were subsumed by an Age × Stimulus interaction, $F(1, 19) = 11.78$, $p < .01$. Post hoc analysis using Tukey's Studentized Range Test revealed a clear pattern: few encumbered anticipations for 8-month-olds when the stimulus event was bears ($M = 4\%$, $SD = 4$) or panels ($M = 6\%$, $SD = 10$), and for 12-month-olds when the stimulus event was bears ($M = 6\%$, $SD = 4$), but significantly more encumbered anticipations at 12 months when the stimulus event was panels ($M = 14\%$, $SD = 8$). Thus, anticipation rarely occurs while the alternative stimulus is still active, and the only appreciable occurrence of encumbered anticipation is at 12 months for the panels. This effect probably reflects the fact that the panels were inherently less interesting than the bears and so were easier to turn away from, and it is compatible with the suggestion of Johnson et al. (1991) that procedural variations such as stimulus materials or the presentation format may affect infants' ability to disengage from a stimulus. The present results also suggest that young infants can direct their gaze toward the location of an upcoming stimulus, but their tendency to do so is markedly reduced when the anticipation requires them to disengage from an ongoing attractive stimulus.

GENERAL DISCUSSION

The goal of the present research was to explore the development of infants' intentional expectations. When infants respond to changes in an ongoing event, their behavior may be based on expectations, but response to contiguous change can be the result of an *as if* mechanism that does not require the sort of explicit mediation that seems intentional in the philosophical sense. In contrast to observations of infants responding to an ongoing event, the VExP imposes a gap between stimulus and action and so establishes a context in which expectation-based behavior may possibly be separated from *as if* intentionality.

The VExP offers two types of measurement that seem relevant to expectations. The first is a facilitation of RT: an infant who has forecast the location of an upcoming stimulus should respond to that stimulus faster once it occurs than an infant who has no such expectations. This process seems similar to the mechanism that Posner and Rothbart have identified as a covert attentional shift—a change in attention toward a particular location that occurs without or before actual gaze shift toward that location (Posner & Rothbart, 1981; Rothbart et al. 1990). In the present study, two effects emerged regarding RT to the stimulus event on trials where infants did not explicitly anticipate the event's onset. First, 4-month-olds respond to stimuli more slowly than either 8- or 12-month-olds both during baseline trials and following considerable experience with a predictable pattern of presentation. Second, 4-month-olds respond to stimuli faster after they have had experience with a predictable pattern of presentation, but 8- and 12-month-olds do not improve over their initial baseline RT.

If one assumes that older infants are more adept at predicting the location of successive events (e.g., because of maturation of the covert attentional system), then RT to a pattern of simple alternation should improve at each contiguous age. Within individual infants, those who detect a predictable pattern in an event sequence should respond faster on later trials. My results support neither of these hypotheses, but there are two explanations that must be considered. First, RT may not be particularly revealing as a measure of infants' covert attention, because it is profoundly affected by development of the ocular-motor control system. It is an established fact that young infants respond faster to patterned than to unpatterned event sequences, but this effect may emerge due to some variance in their ability to control eye movements. The lack of improvement in RT beyond 8 months and its similarity to adult values suggests that by the middle of the first year RT reaches a level of maturation that may limit its usefulness as an indicator of change in the infant's ability to form explicit expectations. A second factor limiting the effect of covert attention is the considerable error in the present measure of infants' RT. Infants seldom maintain a steady state during which stimuli can be presented, and they produce many responses that are irrelevant to the task at hand. Thus, measurement of infants' RT may be too imprecise to reveal robust effects at 8 and 12 months. Further research is needed to contrast infants' response to regular and irregular sequences at these ages.

A second VExP measurement relative to expectations is anticipation. Anticipatory behavior (i.e., shifting gaze to a to-be-active location during an ITI) increases steadily from 4 to 8 months and from 8 to 12 months. If anticipation in the VExP is based on explicit expectations, then the increase in percentage of anticipation suggests that the nature of expectation may be changing gradually during the first year. Unfortunately, behavior in the VExP in this simple alternation condition reveals little about the nature of expectations and how they change with development. For example, expectations could become more firmly articulated or more easily accessed, or they could become a more potent influence on the infant's behavior.

The presence of encumbered anticipations at 12 months is compatible with the suggestion that anticipations become more explicit. That is, an infant who will leave an ongoing stimulus to gaze at a to-be-active site would seem to have an expectation that is relatively potent. That encumbered anticipations occur primarily during the relatively uninteresting stimuli is compatible with this interpretation, but it is unclear whether the mechanism supporting the efficacy of the expectation is an enhanced articulation of the expectation or a greater ability to influence ongoing behavior. One explanatory image is of a fledgling expectation attempting to influence behavior: during an ITI there is little competition, so even 4-month-olds can be swayed. In older infants, the expectation can overcome a relatively boring stimulus but still fares poorly against an interesting ongoing event. Further research will be needed to describe developmental change in the nature of expectations, but the effect of encumbrance may be revealing.

Note that the occurrence of an anticipation in the VExP is not conclusive proof that an infant has formed an explicit expectation. For example, behavior in the VExP could be explained as follows: In a two-choice situation where there is equal payoff for making either choice, infants and nonhumans spontaneously alternate between choices (Feeser & Raskin, 1987; Vecera, Rothbart, & Posner, 1991). In the VExP, a spontaneous alternation mechanism would encourage infants to shift their gaze toward the alternative side after stimulus offset. This strategy is generally efficacious and could be a very basic nervous system characteristic of the brute, blind type described above. However, Canfield and Haith (1991) have discovered that infants can anticipate when the pattern is more complex than a simple alternation. Specifically, they presented 2- and 3-month-old infants with predictable and unpredictable sequences of stimuli, but predictability was based on either simple alternation or an asymmetric pattern such as left-left-right. Three-month-old infants were able to form expectations for asymmetric sequences, which indicates that behavior in the VExP is not just an instantiation of a tendency toward spontaneous alternation. Furthermore, older infants in the present study were able to shift gaze toward the location of the alternative stimulus during an ongoing event. This is a clear violation of the spontaneous-alternation mechanism.

A second nonintentionalist interpretation is that infants' behavior in the VExP is in the service of maximizing exposure to an interesting event. If babies are driven by that mechanism, there is certainly no advantage for them to change sides while an ongoing event remains active. Their shift during the ITI could then be accounted for by a win-stay, lose-shift operant mechanism. Haith (1991) contends that responses in the VExP are gratuitous. That is, a strict definition asserts that operant mechanisms do not apply unless behavior *controls* some outcome. Responses in the VExP do not control the presentation of stimuli, so in that sense the responses in the VExP are gratuitous. But in a different sense, orientation responses during the VExP could be considered efficacious (rather than gratuitous) in that they do at least provide the infant with increased access to the stimulus event. This sense of "operant" is more like the complex mechanisms of later Skinner, for example, in *Beyond Freedom and Dignity* (1971). Simply stated, behavior is shaped by its consequences. Even though behavior in the VExP does not alter the course of the stimulus presentation, it does have consequences for what the infant will see. The 4-month-old who fails to anticipate while an ongoing stimulus is present but does anticipate during a blank ITI is executing a behavior that maximizes exposure to interesting stimuli. On the other hand, by 12 months the pattern of behavior is different. The 12-month-olds can shift to the location of a to-be-active stimulus not only during an ITI but also (on a limited basis) in the midst of active stimulation. If maximization of stimulus exposure is the goal, any encumbered anticipation actually reduces access to the stimulus, which is clearly different from the simple hedonism that drives the win-stay, lose-shift strategy that is the primary mode of operation for 4-month-olds. This interpretation is not unequivocal, but it is at least part of the story.

Infant behavior in the VExP is gratuitous in the sense that the experimenter presents stimuli and the infant happens to gaze at them or not. Thus future-oriented behavior in this context implies some form of expectation about the upcoming event but also some motivation to act on that expectation. This distinction is particularly salient in an analysis of cross-age change: Do expectations become more firmly articulated, or do infants become more motivated to perform? Additional work will be needed to clarify these interpretations of anticipatory behavior in the VExP, but facts begin to accumulate that are relevant for a developmental model of visual expectation. As Haith has shown, RT to fixate a peripheral visual event is facilitated at 4 months when the pattern of presentation of stimulus events is lawful. The present study replicates this effect but suggests that this particular influence on visual expectation is less relevant at older ages. What develops over the first year is the ability to anticipate—to fixate the location of a to-be-active event before the event begins. However, the occurrence of an anticipation depends on the visual context. Eight-month-olds are able to anticipate during a stimulus-free ITI (unencumbered anticipation), but only 12-month-olds anticipate while a second stimulus is present (encumbered anticipation), and the stimulus must be relatively uninteresting. Additional research using the VExP, modifications of the VExP, and other procedures will be required before these facts can be woven into a coherent developmental explanation of infant expectations.

REFERENCES

Aslin, R. N., & Salapatek, P. (1975). Saccadic localization of visual targets by the very young human infant. *Perception and Psychophysics, 17,* 293–302.

Benson, J. B., Cherny, S. S., Haith, M. M., & Fulker, D. W. (1993). Rapid assessment of infant predictors of adult IQ: Midtwin-midparent analyses. *Developmental Psychology, 29,* 434–447.

Bruner, J. S. (1973). Organization of early skilled action. *Child Development, 44,* 1–11.

Butterworth, G., & Hopkins, B. (1988). Hand-mouth coordination in the newborn baby. *British Journal of Developmental Psychology, 6,* 303–314.

Canfield, R. L., & Haith, M. M. (1991). Young infants' visual expectations for symmetric and asymmetric stimulus sequences. *Developmental Psychology, 27,* 198–208.

Dennett, D. C. (1987). *The intentional stance.* Cambridge: MIT/Bradford.

DiLalla, L. F., Thompson, L. A., Plomin, R., Phillips, K., Fagan, J. F. III, Haith, M. H., Cyphers, L. S., & Fulker, D. W. (1990). Infant predictors of preschool and adult IQ: A study of infant twins and their parents. *Developmental Psychology, 26,* 759–769.

Feeser, H. R., & Raskin, L. A. (1987). Effects of neonatal dopamine depletion on spatial ability during ontogeny. *Behavioral Neuroscience, 101,* 812–818.

Fodor, J. (1983). *The modularity of mind.* Cambridge: Bradford/MIT.

Haith, M. M. (1991). Gratuity, perception-action integration, and future orientation. In F. S. Kessel, M. H. Bornstein, & A. J. Sameroff (Eds.), *Contemporary constructions of the child: Essays in honor of William Kessen* (pp. 23–43). Hillsdale, NJ: Erlbaum.

Haith, M. M., Hazan, C., & Goodman, G. S. (1988). Expectation and anticipation of dynamic visual events by 3.5-month-old babies. *Child Development, 59,* 467–479.

Haith, M. M., & McCarty, M. E. (1990). Stability of visual expectations at 3.0 months of age. *Developmental Psychology, 26,* 68–74.

Haith, M. M., Wentworth, N., & Canfield, R. (1993). The formation of expectations in early infancy. In C. Rovee-Collier & L. P. Lipsitt (Eds.), *Advances in infancy research.* Norwood, NJ: Ablex.

Harris, P. L. (1973). Eye movements between adjacent stimuli: An age change in infancy. *British Journal of Psychology, 64,* 215–218.

Hofsten, C. von. (1979). Development of visually directed reaching: The approach phase. *Journal of Human Movement Studies, 5,* 160–178.

Hofsten, C. von. (1980). Predictive reaching for moving objects by human infants. *Journal of Experimental Child Psychology, 30,* 369–382.

Hood, B., & Atkinson, J. (1990). Sensory visual loss and cognitive deficits in the selective attentional system of normal infants and neurologically impaired children. *Developmental Medicine and Child Neurology, 32,* 1067–1077.

Jacobson, S. W., Jacobson, J. L., O'Neill, J. M., Padgett, R. J., Frankowski, J. J., & Bihun, J. T. (1992). Visual expectation and dimensions of infant information processing. *Child Development, 63,* 711–724.

Johnson, M. H. (1990). Cortical maturation and the development of visual attention in early infancy. *Journal of Cognitive Neuroscience, 2,* 81–95.

Johnson, M. H., Posner, M. I., & Rothbart, M. K. (1991). Components of visual orienting in early infancy: Contingency learning, anticipatory looking, and disengaging. *Journal of Cognitive Neuroscience, 3,* 335–344.

Olsen, D. R. (1988). On the origins of beliefs and other intentional states in children. In J. W. Astington, P. L. Harris, & D. R. Olson (Eds.), *Developing theories of mind* (pp. 414–426). Cambridge: Cambridge University Press.

Piaget, J. (1952). *The origins of intelligence in children.* New York: Norton.

Posner, M. I. (1978). *Chronometric explorations of mind.* Hillsdale, NJ: Erlbaum.

Posner, M. I., & Rothbart, M. K. (1981). The development of attentional mechanisms. In J. H. Flowers (Ed.), *Nebraska symposium on motivation, 1980* (pp. 1–52). Lincoln: University of Nebraska Press.

Robinson, N. S., McCarty, M. E., & Haith, M. M. (1988, April). *Visual expectations in early infancy.* Poster presented at the meeting of the International Conference on Infant Studies, Washington, DC.

Rothbart, M. K., Posner, M. I., & Boylan, A. (1990). Regulatory mechanisms in infant temperament. In J. Enns (Ed.), *The development of attention: Research and theory* (pp. 47–66). Amsterdam: North-Holland.

Searle, J. R. (1983). *Intentionality.* Cambridge: Cambridge University Press.

Searle, J. R. (1990). Consciousness, explanatory inversion, and cognitive science. *Behavioral and Brain Sciences, 13,* 585–642.

Shea, S. L., & Aslin, R. N. (1990). Oculomotor responses to step-ramp targets by young human infants. *Vision Research, 30,* 1077–1092.

Skinner, B. F. (1971). *Beyond freedom and dignity.* New York: Knopf.

Stechler, G., & Latz, E. (1966). Some observations on attention and arousal in the human infant. *Journal of the American Academy of Child Psychiatry, 5,* 517–525.

Trevarthen, C. (1977). Descriptive analyses of infant communicative behavior. In H. R. Schaffer (Ed.), *Studies in mother-infant interaction.* London: Academic Press.

Vecera, S. P., Rothbart, M. K., & Posner, M. I. (1991). Development of spontaneous alternation in infancy. *Journal of Cognitive Neuroscience, 3,* 351–354.

Willatts, P. (1984). Stages in the development of intentional search by young infants. *Developmental Psychology, 20,* 389–396.

Wittgenstein, L. (1953). *Philosophical investigations.* Oxford: Basil Blackwell.

PLANNING IN ACTION

Chapter Three

Planning and Perceiving What Is Going to Happen Next

Claes von Hofsten

CONTROLLING ACTIONS

All actions are geared to the future, and controlling them requires predicting future events. We constantly need to know what is going to happen next and how it is going to affect us and our ongoing actions. We also need to know the effects of our own actions on the ongoing and upcoming events in the environment. The problem is that the evolving events in the world, our own actions, and the interactions between our own actions and the events in the world always involve a large number of degrees of freedom and are therefore never totally predictable. Even for a simple limb movement it is impossible to predict all aspects in advance (Bernstein, 1967). As a result, totally preprogrammed movements will not work. On the contrary, plans must be dynamic and flexible. The plan has to evolve with the action, and information has to be picked up under way in order to steer the action adaptively. Perception is needed throughout the execution of any action, and its task is always prospective. It has to inform the actor about upcoming problems so they can be dealt with ahead of time or at an early stage when they are

This article was made possible by funds supplied to me by the Swedish Council for Research in the Humanities and the Social Sciences and the Tercentenary Fund of the Bank of Sweden. I am indebted to Barbara Rogoff for constructive comments and suggestions on an earlier version of this article.

harmless. Consider driving a car. Things are continually happening on the road, and failure to perceive those events clearly may prove fatal. One must attend not only to where all the other cars are on the road, but to where they will end up in the near future and where one's own car will end up relative to them.

There are, of course, differences between different levels of action in the way future-oriented control is achieved. At a sensorimotor level control seems more continuous, as in a servomechanism, whereas more global aspects of actions appear to be controlled in a more steplike fashion—now and then we stop, think, and reconsider. In line with this, Miller, Galanter, and Pribram (1960) used an analog computer metaphor for describing the lower levels of control and a digital computer model for describing the higher levels. Another difference between the prospective control of single movements and the prospective control of larger action sequences concerns deliberate thinking. Deliberate thinking is an important part of tasks like playcrafting but is often insignificant in tasks like reaching or catching. In the control of skilled movements, deliberate thinking might even interfere with performance (Gallwey, 1986). When athletes start thinking about their movements, performance tends to deteriorate. In spite of these and other differences in the control of different kinds of action, however, one basic principle holds true for them all, from the playcrafting of children (Baker-Sennett, Matusov, & Rogoff, 1992) to the reaching and grasping of objects (Hofsten, 1991): a need for flexible planning and a reliance on perceiving what is going to happen next.

In the following sections I discuss the principles of prospective control in the context of action, arguing that action control entails both planning and perceiving what is going to happen next. I show that such control is essential for the interaction with the outer world as well as for the construction of the movement and the maintenance of posture and balance. I then discuss the origins of action and how future-oriented control evolves in ontogeny, arguing that action originates in action and develops through action. The principles of action development are illustrated mainly with examples from the development of reaching, grasping, and catching of objects. Finally, I trace the biological roots of prospective control.

THE NECESSITY OF KNOWING WHAT IS GOING TO HAPPEN NEXT

The smoothness and continuity of movements, so characteristic of adult performance, are completely dependent on our knowing what is going to happen next. There are several reasons for this. First of all, there is a lag between the time information enters into the system and the time adjustments are made. Even if there were no transmission lag in the system, however, knowing about a problem only when it occurs is too late. The inertia of the system introduces a mechanical lag; that is, it takes time before the contraction of a muscle has an effect. These lags will interrupt the flow of action if adjustments are prepared only after problems arise. Finally, some events are irreversible and simply have to be dealt with ahead of time. As we lower a foot toward the ground to take a step, we must foresee the quality of the ground—whether it is hard, soft, or slippery—or else the smoothness of walking will be disrupted. Thus it is quite clear that the motor system could not function ad hoc, because movements would then be discontinuous and jerky. According to Kawato and Gomi (1992), the cerebellar symptoms of hypotonia, hypermetria, and intentional tremor could be understood as a degraded performance when motor control is forced to rely solely on negative feedback after the internal models are destroyed, cannot be updated, or both.

There are three kinds of basic problems to be solved in the production of movements. They have to do with with controlling the body part to be moved, maintaining posture and balance, and interacting with the outer world. First, several forces act on the limb or body segment during a movement. There are, of course, torques originating from muscle contractions aimed at moving the segment in question, but because the body is a mechanically linked system, torques are also generated from other moving segments coupled to it. The form of movement is also affected by the pull of gravity, which will be different for different orientations of the limb in space. The viscoelastic properties of muscles, joints, and tendons will also affect the final form of movement. To produce an intended movement, the passive forces from other segments and gravity must be kept under control by the adjustments of active muscular contractions.

The second problem has to do with maintaining posture and balance. During purposeful movement, the equilibrium of the body must be maintained in a stable orientation to the environment. The problem is that because the body is a mechanically linked system, the movements themselves will affect the body's equilibrium. When a body part is moved, the point of gravity of the whole body is displaced, and if the movement is forceful, it will create a momentum that will push the body out of equilibrium unless the momentum is counterbalanced.

The third set of problems involves coordinating movements with the external world. Since the environment exists independent of ourselves, adaptive coordination is possible only if we can adjust our actions relative to properties of the environment and time them relative to the external events encountered. This holds true whether we are walking in a cluttered terrain, chopping wood, catching a baseball, dancing with a partner, or engaging in social communication.

If we fail to perceive and predict what is going to happen next, continuity of movement is necessarily lost. For instance, when we step on something unexpectedly slippery, our posture is suddenly perturbed, the ongoing activity is interrupted, and attention is focused on regaining balance. It is true that we have a rather efficient way of dealing with this problem, the "stretch reflexes," without which the effects of losing balance would be much worse. However, the stretch reflexes are still ad hoc and they cannot prevent the ongoing action from being interrupted. It would have been much better had we perceived the slipperiness ahead of time. There would then be no interruption. On the contrary, we might even have used the slipperiness to our advantage by, for instance, pushing ourselves forward in a skating movement (as people often do during the long winters in northern Sweden).

The same principles hold true for all induced and passive forces that may arise during production of a movement. If we are prepared for them, we not only can control those forces, but we might also use them to our advantage in producing the desired movement, as Bernstein (1967) once pointed out. Acquiring motor skills is at least partly a question of how the individual handles the contextual forces. The novice "fights" them, whereas the expert, who looks deeper into the future, may "ride" them. Downhill skiing is a good example. Every novice can witness how tiring skiing can be and how clumsy one feels going down the slopes. Not being able to predict the upcoming induced and passive forces, the novice skier tries to counteract them by, for instance, cocontraction, which is both very energy consuming and very inefficient. Expert skiers, on the other hand, who can sense those forces ahead of time, can also use them to support their action. Skiing becomes efficient, the skier is relaxed, and the descent looks easy and elegant (to the envy of the novice).

THE ROLE OF PERCEIVING

Actions are not possible without perception. Perception is needed for fitting movements to the environment, for coordinating movements with external events, and for finding out about the upcoming reactive forces during a movement (Bernstein, 1967). In the context of action, the function of perception is not primarily to evaluate what has been done but to find out what is going to happen next so action can be steered on a stable course. To perceive what has not yet happened may sound paradoxical, but events obeying the law of physics clearly do tell us not only what has already happened but, more important, how they are going to evolve in the near future. For instance, Lee (in press) has shown that the relative expansion of elements in the optic array supplies information about upcoming encounters with external objects and surfaces, time to contact with them, and whether the encounter is going to be rough or smooth. Our perception seems tuned to that kind of information. Lee and associates have shown that hummingbirds use it for homing in on a flower, pigeons guiding their landing, gannets for guiding their dives into the sea, and long jumpers for determining their takeoff point.

PLANNING AHEAD

Planning has to do with organizing the sequence of operations leading up to the accomplishment of a goal. Obviously such activity requires information about the future, some directly perceivable and some accessible only through the individual's earlier encounter with the world. However, to a certain extent the future is always unknown and unpredictable. If we are to cope both with what is known and unknown about the future, efficient planning has to flexible (Miller, Galanter, & Pribram, 1960), opportunistic (Hayes-Roth & Hayes-Roth, 1979), and dynamic. In most cases only a rough outline of the intended action is needed at the outset. As the action proceeds and information is extracted under way, details are added and the plan modified. It has indeed been argued that an efficient action plan has to unfold as a developmental process (Baker-Sennett et al., 1993; Rogoff et al., this volume).

Let's consider a game of chess. On one hand, it is clear that a fixed plan in terms of a sequence of instructions is useless for winning such a game, because the behavior of the opponent is never predictable and every move must take into account what the opponent just did. On the other hand, it is also quite clear that a good chess player looks deeply into the future and knows far ahead of time what actions may end up in a winning configuration and what kind of actions will not. The same holds true for all action plans. They reach into the future based on what aspects the individual expects will remain invariant during the task and what aspects will change. The plan is like a tentative sketch of how the action might unfold, and this sketch must be elaborated and modified under way depending on what one perceives and what one expects is going to happen next at each point in time. Only when the action can evolve dynamically in this way will it be able to serve its purpose efficiently.

To be able to sketch out a plan, we need to integrate organized knowledge of the relatively stable properties of the external world into a system of concepts and relations within which we are located. Such organized knowledge is often thought of in terms of a map of the task space (see, e.g., Hayes-Roth & Hayes-Roth, 1979; Miller et al., 1960; Tolman, 1948). Just like any good geographical map, such a cognitive map should tell us where the goal is located relative to us, note landmarks that might be useful for getting there, tell where difficulties may arise, and show easily accessible routes. In addition, the various constraints of the task, its contingencies, and its contextual opportunities should be represented. Finally, the map of the task space should help one watch for upcoming problems and opportunities and get prepared for them. For instance, when I drive my car to work, I know where I need to watch out for moose, children crossing, merging traffic, and slippery spots in wintertime.

THE ORIGINS OF PROSPECTIVE CONTROL

The variety of movements performed by the neonate may be small, but the task specificity and goal directedness these movements demonstrate warrant referring to them as actions rather than reflexes. Take rooting behavior, for instance—the infant's search for the nipple of the breast. Mechanical stimulation around the mouth makes the infant move the mouth toward the point of stimulation (Prechtl, 1958). Rooting is more than a simple reflex, however, Odent (1979) showed that rooting involves movements not just of the head and mouth but of the whole body. It seems to include exploratory movements of the entire body with all the senses involved. Directly after delivery he placed neonates on the mother's chest and abdomen and recorded the oral seeking behavior of the infant. He reported that caresses, the mother's voice, and the smell of the nipple all played important roles in guiding the newborn to the nipple. These observations were supported by Wiberg (1990).

Sucking is also a prime example of a functioning action system. Apart from using this behavior to acquire food, neonates use sucking, for instance, as a means of access to the mother's voice (DeCasper & Fifer, 1980) or to a visual event (Kalins & Bruner, 1973). Kalins and Bruner found that 5-week-old infants would use sucking as a way to focus a picture. When high-frequency sucking produced a clear focus, the infants quickly detected this contingency and increased their sucking rate. When sucking resulted in a blur, sucking rate dropped instead.

Furthermore, neonates are able to focus their head and eye movements on salient objects and events in the environment. Neonates have been shown to orient their heads toward a human voice and other complex sound sources (Alegria & Noirot, 1978; Field, Muir, Pilon, Sinclair, & Dodwell, 1979; Mendelsson & Haith, 1976) and to follow a visually defined target with head and eye movements (Ball & Tronick, 1971;

Hofsten, 1982). In learning experiments, neonates have been shown to pick up contingencies between head movements and interesting events (Papousek, 1961).

Neonates direct their arm movements toward a visually defined target (Hofsten, 1982) or a proprioceptively defined one (Butterworth, 1986; Rochat, Blass, & Hoffmeyer, 1988). Butterworth found that when neonates directed their arm movements toward their mouths, they were likely to open the mouth before the hand actually arrived there. Early stepping cannot be described as a reflex either. Thelen and colleagues (Thelen, 1985) showed that this basic behavior was modified by a number of task variables, and its disappearance could be explained in terms of the great increase in the weight of the legs during the first months of life.

In summary, actions seem to originate in action, not in reflexes. Neonatal behavior fulfills the basic requirements of actions: it is controlled by the subject, is influenced by environmental opportunities and constraints, and looks to the future for its accomplishment.

DEVELOPMENT OF PERCEPTION AND ACTION

Not only does action originate in action, action also appears to be the means by which it develops. In other words, it is by doing things that infants learn about their own mobility, about the external world, and about the opportunities and constraints of the tasks engaged in. From the beginning of life, infants are deeply engaged in exploring the external world and their ability to act in it (Gibson, 1988).

Exploratory actions have traditionally been thought of as focused on the external world and on objects and events in it, but they may just as well be focused on one's own action systems. It seems quite clear that the way to learn about one's own movement capabilities is to move around. Every voluntary movement, whatever its primary function, is also a means of exploring one's possibilities and limitations. By moving, one may learn about the local contingencies between forces acting on the moving limb. One may learn about properties that change and properties that remain invariant during execution, depending on the posture of the body and how the movements are performed, and one may learn about problems that arise in coordinating with the external world. During the early months of life, infants devote much of their daily activity to exploring their action possibilities. Movements are performed over and over again with slight alterations. Piaget (1953) was so impressed by this fact that he named several of the early developmental stages he described as stages of circular reactions.

Developing action capabilities is also a question of learning to pick up the information that makes it possible to steer the action in a prospective way. This includes distinguishing one's own movements in the environment, evaluating how one moves relative to the stationary and moving objects and surfaces in the environment, and detecting the conditions for smooth encounter with those objects and surfaces.

Research has shown that from an early age infants have the ability to detect and respond to the basic visual flow variables that relate to those problems. Ability to distinguish one's own movements from movements in the environment develops early (Kellman, Gleitman, & Spelke, 1987; Kellman & Hofsten, 1992). Young infants are also sensitive to the expanding visual flow pattern specifying approach. One-month-olds tend to blink to an approaching object (Yonas, 1981), and 3-month-olds react differently to an approaching aperture and an approaching object (Carroll & Gibson, 1981). Carroll and Gibson found that their subjects retracted their heads from an approaching object but had a tendency to lean forward toward an approaching aperture. An expanding visual flow also specifies the time to contact with an object or a surface and tells whether the encounter is going to be rough or smooth (Lee, in press). As infants start to reach and grasp objects successfully, they will also catch moving objects (Hofsten, 1980; Hofsten & Lindhagen, 1979), which seems to require sensitivity to the time-to-contact variable, and as they start to crawl and locomote, sensitivity to the variables specifying smooth or rough encounters seems essential too.

Action development and perceptual development are inseparable. The opening up of new possibilities for action during early development creates new possibilities and new needs for perceiving, and the new possibilities for perceiving will enable infants to master new patterns of movement. The onset of reaching, crawling, and locomotion therefore are milestones not only for motor development but also for perceptual development (Gibson, 1988). As new forms of acting and perceiving open up during early development, the infant will explore those possibilities. For instance, as infants discover they can grasp objects in their surroundings, they devote a considerable part of their waking time to doing so. Through reaching and grasping, they produce the necessary fine structuring of manual space with reference to both vision and proprioception, discover the possibilities and restrictions of manual actions, learn to foresee and control upcoming reactive forces, and coordinate those actions with objects and events in the world. In a series of classic experiments, Held and Hein demonstrated the importance of self-produced movements for establishing coordinated movements in kittens (Hein, 1974; Hein & Held, 1967; Held & Hein, 1963) and coordinated reaching in the rhesus monkey (Bauer & Held, 1975).

Developing skills consequently is to a great extent a question of improving one's perception in the specific context of the task. Perception must inform the actor of upcoming problems so they can be dealt with ahead of time or at an early stage when they are harmless. If this is done, flexibility of movements can be preserved at the same time as smoothness and continuity are maintained. According to Reed (1990, p. 15), "The importance of practice and repetition is not so much to stamp in patterns of movement, but rather to encourage the functional organization of action systems. This principle is constant throughout life: the achievement of an action is not the agent's coming to possess an immutable program, but rather the development of a skill. This means the ability to use perceptual information so as to coordinate movements and postures in a flexible manner that serves to accomplish a desired task."

DEVELOPING PROSPECTIVE CONTROL

The improvement of prospective control can be observed during all phases of action development, from increasing skill in forming movement trajectories to coordinating balance and movement and interacting with the external world.

Trajectory Formation

In a well functioning perception-action system, perception reaches far into the future and movements are smooth and continuous. It has long been recognized that such movements are future oriented and characterized by feedforward control. In a less well functioning system the actor has only limited knowledge of the task space and can perceive the future only very shallowly. Problems are not dealt with sufficiently ahead of time to allow smooth and continuous execution of the movement. Take, for instance, a child learning to write. Constructing letters is slow and requires much more concentration than for the child who has mastered writing. One can easily see that the drawing movements of the novice are chopped up into small segments. Such discontinuous movements are traditionally referred to as feedback regulated. From a functional point of view, however, the only thing that distinguishes "feedforward" regulated movements from "feedback" regulated movements is how far ahead in time the movement is controlled. In other words, the function of "feedback" is not primarily to look back and evaluate what has been done but to look forward and direct the movement in its next phase.

An important aspect of sensorimotor development has to do with creating more continuous and smoother movements, which requires sensing deeper into the future. This is also true for reaching. Reaching trajectories of adults can be divided into two functionally different phases, one larger approach phase occupying about three-fourths of the time and one smaller grasp phase (Jeannerod, 1981). There are good functional reasons for dividing goal-directed movements, even skill-ed ones, into two separate units—a gross movement to the vicinity of the target, followed by a more precise movement to the final destina-tion.

Hofsten (1991) found that early reaching movements were somewhat discontinuous and comprised a number of smaller movements or steps at a base rate of about 4–5 Hz. Each step started with an acceleration and ended with a deceleration. The movements were rather straight within steps and changed in direction at the transitions between steps. These characteristics can be seen in Figure 3.1, which shows a reach by a 19-week-old infant. With development, the structuring of the reaching trajectories changed in several different ways that can be observed in Figure 3.2. Most important, the number of units decreased with age. At 30 weeks of age, most reaches consisted of no more than two units like adult reaching movements. A second kind of development observed concerned the properties of the largest unit. Hofsten (1979, 1991) found that the duration of this unit became greater with age and that it covered a larger proportion of the approach.

The development of trajectory formation in infant reaching parallels in some respects the changes seen in saccadic eye movements during the first months of life. Early eye movements are also composed of several steps with similar length and duration (Salapatek, Aslin, Simons-son, & Pulos, 1980). With age the first saccade increases in the length, and the number of steps decreases. The typical mature pattern is com-posed of one large first saccade and a second small corrective saccade (Becker & Fuchs, 1969; Prablanc & Jeannerod, 1975).

Such coordinating structures continue to form and adjust throughout development. A good example is the grasping and lifting of objects stud-ied by Forssberg, Eliasson, Kinoshita, Johansson, and Westling (1991) in children ranging from 8 months to 15 years of age. One task was to lift a 200 g weight. The way adults and children of different ages ap-proached this problem is illustrated in Figure 3.3. The buildup of grip force and load force are plotted against each other for examples of lifting trials. In adults, grasping and lifting force increase in synchrony, as re-flected in the almost straight diagonal lines (lower far right diagram in Figure 3.3). However, the infants and young children approached the problem in a more or less sequential fashion. During the action, there are periods when only the gripping force increased, resulting in vertical line segments, and there are periods when only the lifting force in-

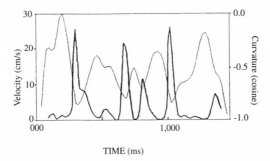

TIME (ms)

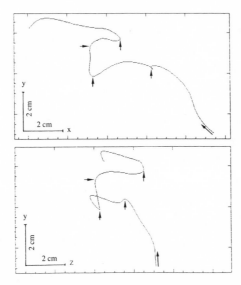

Figure 3.1 A reach of LIB at 19 weeks of age. Duration is 1.45 s. The relative straightness—the covered distance divided by the shortest distance between the end points—is 1.91. The upper figure shows velocity (thin line) and curvature (thick line) as a function of time. Note the coupling between speed valleys and curvature peaks. The movement consists of five action units. Curvature is measured in cosine of the angle. Thus −1.0 equals 180° (i.e., no curvature) and 0.0 equals 90°. The middle figure is a front view of the displacement of the hand during the reach, and the bottom figure is a side view of the same event. The short arrows indicate the borderlines between action units. The direction of the movement is indicated by the long arrow in each figure. (From Hofsten, 1991; reprinted with permission of the Helen Dwight Reid Educational Foundation, published by Heldref Publications, 1319 18th Street N.W., Washington, D.C. 20036-1802.)

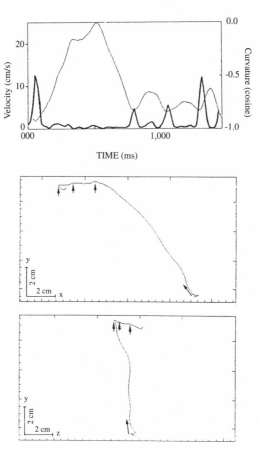

Figure 3.2. A reach by LIB at 31 weeks of age. Duration is 1.47 s. The relative straightness—the covered distance divided by the shortest distance between the end points—is 1.193. The movement consists of four action units. The upper figure shows velocity (thin line) and curvature (thick line) as a function of time. Curvature is measured in cosine of the angle. Thus −1.0 equals 180° (i.e., no curvature) and 0.0 equals 90°. The middle figure is a front view of the displacement of the hand during the reach, and the bottom figure is a side view of the same event. The arrows indicate the borderlines between action units. The direction of the movement is indicated by the long arrow in each figure. (From Hofsten, 1991; reprinted with permission of the Helen Dwight Reid Educational Foundation, published by Heldref Publications, 1319 18th Street N.W., Washington, D.C. 20036-1802).

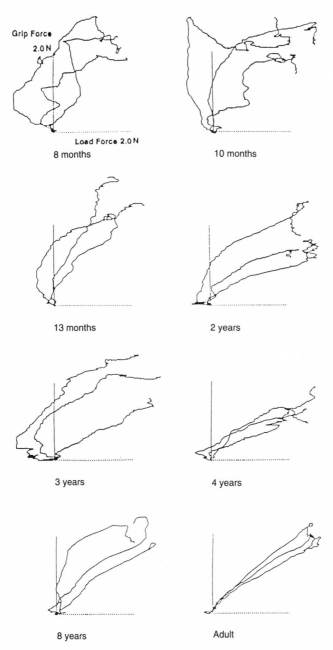

Figure 3.3. Grip force during the preload and the loading phases plotted against load force in children at various ages. Three trials are superimposed for each subject. (From Forssberg, Eliasson, Kinoshita, Johansson, & Westling, 1991, with permission.)

creased, resulting in horizontal line segments. Furthermore, the diagrams of the infants and younger children show that during the beginning of the grasping action, the object was often pressed down instead of lifted up. The fractionation of the grasping and lifting acts can still be observed in children 8 years of age.

Prospective Control of Posture and Balance

To act purposefully, we must be able to maintain balance, equilibrium of the body, and a stable orientation relative to the environment. Postural control is definitely a limiting factor in action development. Whether or not newborn infants will perform visually directed arm movements seems to depend on the postural support they are given. Grenier (1981) found that when the newborn's head was properly supported, the observed arm movements were more mature. In the studies by Hofsten (1982), the neonates who performed aimed reaches were also securely supported. Furthermore, the age when infants start to be successful at reaching—about 4 months—coincides with the age when they can sit and balance with support.

Gravity is a strong force, and disturbances have to be foreseen or detected at an early stage if balance is to be maintained without interruption of activity. The task is even more difficult for the small child than for the adult. When one is standing up, the body acts as a pendulum. The natural sway frequency of a pendulum is inversely proportional to its length; thus a short pendulum oscillates faster than a long one, allowing less time to react to disturbances. For instance, an infant half as tall as an adult has to be twice as fast in organizing actions aimed at maintaining balance. When infants start to be able to stand on their own, by the end of the first year of life, they have mastered a balance problem more difficult than at any time later in life. They also become very sensitive to peripheral visual information for body displacement, as demonstrated by Lee and Aronson (1974). Vision is superior in detecting small body displacements, and with it the subject can be more efficient in using prospective control for controlling balance. It may be argued that vision is too slow for controlling balance because the reaction to a visual perturbation is much slower than to a proprioceptive one (Nashner, 1976). However, the function of vision in this context is to inform the individual about what is going to happen next rather than what has happened. Its importance is especially clear for dynamic postural control—that is, when maintaining balance while moving around. Walking alone is also one of the most clear delays in the motor development of blind infants (Fraiberg, 1977). In a sample of blind children, 90% were delayed past the upper limits of sighted children as given by Bayley

(1969) in walking alone across a room. Although there may be other reasons for blind infants to walk late, deficient postural control is probably an important one.

To keep balance during limb movements, one must know about contingencies between limb movements, the reactive forces that arise during movement, and displacement of the point of gravity. Adults seem to precisely counteract such disturbances to the postural system ahead of time. For instance, when adults prepare to push or pull a handle in front of them, not only will they activate the arm that is doing the job, but just before the arm muscles are fired, the appropriate leg muscles that will resist a displacement of the body are activated (Cordo & Nashner, 1982). For instance, the gastrocnemius muscle is activated about 50 ms before pulling starts.

Hofsten and Woollacott (1990) studied anticipatory adjustments of the trunk in 9-month-old infants reaching for an object in front of them while balancing the trunk. The infant was seated astride one knee of the accompanying parent, who supported the child by the hips. Muscle responses were recorded from the abdominal and trunk extensor muscles as well as from the deltoid muscle of the reaching arm. The results showed that trunk muscles participated in the reaching actions of 9-month-old infants. It seemed to be the trunk extensors that primarily prepared for reaching, the role of the abdominal muscles was less clear-cut. They participated in the reach, but less as a preparation and more as part of bending the body forward toward the end of the reach (see Figure 3.4)

Postural preparations are not separate and independent but should be regarded as an integrated part of the reaching action. Reaching for an object does not involve only the upper limb: the whole body is engaged, and trunk adjustments both before the arm is extended and after it has arrived at its goal are important parts of the process. Figure 3.4 shows that reaching in 9-month-olds is embedded in an envelope of trunk adjustments.

Interacting with the Outer World

In the act of reaching for a stationary object, several problems need to be dealt with in advance if the encounter is to be smooth and efficient. The reaching hand needs to adjust to the orientation, form, and size of the object. The securing of the target must be timed in such a way that the hand starts to close around the target in anticipation of the object encounter and not as a reaction to it. Such timing has to be planned and can occur only under visual control. Tactually controlled grasping is initiated only after contact, and it will by necessity induce an interruption

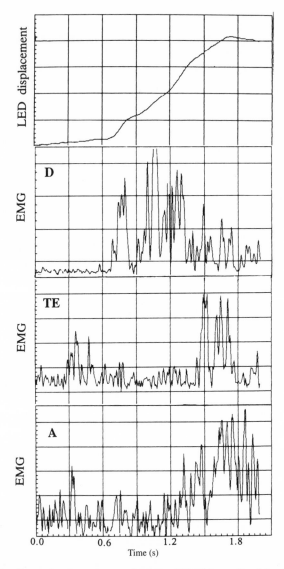

Figure 3.4. Example of responses of subject HAW from the deltoid of the reaching arm, the abdominal muscles, and the trunk extensors plus records of the relative displacements of the reaching hand. In this specific example, the reach was performed with the left hand. It can be seen that the trunk extensor muscles (TE) starts increased firing well before the deltoid (D) muscle. The abdominal (A) muscles have some activation before the deltoid muscle too, but the major activation occurs toward the end of the reach. (Hofsten & Woollacott, unpublished data.)

in the reach-and-grasp act. Thus the emergence of visual control of grasping is crucial for the development of manual skill.

Hofsten and Rönnqvist (1988) studied the timing of the grasp in infants' reaching. They determined when the distance between thumb and index finger started to diminish, and in addition they monitored the position of the target. The target was placed at the end of an elastic rod, and when encountered it was immediately displaced, which enabled them to precisely determine this event too. Five-month-old, 9-month-old, and 13-month-old infants were studied. At all three age levels, the hand started to close in anticipation of the encounter with the object. Figure 3.5 shows the distribution of time differences between starting to close the hand and the arrival at the target for each of the age groups. In the two younger groups, the hand first moved to the neighborhood of the target and then started to close around it. For the 13-month-olds, however, the grasping action typically started during the approach, well before touch. In other words, at this age the grasping movement was starting to become integrated with the approach movement into one continuous approach-and-grasp act.

To coordinate and time one's actions relative to an external event, one must foresee the effects of that event in addition to the effects of the action itself. The first signs of such abilities are seen in infant eye movements. At 3 months of age, infants show their first signs of smooth tracking eye movements, during which the eye is slightly ahead of the target (Aslin, 1981). At the same age, Haith and associates (Canfield & Haith, 1991: Haith, Hazan, & Goodman, 1988; Wentworth & Haith, 1992) demonstrated that infants will start to predict where the next picture in a left-right sequence is going to be shown by moving the eyes there before the picture appears (see also Haith, this volume).

A remarkable ability of infants to time their action relative to an external event is demonstrated in early catching behavior. In a series of studies, I have found that infants possess a remarkable capacity to catch objects (Hofsten, 1980, 1983; Hofsten & Lindhagen, 1979). Infants were presented with a moving object passing in front of them within reach. They reached for this object from the very age they began mastering reaching for stationary ones. Eighteen-week-old infants were found to catch the object moving at 30 cm/s. Hofsten (1983) found that 8-month-old infants successfully caught an object moving at 120 cm/s. The initial aiming of these reaches was within a few degrees of the meeting point with the target, and the variable timing error was only about 50 ms. Figure 3.6 shows an 8-month-old infant catching an object moving at 60 cm/s. Another way to learn about prospective control in infant catching is to suddenly and unexpectedly stop the target while the infant is reaching for it. Such a catch is illustrated in Figure 3.7. Figure 3.7 shows that

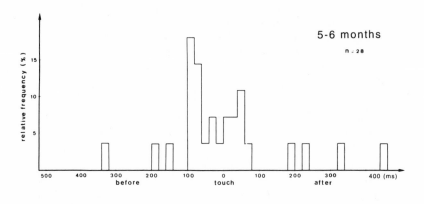

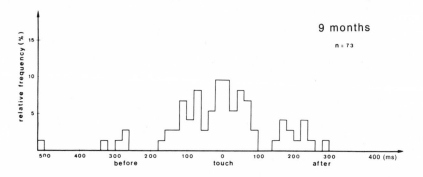

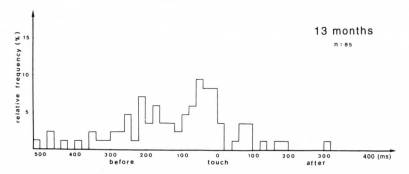

Figure 3.5. The relative frequency distributions of time intervals between starting to close the hand and touch for individuals reaches performed by a group of 5–6-month-old infants, 9-month-old infants, and 13-month-old infants. (From Hofsten & Rönnqvist, 1988; copyright 1988 by the American Psychological Association, reprinted by permission of the publisher.)

Figure 3.6. A 7-month-old infant in the process of catching an object moving at 45 cm/s. The frames are 200 ms apart.

the reach ended at the very point in space where the target should have been had the movement continued.

THE EVOLUTION OF PROSPECTIVE CONTROL

Movements that biological organisms produced in the environments they evolved for are purposeful. There are exceptions to this rule, of course, but they are relatively rare. Even the movements of simple worms are purposeful, as demonstrated by Darwin (1881). Purposes are projected into the future, and the same is true for purposeful movements. The better an animal can look into the future, the better it can master upcoming events and the more favorable are the conditions for its survival. In the perceptual domain, this selective pressure has sensitized the system to parameters in the optical flow corresponding to the dynamics of events (Runesson, 1977) and causal factors between events (Michotte, 1946). It has made animals able to extract optical information about upcoming encounters with external objects and surfaces, time-to-contact with them, and whether the encounter is going to be rough or smooth (Lee, 1992). Finally, it has made at least humans and chimpanzees able to perceive the intentions of other individuals (Premack, 1991).

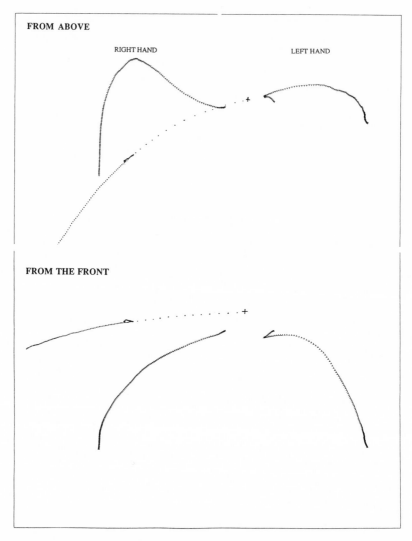

Figure 3.7. An attempt by an 8-month-old infant to catch an object that moves at 60 cm/s and suddenly stops 200 ms before the end of the reach recorded optoelectronically (SELSPOT) at 300 Hz. Observe how the end positions of the two hands, which actually touch each other at that time, coincide with the point in space where the object should have been had the movement continued. Note that the markers were placed on the back of the hands proximal to the index fingers, which explains why the end positions of the markers are slightly below the imagined object position.

Planning serves to expand prospective control beyond what is immediately perceivable. It requires knowledge of the relatively stable properties of the external world, of the opportunities and constraints of the task, and of one's mobility in the specific context of the task. It will indicate what opportunities and problems might arise in the course of action and help one direct one's attention toward the prospective information specifying those events. All the various cognitive activities, like attending, remembering, problem solving, feeling, and thinking, participate. They all evolved to enable us to prepare and organize our behavior for future events and activities. In the guidance of action, they open up a larger window to the past and the future than is available to perception itself. This running window is often refered to as "working memory."

The ability to plan actions does not diminish the importance of direct perceptual guidance, however, and working memory does not enable us "to guide behavior by representations of the outside world rather than by immediate stimulation and thus to base behavior on ideas and thought," as stated by Goldman-Rakic (1990, p. 391). Ideas and thought do not replace perception. On the contrary, the paradoxical consequence of being able to represent the outside world is to make perception more effective. This is not done by adding detail and clarity to perception, as has often been thought in the past (Helmholtz, 1925). Rather, the strength of being able to expand the action sphere in space and time beyond what is immediately perceivable has to do with getting an overview. In an overview, new global structures of the world become distinguishable, providing frames of reference for the more detailed structures embedded within them. Thus, planning and perceiving are complementary. An overview without details is just as insufficient as details without an overview. Planning and perceiving are both necessary for dealing with what is going to happen next.

REFERENCES

Alegria, J., & Noirot, E. (1978). Neonate orientation behavior towards human voice. *International Journal of Behavioral Development, 1,* 291–312.

Aslin, R. N. (1981). Development of smooth pursuit in human infants. In D. F. Fisher, R. A. Monty, & J. W. Senders (Eds.), *Eye movements: Cognition and visual perception.* Hillsdale, NJ: Erlbaum.

Baker-Sennett, J., Matusov, E., & Rogoff, B. (1992). Sociocultural processes of creative planning in children's playcrafting. In P. Light & G. Butterworth (Eds.), *Context and cognition: Ways of learning and knowing* (pp. 93–114). Hemel Hempstead, Eng.: Harvester Wheatsheaf.

Baker-Sennett, J., Matusov, E., & Rogoff, B. 1993. Planning as a developmental process. In H. Reese (Ed.), *Advances in child development and behavior* (Vol. 24, pp. 253–281). New York: Academic Press.

Ball, W. A., & Tronick, E. (1971). Infants' responses to impending collisions: Optical and real. *Science, 171,* 818–820.

Bauer, J., & Held, R. (1975). Comparison of visually guided reaching in normal and deprived infant monkeys. *Journal of Experimental Psychology: Animal Behavior Processes, 1,* 298–308.

Bayley, N. (1969). *Bayley scales of infant development.* New York: Psychological Corporation.

Becker, W., & Fuchs, A. F. (1969). Further properties of the human saccadic system: Eye movements and corrective saccades with and without visual fixation points. *Vision Research, 9,* 1247–1258.

Bernstein, N. (1967). *The coordination and regulation of movements.* Oxford: Pergamon.

Butterworth, G. (1986). Some problems in explaining the origins of movement control. In M. G. Wade & H. T. A. Whiting (Eds.), *Motor development in children: Problems of coordination and control* (pp. 23–32). Dordrecht: Martinus Nijhoff.

Canfield, R. L., & Haith, M. M. (1991). Young infants' visual expectations for symmetric and asymmetric stimulus sequences. *Developmental Psychology, 27,* 198–208.

Carroll, J., & Gibson, E. J. (1981). *Differentiation of an aperture from an obstacle under conditions of motion by three-month-old infants.* Paper presented at SRCD, Boston.

Cordo, P. J., & Nashner, L. M. (1982). Properties of postural adjustments associated with rapid arm movements. *Journal of Neurophysiology, 47,* 287–302.

Darwin, C. (1881). *The formation of vegetable mould through the action of worms, with observations on their habits.* London: J. Murray.

DeCasper, A. J., & Fifer, W. P. (1980). On human bonding: Newborns prefer their mothers' voices. *Science, 208,* 1174–1176.

Field, J., Muir, D., Pilon, R., Sinclair, M., & Dodwell, P. (1980). Infants' orientation to sounds from birth to three months. *Child Development, 51,* 295–298.

Forssberg, H., Eliasson, A. C., Kinoshita, H., Johansson, R. S., & Westling, G. (1991). Development of human precision grip: 1. Basic coordination of force. *Experimental Brain Research, 85,* 451–457.

Fraiberg, S. (1977). *Insights from the blind.* New York: Basic Books.

Gallwey W. T. (1986). *The inner game of tennis.* London: Pan Books.

Gibson, E. J. (1988). Exploratory behavior in the development of perceiving, acting, and the acquiring of knowledge. *Annual Review of Psychology, 39,* 1–41.

Goldman-Rakic, P. S. (1990). The prefrontal contribution to working memory and conscious experience. In J. C. Eccles & O. Creutzfeldt (Eds.), *The principles of design and operation of the brain* (pp. 389–407). Pontificiae Academiae scientiarum Scripta Varia, 78. Berlin: Springer-Verlag.

Grenier, A. (1981). "Motoricité libérée" par fixation manuelle de la nuque au cours des premières semaines de la vie. *Archives Françaises de Pédiatrie, 38,* 557–561.

Haith, M. M., Hazan, C., & Goodman, G. S. (1988). Expectation and anticipation of dynamic visual events by 3.5-month-old babies. *Child Development, 59,* 467–479.

Hayes-Roth, B., & Hayes-Roth, F. (1979). A cognitive model of planning. *Cognitive Science, 3,* 275–310.

Hein, A. (1974). Prerequisite for development of visually guided reaching in the kitten. *Brain Research, 71,* 259–263.

Hein, A., & Held, R. (1967). Dissociation of the visual placing response into elicited and guided components. *Science, 158,* 390–391.

Held, R., & Hein, A. (1963). Movement-produced stimulation in the development of visually guided behavior. *Journal of Comparative and Physiological Psychology, 56,* 872–876.

Helmholtz, J. von. (1925). *Physiological optics* (Vol. 3). (J. P. C. Southhall, Ed.). Washington, DC: Optical Society of America.

Hofsten, C. von. (1979). Development of visually guided reaching: The approach phase. *Journal of Human Movement Studies, 5,* 160–178.

Hofsten, C. von. (1980). Predictive reaching for moving objects by human infants. *Journal of Experimental Child Psychology, 30,* 369–382.

Hofsten, C. von. (1982). Eye-hand coordination in newborns. *Developmental Psychology, 18,* 450–461.

Hofsten, C. von. (1983). Catching the skills in infancy. *Journal of Experimental Psychology: Human Perception and Performance, 9,* 75–85.

Hofsten, C. von. (1991). Structuring of early reaching movements: A longitudinal study. *Journal of Motor Behavior, 23,* 280–292.

Hofsten, C. von, & Lindhagen, K. (1979). Observations on the development of reaching for moving objects. *Journal of Experimental Child Psychology, 28,* 158–173.

Hofsten, C. von, & Rönnqvist, L. (1988). Preparation for grasping an object: A developmental study. *Journal of Experimental Psychology: Human Perception and Performance, 14,* 610–621.

Hofsten, C. von, & Woollacott, M. (1990). *Postural preparations for reaching in 9-month-old infants.* Unpublished manuscript.

Jeannerod, M. (1981). Intersegmental coordination during reaching at natural visual objects. In J. Long & A. Baddeley (Eds.), *Attention and performance* (Vol. 9, pp. 153–168). Hillsdale, NJ: Erlbaum.

Kalins, I. V., & Bruner, J. S. (1973). The coordination of visual observations and instrumental behavior in early infancy. *Perception, 2,* 307–314.

Kawato, M., and Gomi, H. (1992). The cerebellum and VOR/OKR learning models. *Trends in Neuroscience, 15,* 445–453.

Kellman, P. J., Gleitman, H., & Spelke, E. S. (1987). Object and observer motion in the perception of objects by infants. *Journal of Experimental Psychology: Human Perception and Performance, 13,* 586–593.

Kellman, P. J., & Hofsten, C. von. (1992). The world of the moving infant: Perception of motion, stability, and space. In C. Rovee-Collier & L. Lipsitt (Eds.), *Advances in infant research* (Vol. 7, pp. 147–184). Norwood, NJ: Ablex.

Lee, D. N. (in press). Body-environment coupling. In U. Neisser (Ed.), *Ecological and interpersonal knowledge of the self.* Cambridge: Cambridge University Press.

Lee, D. N., & Aronson, E. (1974). Visual proprioceptive control of standing in human infants. *Perception and Psychophysics, 15,* 529–532.

Mendelsson, M. J., & Haith, M. H. (1976). The relation between audition and vision in the human newborn. *Monographs of the Society for Research in Child Development, 41* (No. 167).

Michotte, A. (1946). *La perception de la causalité.* Louvain: Publications Universitaire.

Miller, G. A., Galanter, E., & Pribram, K. (1960). *Plans and the structure of behavior.* New York: Holt, Rinehart and Winston.

Nashner, L. M. (1976). Adapting reflexes controlling human posture. *Experimental Brain Research, 26,* 59–72.

Odent, M. (1979). The early expression of the rooting reflex. In L. Carneza & L. Zichella (Eds.), *Emotion and reproduction* (Vol. 20B). London: Academic Press.

Papousek, H. (1961). Conditioned head rotation reflexes in infants in the first months of life. *Acta Pediatrica, 50,* 565–576.

Piaget, J. (1953). *The origins of intelligence in the child.* New York: Routledge.

Prablanc, C., & Jeannerod, M. (1975). Corrective saccades: Dependence on retinal reafferent signals. *Vision Research, 15,* 465–469.

Prechtl, H. F. R. (1958). The directed head turning response and allied movements of the human infant. *Behaviour, 13,* 212–242.

Premack, D. (1991, October). *Prolegomenon to evolution of cognition.* Paper presented at Dahlem conference "Exploring Brain Functions: Models in Neuroscience," Berlin.

Reed, E. S. (1990). Changing theories of postural development. In M. Woollacott & A. Shumway-Cook Eds.), *Development of posture and gait across the life span.* Columbia: University of South Carolina Press.

Rochat, P., Blass, E. M., & Hoffmeyer, L. B. (1988). Oropharyngeal control of hand-mouth coordination in newborn infants. *Developmental Psychology, 24,* 459–463.

Runesson, S. (1977). On the possibility of "smart" perceptual mechanisms. *Scandinavian Journal of Psychology, 18,* 172–179.

Salapatek, P., Aslin, R. N., Simonsson, J., & Pulos, E. (1980). Infant saccadic eye movements to visible and previously visible targets. *Child Development, 51,* 1090–1094.

Thelen, E. (1985). Developmental origins of motor coordination: Leg movements in human infants. *Developmental Psychobiology, 18,* 1–18.

Tolman, E. C. (1948). Cognitive maps in rats and men. *Psychological Review, 55,* 189–208.

Wentworth, N., & Haith, M. M. (1991). *Event-specific expectations of 2- and 3-month-old infants.* Unpublished manuscript.

Wiberg, B. (1990). *The first hour of life.* Unpublished doctoral dissertation, Department of Applied Psychology, Umeå University.

Yonas, A. (1981). Infants' responses to optical information for collision. In R. N. Aslin, J. R. Alberts, & M. R. Petersen (Eds.), *Development of perception: Psychobiological perspectives: Vol. 2. The visual system.* New York: Academic Press.

Chapter Four

Perception, Action, and Skill
Looking Ahead to Meet the Future

Ralph J. Roberts Jr. and Michael Ondrejko

In this chapter we explore the perceptual and cognitive processes that are involved in the performance of improvisational action skills. We first discuss an important characteristic of many real-world skills—they are adapted quickly and precisely to a varied and often changing environment. Flexibility and precision can be difficult to achieve jointly, especially under tight time constraints. We argue that future-oriented processes are a key component of successful action. Yet skills that are improvisational cannot be entirely scripted in advance but must be organized on line. We suggest that performers actively seek specific perceptual information to monitor ongoing action and to plan upcoming action. To examine these ideas, we present research that utilizes video games and eye-movement recordings to explore the real-time interactions between perceptual selection and upcoming task actions in performers

This research was supported by National Science Foundation grant BNS8618043 and National Aeronautics and Space Administration grant NAG2-737 to Ralph J. Roberts Jr. We would like to thank Scott Wiebke, Laura Valaer, and Brandon Matthias, who helped in the collection and analysis of the data. Thanks are also due to Naomi Wentworth, Claes von Hofsten, Bennett Bertenthal, and the volume editors for providing critical commentaries on an earlier draft of the chapter.

with varying amounts of skill. The findings reveal the characteristics of well-integrated perception-action couplings and suggest important changes in future-oriented processing with the acquisition of expertise.

FLEXIBLE PRECISION IN SKILL

Our ability to learn and perform complex action skills is truly remarkable. From crawling and catching balls to driving and improvising jazz, we acquire a wide variety of skills whose extraordinary complexity is often obscured by the seeming effortlessness of performance. Yet successful action must fit many simultaneous constraints defined by the parameters of the world we act in, the physical construction of our bodies, the processing characteristics of our nervous systems, and the goals that mobilize our actions (Bernstein, 1967/1984; Kugler, Kelso, & Turvey, 1980). Skilled action can be viewed as a solution or set of solutions to the problems of meeting these many simultaneous constraints. Although the difficulty of finding such solutions is mostly transparent once we develop expertise, it is far more apparent to the novice. As an example, consider a common predicament the novice snow skier faces when recognizing that the only available path to the bottom of the mountain is an expert-level run:

> You're still waiting for those butterflies in your stomach to stop fluttering. . . . You've been standing here at the lip of this incredible mogul field (2- to 4-foot bumps) . . . for five minutes and already it seems like an eternity. The bumps below you are big, big and mean, choppy and steep . . . not at all inviting. But they must be so to all those other skiers, creatures from another planet maybe, who smoothly slip by you over the lip and disappear down the fall line, snaking through those bumps . . . legs oscillating like rubber pistons, (upper) bodies motionless, poles deftly picking out a line where all you can see is the possibility of linked disasters. . . . You don't belong up here and you know it. (Tejada-Flores, 1986, p. 125)

Skiing down such a steep, bumpy slope without injuring oneself is unquestionably a complex skill. What makes this sort of skill so remarkable is that performers maintain a high degree of precision in the timing and sequencing of action while continually adapting to a varied and often changing environment. In skiing such a slope, an expert makes two to three turns a second, and each turn is composed of several component actions, including knee flexing, lower body turning, weight shifting, arm reaching, and pole positioning. Successful action requires great precision in the timing of these actions as well as the specific way the actions are executed. Small errors can result in quick disaster. But precision is not enough: action must also be continually adapted to environmental particulars. To carve a path down the slope, the skier must adapt to the position and size of the moguls, the varied surface conditions on each mogul, and obstacles such as bare spots and other skiers. Flexibility is a necessity since no two ski runs are identical; each offers a somewhat different set of challenges.

Thus skiing, like many complex action skills, requires that action occur under tight time pressure and be both precise in its execution and adapted to varied environmental particulars. This is an extraordinary accomplishment. In any behaving system, flexibility and precision can easily be at odds with one another and difficult to achieve jointly. Efforts at optimizing one often degrade the other. For example, it is relatively easy nowadays to design robots that carry out actions with single millisecond accuracy when those actions are scripted and not based on varied environmental circumstances. In such cases, action can be programmed in advance and is relatively inflexible. But if the robot needs to adapt its behavior to changing and somewhat unpredictable circumstances, then it is very difficult to achieve quickly organized and precisely timed behavior (cf. Anderson, 1988). It is much easier to be flexible if the system can evaluate the present context and construe a response without regard to timing.

A central question for understanding skilled action, then, concerns how flexibility and precision are achieved jointly in the multitude of action skills learned in a lifetime. One part of the answer relates to the degrees of freedom problem (Bernstein, 1967/1984). Actors can adapt more quickly and effectively if the many degrees of freedom in action are "compressed" so that the controlled parameters are few. Action theorists have discussed how reductions in the degrees of freedom may result from a variety of sources, including functional muscle synergies, properties of neural computations, and the dynamics inherent in the physical construction of our bodies (for recent reviews see Rosenbaum, 1991; Turvey, 1990). In this chapter we focus on the prospective character of skilled action as a means for understanding flexible precision. In particular we are interested in how perception provides information to allow an actor to prepare for a specific future. We suggest that actors must obtain relevant information at particular moments in action and must also know how to use the information to organize upcoming action. Performers' actions, then, need not follow predefined scripts or react to immediate contexts: they can be based on assessments of future conditions construed from an ongoing interaction with the environment.

PROSPECTIVE CONTROL AND THE PERCEPTION-ACTION CYCLE

The insight that some form of prospective control is involved in producing skilled action has been recognized at least since Bryan and Harter (1899), who studied telegraph operators. These researchers concluded that as operators become more skilled, the units of action become increasingly larger hierarchically organized sequences—from letters to words to common phrases. Predictable sequential interdependencies are profitably used so that the future becomes built in, so to speak, in the organization of the units. A half century later, several researchers argued more directly for the importance of prospective control. Lashley (1951) reasoned that skilled behaviors such as speech, piano playing, and typing occur too quickly for one action to serve as a stimulus for the next; sequences of action must be planned in advance. Miller, Galanter, and Pribram (1960) went further to describe a theoretical framework for specifying how plans and goals organize everyday behavior. Even lower-level motor control, Bernstein (1967/1984) argued, involves anticipation, particularly when "during the course of any given segment of a movement, retrospective control becomes practically impossible" (p. 368). These and other researchers (e.g., Piaget & Inhelder, 1969) pointed the way toward several decades of subsequent research and theory aimed at understanding the cognitive constructs that underlie prospective control, such as schemas, plans, scripts, and motor programs, and the associated feed-forward control processes. This work has shown how advance specification of future action makes precision and speed possible, since action need not be reactive to either prior action or environmental events (also see Haith, this volume; Hofsten, this volume).

Despite this progress, it is still somewhat of a mystery how skilled actors can quickly adapt to constantly changing and often somewhat unexpected environmental circumstances. Paralleling the engineer's efforts at programming skilled action in the robot, the work on the prospective control of action focuses on sequential behavior that tends to be scripted in advance (or relatively simple), but not *continuously* adapted to a varied or changing environment. As described earlier, pre-specification of the sequencing and timing of action is possible when environmental circumstances are irrelevant or perfectly predictable. Yet this is rarely true—most action skills are more improvisational. Simply put, cognitive theorists have tended to neglect the environment, except as it provides stimuli for a response or after-the-fact feedback. In particular, there has been comparatively little work on the perceptual processes that enable the skilled actor to use environmental information to control action. The notable exception to this trend is the work of James Gibson

(1966, 1979) and those influenced by his views (e.g., Hofsten, 1985; Lee, 1980; Reed, 1982; Turvey & Kugler, 1984; Warren, 1984).

Gibson (1966, 1979) and others (e.g., Turvey & Kugler, 1984) have argued that prospective control is accomplished by the pickup or detection of information that is available in the present optical structure, and that this information unambiguously specifies future states. The best worked out example is the optical flow that accompanies self-motion or the motion of an object as it approaches an observer. Lee (1980) has shown that the inverse of the rate of dilation of an optic image specifies time-to-contact, and can be used in a variety of skilled actions, from slowing a car to stop at an intersection to timing the closing of one's hand to catch a ball. Optical structure is not a stimulus for a response, it is a continuous source of information for guiding ongoing activity.

This analysis not only places perception at the center of action, but also highlights the idea that perception is action based. In addition, it dramatically shifts how we think about the environment, from the long-standing perspective that the environment provides "stimuli" to a realization that there is a wealth of perceptual information available to an observer interacting with the environment. In the context of skilled action, it is our view that the actor must also know *how* to use perceptual information to organize activity and must be *selective* in obtaining the relevant information at the appropriate times.

The ability to utilize available perceptual information to organize upcoming action often depends on an actor's knowledge. For example, the state of a traffic light and its relevance for my actions as a driver approaching an intersection is directly related to my knowledge of traffic lights and their role in controlling traffic. Similarly, my expectation that the police will soon be monitoring my speed might be based on seeing an oncoming motorist flash his or her headlights. I make an inference about the meaning of the flashing lights based on my knowledge of how motorists sometimes communicate with each other. Thus, perceptual information for guiding future action can involve knowledge as well as inference for its effective use.

The optic array typically offers a great deal of information, much more than is relevant for a specific action or action sequence. Thus, perceptual selection may be necessary to obtain appropriate information at the appropriate times. As action unfolds, an actor's goals and subgoals change, as does the information that is most relevant for accomplishing those goals. The most important information may come from different places at different times. As an example, reconsider the expert skier maneuvering down the mogul run. The closest mogul provides information about a turn in progress, adjacent moguls provide information about possible upcoming turns, and skiers, trees, and rocks scattered farther down the mountain provide information about possible future paths. Depending on the skier's current and upcoming goals (e.g., initiating a turn, figuring out which path leads to a particular chairlift, finding a companion in a crowd of skiers), different kinds of information are more or less relevant. We expect that selection is active and knowledge based.

Thus we take the view that contexts of action provide a rich source of perceptual information for determining and calibrating upcoming action. Some information directly specifies upcoming environmental events, other information is useful because a skilled actor can infer the relevance of the information for future action. Perception is also selective in terms of what is most important at any given moment, and what is most important is partially determined by the changing goals and subgoals the actor constructs as action unfolds.

This perspective on the interaction between action, cognition, and perception is similar to the views espoused by Arbib (1980, 1989) and Neisser (1976) when describing the perceptual cycle. In the context of skilled action, the actor's goals for upcoming action direct perceptual selection. Information gathered, in turn, helps organize action planning and modifies the unfolding goals and subgoals for action, which further direct perceptual selection, and so on. Perceptual information is used prospectively; as Arbib (1989, p. 26) notes: "Perception is oriented toward the future as much as the present—not only to interacting with the environment in some instrumental way, but also to updating an *internal model of the world* to be used to guide future action."

Although this approach to the close interconnections between perception and action seems sensible, there are few well-developed methodological approaches readily available for studying such relations. The perception-action cycle is more of a general hypothesis than an empirically established fact. Historically, perception and action have most often been studied separately, and the two have evolved into somewhat different disciplines. In addition, there are practical problems for studying the kind of perception-action cycle described above. In an effort to maintain experimental control, we normally develop tasks that are far less complex than the real-world contexts they are designed to inform us about. Although we eschew stimulus-response theories of learning and performance, most of our experimental paradigms employ a stimulus-response methodology: subjects perform individual trials where a response is made to some stimulus. The interdependent cycling of perception and action may not be evident or even necessary in such simplified settings. Another problem concerns how to measure both perception and action continuously in more realistic, complex settings.

These are problems we have been grappling with in our own research, and in the rest of the chapter we describe an approach we have developed for examining the perception-action cycle. The approach uses specially designed video games as the context of action and the spatiotemporal patterning of eye movements as an indicator of perceptual selection.

CORRESPONDENCES BETWEEN EYE MOVEMENTS AND SKILLED ACTION

Skilled behavior occurs in environments that are often cluttered and dynamic, and the sources of information about various aspects of the environment also vary across place and time. Since we are able to extract detailed visual information only from the fovea, which occupies a relatively small part of the visual field, we move our eyes to reposition the fovea to those areas of the scene that are presumably most informative. Thus in many situations eye movements can be a relatively straightforward indicator of perceptual selection (cf. Loftus, 1983; Stark & Ellis, 1981). In such cases one would expect that the pattern of fixation locations and the timing of saccadic movements should correspond in some regular fashion with the flow of action, and that the form of this correspondence should reveal the ways skilled performers gather visual information to anticipate future states and plan action accordingly.

There is very little research that examines eye movements in the context of ongoing action (although see Bahill & LaRitz, 1984; Shapiro & Raymond, 1989). A notable exception to this trend is the work on reaching and pointing, where researchers have examined correspondences between hand, head, and eye movements (e.g., Biguer, Jeannerod, & Prablanc, 1982; Carnahan & Marteniuk, 1991; Gielen, Van den Heuvel, & Van Gisbergen, 1984). This work indicates that in pointing and reaching tasks, movements of the eye and hand are tightly coupled in time, with the eye beginning slightly before (60–100 ms) or close to the same time as the hand and arriving at the target consistently about 200 ms before the hand arrives (Angel, Alston, & Garland, 1970; Carnahan & Marteniuk, 1991). Early arrival of the eye is viewed as anticipatory, since it allows for late corrective feedback for the hand movement. Several models have been constructed to explain this tight coupling between eye movements and arm movements, yet it is entirely unclear whether the correspondences found in these relatively simple and discrete pointing tasks are representative of what occurs in more complex contexts, where perception and action are continuous and environments are cluttered and nonstatic. A goal for our work was to examine such correspondences in a more complex, less constrained setting as a starting point for exploring the real-time characteristics of the hypothetical perception-action cycle.

SUMMARY AND OVERVIEW OF THE VIDEO GAME STUDY

The perspective on perception and action just reviewed can be summarized as follows, and it acts as a set of guiding assumptions for our work: Skilled action is both flexible and precise in how it is organized in accordance with a varied and changing environment. Action sequences cannot be primarily reactive to environmental particulars because responses would often be too late—some form of prospective control is necessary. Yet action sequences cannot be planned too far in advance, since not all relevant contextual information for planning action can be known in advance. The optic array provides a wealth of information about current and upcoming conditions, and this information can be used for adapting action to an upcoming environment. To use perceptual information effectively, the skilled performer must know what information is relevant at what points in time during the flow of action. Just as action must often be anticipatory, so must perceptual information gathering that subserves that action. Thus action and perception interact in a continual cycle, with the goals of action influencing perceptual selection and the information gained influencing subsequent action planning.

The primary purpose of our research was to examine the perception-action cycle in a reasonably complex task in which behavior was continuous and relatively unconstrained. We examined the spatiotemporal characteristics of eye movements as an index of perceptual selection and the sequence of task actions as an index of the actor's unfolding action goals. Since there is little previous work that examines eye movements in the context of ongoing skilled action, our initial work was necessarily exploratory and descriptive. The research focused on the following questions:

- How is perceptual selection, as evidenced by eye movements, related to ongoing action? In particular, to what degree do the locations of foveal regard and the timing of changes in looking location correspond to what the actor is trying to accomplish?
- If regular correspondences occur, what do they reveal about how visual information is utilized? To what degree does perceptual selection anticipate action? Is there evidence that performers actively look ahead to gather perceptual information to select and calibrate future action?
- Are there differences in perception-action correspondences as a function of expertise? And if so, what do such differences suggest about what is acquired with the acquisition of skill? For example, do novices show a less consistent relation between perception and action? Are they less able than more experienced players to use visual information to plan action appropriately?

To examine these questions, we used a specially designed video game in conjunction with an infrared eye-movement recording system (Roberts, Brown, Wiebke, & Haith, 1991). We used the video game because, although it is a somewhat constrained perception-action context, it shares a number of important similarities with other complex perception-action skills: expertise cannot be acquired quickly and requires both precision in the timing and sequencing of actions and flexibility in the face of a continually changing context.

METHOD

Experimental Setup

The task was presented to subjects in an arcade style video game cabinet (see Figure 4.1). Subjects sat on a stool in front of the cabinet and rested their heads on a chin-forehead support. Subjects' hands rested on a panel that contained three buttons, two for the left hand (middle and index fingers) and one for the right hand (index finger). Subjects viewed a half-silvered mirror tilted 60° from horizontal. The task monitor was a 19-in. (48.3 cm) x-y vector monitor with a $1,024 \times 768$ resolution that was positioned under the mirror and angled 20° from the horizontal. With this arrangement, the monitor appeared to be directly in front of the subject's face at a distance of 66 cm; 1 cm on the game monitor equaled 0.87° of visual angle. An infrared light and an infrared-sensitive video camera were positioned behind the mirror and aimed at the subject's left eye.

The video output from the camera was fed to an automatic eye tracker that processed the video signal to find the locations of the center of the pupil and the center of the corneal reflection of the infrared light. The difference between these values relates monotonically to looking location (with an accuracy of approximately ½° of visual angle). These data were output to a computer that sampled the data at 60 Hz. The computer also received input from the video game's processor and collected, synchronously with the eye-movement data, a complete digital record of the video game's display and the button presses. (For a more complete description of the hardware and software, see Roberts et al., 1991.)

Video Game Task

The task was based on a commercially available game called Asteroids (see Figure 4.2). The subject controlled the actions of the "ship," a triangle displayed at the screen center (0.7 cm at the base, 1.2 cm high). The two left-hand buttons controlled the ship's orientation by rotating it counterclockwise or clockwise. As long as a turn button was pressed, the ship rotated around its center axis at a rate of 250°/s. The ship always remained at the center of the screen. A "shot" could be released from the nose of the ship when the fire button was pressed. A shot moved

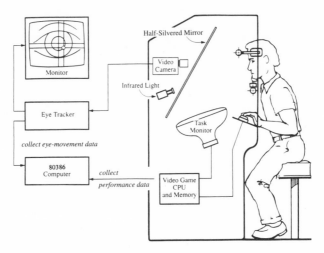

Figure 4.1 A schematic diagram of the data collection system (adapted from Roberts, Brown, Wiebke, & Haith, 1991). The cutaway of the video game booth shows a subject viewing a reflection of the task monitor on a half-silvered screen. Behind the one-way mirror an infrared-sensitive video camera focuses on the subject's left eye, which is illuminated by a near-infrared light. The video signal from the camera is fed to an automatic eye tracker that outputs x-y locations of the centers of the pupil and corneal reflection of the infrared light to an 80386 personal computer. The 80386 PC also collects synchronous performance data from the video game central processing unit.

across the screen in a straight line at 17.7 cm/s and disappeared when it intercepted a target or traversed the length of the screen. Potential targets were moving "asteroids" (jagged circles with a 0.5 cm radius), that also moved in a straight line across the screen at constant velocities. When an asteroid moved off the edge of the screen, it "wrapped around" to immediately reenter on the opposite edge. Each asteroid's velocity and trajectory angle were determined randomly within a range of values. Thousands of combinations were possible.

The subject's task was to avoid letting an asteroid intercept the ship and to successfully shoot as many asteroids as possible. To discourage rapid "blind" shooting, we programmed the task so that only one shot could be displayed on the screen at a time—pushing the fire button had no effect until the previous shot either intercepted an asteroid or disappeared from the screen. When a shot intercepted an asteroid, an explosion sequence was displayed and the asteroid disappeared. A replacement asteroid was immediately generated on the edge of the screen, with a new velocity and trajectory. This arrangement ensured that the subject received feedback on the success of each shot and that

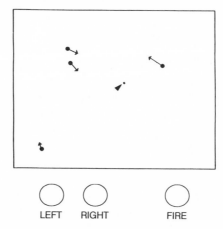

Figure 4.2   A representation of the video game task. The circles represent the asteroids, and the triangle represents the ship. The lines are not displayed on the screen but are shown here to represent the motions of the objects. The circles at the bottom of the figure show the positions of the buttons that control the ship.

the number of potential targets remained constant, regardless of the subject's level of expertise. When an asteroid intercepted the ship, the ship exploded and a new ship was displayed.

We felt that the task, designed with these features, required the key characteristics of perception-action skills that were of interest. First, successful performance (many hits, few asteroid-ship interceptions) required integrating several perception and action components, such as selecting targets, determining intercept times and positions, reorienting the ship for aiming, and timing the release of the shots. Flexibility was required, since the context was continually changing and it was very unlikely that two games would ever be identical. Precision in the timing of action was also required; for example, many targets moved quickly across the screen and had brief intercept windows (30–500 ms) for a given orientation of the ship.

Subjects and Procedure

We tested 13 college-age subjects who were divided into two groups based on their previous experience with video games and their performance on a pretest. The novice group (three males and four females) reported that they had played video games only on a few occasions, whereas the experienced group (five males and one female) said they were avid video game players. Subjects were tested on a pretest that was similar to the experimental task. The pretest consisted of thirty 15-s trials. Subjects in the experienced group obtained an average of 6.6 hits per trial (the range of subject averages was 6.2–7.6), and those in the novice group averaged 2.7 hits (range = 2.0–3.7), $t(11) = 11.2$, $p <$ .001. Although the subject partitioning clearly distinguished players of different levels of skill and experience, it is important to note that the experienced players were not true experts on our task, since they had never played our constrained version of the Asteroids game before coming to the lab. Additionally, our novices were not complete beginners, since they had already practiced 30 trials of the game before testing began. With these caveats in mind, we will refer to the groups as experts and novices.

Subjects performed 20 test trials, divided into four blocks. Each block contained randomly ordered trials with 1, 4, 7, 10, and 13 asteroids per trial. These different "clutter" conditions allowed us to sample performance across a range of contexts and to assess how such changes influenced performance. Trials lasted 20 s, which excluded the time the ship was not displayed on the screen after an asteroid-ship interception. At the end of each trial, performance feedback was provided on the screen that showed the number of hits and ship "deaths."

Coding and Dependent Measures

During performance, two 60 Hz streams of data were collected: one contained performance and task-environment information, and the other contained eye-movement information. These data were further processed to obtain the relevant performance variables. Global variables that described summary aspects of task actions for a single trial were straightforward to extract from the performance data. Such variables included the frequency and duration of button presses, the number of hits, the number of shots, the number of asteroid-ship interceptions, and the distances between objects at various points in time (e.g., ship-asteroid distance of hit targets).

Obtaining variables that reflected the relations between eye movements and task actions was more involved. First, the eye-movement data were linearized and transformed into the task-monitor coordinate space (Roberts et al., 1991; Sheena & Borah, 1981). These data consisted of looking locations specified in x–y coordinates of the task monitor for each $\frac{1}{60}$ s. These data did not specify what object a subject was looking at, since the objects on the screen, except for the ship, were always moving. In addition, the data did not directly specify the eye's state (fixation, saccade, or smooth pursuit), the timing of the transitions between states, or the relations between eye movements and task actions. The next step in data reduction provided these missing pieces.

The performance data contained the x-y locations of each object and the status of the three buttons (pressed/not pressed) for each $\frac{1}{60}$ s. These data allowed us to create a complete replay on a computer screen of a performance trial, in real time, slow motion, or stopped frame. Since the transformed eye-movement data were in the same coordinate space, we developed a program that superimposed a crosshair on the game screen to show the looking location for each frame. Thus we could view a replay of a trial with a moving crosshair showing the player's changing visual regard. The replay program simultaneously displayed, on a separate monitor, a plot of the coordinates of the direction of gaze, highlighting the current frame of data displayed on the task monitor. This replay program provided the core for a computer-assisted coding system (for more detail, see Roberts et al., 1991).

Coders examined replays and the corresponding visual-regard plots of every trial and made judgments about the beginning of saccades (rapid shifts in point of regard), fixations (relatively stationary point of regard), and smooth pursuit or tracking (relatively continuous movement of gaze direction). Coders also indicated, with a cursor on the task screen, the object of visual regard (an asteroid, the ship, the shot, or empty areas) in conjunction with the fixation and tracking codes. Also coded were blinks and other types of noise in the data. All codes were stored with information on the objects of regard (e.g., asteroid distances from ship) and synchronous task performance data (e.g., onset and offset of the button presses). Interrater reliability on the codes was very high: two scorers coded the same 20% of the data set, distributed across all subjects. Coder agreement on the choice of code and the frame to mark the code ($+/-$ 1 frame) was always above 95%. Agreement on the object of regard was always above 90%.

RESULTS

We first describe general characteristics of task performance and then describe activity from a more sequential, time-based perspective. For this latter analysis, we present a framework for segmenting the behavioral stream and a detailed example of typical expert performance. We then present group data for experts and novices that describe the correspondences between eye movements and task actions during each of the behavioral segments.

Performance Overview

The results reported in this section describe global characteristics of task behaviors and eye movements without reference to their moment-to-moment sequencing or interactions. For task behaviors, success at playing the game was expected to reflect expertise. Global measures of eye-movement behavior, such as the percentage of time spent looking at various locations, provided an index for determining how players generally distributed their visual attention. We expected fewer differences in these global indexes of eye movements than in measures that reflected the spatiotemporal interactions between eye movements and task actions. These latter measures, reported in later sections, were expected to better reflect characteristics of the perception-action cycle.

Each subject performed 20 trials, four at each of the five levels of clutter (1, 4, 7, 10, and 13 asteroids). Performance variables were obtained for each trial and then averaged within level of clutter so that there was a single score for each clutter level. We examined performance with mixed analyses of variance with expertise as a between-subjects factor and amount of clutter as a within-subject factor. Since the effects due to clutter were few and not the primary focus of the study, we report these effects only in a few cases.

Task Performance

As would be expected, the experts performed better than the novices. Experts successfully shot more asteroids ($M = 5.9$, $SD = 0.6$) than novices ($M = 2.6$, $SD = 0.8$), $F(1,11) = 61.5$, $p < .001$, although both groups obtained more hits as the amount of clutter increased, $F(4,8) = 56.7$, $p < .001$. A significant interaction between expertise and clutter, $F(4,8) = 8.5$, $p < .01$, indicated that experts were better able than novices to obtain more hits with increasing clutter. Part of the reason experts got more hits was that they fired more shots, $F(1,11) = 26.1$, $p < .001$. On average, experts fired 11.3 shots per 20-s trial while novices fired 7.6. Experts were also more accurate in their shooting: the percentage of shots that successfully intercepted a target was higher for experts ($M = 51$, $SD = 5$) than novices ($M = 33$, $SD = 8$), $F(1,11) = 26.6$, $p < .001$. As would be expected from their superior shooting, experts also had fewer ship-asteroid interceptions per trial ($M = 0.10$, $SD = 0.05$) than did novices ($M = 0.41$ $SD = 0.26$), $F(1,11) = 7.2$, $p < .05$.

The turn buttons allowed subjects to reorient their ship before shooting, and experts tended to use the buttons more frequently than novices ($Ms = 17.2$ and 14.4; $SDs = 1.8$ and 2.9, respectively), $F(1,11) = 4.0$, $p = .07$, but they pressed the buttons for somewhat shorter durations (in milliseconds: $Ms = 180$ versus 235; $SDs = 27.1$ and 28.0, respectively), $F(1,11) = 11.6$, $p < .01$. Experts and novices did not differ, however, in the average number of turns per shot (overall $M = 1.8$, $SD = 0.6$). Thus, experts turned more frequently because they fired more shots, but both experts and novices made the same number of ship orientation adjustments per shot.

To summarize, experts performed more quickly and more accurately than the novices, although the novices were reasonably successful at obtaining hits and avoiding ship deaths.

Eye Movements

In contrast to task performance, there were very few global differences between experts and novices in where they looked or in how long they looked at various locations. To examine how performers distributed their looking across various possible locations, we collapsed the coded eye movements into the following six categories:

- Fixate on ship: fixation with 2° of visual angle of ship.
- Track target: smooth pursuit of upcoming target.
- Track nontarget: smooth pursuit of nontarget moving asteroid(s).
- Fixate between ship and target: fixate on a blank area of the screen that is near halfway between the ship and the target.
- Fixate between ship and nontarget: fixate on a blank area of the screen between ship and asteroid(s).
- Fixate other: fixate on areas of the screen not covered in the other categories, such as watching the moving shot or the brief animated explosion sequence when an asteroid is hit.

For each trial, we summed the frequencies and durations of fixations and tracking for each category. We present the findings averaged across clutter condition, since there were only a few minor differences related to clutter.

Overall, subjects spent the most time (duration) tracking targets (41%) and fixating on the ship (33%). Interestingly, subjects sometimes looked at a location between the ship and target (9%), perhaps to minimize both objects' distance from central vision. Nontarget asteroids were not looked at as long as the targets (track nontarget = 8%, fixate between nontarget and ship = 3%). The duration of looks at other locations summed to 5%. As shown in Table 4.1, the frequency and average duration of looks at the various locations were almost identical in experts and novices.

The preceding analyses show that experts were indeed better players, in terms of accuracy of shooting, number of shots fired, and avoiding asteroid-ship interceptions. Players were not so different, however, in the general characteristics of their eye movements. Both groups tended to look most often at the ship or the moving target. This global analysis of performance does not inform us, however, about the correspondence between eye movements and task actions.

Segmenting the Flow of Perception and Action

Subjects' actions were not constrained during each trial and consisted of a continuous stream of eye movements and task actions. To examine

TABLE 4.1 Averages for Looking Measures for Experts and Novices

									Visual tracking			
			Between ship and target		Between ship and nontarget		Other		Target		Non-target	
	Ship											
	M	*SD*	*M*	*SD*	*M*	*SD*	*M*	*SD*	*M*	*SD*	*M*	*SD*
Frequency												
Expert	10.6	2.3	4.8	1.7	1.3	0.6	5.8[a]	0.7	12.7[a]	2.4	3.1	0.5
Notice	10.2	1.5	3.4	0.9	2.1	0.9	3.3	0.8	9.2	1.3	4.6	1.7
Duration (ms)												
Expert	645	91	442[b]	65	365	117	256	46	731	77	377	46
Novice	555	142	343	50	302	54	210	39	671	78	388	62

LOOKING LOCATIONS / Fixations

Note. Numbers represent averages across 20 trials.
[a]Expert/novice difference, $p < .01$.
[b]Expert/novice difference, $p < .05$.

naturally occurring correspondences between eye movements and task actions, we developed a means for segmenting the stream of behavior so that common points of action could be compared within and between subjects. A simple task analysis of the video game suggested three basic components or subgoals of performance. The first component was *selecting a target*. In the multiple-asteroid trials there were 4 to 13 potential targets on the screen. Before releasing a shot, the players needed to determine which asteroid would be the next target. As described below, players routinely made an eye movement to the target before acting on it, in terms of turning the ship toward the target or shooting at it. The next component was *reorienting and aiming*. Before shooting, players typically reoriented the ship, presumably to position the angle of the upcoming shot's trajectory to intercept the selected target. The final component was *timing the interception*. After reorienting the ship, there was typically some time lag before the shot was released. The timing had to be precise, often within tens of milliseconds, to obtain a hit. At some point after the shot was released (or perhaps before), the player would cycle back to the first component—selecting a target.

As described previously, our computer setup allows us to replay performance in slow motion with a crosshair indicating the position of the player's changing visual regard. When viewing such a replay, the observer immediately gets a sense of these sequenced action components, as well as how the shifting of visual regard corresponds to the player's unfolding action goals. We briefly describe an example of such a replay to convey a sense of the flow of action.

Figure 4.3 presents a sequence of still-frame samples of a 1,900 ms

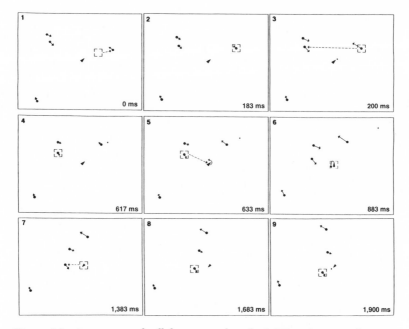

Figure 4.3   A sequence of still-frame samples of a 1,900 ms excerpt of an expert performance. Each panel represents a snapshot in time when some aspect of performance changed: the person either used one of the buttons or made an eye movement to a new object of regard. Shown are the positions of the asteroids (dots) and the shot (small dot), the orientation of the ship (triangle), and the position of foveal regard (box). The lines and arrows on each of the objects indicate the position of the object in the *next* panel. Panel number and elapsed time (beginning from the first panel) are shown in the upper left and lower right corners, respectively. See the text for a description of the sequence of events.

excerpt of expert performance. The excerpt represents nothing remarkable or unusual; it is typical of good performance. Each panel represents a snapshot in time when some aspect of performance changed; the person either used one of the buttons or made an eye movement to a new object of regard. Shown are the positions of the asteroids (dots) and the shot (small dot), the orientation of the ship (triangle), and the position of foveal regard (dotted box). The lines and arrows on each of the objects indicate the position of the object in the *next* panel. Panel number and time elapsed (beginning from the first panel) are shown in the upper left and bottom right corners, respectively.

The panels show the player shooting twice. In panel 1, the player had already reoriented the ship and was fixating on the blank area between the ship and the target. In panel 2, 183 ms later, the player made an eye movement to the target and tracked its movement. Shortly thereafter (17 ms, panel 3), the player fired the shot (as indicated by the dot above the ship). Notice that the shot was fired *before* the target reached its intercept point, although the shot was still too late for an interception. Less than half a second later (417 ms, panel 4) the player made an eye movement to another asteroid on the other side of the screen, which became the next target. Two points are worth noting. First, the player did not foveally examine several asteroids before selecting the next target. The selection must have been made peripherally, since the player had not viewed the new target foveally. Second, the selection occurred quickly—the eye movement to the new target began after the shot passed the intercept line of the old target but before the shot traversed the rest of the screen. Given that it takes some time to program an eye movement, the selection had to occur even earlier. In this case it most likely occurred before the shot reached the intercept line. Shortly after the eye movement to the new target (16 ms, panel 5), the player pressed the left turn button, which started the ship's rotation toward the new target. Notice that during the initiation of the turn, the subject was foveating on the target, not the ship. But 250 ms later (panel 6), the player made a saccade to the ship while the turn was in progress. The turn continued for another 500 ms (panel 7), and 300 ms after the turn was completed, the player made a saccade back to the moving target (panel 8). As decribed below, this pattern was very common—players determined turning direction without the benefit of foveal examination of the ship, but they almost always shifted to examining the ship during the turn and for several hundred milliseconds after the turn was completed before saccading back to the target. The pattern suggests that looking at the ship is not necessary for deciding which direction to turn it but is important for determining when to stop the turn and for encoding the ship's new orientation. Returning to the example, the player released the shot 217 ms after returning to tracking the target (panel 9).

This example scenario exemplifies the kind of correspondence we found between eye movements and task actions. Performers moved their eyes to gather visual information that was important for organizing upcoming action. The following analyses cover the entire data set and were aimed at examining the generality of the patterns just described and exploring the similarities and differences between the two expertise groups. For these later analyses, we were interested in comparing the patterns of correspondences as well as the relative consistency in the couplings between eye movements and task actions.

In the following analyses the shot was the unit of analysis. Each shot defined an *episode* that covered the period extending from the firing of the previous shot to the firing of the current shot. In several of these analyses we excluded the one-asteroid trials. Medians were calculated for all time and distance variables within each trial and were then averaged for each clutter condition. Times are reported in milliseconds. In instances where we were interested in the degree of variability in the timing between eye-movement onsets and task events, we calculated standard deviations for each trial and then averaged the deviations within each clutter condition. Most of the analyses consist of mixed ANOVAs, with expertise group as a between-subjects factor and degree of clutter as a within-subject factor, although we report clutter effects in only a few cases. The findings are presented in order of the three subgoals of action: selecting a target, reorienting the ship, and timing the interception.

Target Selection

The coding system differentiated between looking at targets and looking at nontargets. This was a relatively simple, highly reliable judgment because subjects tended to foveally examine only one or two potential targets in an episode. All subjects tended to visually track at least one asteroid in over 90% of the episodes (experts: $M = 96\%$, $SD = 4$; novices: $M = 93\%$, $SD = 2$, n.s.). In these episodes, where the target was identified, we calculated the number of asteroids that were considered foveally (tracking an asteroid) or close to the fovea (fixating between an asteroid and the ship). Both groups of subjects rarely looked at more than two potential targets, although experts looked at significantly fewer ($M = 1.2$, $SD = 0.06$) than novices ($M = 1.6$, $SD = 0.34$), $F(1,11) = 5.1$, $p < .05$. Remarkably, the number of potential targets looked at did not increase with increasing clutter (4 to 13 asteroids), $p > .3$. One could argue that performers looked at so few asteroids because they were pursuing the same target across several episodes. In fact, however, both groups chose the last episode's missed target on only 15% of the episodes. When these episodes were removed from the analyses, the pattern of results did not change.

The preceding analyses suggest that players limited their foveal examination to only a few asteroids before deciding which one would be the actual target. It appeared that deciding which asteroid to choose was based on visual information obtained outside the fovea. We examined the first eye movement to the target in cases where the target was not the same as in the previous episode. The average visual angle between the point of regard immediately before the eye movement and the target was $7.6°$ ($SD = 0.9°$), well outside the foveal region. This distance did not differ as a function of expertise.

The first saccade to the new target also occurred relatively quickly after the previous shot was fired, and experts were faster than novices (experts: $M = 714$, $SD = 148$; novices: $M = 1247$, $SD = 397$), $F(1,11)$ $= 9.5$, $p < .05$). The time between the previous shot and the first look to the target was also more variable in novices than in experts (mean trial standard deviations, novices: $M = 1445$, $SD = 445$, experts: $M = 683$, $SD = 94$, $F(1,11) = 16.5$, $p < .005$.

It did not appear that the choice of target was random or haphazard for either group of subjects, and our impressions from observing many replays was that the choices were in fact good ones—players seemed to choose targets that were most likely to intercept or come close to the ship. Such targets not only were more dangerous but were often easiest to hit. A comparative analysis of all the asteroids on the screen immediately before the first look to the target showed that players looked at the asteroid closest to the ship in 50% of the episodes ($SD = 8\%$). Players also seemed to take direction of movement into account: when the asteroid closest to the ship was moving toward the ship, it was chosen 64% of the time ($SD = 8\%$), but when it was moving away it was chosen only 17% of the time ($SD = 9\%$). These selection percentages did not differ between the two groups.

To summarize, players did not foveally examine several possible targets among the many moving asteroids. Instead, they visually identified one or two possibilities soon after shooting at the previous target. The target selection was most often made from information gained in the periphery and seemed to reflect good choices. Compared with the novices, the experts foveally considered fewer alternatives, shifted visual regard to the target more quickly, and were less variable in the timing between the previous shot press and initial saccade to the new target.

Reorienting and Aiming

The first look to the new target occurred before shooting at the target and was the first straightforward behavioral indication that the player had started preparing for the next hoped-for interception. The time between the first look and the eventual shot was often used for repositioning the ship and presumably for obtaining visual information about the target's trajectory, velocity, and position for timing the release of the shot (see below). The median time lag between the first look to the target and the shot was shorter for experts ($M = 989$ ms, $SD = 178$) than for novices ($M = 1560$ ms, $SD = 579$), $F(1,11) = 5.3$, $p < .05$, and it decreased with increasing amounts of clutter, $F(3,9) = 4.3$, $p < .05$. Experts were also less variable in the time lag between the first look and the shot; the averaged within-trial standard deviations of this lag were 539 ms ($SD = 28$) and 821 ms ($SD = 62$) for experts and novices, respectively, $F(1,11) = 59.4$, $p < .001$.

As would be expected, experts were more effective at turning the ship to increase the likelihood of an interception. A straightforward measure of turning effectiveness is whether a possible intercept existed before the first turn and after the last. Intercepts did not exist for a given orientation when the target would not cross the intercept line, such as when the asteroid had already passed the ship. The percentage of such "impossible" targets before the first turn was high and did not differ between the groups (experts: $M = 54$, $SD = 6$; novices: $M = 56$, $SD = 8$), $p > .5$. After the last turn, the percentage of impossible targets was low, and experts had a significantly lower percentage ($M = 3$, $SD = 2$) than novices ($M = 10$, $SD = 3$), $F(1,11) = 13.7$, $p < .005$.

Turning the ship appropriately for an interception required taking into account characteristics of the target, such as its trajectory, velocity, and distance from the ship; thus, visually tracking the target provided important information for determining an appropriate ship orientation. Foveating on the ship, however, was also important for preparing for an eventual interception, since looking at the ship provided information on the direction it was pointing, which was especially important when turning. The timing of when to stop turning needed to be precise, since pressing the turn button for even a short duration had a large effect: a 200 ms press changed the ship's orientation by 50°. Thus both ship and target provided important information for calibrating action, and these locations could often not be examined foveally at the same time. Players shifted their gaze, on average, 1.7 times during an episode ($SD = 0.87$). Shifting of visual regard between ship and target would presumably increase when both locations could not be placed at or near the foveal region, that is, when the distance between the objects increased. To examine whether this was indeed the case, we divided episodes into two groups using a median split of target-asteroid distances early in the episode (the median distance was 7.3° of visual angle, which did not differ between groups, $p > .3$). Those episodes with targets farther from the ship averaged 2.0 shifts ($SD = 0.9$), while those with closer targets averaged 1.0 shifts ($SD = 0.7$), $F(1,11) = 87.6$, $p < .001$. This effect did not interact with expertise.

When subjects did turn the ship before shooting, they tended to make an eye movement to the ship sometime during the turn, although this tendency varied somewhat depending on the context, such as the degree of clutter, the distance from the target, and the extent of the turn. Subjects looked at the ship on 76% of the turns ($SD = 9$). This percentage did not differ as a function of expertise, $p > .2$, but it did decrease linearly with increasing clutter, from 89% of the turns ($SD = 9$) with 1 asteroid, to 68% of the turns ($SD = 14$) with 13 asteroids, $F(1,11) = 23.3$, $p < .005$. Shifting of visual regard between ship and target would presumably increase when both locations could not be placed at or near the foveal region, that is, when the distance between the objects increased. A comparison of the turns at which subjects did and did not look at the ship showed that turns including an eye movement to the ship involved targets that were significantly farther from the ship (Ms = 8.2° versus 6.1°, SDs = 0.5 and 0.7), $F(1,11)$ = 160.4, p < .001. Turns that incorporated an eye movement to the ship were also significantly larger (Ms = 74° versus 57°, SDs = 13 and 14), $F(1,11)$ = 33.3, p < .001. Thus, subjects most often looked at the ship sometime during a turn, and looking was more likely with fewer asteroids on the screen, when the ship and the target were farther apart, and when the player was making larger turns.

When subjects did look at the ship during a turn, the saccade to the ship occurred close to the start of the turn, while the eye movement away from the ship usually occurred well after the turn was completed. On average, saccades started 92 ms (SD = 87) before the turn began; in 44% of these cases the fixation began after the turn had started. This timing suggests that subjects usually decided which direction to turn the ship when not foveally examining the ship's orientation. There were no differences in this timing across groups. Eye movements away from the ship began after the completion of the turn in 92% (SD = 3) of the cases. The lag between the end of the turn and the look away from the ship was remarkably long in both groups, although the lag was shorter for experts than for novices (Ms = 422 versus 565 ms, SDs = 128 and 99), $F(1,11)$ = 5.1, p < .05. The long lag suggests that subjects almost always watched the end of the turn and continued to foveate on the ship to encode the new orientation before shifting visual regard back to the target.

Experts were less variable in the timings between looking and turning. The average trial standard deviation for the timing between the saccade to the ship and the start of the turn was greater in novices (M = 528 ms, SD = 110) than in experts (M = 395 ms, SD = 71), $F(1,11)$ = p < .05. Similarly, the average trial standard deviation for the timing between the end of the turn and the look away from the ship was greater in novices (M = 535 ms, SD = 96) than in experts (M = 397 ms, SD = 100), $F(1,11)$ = 6.2, p < .05.

To summarize, between the first look to the target and the eventual shot, players most often reoriented the ship. Both the ship and the target provided important information for determining the final orientation, and players shifted visual regard between the two locations. Changes in looking location seemed to occur when updated information was needed most: shifts from target to ship were most likely when the target and ship were far apart and farther out of alignment. Saccades to the ship occurred near the beginning of the turn, but saccades away occurred well after the completion of the turn, suggesting that foveal information was not needed for initiating the turn but was used for monitoring changes in orientation and updating information on the postrotated position. Overall, experts were faster and less variable in the timings between shifting visual regard and task actions.

Timing the Interception

After the last turn players needed to determine the best time to release the shot. As in the example scenario described earlier, shots usually needed to be fired before the target reached the intercept line, since it took time for the shot to reach the intercept (the shot traveled at 1.4° of visual angle per 100 ms). In many cases firing when the target was at the intercept would be too late, since the target would have passed the intercept point by the time the shot arrived. The best time to release the shot varied as a function of the target's velocity and trajectory (which determined the time for the target to reach the intercept) and the distance between the intercept and the ship (which determined the time for the shot to reach the intercept).

The time lag between the last turn and the fire button press varied from 0 to 4702 ms. Experts generally pressed the fire button earlier ($M = 551$, $SD = 122$) than did novices ($M = 827$, $SD = 158$), $F(1,11) = 12$, $p < .005$, and were also significantly less variable in this timing ($M = 363$, $SD = 51$) than were novices ($M = 512$, $SD = 115$), $F(1,11) = 7.8$, $p < .05$. Determining the right moment to release the shot required precise trajectory and velocity information about the target, and performers' visual regard immediately before shooting suggests that the moving target provided the most relevant immediate data for timing the interception. Both groups of players tended to visually track the target immediately before pressing the fire button, although experts did so significantly more often than novices ($Ms = 86\%$ versus 71%, $SDs = 5$ and 6), $F(1,11) = 14.2$, $p < .005$. There was also evidence for a functional relation between looking at the target before shooting and the likelihood of a successful hit. When tracking the target before shooting, players were almost twice as likely to hit the target ($M = 0.40$, $SD = 0.14$) as when looking elsewhere on the screen before shooting ($M = 0.22$, $SD = 0.11$), $F(1,11) = 50.6$, $p < .001$, and this relation did not differ between groups.

We also examined the timing characteristics of missed shots. For each target, we calculated the best time to release the shot given the ship's orientation before shooting. Misses by experts were closer to a hit ($M = 531$ ms off, $SD = 90$) than were the misses of novices ($M = 760$ ms off, $SD = 153$), $F(1,11) = 10.6$, $p < .05$. Missed shots by novices tended to be late rather than early. The average percentage of late misses was 68% (SD = 7) for novices, but 47% (SD = 9) for experts, $F(1,11)$ = 19.3, $p <$ .005. Experts were also less variable in the timing of their misses (mean of trial standard deviations = 594 ms, SD = 110) than novices (M = 767 ms, SD = 84), $F(1,11)$ = 9.2, $p <$ .05.

To summarize, determining the best time to fire the shot required information about the target's trajectory and velocity, and subjects tended to track targets visually before shooting. Tracking the target was related to increased probability of a hit, and experts tracked the target more often than novices. Novices also tended to fire too late, so that when the shot reached the intercept, the target had already passed. Experts' misses were almost equally divided between being late and early. As in other aspects of performance, experts were less variable in the timings between actions.

DISCUSSION

The findings suggest that the patterning of eye movements during performance was well integrated with ongoing action. The timing of shifts in visual regard in relation to the subjects' actions and events on the game screen was well coordinated, even in the less skilled players. The probabilities of shifting visual regard at particular points in the sequence of action and the relatively low variability in the timings between looking and acting reflected relatively stable looking-acting correspondences. These coordinations were not, however, as tightly synchronized as is typically found in reaching and pointing studies (e.g., Biguer et al., 1982; Carnahan & Marteniuk, 1991). In less constrained settings, such as the one examined here, eye movement and other action systems may be more flexibly coordinated by adapting to variations in context and the goals of action.

Obtaining visual information via eye movements also seemed remarkably efficient. For example, players did not foveate on more than one or two potential targets, even when there were many possibilities. Players used peripheral information to make the selection and usually made a saccade to the new target less than a second after the previous target was shot. In many such cases, the peripheral selection must have occurred before the previous shot reached its target.

Another example of the efficiency of visual selection was shifting between looking at the target and looking at the ship when setting up for the next shot. There was an implicit competition between looking at the two locations. The target provided critical time-varying information for organizing action to obtain an intercept, but the ship usually needed to be turned, and the player needed to precisely gauge the ship's new orientation to accurately time the release of the shot. Most of the time players tracked the target, but when a turn began they usually shifted to looking at the ship, especially in cases where foveal information was particularly needed (when the ship was farther from target and when the new orientation was significantly different from the old one). Deciding which direction to turn the ship did not require detailed foveal information on the ship's orientation, so players usually shifted visual regard to the ship about the beginning of the turn; they did not waste time looking at the ship before the turn. Alternatively, players needed to determine the ship's new orientation accurately to obtain a hit; a miscalculation of just a few degrees could misplace the intended intercept point by several centimeters. Yet if players returned to tracking the target before releasing the shot (which they usually did), they could determine the ship's orientation only from peripheral vision or from memory. Our guess is that memory was important, since peripheral vision often would not provide detailed enough spatial information to determine the orientation within several degrees. These ideas are consistent with player performance: players almost always continued to foveate on the ship for several hundred milliseconds after the turn was completed before making a saccade back to the target. In the context of the game, several hundred milliseconds was a long time to stare at the only stationary object on the screen, but that amount of time would be required if one wanted to encode the ship's new orientation into memory.

These examples illustrate the fact that perceptual selection was efficient and well organized for regulating action. Knowing something about what the subject was doing was very instructive in determining where the subject would be looking and when shifts in foveal regard were likely to take place. In the context of the perception-action cycle discussed in the chapter opening, the findings suggest that visual information gathering was used to regulate ongoing action and, most significantly for the present purposes, to *prepare for upcoming action*. Almost every shift in looking location can be viewed as future oriented: one selects a new target to determine a new ship orientation, one looks at the start of the turn to determine when to stop the turn, one looks at the ship after the turn to acquire information that will be used later to time the shot release, one tracks the target to determine when to release the shot, and one continues to track the target after the shot is released to see if it will hit the target.

Perceptual information was used in preparing for future action, but action was also based on anticipated future states, determined from current visual information and from task knowledge. For example, the ideal time to release the shot most often was before the target reached the intercept point. In such cases the shot would be released based on some estimate of when the target would reach the intercept, which would be the same time it should take the shot to reach the intercept. The time for the target to reach the intercept involved examining the velocity, trajectory, and current position of the asteroid. Determining the time it would take to take the shot to reach the intercept entailed combining the perceived distance between the ship and the intercept with one's knowledge of the shot speed. Anticipating future states was also involved in determining the new orientation of the ship when setting up for a new target. There was usually a time lag of several hundred milliseconds between the end of the last turn and the firing of the shot. Players positioned the ship in an orientation that provided enough time to encode the ship's final orientation, saccade back to the target, and track the target. Thus players needed to determine how far ahead to turn the ship based on the target's velocity, trajectory, and current position as well as some determination of the amount of lead time required for "setting up" for the interception.

The ability to use visual information to anticipate upcoming events and plan action accordingly was undoubtedly important in allowing action to be both flexible and precise. Players adapted to the particulars of each episode by quickly and efficiently repositioning their foveae to obtain the relevant information for organizing action. Precision was possible when players organized their actions appropriately to an accurate appraisal of the near future. Yet players did not always perform effectively, and the novices were clearly less effective than the experts. Our findings suggest several hypotheses about what is acquired with increasing levels of expertise.

Experts and novices did not differ in many of the general characteristics of eye movements; they were also quite similar in how task actions corresponded to eye movements. (Although as described in the methods section, these groups were not as disparate in skill level as would be expected with genuine experts and novices.) For example, despite some group differences, novices were surprisingly good at using peripheral vision to select the next best target and at efficiently moving visual regard to and from the ship during turning. Given that our task was fairly novel for those who were not video game players, these findings suggest that the novices employed well-developed perceptual skills that could quickly be adapted to the particulars of the game.

Although general perceptual processes did not appear to differ across the groups, there were aspects of performance that were consistently different. Experts were faster than novices in almost every respect: they took less time to find a new target, to orient the ship, to move visually between ship and target, and to time the interception. Experts' actions were also better tuned to the task environment: their shots were more accurately timed, and their turning was more effective in setting up for the next target. Novices' actions were often too late. In shooting, novices tended to release the shot when the target had already moved too close to the intercept. We also noticed that subjects often pushed the turn button too long and consequently turned the ship too far. This would occur if players did not take into account their own reaction time in determining when to stop pressing the button. Perhaps the most salient expert/novice difference was the within-subject variability in the timing between eye movements and task actions. Almost every measure of the variability in the time lag between an action and the initiation of an associated eye movement was significantly higher in novices.

Taken as a whole, the pattern of expert/novice differences in behavior suggests several important differences in cognitive and perceptual processing. First, novices have greater difficulty using current perceptual information to determine future states, such as where a particular target will be at some future time. This difficulty often results in action that is based relatively more in the present time frame—that is more reactive to current conditions. In such cases action will be late. Second, novices are also less knowledgeable about the properties of their "tools" for action, such as the rotation rate of the turn button and the velocity of the shot. Increased uncertainty about how to use current information for planning upcoming action and about the properties of one's tools for action would contribute to increased variability in performance. Such variability may be an essential part of eventually determining appropriate mappings between action, perception, and context (Freedland & Bertenthal, 1994; Siegler, 1989). With practice, however, uncertainty and variability are reduced and perception-action components become increasingly "automatic." Automatized components should reduce the degrees of freedom that require explicit control and increase overall speed.

Our findings, when examined along with related research, suggest a more speculative set of hypotheses about future-oriented processing and the acquisition of complex perception-action skills. Novices are not as adept as experts at using current contextual information to determine future states and organize upcoming action appropriately, and consequently they appear less future oriented. Yet less experienced performers might actually commit *more* cognitive resources to future-oriented processes, such as in planning action or determining what will happen next. As one develops expertise, the future gets built in to increasingly automated perception-action modules (cf. Bryan & Harter, 1899). During skill acquisition, the performer learns the implications of specific perceptual information for upcoming action and develops perception-action modules that embody those regularities. As the modules become well developed, performers can quickly adapt to new situations, since they have a repertoire of well worked out components that can be rapidly chosen and implemented. Thus experts do not need to plan far into the future (cf. Simon, 1981) and may spend fewer resources on "scenario spinning" (Calvin, 1990) than novices. Returning to the example discussed at the outset, when novices learn to ski moguls, instructors often teach them to plan four or five turns ahead. Yet the goal of the training is to ski like experts, who can adapt very quickly to the particulars of the slope and rarely look more than two turns ahead (Tejada-Flores, 1986). Thus we are suggesting that expert action is better adapted to the future, but that experts may allocate fewer resources to future-oriented processes than novices do. Novices are not as successful at taking the future into account and, at least at particular points in learning, will devote a great deal of effort to trying to predict future states and plan accordingly.

Two other studies of video game performance (using different tasks) support this view. In one study, Logie, Baddeley, Mane, and Donchin (1989) examined the role of working memory in the performances of more or less skilled players. Working memory is seen as a limited resource for holding transient information on line and performing simple computations, and it is viewed as essential for future-oriented behavior in general and short-term planning in particular (Baddeley, 1986; Goldman-Rakic, 1987; Pennington, this volume; Roberts, Hager, & Heron, in press). Logie et al. (1989) found that the performance of less skilled players was disrupted more by secondary working-memory tasks than the performance of more skilled players. It is worth noting that not all interference tasks showed this pattern; for example, a motor-timing task was more interfering for more experienced players than for less experienced ones. The findings suggest that working memory, which may be essential for future-oriented processes, is more heavily utilized at lower levels of skill. In another study, Haier et al. (1992) found that more skilled players showed less overall cerebral activity (measured by PET) while playing a video game than did novices. Taken together, these studies give some support for the somewhat paradoxical idea that as they acquire skill performers commit fewer resources to future-oriented processing but are nevertheless better able to adapt to the future.

From a neuropsychological perspective, the prefrontal cortex, which is viewed as essential for working memory and future-oriented processes (Goldman-Rakic, 1987; Weinberger, Berman, Gold, & Goldberg, this volume), may initially be more involved during learning than at higher skill levels. Acquiring a new skill, such as playing a video game, is a problem-solving exercise that requires learning new relations and integrating perceptual, motor, and strategic components. This sort of deliberate problem solving in novel contexts has traditionally been associated with frontal functions (for reviews, see Fuster, 1989; Shallice, 1988).

With increasing automatization, however, other motor areas, such as the basal ganglia or the cerebellum, may assume increasing control over larger units of automated behavior. Further research will be required to elaborate the changes in processing that occur during the learning of complex perception-action skills.

CONCLUSION

The relatively unconstrained flow of skilled activity in the work reported here reveals a remarkably intricate interweaving between the past, the present, and the future. Performers are continually gathering visual information for determining the outcomes of past acts, for monitoring the progress of ongoing acts, for determining what will happen next, and for planning and calibrating upcoming action. At the same time, the performer is producing a stream of activity that is based on the continual flow of perceptual information. All of this occurs quickly and, at least in the expert, relatively effortlessly. This chapter provides a descriptive window into how perceptual selection, via eye movements, is used to adapt flexibly and precisely to a changing and indeterminate context.

REFERENCES

Anderson, R. L. (1988). *A robot Ping-Pong player.* Cambridge: MIT Press.

Angel, R. W., Alston, W., & Garland, H. (1970). Functional relations between the manual and oculomotor control systems. *Experimental Neurology, 27,* 248–257.

Arbib, M. A. (1980). Perceptual structures and distributed motor control. In V. B. Brooks (Ed.), *Handbook of physiology: Sec. 1. The nervous system: Vol. 2. Motor control* (pp. 1449–1480). Baltimore: Williams and Wilkins.

Arbib, M. A. (1989). *The metaphorical brain: 2. Neural networks and beyond.* New York: Wiley.

Baddeley, A. (1986). *Working memory.* Oxford: Oxford University Press.

Bahill, T. A., & LaRitz, T. (1984). Why can't batters keep their eyes on the ball? *American Scientist, 72,* 249–253.

Bernstein, N. (1984). *The co-ordination and regulation of movements.* Reprinted in H. T. A. Whiting (Ed.), *Human motor actions: Bernstein reassessed.* Amsterdam: North-Holland. (Original work published 1967)

Biguer, B., Jeannerod, M., & Prablanc, C. (1982). The coordination of eye, head, and arm movements during reaching at a single visual target. *Experimental Brain Research, 46,* 301–304.

Bryan, W. L., & Harter, N. (1899). Studies on the telegraphic language. *Psychological Review, 6,* 345–375.

Calvin, W. H. (1990). *The cerebral symphony: Seashore reflections on the structure of consciousness.* New York: Bantam Books.

Carnahan, H., & Marteniuk, R. G. (1991). The temporal organization of hand, eye, and head movements during reaching and pointing. *Journal of Motor Behavior, 23*, 109–119.

Freedland, R. L., & Bertenthal, B. I. (1994). Developmental changes in interlimb coordination: Transitions to hands-and-knees crawling. *Psychological Science, 5*, 26–32.

Fuster, J. M. (1989). *The prefrontal cortex: Anatomy, physiology, and neuropsychology of the frontal lobe.* New York: Raven Press.

Gibson, J. J. (1966). *The senses considered as perceptual systems.* Boston: Houghton Mifflin.

Gibson, J. J. (1979). *The ecological approach to visual perception.* Boston: Houghton Mifflin.

Gielen, C. C. A. M., Van den Heuvel, P. J. M., & Van Gisbergen, J. A. M. (1984). Coordination of fast eye and arm movements in a tracking task. *Experimental Brain Research, 56*, 154–161.

Goldman-Rakic, P. S. (1987). Circuitry of primate prefrontal cortex and regulation of behavior by representational memory. In F. Plum (Ed.), *The Handbook of Physiology: Section 1. The Nervous System: Vol. 5. Higher Functions of the Brain* (pp. 373–417). Bethesda, MD: American Physiological Society.

Haier, R. J., Siegel, B. V. J., MacLachlan, A., Soderling, E., Lottenberg, S., & Buchsbaum, M. S. (1992). Regional glucose metabolic changes after learning a complex visuospatial/motor task: A positron emission tomographic study. *Brain Research, 570*, 134–143.

Hofsten, C. von (1985). Perception and action. In M. Frese & J. Sabini (Eds.), *Goal directed behavior: The concept of action in psychology* (pp. 80–96). Hillsdale, NJ: Erlbaum.

Kugler, P. M., Kelso, J. A., & Turvey, M. T. (1980). On the concept of coordinative structures as dissipative structures: I. Theoretical lines of convergence. In G. E. Stelmach & J. Requin (Eds.), *Tutorials in motor behavior* (pp. 3–47). New York: North-Holland.

Lashley, K. S. (1951). The problem of serial order in behavior. In L. A. Jeffress (Ed.), *Cerebral mechanisms in behavior: The Hixon symposium* (pp. 112–146). New York: Wiley.

Lee, D. N. (1980). Visuo-motor coordination in space-time. In G. E. Stelmach & J. Requin (Eds.), *Tutorials in motor behavior* (pp. 281–295). New York: North-Holland.

Loftus, G. R. (1983). Eye fixations on text and scenes. In K. Rayner (Ed.), *Eye movements in reading: Perceptual and language processes* (pp. 359–376). New York: Academic Press.

Logie, R., Baddeley, A. D., Mane, A. M., & Donchin, E. E. A. (1989). Working memory in the acquisition of complex cognitive skills. Special issue. The Learning Strategies program: An examination of the strategies in skill acquisition. *Acta Psychologica, 71*(1–3), 53–87.

Miller, G. A., Galanter, E., & Pribram, K. H. (1960). *Plans and the structure of behavior.* New York: Holt, Rinehart and Winston.

Neisser, U. (1976). *Cognition and reality: Principles and implications of cognitive psychology.* San Francisco: W. H. Freeman.

Piaget, J., & Inhelder, B. (1969). *The psychology of the child.* New York: Basic Books.

Reed, E. S. (1982). An outline of a theory of action systems. *Journal of Motor Behavior, 14*(2), 98–134.

Roberts, R. J., Brown, D., Wiebke, S., & Haith, M. M. (1991). A computer-automated laboratory for studying complex perception-action skills. *Behavior Research Methods, Instruments, and Computers, 23*(4), 493–504.

Roberts, R. J., Jr., Hager, L. D., & Heron C. (in press). Prefrontal cognitive processes: Working memory and inhibition in the antisaccade task. *Journal of Experimental Psychology: General.*

Rosenbaum, D. A. (1991). *Human motor control.* New York: Academic Press.

Shallice, T. (1988). *From neuropsychology to mental structure.* Cambridge: Cambridge University Press.

Shapiro, K. L., & Raymond, J. E. (1989). Training of efficient oculomotor strategies enhances skill acquisition. Special issue. The Learning Strategies program: An examination of the strategies in skill acquisition. *Acta Psychologica, 71*(1–3), 217–242.

Sheena, D., & Borah, J. (1981). Compensation for some second order effects to improve eye position measurements. In D. F. Fisher, R. A. Monty, & J. W. Senders (Eds.), *Eye movements: Cognition and visual perception* (pp. 257–268). Hillsdale, NJ: Erlbaum.

Siegler, R. S. (1989). Mechanisms of cognitive development. *Annual Review of Psychology, 40,* 353–379.

Simon, H. A. (1981). *The sciences of the artificial* (2nd ed.). Cambridge: MIT Press.

Stark, L., & Ellis, S. R. (1981). Scanpaths revisited: Cognitive models direct active looking. In D. F. Fisher, R. A. Monty, & J. W. Senders (Eds.), *Eye movements: Cognition and visual perception* (pp. 193–226). Hillsdale, NJ: Erlbaum.

Tejada-Flores, L. (1986). *Breakthrough on skis: How to get out of the intermediate rut.* New York: Vintage Books.

Turvey, M. T. (1990). Coordination. *American Psychologist, 45,* 938–953.

Turvey, M. T., & Kugler, P. N. (1984). An ecological approach to perception and action. In H. T. A. Whiting (Ed.), *Human motor actions: Bernstein reassessed* (pp. 373–412). Amsterdam: North-Holland.

Warren, W. H. (1984). Perceiving affordances: Visual guidance of stair climbing. *Journal of Experimental Psychology: Human Perception and Performance, 10,* 683–703.

Chapter Five

Learning, Prediction, and Control with an Eye to the Future

Duane M. Rumbaugh, E. Sue Savage-Rumbaugh, and David A. Washburn

To speak of *Vegetable Psychology* would cause a smile to ripple over the faces even of those who have granted the identity of the intelligence between man and the brute. But the near future may have occasion to show there can be no life absolutely without *psychological* action—that the latter is the result of the former. It may some day be shown that life is conditioned by psychological action; and that there is in plants the equivalent of "instinct" in animals—the power of gaining individual experience, and of transferring such experience to descendants to profit thereby, not altogether unconsciously! (Taylor, 1884, pp. 4–5)

Behavior is a marvelous idea, one reserved in nature—Taylor's quaint view notwithstanding—for animals. Although plants might be said to behave in the limited sense that, for example, the orientation of their leaves and growth is sensitive to the source and intensity of light, such "behavior" is slow and boring to the casual observer. Indeed, the behavior of vertebrates is very quick compared even with the very best "mur-

Preparation of this chapter was supported by grants from the National Institute for Child Health and Human Development (HD06016) and from the National Aeronautics and Space Administration (NAG2-438) to Georgia State University. Additional support was provided by the College of Arts and Sciences of Georgia State University.

derous, cooperative, and competitive" (Taylor, 1884, p. 5) behaviors that plants might be said to employ in achieving their adaptive ends.

Animal behavior is also uniquely subject to rapid and at times inexplicable shifts in goals and in the basis of control. Examining these shifts and positing their goals constitute the focus of the present chapter. There are of course always reasons for such changes, and these changes and their underlying motivations provide the impetus for much psychological research. We will discuss response patterns that result from the ability to discern reliable relations in the environment, from perceiving and benefiting from control, from the motivation to perform, and from the ability to anticipate future events. However, before considering in some detail these behaviors and how they illustrate the future orientation of much of cognition, it will be useful to contrast the notion of future-oriented processes with the past-oriented perspectives that, until recently, were dominant in the field of animal behavior.

CHANGING PERSPECTIVES

The reasons posited to explain particular behaviors may be relatively obscure—particularly if one retains the perspectives of staunch behaviorism that have held sway within psychology for much of the past century. In efforts to understand animal behavior, the primary questions of behaviorism have historically been, What are the stimuli that now control an animal's responding? and What is the history of reinforcement that causes them to do so? A main reason for this emphasis has been, of course, to avoid attributing to animals any role as "initiating agents of actions" or any form of mentalistic ability such as thinking, planning, weighing options, and so on. The "instigators of behavior" were to be attributed to environmental stimuli and events and not to any initiative animals might generate as agents of action. Such an approach might have enhanced psychologists' standing as scientists (e.g., as objective and hardheaded), but only at the expense of the richness and complexity of behavior. In the attempt to simplify the study of behavior, psychology became a science of simple actions. The behavior left to explain was for many no more fascinating than "vegetable psychology."

It is undeniable that the stimuli of the here and now and the experiences of the past do influence behavior. Notwithstanding, it is now held that some organisms, notably those that have relatively large brains with elaborated cortices, declare their own contributions to behavior. Such organisms have the ability not only to acquire knowledge quickly and abundantly, but also to transcend stimulus-response associations and derive general, rulelike relations. To do so, they generally must have had enriched rather than impoverished early environments, ones that foster the perception of predictive relations between what is happening now and what will happen in the future.

This resurgence of investigation of complex and future-oriented behavior is also reflected in the increased concern for the psychological well-being of animals across species. To the degree that the empty-organism model of behavior succeeded, it also—perhaps quite inadvertently—fostered indifference toward the animal, and what now would be called abuse of animals in laboratories and elsewhere was of little concern. After all, the animals were just "empty" things that, in keeping with the Cartesian perspective (Descartes, 1637/1956), had no feelings or abilities to reason regarding their present, past, or future plight. Though they responded, they had "no psyche."

Continuity of Behavior

Closely related animal species look alike because of their shared genes. They also behave in similar ways because of their shared genes. Complex anatomical expressions, such as the ability to see and the ability to fly, have emerged from the integration of simpler structures and systems. Similarly, the complex psychological expressions of our species are manifested as simpler, more basic ones in nonhuman species. Fortunately, traces of the attributes in our species that have been selected and honed throughout history are also to be found in other animal forms (see extensive reviews by Gallistel, 1990; Leger, 1992; Roitblat, 1987). In this chapter we will focus on these species that are most closely related to us, the great apes and other primates.

Research of the past decade has put in place the evidence needed to argue for the correctness of the Darwinian perspective (Darwin, 1859) and the incorrectness of the Cartesian view. Basically, humans are not all that different from other primates. They are singular less in their attributes than in how far certain attributes have been elaborated. For instance, there is now strong evidence that apes have substantial language skills and that they can acquire those skills best if they are reared in ways uncommon in their natural histories. More specifically, if they are reared much as one cares for a human child, one observes what is common to the development of the human child—the spontaneous acquisition of skills with which to understand speech (Savage-Rumbaugh et al., 1993) followed by their competent use of symbols to "talk." Thus reared, they have the potential to comprehend novel sentences of request at the level of a 2½-year-old child. Their comprehension is instated not by their own use of language, but rather by their perception of how the utterances of their caretakers predict the nature and course of imminent events of special interest (e.g., diapering, feeding, food preparation, arrivals). And though no nonhuman primate literally "speaks," one bonobo (*Pan paniscus*), Kanzi, has manifested marked changes in his vocal repertoire that probably reflect his particular sensitivity to the human speech of the environment in which he was reared (Hopkins & Savage-Rumbaugh, 1991).

Computers and Their Impact

The rapidly accruing literature generated by such methods has significantly redefined and upgraded our estimation of primate cognition. The growth of computer science over the past decade now provides the comparative psychologist with new and powerful technology for studying primates' abilities, as illustrated by their performance on complex video-formatted tasks.

Primates' performance on video tasks clearly shows that they do more than just respond to tasks simplistically and mechanically. Rather, as we shall discuss, they can come to predict events and learn how their responses must be altered if they are to succeed in a given task. Their behavior can be new and fresh on each trial when each trial is novel. As we will discuss later in this chapter, their efficiency in learning and their "work ethic" appear to be enhanced by giving them control over when they work, what they work for (incentive), and what they work on (the specific task). Eventually it matters little if they are hungry and get food pellets for correct performances; instead, they work because of nonnutritive incentives associated with the tasks. Although their initial work on the computer-based tasks is surely "pellet driven," gradually it becomes task driven. In other words, although rhesus monkeys' initial work on computer tasks surely depends on their receiving tangible incentives appropriate to biological needs, gradually their readiness to work becomes psychologically rather than biologically driven. Their behavior is refined to the ends that they exercise opportunities to work and to learn, to do things that challenge their abilities, and to avoid indolence.

Behavior can be both formed and limited by the instruments of measurement used for its study. Accordingly, psychologists' perspectives on a species' learning ability are delimited by their methods of inquiry. If a rat is tested in a simple maze with a single right/left choice point, then both the rat's learning and the psychologist's view of the rat's ability to learn might be unduly circumscribed. If a monkey is tested in the standard Wisconsin General Testing Apparatus (WGTA; Harlow, 1949), one might observe how it develops learning skills that enhance efficiency. One would also see how fragile those skills are, noting profound disruption in learning whenever the locus of response is moved even slightly away from the stimulus (see Rumbaugh et al., 1989). The temptation is strong to interpret these effects as a species attribute (e.g., as rhesus monkeys' inability to cope with stimulus-response spatial discontiguity) rather than as an artifact of the test situation. However, uncompromised learning by monkeys with similar stimulus-response spatial separations within a different testing paradigm, as has been reported using the joystick technology (Rumbaugh et al., 1989), reveals that these earlier reports reflect limitations of the WGTA, not the monkeys. Similar technological modifications have permitted us to see the monkeys' ability to learn to predict the outcome or resolution of a highly dynamic field— skills previously reported to be beyond the capacities of nonhumans (see Washburn & Rumbaugh, 1992b). Indeed, the WGTA and other conventional technology would not even permit the experimenter to ask whether the rhesus might be able to do such things, because the apparatus could not possibly provide such opportunities. However, the point here goes beyond noting that advancing technology empowers scientists to ask new questions; new research technology is also producing new, exciting answers to old questions!

A New Research Era

Laboratory animals of past decades generally have been maintained and studied as though their learning and cognitive operations were fixed and not markedly influenced either by their early rearing or by methods of scientific inquiry. The idea seemingly was that if one would just keep the animals alive and healthy, one could study them without concern that the way they were maintained and studied would affect their ability to learn, and so on. We now know that how animals are reared and maintained and how their learning abilities are researched can markedly change the most basic dimensions of their abilities and psychology. The kind and intensity of experiences that can be extended to our nonhuman primates via new technology can alter the very nature of their learning processes and abilities (Washburn & Rumbaugh, 1992a) and can produce animals whose cognitive operations are quite different from those previously associated with their species.

The subject is very much at center stage as an agent of action in the new era that we now work in. As we stated above, stimuli of the environment and reinforcements of the past remain important, but in new ways—ways that extend to the subject's *informational bases* and *predictive relationships* that can be referenced in selecting one of several behavioral options rather than determining each behavioral response. All these points probably hold with a large variety of animals, but they particularly apply when one has an animal form with a highly encephalized brain and an elaborated cortex—such as the larger monkeys and the great apes (for excellent reviews of the neuropsychology of future-oriented processes, see Goldman-Rakic, 1992, 1993).

ON THE EVOLUTION OF AND SEARCH FOR CONTROL

Relational Learning

Within the order Primates, there is systematic evidence that with enhanced encephalization of the brain and in particular with elaboration of the cortex there is a gradual shift from rather straightforward stimulus-response associative learning (characteristic of prosimians and most monkeys) to a relational or mediational form of learning (characteristic of some rhesus monkeys, apes, and humans) that by comparison is more abstract, general, and comprehensive (Rumbaugh & Pate, 1984). This is not to say that the great apes, or indeed humans, cannot or do not learn by stimulus-response associative learning. Rather, under certain conditions they can discern the relations between stimuli/events and abstract rulelike principles that can be used to execute correct responses in complex tasks or situations even when more basic associative principles would dictate other, incorrect responses. This distinction requires more than a disambiguation of associative and relational memory processes, for it entails the ability to break the stimulus-response bond and to favor mediational strategies for responding vis-à-vis habits and local contingencies.

Perceptions of the Learner

The nature of the shift in learning process is noted and relevant here because of its implications for how the learner might, in a sense, "perceive" itself in the situation—assuming for the moment that the subject does perceive itself in accordance with changing situations. At best, a stimulus-response learner might perceive itself only as responding based on what has happened in the recent trials, a reflection of its recent record of reinforcement in that situation. Its behavior would be "pellet driven," that is, completely contingent on the economics of obtaining pellets.

By contrast a mediational learner, one capable of abstracting rules and relations among things and events, might see itself as positing predictive or even cause-effect relationships about the task it works on. Beyond just learning to "do behavior X contingent on the presence of stimulus Y," it might be discerning rules or regularities that, when tested, suggest at least a perceived sense of control.

What evidence is there that an animal might perceive when it does and does not have an element of control? There is, of course, the vast literature pertaining to "learned helplessness," which attests that animals can become listless and depressed if they can do nothing other than endure the inescapable consequences of noxious events imposed on them (Overmier & Seligman, 1967). There is also the literature indicating that if a noxious event is inevitable, then subjects prefer at least to have a signal that the event is imminent (Abbott, 1985), perhaps allowing them to prepare for the worst and then relax.

Recently in our laboratory we have demonstrated with a task called Select (Washburn & Rumbaugh, 1991) that rhesus monkeys (*Macaca mulatta*) can learn to use icons representing a number of familiar tasks. There was, for example, a unique icon for Task A, another unique icon for Task B, and so on. Once selected, a task was presented for five trials, whereupon the menu of icons was presented again (either with or without replacement of the task last chosen, depending on the purpose of the study). With such icons randomly selected and randomly arranged on a monitor, the monkeys could choose a task to work on. Under those conditions, they not only learned the icons, they performed significantly better (more rapidly and accurately) on tasks of their own choosing than when the experimenter assigned the next task. The finding is, then, similar to that obtained from research with humans (e.g., Monty & Perlmuter, 1986). Within limits, performance is enhanced if humans—and apparently rhesus monkeys—perceive that they have a choice of what to do.

Why should giving the subject a choice of what to do enhance performance? Why should a young chimpanzee try repeatedly to test its abilities, such as leaping from one point to another? Why, as we will discuss later in this chapter, should a rhesus monkey come to work on computer tasks during times when it has access to more food than it could eat in an entire day? To better understand these important effects and behaviors, let us assume that *control*, either perceived or real, can become a controlling dimension of reinforcement for certain organisms as they work on certain kinds of tasks. Why, we then ask, does the perception of control enhance that organism's best efforts?

Rumbaugh and Sterritt (1986) suggested that motivation to control one's environment might have been a driving force in the evolution of intelligence. By "intelligence" we mean the ability to learn quickly and in a comprehensive, relational manner as opposed to learning slowly in what appears to be a stimulus-response associative manner.

In the development of control theory, Rumbaugh and Sterritt (1986) made the following assumptions:

1. Even the most basic physiological and behavioral processes help maintain homeostatic requisites for life. When homeostatic states are disturbed, strong drives can be induced. Behaviors that restore states of balance are selectively reinforced.

2. The evolution of more complex forms of life has been coupled with the preference for exercising individual control over outcomes

rather than accepting those that are under random control or are controlled by others. There is a continuum from the simple behaviors designed to maintain homeostatic equilibria (see assumption 1) to more complex behaviors for control that are the products of cognition. Here the implication is that those behaviors that instate either a real cause-and-effect control of behavior or even a perceived sense of control will be strongly reinforced because they sustain and satisfy a need state coupled with the evolution of complexity—a motivation to establish perceived control over the events and consequences of the environment.

3. The reinforcement value of control has at least two vectors: Perceived control, valid or not, substitutes quiescence for the anxiety that can be induced by exposure to extraordinary and intense novel events. And control can conserve energy. Although a little novelty may induce curiosity, large amounts can induce fear and anxiety because the environment is then seen as unstable and unpredictable. Under such conditions, the perceived control (regardless of whether the control is real) is assumed to attenuate such fear and anxiety. With reference to the second vector, any organism has a finite amount of energy and strength it must budget to produce behavior that is likely to meet basic needs, as noted in assumption 1 above. Only when basic needs are met can the organism afford to experiment with its behaviors to determine, within limits, what effects it can achieve and what other dimensions of control it might perfect. Thus genuine control might have been a primary requisite for providing the early hominids with the necessary time for documenting the first discoveries, for inventions, and for steps toward the development of complex cultures.

Thus all perceived control is reinforcing, according to control theory, because at a minimum it modulates arousal levels and the anxiety or apprehension induced by extraordinary amounts of novel, unpredictable stimuli of the natural world. Rituals that could have given the early hominids perceived control over weather and over the supply of game, fruits, berries, and so on would be reinforced from time to time by such coincidences as the termination of severe storms and the appearance of game and edible plants. As the control became real rather than just perceived or believed, the early hominids were given genuine behavioral options for enhancing the supply of things or conditions they needed (food, water, shelter, escape/avoidance of danger, etc.) or could readily develop an appetite for (various comforts that might be discovered or invented and other quality-of-life factors that, though "enjoyable," were substantially more than was needed to sustain life and reproduction). As the hominids became more efficient through exercising valid means of control, they came to have the time and energy to document discoveries (e.g., how to produce and control fire) and to invent (e.g., stone tools, improved means of transport).

Selection for "intelligence," and the attendant ability to infer contingencies or consequences as a function of various behaviors, would have increased the probability that the homeostatic needs (assumption 1) would be met and attendant states maintained with minimal energy expenditure (assumption 3) through the identification and selective use of *genuine* cause-and-effect relationships (e.g., predictive relations that entailed the selective use of behaviors that literally produced the prized consequences or contingencies). Invalid, specious relations would be sustained only by the chance coupling of desired consequences with the exercise of rituals or superstitious behaviors.

A variety of findings attest to the validity of assumption 2. Several species have demonstrated an aversion to "freeloading" (e.g., Osborne's literature review [1977] indicates animals' preference for earned rather than free reinforcements). Animals prefer predictable to unpredictable shock (Abbott, 1985). Bees predict when and how far they must fly each day to find food placed by the experimenter (Gould, 1983). Animals benefit most from active rather than passive experiences (e.g., Held & Hein, 1963). Additionally, animals' ingestive responses and their natural consequences (e.g., the consumption of food) are synergistically effective in determining the reinforcement value of rewards in learning tasks (Sterritt & Smith, 1965, found that chicks that had never eaten by pecking from the time of hatching learned a maze task optimally when pecking and infusion of food to their crops through a tube were temporally coupled rather than separated). By contrast, animals do not thrive in situations where, regardless of what they do, they must endure noxious consequences (e.g., "learned helplessness" as originally formulated by Overmier & Seligman, 1967, and by Seligman & Maier, 1967, and as revised and reviewed by Abramson, Seligman, & Teasdale, 1978, and by Peterson & Seligman, 1984).

Control for the Future

Control and the quest for control are inherently future oriented in that they imply choice, or degrees of freedom for future action and consequences. As noted earlier in this chapter, when rhesus monkeys are given choices (control) over the tasks they work on for fruit-flavored food pellets, they do significantly better than when the tasks they encounter are either determined by the experimenter or yoked to actual choice patterns (Washburn, Hopkins, & Rumbaugh, 1991). If the monkeys' behavior were solely pellet driven, *what* task they work on seemingly would be of no consequence to them as long as the payoff (e.g., pellets per unit of time) was held constant. But tests indicate that it does matter to them, suggesting that they make predictions regarding what the future holds for them by way of challenge (e.g., via choice of tasks), and that if there is no concordance between their expressed choice and the tasks they then encounter, performance decays. There is much more to learning and what is learned than selecting motor responses contingent on receiving food pellets from the experimenter's equipment.

Learning Can Become Rewarding

One implication of the view that complex learning is future oriented is that *opportunities* to learn can become inherently motivating and reinforcing. The literature on "mastery motivation" and related topics bears out this point with human learning (e.g., Harter, 1978a,b). Research with rhesus monkeys at our laboratory has yielded comparative findings that support this implication.

Washburn, Hopkins, and Rumbaugh (1991) reported performance of rhesus monkeys in a variant of one of their several video-formatted tasks, called Select, mentioned above. It is in the Select task that the monkeys can choose from a menu of available tasks the specific task they will work on for the next five trials. Upon completion of those trials, the menu of tasks (each represented by an icon) is again presented, and the monkeys can choose another. In the study at hand, the monkey could choose the option "free food," whereupon the animal received five pellets distributed at a rate comparable to that characterizing task performance (five pellets per minute). Thus the monkeys were given a choice of *not* working, but receiving food as though they had been working.

Gradually the free food option came to be preferred, until the monkeys were "on the dole" more than on the payroll. Of course it was not certain whether the monkeys viewed free food as freeloading or as a richly rewarded single-response task (much like the number-related research described below, in which selecting a single digit resulted in paced delivery of multiple pellets).

To clarify the choice between free food and working for rewards, a cost was introduced for exercising the free food option. Selecting the "free food" icon brought "free" delivery of pellets (not contingent on performance) for 30 min; however, during that interval the screen was blank and no other task option was available. In other words, the menu for the Select task did not reappear during "free food." Food, food everywhere—more than enough to eat during quite a spell! (The 150 97-mg pellets thus delivered would constitute about 5% of their daily ad libitum food intake.) Under these conditions, the preference for free food rapidly diminished, and the "work ethic" was reinstated. In other words, it seems that the free food option was very attractive to the monkeys so long as it was an option that they could choose or not, and one that did not impede the opportunity to work. But when choice of free food was at the protracted expense of their being unable to choose and to work on tasks of their choice for 30 min, it became a very unattractive option. Their choice of the free food option dropped to below chance (to 18% from a high of about 70%). By contrast, when *other* tasks (not "free food") were selected and continued for 30 min, rather than for just five trials, there was no drop in preference for them.

Though pellets might be the staff of our monkeys' lives, clearly they do not live by pellets alone. "Free food" seems to be attractive only if it remains a short-lived option that does not significantly interfere with access to tasks of choice. When the option of free food competes with other important motivations, including those to work and to exercise control over their activities, it apparently becomes aversive.

Predictive Skills

Thus viewed, complex learning is very much *future oriented.* Supporting this conclusion are recent findings regarding animals' ability to predict future events. Washburn and Rumbaugh (1992b) report that rhesus monkeys are, in fact, capable of anticipating events in the future. In two computerized tasks, called Chase and Laser, the monkeys predicted where a target was going based on its location, speed, and direction of movement. The monkeys' responses tended to approximate the paths of most efficient intersection with the moving targets, irrespective of the targets' actual course. Although not always as adroit as humans, the monkeys responded as predictor-operators in the Chase task, meaning that their responses—like those of human subjects—were a complex function of perceptual, motor, and cognitive factors, including prediction. Similarly on the Laser task, humans and rhesus monkeys were both able to "shoot" a moving target by aiming a turret at where a target was going rather than at where the target was (Washburn, 1993). Moreover, both species could efficiently and accurately abort errant shots; rarely did human or monkey subjects abort a shot that would, in fact, have hit the target (fewer than 5% of such shots).

Chimpanzees' predictive skills might well be intermediate between those of rhesus monkeys and of humans. Rhesus monkeys, chimpanzees, and humans were tested on a novel condition of the Chase task in which the familiar target traveled a new path, a perfect circle around the middle of the screen (Washburn & Rumbaugh, 1992b). Initially, all subjects simply chased the target (which moved slightly faster than the cursor) around the circle (see Figure 5.1). The human subjects, with their lifetime of experience with circles, generally recognized the circular path within the first few trials; hence they solved the problem quickly by

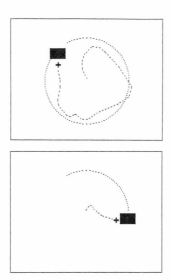

Figure 5.1   The task for the subject was to capture the rectangular target
with the cursor, movements of which were controlled by the subject's use of a
joystick in two video-formatted problem situations. The top section portrays
the characteristic pattern of responding for rhesus monkeys, and the lower section that for humans and chimpanzees.

moving across the arc of an efficient point of intersection. By contrast,
the rhesus monkeys captured the target only with the greatest difficulty,
requiring several hundred trials to learn the regularity of circular movement. Chimpanzees tested under similar conditions learned significantly
more quickly than rhesus monkeys to anticipate a target's movement
along a circular path. The efficiency of mature performance was comparable for all three species, but the rate of learning to predict the movements of a target (to abstract the regularity inherent in a circular path)
differed profoundly in accordance with brain complexity.

In a related task, called Hole, the subject was faced with another
novel challenge. The Hole task is similar to Chase, but each trial features
a large circle presented in the center of the screen. The target could
pass through this circle, but the cursor could travel only around the
outside of its circumference. Thus subjects had to catch a moving target
on each trial despite this semipermeable obstacle. Once a target entered
the circle, it either remained visible or disappeared; in either case, the
target continued to move along the same angle that characterized its
entry.

Under these conditions the optimal tactic is to go around the circle
and place the cursor in a strategic spot, aligned with the vector according

to which the target entered the circle, so as to capture the target just as it exits the perimeter. A chimpanzee (*Pan troglodytes*) subject, Austin, employed exactly this strategy and was markedly superior to all of our rhesus monkeys in doing so. In the condition in which the target disappeared when it entered the circle (reappearing only once it exited the obstacle), rheses monkeys were inclined to do nothing until the target reappeared. Only with additional experience in which target movement was made contingent on cursor movement did they provide evidence of anticipating, as did Austin the chimpanzee, the exit point of invisible targets.

SUPRALEARNING IS THE RULE

Numerical Skills

Primates learn more—generally much more—than they must know to optimize their receipt of pellets, as illustrated by two studies from our laboratory. In the first study, we gave Sherman and Austin, two adult male chimpanzees, the opportunity to select between two *pairs* of food wells that held their favorite M&M chocolate candies (Perusse & Rumbaugh, 1990; Rumbaugh, Savage-Rumbaugh, & Hegel, 1987; Rumbaugh, Savage-Rumbaugh, & Pate, 1988). The food wells were evenly spaced, and the rule was that if the chimpanzees selected either of the two on their right, they were given the contents of *both* wells. Similarly, if they chose either of the two food wells on their left, they got to eat the contents of both those wells. In each case the unselected pair of wells (right or left) were withdrawn from reach, though they remained in view.

It is important to note that in no case were the chimpanzees required to choose the pair of wells that would yield the greater total number of chocolates. Rather, they always got chocolates; their selection determined only whether they would get the maximum number on a given trial. They gradually came to choose the right or left pair of M&M-baited wells that netted the greater total. Thus, although they did not have to learn to select the greater total, they did so and could differentiate even 9 chocolates from 10 (Perusse & Rumbaugh, 1990). As one might expect, the coarser the ratio of numbers of chocolates, as defined by the right and left pairs of food wells, the more probable it was that they would succeed in selecting the pair that netted the higher total.

Washburn and Rumbaugh (1991) found similar evidence that primates learn far more than is necessary when given the opportunity to choose between numerals 0 through 9 in a video-formatted task. When a numeral was selected, the monkey received a corresponding number of pellets. For example, on a trial in which 3 was paired with 5, choosing the former would bring three pellets whereas choosing the latter brought five. When 0 was present and chosen, the monkeys received no pellets. Thus the monkeys received pellets irrespective of which nonzero numeral they selected; they did not have to choose the larger numeral to obtain food.

The monkeys quickly came to select the larger of two numerals, however, despite having only the relative number of reinforcers to discriminate the stimuli. After the rhesus monkeys had manifested overall preference for the larger of two paired numerals, they were presented seven novel trials on which, for the first time, selected numerals were paired in their presentation. One rhesus made no errors, and the second made only two: their performance was significantly beyond chance. Thus it was concluded that the monkeys had learned *more* than simply to select numerals for rewards, or even which of two numerals for every pair previously presented to them was the "correct" one to select (for the optimum amount of food to be received). What they learned can be summarized as a complex relational matrix—both of the relation between numeric symbols and numbers of pellets and between each of the numeric symbols and the others. They learned to treat these numeric symbols in accordance with their values and ordinal ranks in a situation where their ordinal ranks differed minimally—that is *by one pellet*. That the monkeys had learned the relative values of numerals and, furthermore, had learned the relative ordinal ranks, if not the cardinal values, of each numeral attests to the proclivity of the primate's brain for organizing par excellence all information that is orderly and reliably encountered in an environment within which its most basic needs are to be met.

Thus chimpanzees and rhesus monkeys prefer to control what they do, and they learn far more than is required for them to do well even in a complex-learning task. They are inclined to learn more than task minima. Rather, they are likely to learn all that is "learnable" (regular or predictable) in the environment, bringing to bear any past experience that helps them organize events. Once it is stated thus, one recognizes that there is a large body of evidence to support the general principle that animals (including humans) learn more than they must in order to handle the immediate demands of specific tasks. Why they do so is not a trivial question. If for no other reason, it might seem that the conservation of energy and the principle of least effort would restrict what is learned and how well it is learned to a value that would simply ensure optimal cost-effective performance.

On the other hand, if we view learning in a new key—namely, suppose that the learner tends to exploit as optimally as biology permits all that might be learned in a situation—we get a new perspective on learning, behavior, and the selective pressures for large brains that have evolved in some animals, notably in the order Primates. This view implies that large brains were not selected just to provide the power to learn and to adapt to the environmental challenges of the moment. Rather, large brains might have been selected in substantial measure because they afford maximum learning and integration of new learning with past learning. They also afford effective memory storage systems that "pack and transport learning" to the future for possible use in solving related problems. Thus energy was conserved in the long run without limiting the amount that might be learned in the short run.

Participation in Routines

Consonant with the principle that primates learn substantially more than they must. Savage-Rumbaugh (1991) detailed analysis of the process by which a bonobo, Panbanisha, and a chimpanzee, Panzee, came to comprehend specific spoken words and lexigrams through being participant-observers in a variety of "routines," many of them designed to provide the care necessary for their well-being and comfort.

Typical routines included getting ready to go outdoors, taking a bath, looking at pictures in a book, playing games, going to specific sites in the woods, and so on. For infant apes, some routines are far too abstract to comprehend at all; but others, such as having diapers changed, are so frequent and concrete that they do come to participate in that routine. One of the first signs of their becoming participants is that they accept the positioning imposed by their caretaker. Eventually they might come to comprehend their caretakers' speech regarding diapers—getting a clean one, lying down for the change, distinguishing "dirty" and "clean" diapers, and so on.

A detailed analysis was offered regarding the learning that took place in the "blowing bubbles" routine. That routine has many components, which include finding, and opening the bottle of bubble solution, finding and using the bubble wand, watching and chasing the bubbles, and so on. As this playful routine is executed time and again, the ape eventually comes to behave as if it knows what must happen next for the routine to be satisfying. It even learns that it can initiate the routine by selecting the bottle of bubble solution from other options, showing it to the caretaker, putting the wand to the caretaker's mouth, and so on. Thus a transition is made from passive-receptive comprehension of the routine to becoming an active participant.

The ape learns without the caretaker's being the driving force. Initially it learns the simplest aspects of the task, but gradually it comes first to comprehend and later to use language markers (speech heard and/or use of word lexigrams, or symbols, at the keyboard). What the very young ape cannot formally request through its own speech or through use of lexigrams, it will attempt to request through actions—such as putting the bottle of bubble solution in the caretaker's hands after making unsuccessful attempts to open the bottle on its own. Still later it can comply with novel requests, such as getting the bubble bottle, putting it in the backpack, and carrying it out into the woods. On a walk in the woods, the bottle might be requested by the ape or by any other member of the traveling party and used for play.

Comprehension of verbal markers typically occurs first within established or familiar routines, yet across time those markers can be used appropriately/intelligently in variations on familiar routines and even as they are experienced within other routines that have not included blowing bubbles. Table 5.1 shows the developing competence of the two infant apes (one *Pan paniscus* and the other *P. troglodytes*) obtained from the "blowing bubbles" routine. These two apes were not required to learn anything, nor were they given specific training drills or teaching sessions. Rather, they were observer-participants—encouraged to watch, encouraged to participate in and enjoy a visit to the forest, or the eating of food, or a social game (such as hide-and-seek) that was "predicted" by someone speaking and using the symbol-embossed keyboard.

These apes learned, and they learned a great deal more than we had expected. They learned because they could. The learned because their brains kept "taking the initiative" in terms of both absorbing the experiences of life and integrating them—so that in due course, they responded intelligently to the word "bubbles" and other words regardless of the specifics of the context. And in our view, it is that function for which their large brains evolved.

What was the driving force impelling the apes to learn to comprehend and master the use of verbal markers? We believe it was their predictive value. The verbal markers became worthy of focused attention, and once mastered they allowed the infant apes to predict, in part, their world—including the behavior of others and what they themselves would have to do to participate in or avoid the consequences of others' behavior.

SUMMARY

Human competencies have their foundations in the biopsychology of our ancestors. We and chimpanzees have a common ancestor of about five million years ago. There are strong continuities between the potential competencies of the great apes and humans—with the qualifier *potential* allowing for the specific effects that early rearing must have on the optimal cultivation of the most complex competencies.

TABLE 5.1 Increasingly Competent Levels of Symbol Usage in Two Species of Apes

Action	Panbanisha (*Pan paniscus*)	Panzee (*Pan troglodytes*)
Imitative touching	13 months, 29 days	14 months, 6 days
Earliest evidence of beginning comprehension of the relation between spoken word and object or symbol and object	13 months, 29 days (word and object)	14 months, 14 days (symbol and object)
Exploratory touching of different symbols on the board	—	17 months, 18 days
Imitative use to indicate agreement with teacher	16 months, 30 days	27 months, 29 days
Imitative use of communicative request during bubble-blowing routine	17 months, 5 days	22 months, 21 days
Nonimitative use of bubbles in response to teacher's query	—	29 months, 22 days
Nonimitative communicative request in old context—bubbles are not being blown but are present	17 months, 2 days	—
Nonimitative communicative request in new context—bubbles are absent	17 months, 5 days	29 months, 21 days
Nonimitative addition of modifier to request a particular type of bubbles (bubble gum)	—	30 months, 3 days
Nonimitative use of bubbles to alter planned activity	17 months, 10 days	34 months, 22 days
Nonimitative use of bubbles to comment on actions of teacher	20 months	—
Practices touching bubbles	21 months, 5 days	—
Nonimitative generalized comment in new context		

Source. Savage-Rumbaugh, 1991. Reprinted by permission of Lawrence Erlbaum Associates.

Just as mechanisms have evolved to maintain equilibria of biological states, other processes evolved to modulate evolving curiosity and the consequences of an organism's appetite for enhanced complexity and novelty—which in large amounts could bring both fear and danger. The opportunity was at hand for mechanisms of *control* to evolve, or at least the perception of control (posited cause-and-effect relations). Concurrently, the selection for intelligence, serviced by large brains and elaborated cortices, rapidly advanced. Such brains, though metabolically very expensive, were the only route to really effective, masterful control in a generalized sense. New forms of generalized observational learning became instated in the infant ape and human child that could, in turn, formulate a large knowledge base of predictive relations between things (e.g., between responses, between responses and events, between stimuli), and even between arbitrary symbols such as words and what would probably occur next. Such an information base could thus be developed even though the infant ape, hominid, or human was motorically constrained by its immaturity. The conservation of energy on behalf of the infant was enormous, as was the complex information base it accrued— information it would use when it became an "older infant" and adult. The competencies of the future for the ape lay in the experiences of infancy. And we suspect the same is true for our own species' infants.

In brief, according to the perspective of this chapter, the more complex aspects of great apes' and humans' psychologies became, in essence, future oriented. In turn, both the apes and we became future-oriented beings—capable of inventions, culture, and even language.

We close with one more view expressed by Taylor (1884, pp. 4–5):

> Many people still regard even the higher animals as automata. They are unwilling to allow that the various intelligent acts they perform proceed from cerebration, exactly in the same way as the intelligent and rational actions of men. They formulate the existence of a different kind of mentality, which they frequently call "instinct," "sagacity," etc. But this old-fashioned way of disposing of the psychology of the lower animals will soon become extinct. Comparative animal psychology is rising to the dignity of a special science, and it has already fairly demonstrated that the intelligence of the dog, horse, and elephant, differs mainly in degree, and not in kind, from that displayed by man.

We share Taylor's anticipation that particular views of behavior will become "extinct"—as have several of his own! Thus science itself, like so many of the very behaviors we study, is a future-oriented process.

REFERENCES

Abbott, B. B. (1985). Rats prefer signaled over unsignaled shock-free periods. *Journal of Experimental Psychology: Animal Behavior Processes, 11,* 215–223.

Abramson, L. Y., Seligman, M. E. P., & Teasdale, J. D. (1978). Learned helplessness in humans: Critique and reformulation. *Journal of Abnormal Psychology, 87,* 49–74.

Darwin, C. (1859). *The origin of species.* New York: Hurst.

Descartes, R. (1956). *Discourse on method.* New York: Liberal Arts Press. (Original work published 1637)

Gallistel, C. R. (1990). *The organization of learning.* Cambridge: MIT Press.

Goldman-Rakic, P. S. (1992). Working memory and the mind. *Scientific American, 262,* 111–117.

Goldman-Rakic, P. S. (1993). The issue of memory in the study of prefrontal function. In A. M. Theirry, J. Glowinski, & P. S. Goldman-Rakic (Eds.), *Research and perspectives in neurosciences.* Berlin: Springer-Verlag.

Gould, J. L. (1983, April). *The invertebrate mind.* Paper presented at the Second National Zoological Park Symposium, Washington, DC.

Harlow, H. F. (1949). The formation of learning sets. *Psychological Review, 56,* 51–56.

Harter, S. (1978a). Effectance motivation reconsidered: Toward a developmental model. *Human Development, 21,* 34–64.

Harter, S. (1978b). Pleasure derived from challenge and the effects of receiving grades on children's difficulty level choices. *Child Development, 49,* 788–799.

Held, R., & Hein, A. (1963). Movement-produced stimulation in the development of visually-guided behavior. *Journal of Comparative and Physiological Psychology, 56,* 872–876.

Hopkins, W. D., & Savage-Rumbaugh, E. S. (1991). Vocal communication as a function of differential rearing experiences in *Pan paniscus:* A preliminary report. *International Journal of Primatology, 12*(6), 559–583.

Leger, D. W. (1992). *Biological foundations of behavior: An integrative approach.* New York: HarperCollins.

Monty, R. A., & Perlmuter, L. C. (1986). Choice, control and motivation in the young and aged. In M. L. Maehr & D. A. Kleiber (Eds.), *Advances in motivation and achievement* (Vol. 5). Greenwich, CT: JAI Press.

Osborne, S. R. (1977). The free food (contrafreeloading) phenomenon: A review and analysis. *Animal Learning and Behavior, 5,* 221–235.

Overmier, J. B., & Seligman, M. E. P. (1967). Effects of inescapable shock upon subsequent escape and avoidance learning. *Journal of Comparative and Physiological Psychology, 63,* 28–33.

Perusse, R., & Rumbaugh, D. M. (1990). Summation in chimpanzees (*Pan troglodytes*): Effects of amounts, number of wells, and finer ratios. *International Journal of Primatology, 11*(5), 425–437.

Peterson, C., & Seligman, M. E. P. (1984). Causal explanations as a risk factor for depression: Theory and evidence. *Psychological Review, 91,* 347–374.

Roitblat, H. L. (1987). *Introduction to comparative cognition.* New York: Freeman.

Rumbaugh, D. M., Hopkins, W. D., Washburn, D. A., & Savage-Rumbaugh, E. S. (1991). Comparative perspectives of brain, cognition, and language. In N. A. Krasnegor, D. M. Rumbaugh, R. L. Schiefelbusch, & M. Studdert-Kennedy (Eds.), *Biological and behavioral determinants of language development.* Hillsdale, NJ: Erlbaum.

Rumbaugh, D. M., & Pate, J. L. (1984). The evolution of cognition in primates: A comparative perspective. In H. L. Roitblat, T. G. Bever, & H. S. Terrace (Eds.), *Animal cognition* (pp. 569–587). Hillsdale, NJ: Erlbaum.

Rumbaugh, D. M., Richardson, W. K., Washburn, D. A., Savage-Rumbaugh, E. S., & Hopkins, W. D. (1989). Rhesus monkeys (*Macaca mulatta*) video tasks, and implications for stimulus-response spatial contiguity. *Journal of Comparative Psychology, 103,* 32–38.

Rumbaugh, D. M., Savage-Rumbaugh, E. S., & Hegel, M. T. (1987). Summation in the chimpanzee (*Pan troglodytes*). *Journal of Experimental Psychology: Animal Behavior Processes, 13,* 107–115.

Rumbaugh, D. M., Savage-Rumbaugh, E. S., & Pate, J. L. (1988). Addendum to "Summation in the chimpanzee (*Pan troglodytes*)." *Journal of Experimental Psychology: Animal Behavior Processes, 14,* 118–120.

Rumbaugh, D. M., & Sterritt, G. M. (1986). Intelligence: From genes to genius in the quest for control. In W. Bechtel (Ed.), *Integrating scientific disciplines.* Dordrecht: Martinus Nijhoff.

Savage-Rumbaugh, E. S. (1991). Language learning in the bonobo: How and why they learn. In N. A. Krasnegor, D. M. Rumbaugh, R. L. Schiefelbusch, & M. Studdert-Kennedy (Eds.), *Biological and behavioral determinants of language development.* Hillsdale, NJ: Erlbaum.

Savage-Rumbaugh, E. S., Murphy, J., Sevcik, R. A., Williams, S., Brakke, K., & Rumbaugh, D. M. (1993). Language comprehension in ape and child. *Monographs of the Society for Research in Child Development, 58* Nos. 3 & 4.

Seligman, M. E. P., & Maier, S. F. (1967). Failure to escape traumatic shock. *Journal of Experimental Psychology, 74,* 1–9.

Sterritt, G. M., & Smith, M. P. (1965). Reinforcement effect of specific components of feeding in young leghorn chicks. *Journal of Comparative and Physiological Psychology, 59,* 171–175.

Taylor, J. E. (1884). *The sagacity and morality of plants.* New York: Dutton.

Washburn, D. A. (1993). Human factors with nonhumans: Factors that affect computer-task performance. *International Journal of Comparative Psychology, 5,* 191–204.

Washburn, D. A., Hopkins, W. D., & Rumbaugh, D. M. (1991). Perceived control in rhesus monkeys (*Macaca mulatta*): Enhanced video-task performance. *Journal of Experimental Psychology: Animal Behavior Processes, 17,* 123–127.

Washburn, D. A., & Rumbaugh, D. M. (1991). Ordinal judgments of numerical symbols by macaques (*Macaca mulatta*), *Psychological Science, 2*(3), 190–193.

Washburn, D. A., & Rumbaugh, D. M. (1992a). The learning skills of rhesus revisited. *International Journal of Primatology, 12*(4), 377–388.

Washburn, D. A., & Rumbaugh, D. M. (1992b). Comparative assessment of psychomotor performance: Target prediction by humans and macaques (*Macaca mulatta*). *Journal of Experimental Psychology: General, 121*(3), 305–312.

PLANNING IN
PROBLEM SOLVING

Chapter Six

Developmental Transitions in Children's Early On-Line Planning

Thomas R. Bidell and Kurt W. Fischer

Planning is perhaps the most prominent of future-oriented activities as well as a fundamental cognitive skill in its own right. Yet surprisingly little is known about the way children acquire planning skills and how those skills change during childhood. The large literature on problem solving and strategy learning (Klahr & Wallace, 1976; McCormick, Miller, & Pressley, 1989; Miller, Galanter, & Pribram, 1960; Siegler, 1989) assumes that children's behavior is guided by anticipation or planning of action sequences, but the nature of anticipation or planning has received little direct attention (Friedman, Scholnick, & Cocking, 1987). Developmental research in planning thus lags behind work in many other do-

This chapter is based in part on presentations given at the Conference on Future-Oriented Processes of the MacArthur Network on Early Childhood in Breckenridge, Colorado, April 1992, and at the Twentieth Annual Symposium on the Jean Piaget Society in Montreal, May 1992. Parts of the chapter are also based on a doctoral dissertation carried out by Thomas R. Bidell at Harvard University under National Institute of Mental Health predoctoral fellowship 5 F31 MH09265-02. Other sources of support for this work include the MacArthur Network on Early Childhood, the Carnegie Corporation, Harvard University, and the Center for Advanced Study in the Behavioral Sciences. We thank Daniel Bullock, Nira Granott, Ralph J. Roberts Jr., Elaine Rotenberg, Dan Simons, and William Wansart for their contributions to the work presented here. Special thanks go to Marshall M. Haith, Ralph J. Roberts Jr., and Janette B. Benson for their extensive and thoughtful editorial reviews of earlier versions of the chapter.

mains where both detailed age-related developmental sequences (Case, 1985; Fischer, 1980b; Siegler, 1981) and microdevelopmental changes in learning and problem solving (Fischer, 1980a; Granott, 1993; Siegler & Crowley, 1991) have been described.

A few important pioneering studies have shown that young children can form sophisticated plans before performance (Klahr, 1978), that children's planning abilities improve with age (DeLisi, 1987; Klahr & Robinson, 1981) and instruction (Casey, 1990), and that planning development is strongly context dependent (Rogoff, 1990). Yet so far researchers have not provided systematic developmental models or frameworks with which to interpret developmental findings about planning and inform systematic research into developmental processes. Without such a systematic developmental framework, researchers lack the conceptual and empirical tools needed to understand how planning capacities described in different studies and at different age levels may relate to one another, or how findings from diverse fields of research such as problem solving, neuropsychology, or infant development may relate to developmental changes in children's planning.

As a contribution to building a developmental framework for planning, we propose a model of young children's planning development based on dynamic skills theory (Fischer, 1980b; Bidell & Fischer, 1991). Dynamic skills theory provides theoretical and methodological tools with which to systematically describe both mechanisms and outcomes of developmental change in children's planning processes. And because it uses a task-analytic approach, it permits the study of planning development across a range of tasks and contexts. Moreover, by framing the development of planning within a broader context of neo-Piagetian developmental theory, it may be possible to better understand the developmental relations between planning and other domains of cognitive skills.

Skills are dynamic because they are determined by multiple, interacting factors that produce wide variability in action and thought. Skill growth functions follow the principles of dynamic systems theory (Fischer & Rose, 1993; Van der Mass & Molenaar, 1992; Van Geert, 1991): The organization of skills changes dynamically as children actively construct new skills through integrating (coordinating) previously constructed skills in relation to specific tasks, situations, and emotional states.

In the present model of planning development, the general constructivist principles of skill theory have been adapted to the domain of planning by relating them to central concepts and findings in the planning and problem-solving literature. The starting point of our model is the body of research on problem solving and frontal functions that points to the central role of *working memory* in the representation of anticipated action sequences (Goldman-Rakic, 1987). The ability to hold action sequences on line in working memory so as to anticipate and guide performance is called *on-line planning* and is viewed as a specialized cognitive skill subject to the constructive developmental mechanisms described by dynamic skills theory. The first on-line anticipation and guidance of planned action sequences develops early—by mid- to late infancy (Piaget, 1952; Uzgiris & Hunt, 1975)—and may provide a foundation for later forms of planning (DeLisi, 1987). Development of on-line planning capacities involves qualitative changes in the organization of relations among anticipated action sequences in working memory. From age two to twelve years, on-line planning develops through a series of major reorganizations moving from the early anticipatory guidance of action sequences, to representations of anticipated action sequences, then to representations of simple relations among sequences, and finally to representations of complex systematic relations among action sequences.

However, the core of our model is not the description of planning skills at different ages, but the description of microdevelopmental *mechanisms* by which planning skills are dynamically reorganized. In accord with other contemporary cognitive developmentalists (Siegler, 1989; Siegler & Crowley, 1991; Sternberg, 1984), we consider an account of the mechanisms of change more fundamental than the simple documentation of developmental levels. For dynamic skills theory, the central process involved in the transition to new levels of organization in on-line plans is the *coordination* of skill components in working memory, as opposed to their mere successive juxtaposition. Dynamic skills theory specifies how coordination replaces juxtaposition to produce specific skills at organizing on-line plans. The microdevelopmental aspects of the present model therefore addresses the complex set of mechanisms involved in a child's coordination of lower level component skills to form a new on-line planning capacity for a given task.

Because the microdevelopmental mechanisms of construction are central to the model, the chapter opens with a discussion of the mechanism of skill coordination in producing qualitative developmental changes in working memory capacity. Following this we present our model of dynamic skills development in on-line planning, describing a process in which microdevelopmental constructions lead to macrodevelopmental shifts in children's ability to organize plans and hold them on line. Finally, we devote a major portion of the chapter to elucidating the microdevelopmental model and the relations between micro- and macrodevelopment in a study (Bidell, 1990) of children's first-time encounters with the Tower of Hanoi, a task widely associated with planning demands (Karat, 1982; Klahr & Robinson, 1981; Spitz & Borys, 1982; Welsh, Pennington, & Groisser, 1991).

Note that the model has been devised especially for problem-solving tasks like the Tower of Hanoi, in which children must carry out a series of movements of objects to reach a particular goal configuration. Although the Tower of Hanoi has been specifically associated with planning, the model may be applied to many other tasks requiring the on-line mental anticipation of actions on objects. An example we refer to in this chapter is classification by sorting, in which children must anticipate specific configurations and then carry them out.

THE PROCESS OF COORDINATION IN WORKING MEMORY

The main process at the foundation of both long-term changes in cognitive development (macrodevelopment) and short-term changes in learning or problem solving (microdevelopment) is the ability to integrate or coordinate items held on line in parallel co-occurrence in working memory (Fischer & Rose, 1994). Co-occurrence allows a child to integrate or coordinate the items, which is distinct from merely shifting from one to another in succession. When two actions or representations occur in succession, they are independent and can even compete with each other as alternative foci of attention. When they co-occur on line in working memory, they can be linked and coordinated so that they can collaborate within a single skill.

Change from shifting to coordination marks the major developmental reorganizations in working memory—and therefore in planning tasks, where coordination of components is especially important. This means that working memory develops through a series of qualitatively different organizations of items held on line, not just through increases in the number of items.

Transition from Shifting to Coordination

People's strategies for simplifying difficult tasks show that earlier developmental levels are characterized by shifting between components that need to be coordinated. In research with dozens of different tasks across the entire age range from infancy to adulthood, people show a common type of error or simplification before they develop a capacity for coordinating co-occurrence: they keep components separate that need to be coordinated, shifting between them instead of coordinating them into a unit (Fischer & Elmendorf, 1986; Fischer, Hand, & Russell, 1984; Gottlieb, Taylor, & Ruderman, 1977; Perry, Church, & Goldin-Meadow, 1988; Roberts, 1981). For instance, when 13-year-olds are asked how addition and multiplication relate to each other in general, they first explain one operation and then shift to the other, not specifying the general relation between the two. When 5-year-olds explain a story about a doctor helping his sick daughter, they likewise split the story in two, telling one story about father and daughter and a second one about doctor and patient (Watson & Fischer, 1980).

This sort of simplification plays a major role in on-line planning tasks, where children coordinate anticipated movements of objects to produce a goal configuration. Upon encountering a planning task that is too complex for them, children commonly simplify the task by splitting it into separate pieces and therefore not coordinating all the anticipated movements. For example, in a series of studies where 4- and 5-year-olds were asked to produce a classification matrix of blocks varying in shape and color, the children commonly shifted between sorting by shape and sorting by color, thus producing a mixed-up matrix (Fischer & Roberts, 1991).

The strategy of shifting between dimensions usually produces an inconsistent matrix, but in special circumstances it can produce a correct one. In several studies, we taught many preschoolers to shift systematically, first sorting all blocks by shape and then sorting them by color, taking one pile (all of a given shape) at a time. With this new strategy, they could sort the matrix correctly while dealing with only one dimension at a time. Still, after this training, when we asked the same children to deal with both dimensions simultaneously, they remained unable to build a correct matrix. Controlled juxtaposition did not immediately induce coordination.

Similarly in the Tower of Hanoi, children who fail the task organize a few moves at a time and then shift to organize a few more. They do not organize the entire sequence of moves into one coordinated skill. Coordinating separate skills into an integrated unit is a major developmental achievement.

Role of the Frontal Cortex

Support for this integrative view of working memory development comes from research on the role of frontal cortex function. Recent evidence about brain development in both monkeys and human infants supports the argument that the frontal cortex is a source of the developing capacity for holding co-occurring information in working memory so it can be integrated.

Research by Goldman-Rakic (1987) and her colleagues demonstrates that specific columns of cells in the prefrontal cortex of the rhesus monkey hold information on line about an object that a monkey has seen hidden under a cloth. If these cells do not fire, the monkey cannot find the hidden object. Bell and Fox (1992, 1993) have shown via electroencephalographic (EEG) recordings that the frontal cortex is also active when this search skill develops in human infants during the first year.

Growth spurts in connections between the frontal cortex and other cortical areas correlate strongly with developmental changes in working memory capacity. In rhesus monkeys the frontal cortex (as well as other cortical areas) shows a sharp jump in synaptic density during the time when they develop successful search for a hidden object (Goldman-Rakic, 1987). Human infants who develop this search skill show a concurrent increase in EEG coherence for connections between frontal and occipital cortical areas (Bell & Fox, 1992, 1993). (Coherence is an index of connectivity between cortical areas.) For later ages in human beings, Thatcher's (1991, 1994) large study of the development of EEG coherence found that the frontal cortex was involved in over 90% of the coherence patterns that showed systematic development. In general, the emergence of each new cognitive-developmental level seems to be associated with a major discontinuity in the EEG, probably reflecting a change in connections with the frontal cortex, among other things (Fischer & Rose, 1994).

Coordination and Qualitative Changes in Working Memory

The concept of coordination as a mechanism leading to changing organization of working memory capacity adds a new dimension to theory and research on working memory. In the dynamic skills model, changes in working memory capacity depend more fundamentally on the nature of the structural relationships among the parts of a working memory representation than on quantitative increments in information storage. The emergence of new forms of structural relations in working memory is explained by an active process of coordination of component representational skills. The coordination of component skills leads not only to increased information capacity, but also to qualitative changes in the ability to organize information on line. Dynamic skills theory provides tools for describing and predicting such changes both micro- and macro-developmentally (Fischer & Pipp, 1984; Fischer & Rose, 1994).

In most cognitive approaches, limitations on working memory capacity are characterized in primarily quantitative terms (e.g., Case, 1980; Pascual-Leone, 1970). Concepts such as Miller's (1956) magic number 7 ± 2 information units or Pascual-Leone's (1970) and Case's (1980) M-space describe the number of items held on line at a given moment in working memory or its historical precursor, short-term memory (Atkinson & Shiffrin, 1968). As a result, changes in working memory are construed mainly as linear numerical increases in the number of items that can be held on line. While most theorists recognize the empirical reality of discontinuities in working memory capacity at different age levels (Klahr & Robinson, 1981), current theories of development of

Start

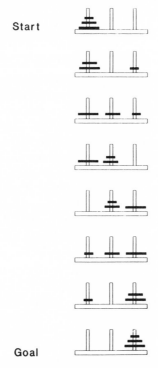

Goal

Figure 6.1   Optimal seven-move solution of the three-disk Tower of Hanoi.

working memory capacity do not address *structural* changes in the organization of working memory capacity that might lead to such qualitative
shifts. Qualitative change in working memory is generally accounted for
with concepts such as "chunking" (Miller, 1956), in which extensive
practice allows people to group items into units, as when the three
numerals 4, 9, and 5 are chunked as a unit for a telephone exchange,
495. But such concepts specify little about the organization of relations
among or within information units.

   For example, in research on problem solving with the Tower of Hanoi
and related tasks, working memory limits in on-line planning have been
characterized quantitatively in terms of depth of search, defined as the
number of moves an individual can anticipate in advance of performance
(Karat, 1982; Klahr & Robinson, 1981; Spitz & Borys, 1982). For the
tower task, a child is presented with three doughnut-shaped disks of
differing diameters, stacked in a pyramid on one of three posts fixed to
a wooden base, as shown at the top of Figure 6.1. The child is asked to
transfer the stack of disks from the initial post (Start) to another post

(Goal) by moving only one disk at a time and avoiding placing a larger disk on top of a smaller one. Achieving this goal requires using the third post (Rest) to store two disks in a temporary subtower.

Calculations of the number of moves are based on researchers' specification of a problem space, typically defined as including representations of the initial task configuration, the goal configuration, the intended actions, the possible actions in the task environment, and rule constraints on the actions, among other things (Newell & Simon, 1972). Many aspects of the problem space, such as rule constraints, previous moves, or even the final goal configuration, may be handled by forms of intermediate storage, but the potential actions under immediate consideration must be held on line in working memory in order to anticipate outcomes and compare alternative courses of action. The series of steps in Figure 6.1, representing the minimum sequence of moves to solve the problem, is typically used to calculate depth of search in the tower task. As Klahr and Robinson (1981, p. 133) wrote in regard to their models of children's strategies in the Tower of Hanoi, "Each move . . . is selected with respect to a sequence of moves computed to achieve a specified subgoal. . . . If the number of required moves exceeds the depth to which the child is willing or able to search, then he cannot compute the first move of a subgoal achieving sequence."

The number of moves is certainly important for working memory, but we argue that the structural *relations* among anticipated moves are equally important. A given number of moves can place very different requirements on working memory, depending on how they are organized. For instance, as we will show shortly, the first four moves in the Tower of Hanoi require representation of complex interdependencies, whereas the last four moves require much simpler relations to be represented. Over 40 years ago, Lashley (1951) argued that models of sequentially organized behavior must account for not only the number of items in a sequence but also the cognitive control structure relating the items. Making an effective plan for shopping from a shopping list requires representation in working memory not only of a number of items but also of the relations among anticipated actions for finding the items.

The ability to hold such specific relations among representations on line requires a specific form of cognitive control structure. Our model provides an account of the development of cognitive control structures for anticipated actions in which changes to new developmental levels of on-line planning involve qualitative changes in organization of relations among actions (and secondarily correlated quantitative changes). The qualitative changes between levels are evident not only in development of new capacities at certain ages (macrodevelopment) but also in changes in behavior during problem solving and learning (microdevelopment) (Bidell & Fischer, 1991; Fischer, 1980a; Granott, 1991, 1993).

MODEL OF DEVELOPMENT OF ON-LINE PLANNING SKILLS

Dynamic skills theory posits complex relations between macro- and microdevelopment. In contrast to traditional stage theory, which conceived major developmental transitions as all-or-nothing leaps, we view transitions as products of multiple constructive acts, leading to constructive generalization (Bidell & Fischer, 1991; Fischer & Farrar, 1987) or extension of a current skill to a new task or domain. Moreover, even within a task or domain the constructive process is not an all-or-nothing event. Cognitive skills of planning and problem solving are constructed gradually, over a number of trials, in a manner similar to physical skills such as bicycle riding or tennis (Fischer, 1980b; Fischer & Farrar, 1987). Through repeated active attempts to master tasks or situations, people gradually integrate component skills into qualitatively new cognitive abilities, which in turn must be exercised, consolidated, and automatized.

From this perspective, developmental transitions must be seen as involving both macro- and microdevelopmental processes. Neither can be explained in isolation from the other, and an adequate model of developmental transitions must describe the contribution of both. Therefore, in the present model of on-line planning skill development, macrodevelopmental acquisitions in the form of previously constructed and consolidated planning skills both support and constrain the microdevelopmental process of constructing new skills because they determine the nature of the component skills available for coordination into a new skill. At the same time, the microdevelopmental process of skill integration, extension, and consolidation contributes to macrodevelopmental transitions to new levels of planning abilities.

In the following subsections we outline this model. We first define on-line planning skills and then present a framework for describing the organization of planning skills at different developmental levels and for predicting the outcomes of developmental transitions. Finally, we outline implications of microdevelopmental mechanisms and their relation to macrodevelopmental levels. Then, in subsequent sections, the outline is elaborated in relation to a task analysis of the Tower of Hanoi problem and research on children's performance with the task.

Defining On-Line Planning Skills

On-line planning skills are defined as cognitive control structures that hold working memory representations on line in the organizations needed to anticipate a course of action, in a manner analogous to the physical skills needed in juggling or balancing several objects simultaneously. The complexity of the skill needed to anticipate actions in a given situation depends on the complexity of the task. Simple tasks may require only that an individual hold two actions on line in a sequential relation. More difficult tasks may require that several actions be sequenced or that more than one sequence be organized and compared simultaneously.

Because cognitive skills are task and context specific, developmental sequences and the mechanisms of skill integration that produce them are always specified in terms of a particular task and context. Measuring the relative level of skill complexity requires doing careful task analysis, specifying the variations a person must control to perform the task. Developmental analysis involves breaking down the task into a series of task variations representing different steps in the complexity of skills needed to perform the full task. Analysis of the relations among actions that must be held on line in these task variations produces a predicted developmental ordering of the on-line planning skills an individual can bring to bear in a given situation.

Four Levels of Development of On-Line Planning

Our general model of development of on-line planning is based on a number of such task analyses. Skills for on-line planning during childhood develop through four levels, each reflecting a different type of organization of skills in working memory, as shown in Table 6.1. Each level defines an upper limit on the complexity of skills that a child can control, the *optimal level* (Fischer & Pipp, 1984). As a new optimal level emerges, the upper limit grows precipitously, thus producing a cluster of spurts in optimal performance for familiar tasks under supportive assessment conditions. For each level, a spurt in cortical connections is hypothesized at the same ages, producing more complex neural networks that can sustain the new type of working memory characteristic of the level (Fischer & Rose, 1994). The age ranges when each optimal level emerges according to prior research are shown in the right-hand column of Table 6.1. Most of the time, however, children do not function at their optimal level but instead show a lower limit, their *functional level*. In ordinary behavior, without strong contextual support, children typically operate at this functional level in most domains. They show their optimal level primarily when some event evokes it, as when an adult or a skilled peer demonstrates a more complex behavior or a context primes it (Fischer, Bullock, Rotenberg, & Raya, 1993).

Understanding the levels in Table 6.1 and the skill analyses to be presented later requires some background concepts. Dynamic skills the-

TABLE 6.1 General Levels in Development of On-Line Planning Skills in Early Childhood

		SKILL STRUCTURE[a]		
LEVEL	PLANNING SKILL	Sensorimotor actions	Representations	AGE OF EMERGENCE[b]
S3: sensorimotor systems	Anticipation of a means-end action	$\left[L_R^P \longleftrightarrow M_S^Q \right]$		1 year
S4/Rp1: systems of sensorimotor systems, which are single representations[c]	Representation of an anticipated action plan: moving an object from one location to another	$\begin{bmatrix} L_R^P \longleftrightarrow M_S^Q \\ \Updownarrow \\ N_Y^W \longleftrightarrow O_Z^X \end{bmatrix} \equiv$	$[A]$	2 years
Rp2: representational mappings	Representation of two or more anticipated actions linked in a dependency relation to each other		$[A \longrightarrow B]$	4 years
Rp3: representational systems	Representation of several anticipated actions linked in two connected dependency relations		$[T_A^C \longleftrightarrow U_B^D]$	6 years

[a]In skill structures, each letter designates a skill component, with each full-size letter designating a main component (set) and each subscript or superscript a subset of the main component. Bold letters designate components that are sensorimotor actions, and italic letters components that are representations. Lines connecting sets designate relations between components forming a mapping, single-line arrows designate relations forming a system, and double-line arrows show relations forming a system of systems. Examples of specific skills and their components are elaborated in Table 6.2.

[b]This column specifies the age when skills at each level first become common, based on research with middle-class American and European children.

[c]At this level, children coordinate two or more sensorimotor systems from the previous level to produce a new kind of skill unit, a representation. The single representation A is therefore composed of at least two sensorimotor systems like that shown for level S3.

ory provides a general developmental framework for scaling the complexity of cognitive skills, with three kinds of increments in complexity at different degrees of coarseness. At the coarsest degree there are *tiers*, the four major types of skills organized at different points in the life span—reflexes in early infancy, sensorimotor skills in later infancy, representational skills in childhood, and abstract skills in adolescence and adulthood. Parts of the sensorimotor and representational tiers are included in Table 6.1.

Within each of these tiers there are four finer gradations of developing skill organization called *levels*. For the representational tier, which is the primary focus of this chapter, the four levels are single representations (Rp1), representational mappings (Rp2), representational systems (Rp3), and systems of representational systems (Rp4), which are also single abstractions. The fourth level produces a new kind of unit in skill organization and thus starts a new tier: in Table 6.1 level S4/Rp1 is both the fourth sensorimotor level and the first representational one because the coordination of sensorimotor systems produces a single representation.

For a given task or situation, even finer gradations of skill organization can be specified, called *steps*, which involve small transformations in skills within a level. Each transformation is produced by a coordination or integration of skills from previous steps. The theory specifies a limited set of transformation rules that describe the possible ways lower level component skills may combine to produce new skills. This limited set of combination rules allow a potentially large number of developmental steps, with the number depending on task, context, and person. A series of small steps is commonly seen in problem-solving situations. The analysis we will present of development and problem solving in the Tower of Hanoi involves seven steps moving across the three representational levels (Rp 1 through 3) shown in Table 6.1.

At the first level in Table 6.1, sensorimotor systems, infants can *anticipate a flexible means-end action,* such as picking up a disk to place it over a post in the Tower of Hanoi, varying their actions until they get the post through the hole in the disk. The skill structure diagramed in Table 6.1 shows that a child coordinates at least two variations of one action (**P** and **R** of action **L**), such as looking at the disk and the post, with at least two variations of a second action (**Q** and **S** of action **M**), such as manipulating the disk in relation to the hole in the disk and the post. One-year-old infants can carry out these fundamental precursors of planning skills, although planning researchers have seldom assessed such young children. An exception is our research on the development of classification skills, in which a prediction about this level was tested and supported: children 1 year of age were able to use an on-line plan to pick out blocks of a simple shape (or color) in order to place them in a box (Fischer & Bidell, 1991; Fischer & Roberts, 1991).

The level of single representations, which is the first one involved in the Tower of Hanoi in most research with young children, involves a major reorganization of sensorimotor systems: two sensorimotor systems are coordinated to form a *single representation of an anticipated action plan.* For the tower, a child of approximately age 2 years or older moves an object systematically from one place to another, such as removing a disk from one post in order to place it on another, which is called a "transposition" in the research literature. This skill coordinates the sensorimotor system for placing the disk over a post (actions **L** and **M**, each with two variations) with a second sensorimotor system for manipulating the disk to remove it from a post. In the second system, looking at the disk and looking at the post (**W** and **Y** of action **N**) are coordinated with removing the disk from the post (**X** and **Z** of action **O**).

The coordination of sensorimotor systems produces a representation because a child can use one system to evoke the other. For example, while removing the disk from one post (top system in the structure for level S4/Rp1 in Table 6.1), the child can represent placing the disk on another post (bottom system). This anticipation of one action system while using another separate action system constitutes a single representation.

The third level, representational mappings, involves reorganizing two single representations by *coordinating two represented actions so that one action is dependent on the other,* thus forming a one-dimensional dependency relation. For instance, a child of approximately 4 years or older can represent that for two disks stacked on top of each other, moving the one on the bottom to the goal post requires first moving the one on top to some other post. The transposition of the second disk, *B,* is dependent on first doing the transposition of the first disk, *A.*

At the fourth level, representational systems, children coordinate two representational mappings, thus *linking two represented dependency relations* in a two-dimensional relation. In the tower, a child of 6 years or older can represent the series of actions in which disks are moved to posts where they are not supposed to end up so that other disks can be moved into positions that will allow moves to the final goal configuration. That is, they can coordinate dependent movement of four disks, such as moving one disk, *A,* in order to be able to move a second disk, *B,* so that a third disk can be moved, *C,* in order to move a fourth disk into its correct position, *D.*

Recall that each level is predicted to produce spurts in optimal performance at specific ages. Research by Welsh, Pennington, and Groisser

Figure 6.2   Spurts in performance on the Tower of Hanoi at predicted ages 3–4 and 5–7 years. Data from Welsh, Pennington, and Groisser (1991). Planning efficiency score assigns 6 points for an optimal solution in Trials 1 and 2, 5 points for an optimal solution in Trials 2 and 3, etc., with a resulting range of 0 to 36 points.

(1991) supports these predictions for the levels of mappings and systems in Table 6.1. Our reanalysis of data they report shows spurts in Tower of Hanoi performance at 3–4 and 5–7 years, as shown in Figure 6.2.

    In addition, changes in strategy occur at the times of these predicted transitions in on-line planning skills. At the 3- to 4-year transition to representational mappings when, according to our model, children become capable of plans involving dependent moves, researchers report sudden transitions to strategies involving simple subgoals (Klahr & Robinson, 1981; Welsh, 1991). Similarly, at the 6- to 7-year transition to systems, when children begin to anticipate action sequences involving dependencies among dependencies, researchers report a second shift to strategies involving nested subgoals, such as building a temporary two-disk tower on the Rest post (Figure 6.1) in order to move the third disk to the Goal post (Piaget, 1976; Spitz & Borys, 1982; Welsh, 1991).

Developmental Steps within a Level

Besides these basic structures for each level, the transformation rules describe how children can recombine the basic components in small steps to construct increasingly complex skills within a level. Our analysis of the Tower of Hanoi involves several of these transformations. In one of the simplest transformations, shifts of focus, children simply shift from one skill to another in succession. Children first represent the transposition of disk A to be able to transpose disk B, a mapping. Then they shift to representing the transposition of disk A to another post, which by itself involves only a single representation. This skill is diagramed as follows:

$$[A_2 \text{———} B] > [A_1] \quad \text{(shift of focus)}$$

The numbers are sequenced in reverse order, with the final move numbered 1. In another common transformation, called compounding, children coordinate more than two components at the same level. For example, a child anticipates moving disk B and then disk A to one post in order to move disk C to another post:

$$[B \text{———} A \text{———} C] \quad \text{(compounding)}$$

Together, the levels and transformations are used to predict and describe sequences in both development with age and microdevelopment during problem solving.

Microdevelopment of On-Line Planning Skills

Acquisition of on-line planning skills is a structural integration process in which lower level skills serve as components for the construction of developmentally more complex on-line planning skills. The organization of plans and performance is constrained by the previously reached macrodevelopmental level of control structures (skills) governing representations of actions in working memory. Within each major step in problem solving a new set of relations between main goal, subgoals, and actions emerges, constructed according to the skill transformation processes. Some steps involve relatively small, within-level gains in plan complexity, and some involve larger jumps to new levels of complexity.

There are two major developmental constraints on on-line plans: an *entry-level* of planning skill, which is the level of skill the child initially brings to bear on first encountering a task, and an *optimal level*, which is the most complex structure the child can construct under optimal conditions, including practice and contextual support. If the task is unfamiliar, the entry level is usually below the optimal level, since the child has not yet extended optimal level skills to the new domain. Successful problem solving usually involves building on-line plans that move from the entry level toward a higher level.

Moreover, a given individual's entry level will vary as a function of age and experience in a given domain. Children who have had an opportunity to practice and consolidate or automatize their planning skills on a given type of task will be able to apply more complex entry level skills to a related task. Children with less automatized skills will find their plans breaking down when confronted with new cognitive demands and will therefore be operating with less complex entry level skills on the new task.

When optimal level planning skills have been constructively generalized to a wide range of tasks in a given domain, and highly automatized, they may become the entry level skills of a new set of tasks requiring a higher optimal level of planning skill. Such constructions may at first be temporary, but with practice and repeated constructive activity, they can become automatized, extending the individual's optimal planning skills to a new macrodevelopmental level for the domain.

For 10- to 11-year-old children, entry level skills on a task requiring systems level skills are likely to be close to or at the systems level, since their systems level skills should be highly automatized. Children in this situation would need little constructive activity to perform the task. On the other hand, 6- to 7-year-olds typically are just in the process of constructing representational systems level skills in a range of domains. Entry level skills for these children would usually be either mappings or single representations (as shown in Table 6.1). In this case children must construct the representational system skills needed for a novel task from mapping level components—and perhaps even construct the component mappings.

When children must construct the planning skills needed for a new task, they first try out alternative plans at their entry skill level, and there is competition among these entry level alternatives, with no clear winner since none are capable of organizing the required relations among action sequences.

These alternatives serve as components for a new, more complex skill that the child constructs. Two or more of the alternatives that have been used successively are held on line simultaneously and coordinated into a more complex plan. This process often occurs gradually through laborious small steps of construction, and when the coordination is achieved, there are typically also rapid changes in performance.

The higher level coordination is often not stable when it initially appears, because the immediate problem-solving context has primed the coordination, moving a child temporarily toward his or her optimal level of performance. Once the effects of that supportive context dissipate, the child cannot sustain the coordination without further opportunities to repeat and consolidate the construction. This property reflects the developmental range between optimal and functional levels that is basic to cognitive functioning (Fischer et al., 1993).

Prior research on microdevelopmental transitions in strategy type for the Tower of Hanoi fit the skill integration model (Anzai & Simon, 1979; Kotovsky, Hayes, & Simon, 1985; Simon & Reed, 1976; Wansart, 1990). For instance, Wansart found that for the three-disk task in Figure 6.1, 10-year-old children followed a microdevelopmental sequence of strategy transitions from brief global attempts at moving the whole stack to strategies recognizing a subgoal and then to successful nested subgoal strategies. This sequence of strategy transitions follows transitions from single representations to mappings and finally to systems in on-line planning skills.

In the remainder of this chapter, we present a detailed analysis of these transitions in on-line planning skill in children's solutions of the Tower of Hanoi task. We begin with a developmental task analysis of the Tower of Hanoi and in the subsequent section present evidence of the micro- and macrodevelopmental processes involved in cognitive transitions.

TASK ANALYSIS OF ON-LINE PLANNING SKILLS IN THE TOWER OF HANOI

The Tower of Hanoi provides a convenient task for building a specific model of on-line planning development because the task structure is straightforward and there have been a number of studies of problem solving with the task. The standard analysis of the problem space for the three-disk tower, shown in Figure 6.3, organizes all possible configurations of disks that a person can produce under the rule constraints (Karat, 1982; Klahr, 1978). Each line connecting problem states indicates a possible move of a single disk. For the starting configuration shown at the top of the triangular diagram, the optimal seven-move solution proceeds down the right side to the goal state at bottom right (also shown in Figure 6.1). Bars divide the problem space into classes of task variations with the same optimal number moves to the goal. Step 3 tasks may be solved in a minimum of three moves, step 4 tasks in four moves, and so forth.

Moving up from step 1, each step adds one move to the optimal path length and so requires greater complexity in the working memory representation for solving the task. According to our model, task complexity increases qualitatively as well as quantitatively, requiring representation of specific relations between moves, which is not captured by Figure 6.3. The addition of one action to a sequence sometimes simply involves adding a move but at other times requires a reorganization of relations among moves in the sequence, such as a detour.

Table 6.2 describes a dynamic skills model of the seven steps to solve the tower, the structures of moves-in-relation that must be held on line in each task variation. All examples are for the optimal solution path running along the right side of the triangle in Figure 6.3. The skill structures involve not only the single move for a given step but also the

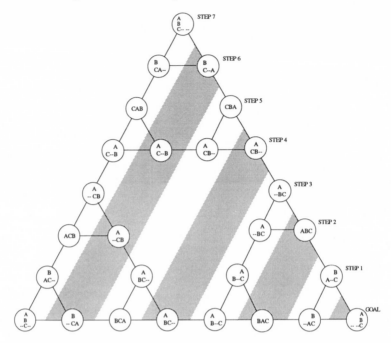

Figure 6.3 Problem space diagram for the Tower of Hanoi. Within each circle the small, medium, and large disks are labeled A, B, and C, respectively.
Their positions on the three posts are indicated in three horizontal places,
with a dash indicating an empty post. A vertical stack of letters represents a
stack of disks. Each line connecting problem states indicates a possible move
of a single disk transforming one state into another. Thick lines demarcate
forms of the task that require the same minimum number of moves to solution. Those labeled step 5, for example, require a minimum of five moves.

remaining moves required to complete the solution. For each step, the
child is faced with the array of disks shown in the far right circle for
that step in Figure 6.3.

According to our skill analysis, a step 1 task can be solved in two
ways, depending on specific task requirements. A child as young as about
1 year can control a means-end system of actions, picking up a disk and
placing it on a specific post. Controlling these actions requires a minimum of a sensorimotor system (level S3, diagramed in Table 6.1), which
children can construct by about 1 year of age.

In standard versions of the Tower of Hanoi, however, the child must
be able not only to carry out these actions but to represent them by
relating the removal of the disk from one peg to placing it on another
peg, as described for Table 6.1 above. Just as children can walk before
they can represent themselves or other people as walking (Fischer &

Jennings, 1981; Watson & Fischer, 1977; Wolf, 1982), they can move a disk before they can construct a separate representation of moving it. The representation of this action sequence requires a skill at the next level, single representations (level Rp1, the first level of the representational tier), which typically emerges at about 2 years. Children represent placing disk A on the Goal post while they are removing it from the Start post, which is symbolized by A_1 in Table 6.2.

The tasks in step 2 require representation of a sequence of two disk actions, moving disk B to Goal and then disk A to Goal (on top of B). To anticipate this sequence of actions, a child must hold on line two action sequences in succession, B_1 and A_1. The minimum skill needed to hold this relation on line is a shift between two single representations, which is a more complex skill at level Rp1. All steps after number 1 require shifts between skills as part of the minimum needed to perform them (Table 6.2).

Step 3 tasks produce a new dimension of complexity because for the first time a disk is blocking the appropriate action: disk A is blocking the movement of disk B to the Goal post. The solution therefore entails a major qualitative change, representing a *dependency relation*, first moving disk B to a new location in order to free disk A to be moved to Goal. This skill requires a representational mapping (level Rp2), $[A_2 \text{———} B_1]$. A person holds on line in working memory a mapping relating the two moves (disk A off disk B, A_2, so that disk B can move to Goal, B_1). Once this set of actions has been accomplished, disk A can be easily moved to the Goal post, which requires shifting to single representation A_1 as in step 1.

The skills required for steps 4, 5, and 6 involve increasingly complex dependency relations (representational mappings), as shown in Table 6.2. Step 4 adds to step 3 the requirement of moving disk C to Goal, C_1, before making the three-move sequence of step 3. Step 5 increases the complexity of the problem by adding a second blockage (disk A blocking disk C's movement to Goal) and so requires a second mapping, $[A_3 \text{———} C_1]$: a person must hold on line a dependency relation between the moves of disks A and C in order to anticipate the necessary movement of disk C. Then there is a shift to the skill in step 3. At step 6, disks A and B both block movement of disk C to Goal. Anticipation of the dependent moves requires coordination of three transpositions in a compound mapping, $[B_2 \text{———} A_3 \text{———} C_1]$, followed by a shift to the skill in step 3.

Step 7 entails another major qualitative change in complexity, movement to the level of representational systems (level Rp3), which emerges at about 6 years and is related to what Piaget (1976) called concrete operations. Besides the blockages present at step 6, the additional re-

TABLE 6.2 General Levels in Development of On-Line Planning Skills in Early Childhood

Step	Name	Skill structure[a]	Skill description and example of on-line planning
Level Rp1: single representations			
1	Single representation	$[A_1]$	Represent one transposition of a disk from one position to another (start state/change/end state), A_1. Example: Plan to move disk A from the Start post to the Goal post (on top of disks B and C).
2	Shift between representations	$[B_1] > [A_1]$	Represent a single transposition, B_1. Then shift to represent single transposition A_1. Example: Plan to move disk B from Rest to Goal (on top of disk C). Then plan to move disk A from Start to Goal.
Level Rp2: representational mappings			
3	Representational mapping with shift to a single representation	$[A_2 \!-\!\!-\!\!-\! B_1] > [A_1]$	Represent a transposition, A_2, as a simultaneous function of transposition B_1. (The specific effects of one transposition depend on those of another.) Then shift to represent single transposition A_1. Example: Plan to move disk A from Rest to Start in order to move disk B from Rest to Goal. Then shift to plan for moving disk A from Start to Goal.
4	Representational mapping with two shifts to single representations	$[C_1] > [A_2 \!-\!\!-\!\!-\! B_1] > [A_1]$	Represent a single transposition, C_1. Then shift to represent transposition A_2 as a function of transposition B_1. Then shift to represent single transposition A_1. Example: Plan to move disk C from Start to Goal. Then shift to plan to move disk A from Rest to Start in order to move disk B from Rest to Goal. Then shift to plan to move disk A from Start to Goal.

Step	Description	Skill structure	Analysis and example
5	Shifts between two mappings and a single representation	$[A_3 \text{———} C_1] >$ $[A_2 \text{———} B_1] > [A_1]$	Represent a transposition A_3 as a function of transposition C_1. Then shift to represent transposition A_2 as a function of transposition B_1. Then shift to represent single transposition A_1. Example: Plan to move disk A from Goal to Rest (on top of disk B) *in order* to move disk C from Start to Goal. Then shift to plan to move disk A from Rest to Start *in order* to move disk B from Rest to Goal. Finally, shift to plan for moving disk A from Start to Goal.
6	Shifts from a compound mapping to a simple mapping and then to a single representation	$[B_2 \text{———} A_3 \text{———} C_1] >$ $[A_2 \text{———} B_1] > [A_1]$	Represent two transpositions, B_2 and A_3, as a function of transposition C_1. Then shift to represent transposition A_2 as a function of transposition B_1. Then shift to represent single transposition A_1. Example: Plan to move disk B from Start to Rest *and* disk A from Goal to Rest *in order* to move disk C from Start to Goal. Then shift to plan to move disk A from Rest to Start *in order* to move disk B from Rest to Goal. Finally, shift to plan for moving disk A from Start to Goal.

Level Rp3: Representational systems

Step	Description	Skill structure	Analysis and example
7	Shifts from a representational system to a mapping and then to a single representation	$[T_{A_3}^{A_4} \longleftrightarrow U_{C_1}^{B_2}] >$ $[A_2 \text{———} B_1] > [A_1]$	Represent a system of four transpositions, A_4 and B_2 allowing or *compensating* with A_3 and C_1. Then shift to represent transposition A_2 as a function of transposition B_1. Then shift to represent single transposition A_1. Example: Plan to move disk A from Start to Goal *in order* to move disk B from Start to Rest and then disk A from Goal to Rest *in order* to move disk C from Start to Goal. Then shift to plan to move disk A from Rest to Start *in order* to move disk B from Rest to Goal. Finally, shift to plan for moving disk A from Start to Goal.

Note. All skill analyses and examples are for the optimal solution path along the right side of the triangular diagram in Figure 6.1. The skill structures for each step involve not only the new move required at that step but also the moves required to complete the solution.

[a]Representations of disk transpositions are indicated by letters A, B, and C for the respective disks and subscripts 1 to 4 for moves of the disk, with lower numbers indicating later moves (and therefore lower steps).

quirement of moving disk A from Start creates a situation in which disks A and B block not only disk C but also one another. A child must represent a dependency between dependencies, a two-dimensional dependency relation of four moves, A_4, B_2, A_3, and C_1, which requires a representational system (level Rp3) as shown at the bottom of Table 6.2. To anticipate the correct movement of disk C to Goal, the following information must be held on line: (a) disk A should be moved to Goal (a counterintuitive move if your plan is based on mappings) so that disk B can be moved to the Rest post, and (b) these moves are necessary in order to allow moving disk A to Rest in order to move disk C to Goal. All four moves must be simultaneously controlled in working memory to generate the specific order in which to make the first four moves of the task. Then the rest of the moves can be made with a shift to the skill in step 3.

One of the implications of the qualitative differences between steps in this model is that tasks judged to have the same complexity with standard metrics for depth of search have different complexities. As an example, consider two sets of task variations, each with a depth of search of four moves. In these tasks, children are asked to start with one of the configurations in Figure 6.3 and to end with another, not necessarily the standard Goal. In one task children move from step 7 to a goal of the configuration at step 3. In the second task, children move from step 4 to the standard Goal. According to the skill analysis in Table 6.2, constructing a plan for the latter task requires holding on line only two dependency relations in a sequential relation with one another—a mapping, which children are capable of by approximately age 4. Constructing a plan for the former task requires holding on line two dependency relations that are dependent on each other—a system, which children are optimally capable of by approximately age 6. In this way, the skill model makes different predictions from the traditional problem-space model in Figure 6.3.

A MICROANALYTIC STUDY OF COGNITIVE TRANSITIONS IN THE TOWER OF HANOI

In this section we illustrate and elaborate our model of cognitive transitions in on-line planning in relation to an exploratory study (Bidell, 1990) of children's problem-solving performance on the Tower of Hanoi task. The study employed a microanalytic methodology in order to better observe fine-grained changes in behavior associated with cognitive transitions (Siegler & Crowley, 1991). We reasoned that, since children solving a problem must make a transition from an inadequate to an adequate plan (Newell & Simon, 1972), a good place to observe behavior related to the construction of new plans would be children's first encounter with a problem-solving task such as the Tower of Hanoi. Children aged 6 to 11 years were studied, since they are typically capable of an optimal skill level of at least representational systems (Rp3) (the older children in this age range are presumed to have constructed more complex skills within the Rp3 level). It was expected that observations of their first-encounter performances would provide data related to the transition from entry level to optimal level planning skills, and that age-related differences in that transitional process would shed light on the relations between macro- and microdevelopment in the transition to new planning skills. Finally, by understanding something about the transitional mechanisms involved in moving from entry to optimal level, we might gain some insight into the more complex process of moving to new optimal levels in a given domain.

Twenty-five children, 12 boys and 13 girls, approximately matched for age, were videotaped while solving the three-disk version of the tower for the first time. After one to three further practice trials they were asked to give postperformance verbal and gestural descriptions of their plans for the task. Plans were not collected before problem solving because we wanted to observe the children's problem-solving behavior as they formulated their first on-line plans. First trials were videotaped and coded for move sequences, move durations, move latencies, and behavioral indicators of cognitive demand such as tapping the fingers, verbalizing, and breaking task rules (called infractions). (Later practice trials will not be analyzed in this chapter.) Postperformance plans were coded for move sequences and types of rule infractions.

Qualitative Transitions in Planning Activity

Of the 25 children, 4 (among the oldest) solved the task perfectly (minimum seven-move solution) on the first trial. This group will be called the "efficient" problem solvers. The entry level for these subjects appears to have been essentially the same as the level required by the task, so only a little constructive activity was required to achieve an adequate plan. Therefore we will be concerned primarily with the performance of the 21 subjects who did not solve the task in the minimal number of moves ("inefficient" problem solvers) and therefore presumably underwent a constructive transition during their first trial.

All of the 21 inefficient problem solvers exhibited a sudden behavioral change from inefficient to highly efficient problem solving during the course of their first trial. Figure 6.4 presents an individual profile of first-trial problem solving showing one such transition. Move durations and latencies are plotted as a function of move number. Durations and latencies greater than 2.5 s (indicated by the dotted reference line la-

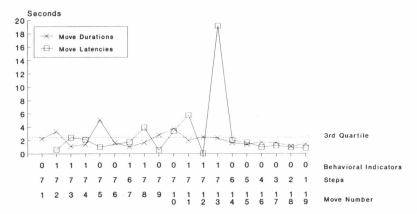

Figure 6.4   Typical individual profile showing sudden transition to efficient problem-solving behavior.

beled 3rd Quartile) were longer than 75% of the other moves and were designated as pauses. The two lines plotted below the horizontal axis show the presence or absence of behavioral indicators (upper line, 1 = present) and the step at which each move originated (which is also distance from the goal).

During the first part of the trial, called Period 1, these children's moves were consistently nonoptimal. For example, the moves of the child in Figure 6.4 all remained in or returned to step 7 task variations— those requiring two-dimensional dependency relations (representational systems) in the model. Of 144 moves made in Period 1 by the 21 children, only 4 (3%) reduced the number of moves to the goal despite a chance expectancy of 33.3% on most moves. Every one of these 4 was followed by reversals that returned to step 7 tasks. Moreover, on the very first move made, not one of the 21 children moved correctly, even though this task affords only two choices, as shown in Figure 6.3, so that the chance expectancy is 50%.

The transition to the second part of the trial, Period 2, was marked by a sudden change from the ineffective Period 1 pattern to perfect or nearly perfect performance. Period 2 was defined as all those moves in a trial after and including the first two optimal moves in a row. This criterion marked a clear turning point in all the children's move profiles, as exemplified by the protocol in Figure 6.4. For most children, once they made two optimal moves in a row, all further moves were optimal, in stark contrast to their nonoptimal responding in Period 1. Only two of the youngest children made one or two nonoptimal moves during Period 2, but even these were subsequently reversed, as the children resumed a chain of optimal moves leading to the goal.

Furthermore, during Period 1 children exhibited high frequencies of pauses, behavioral indicators, and rule infractions compared with Period 2. Pauses were associated with 42.7% of the children's Period 1 moves, but only 10.9% of Period 2 moves, a highly significant drop (χ^2 [1] = 36, p < .0001). Similarly, behavioral indicators were associated with 40.6% of Period 1 moves, but only 12.7% of Period 2 moves (χ^2 [1] = 28.8, p < .0001). Of a total of 16 rule infractions by nine children, all occurred in Period 1, when children were confined to step 7 task variations.

This major transition, occurring only at step 7 task variations, clearly indicated that not just the first move, but the whole set of step 7 task variations presented a special cognitive challenge. The children were unable to proceed until they solved one of the step 7 variations predicted to require a representational systems level plan. But once they did, they were able to solve with relative ease the lower level task variations encountered en route to the goal.

Yet even after children solved the step 7 task variation, they often seemed to continue their planning activities. A comparison of the proportion of moves with behavioral indicators across classes of task variations suggests continued but decreasing cognitive activity, with two significant drops, one from step 7 to step 6 variations, and one from step 3 to step 2 variations. The proportion was significantly lower for moves originating in combined steps 5 and 6 (χ^2 [1] = 10.9, p < .001) than in step 7 variations, and significantly lower for steps 1 and 2 (χ^2 [1] = 9.01, p < .003) than step 3 task variations.

These findings suggest that once children constructed a systems level plan, planning activity continued but dropped off at two key points in the task. First, after successful achievement of the systems level plan, behavioral indicators dropped, but the proportion remained relatively high until children passed the step 3 task variation, where the proportion dropped to near zero. The task analysis showed that step 7 variations each require a plan of four moves related in a two-dimensional dependency (system). Thus once children succeed in constructing the systems level plan, they have anticipated four moves ahead, which brings them to one of the step 3 variations. Step 3 tasks require a one-dimensional dependency or mapping level plan. It appears that if the children have not already anticipated this additional mapping level plan for the step 3 task, they are confronted again with the need to construct a plan, albeit a less complex one. Most children, having constructed mapping level component skills, seem to make this second, less complex transition smoothly. However, some children, possibly those with lower initial entry level skills, seem to require more cognitive effort in constructing the second part of the plan, showing behavioral indicators.

Variations in Transitional Behavior

Although all 21 inefficient problem solvers seemed to undergo a cognitive transition to successful problem solving, they did not all pass through this transition in the same way. They showed different patterns of behavior during the transition, and these were related to age.

To describe variability in transitional behavior we created a rough scale, classifying children's behavior into four transition patterns according to the number of pauses in the two phases of the first trial. Pattern 1 responses had more than two pauses in the first period and at least one pause in the second period. Pattern 2 had more than two pauses in the first period and none in the second. Pattern 3 had two or fewer pauses in the first and none in the second. Pattern 4 had no pauses in either period.

Comparison of these transition patterns across children showed a sharp discontinuity in the number of moves to criterion. Children showing Patterns 1 and 2 took more moves to reach criterion, with means of 13.2 and 17.1, respectively, which did not differ statistically. Children showing Patterns 3 and 4 averaged 10.4 and 7 moves, differing significantly from the average of the first two patterns (Duncan, $a = 0.05$). Since 7 is the minimal solution, Patterns 3 and 4 involved few or no nonoptimal moves. Children who took more moves and made more pauses tended to be younger. Pattern 1 and 2 children were significantly younger than those showing Patterns 3 and 4, with mean ages of 8.7, 9.3, 10.9, and 11.2 years, respectively—a 1.6-year difference between Groups 2 and 3.

Consistent with our model, younger children, who are likely to construct less complex entry level planning skills, took longer to make the transition from entry to optimal level and showed more signs of stress. This suggests that Pattern 1 and 2 children, who took longer to make the transition, spent Period 1 of their first trial constructing the necessary component skills, while Pattern 3 and 4 children, who entered the task with more consolidated and automatized component skills, were able to construct a systems level plan with little or no effort at constructing component skills.

Structures of Children's Entry-Level Planning Skills

The study included two more direct methods of assessing the organization of children's plans using error analysis. First, during their initial task performance the nonoptimal moves and rule violations or infractions were used to infer the structure of on-line plans involved at the time of the error. Second, during the postperformance assessment of verbal and gestural plans, children also committed infractions that could be structurally analyzed. Both assessments indicated that children's plans began

Infraction: Big on Little

Figure 6.5   Typical rule infraction committed during performance trials.

as simple representational mappings or single dependency relations similar to the one diagrammed for step 3 in Table 6.2.

First, analysis of the inefficient problem solvers' infractions and nonoptimal moves during initial performance trials demonstrated that the children initially lacked the representational system (Table 6.2) needed to anticipate appropriate action sequences in the step 7 task variations. The children moved back and forth among step 7 task variations during Period 1 of the protocols, attempting to anticipate an adequate path to the goal. Why would these children remain so systematically within step 7 tasks, reversing optimal moves and defying probabilities that would have given them one out of two or three optimal moves by chance alone? The systematic quality of this behavior indicates that the children were not simply giving up and turning to trial-and-error response patterns. Their behavior was clearly guided by plans of some kind, but plans that were inadequate to the task.

The character of these inadequate on-line plans can be inferred from the nature of the infractions committed during the problem-solving trials. Different types of infractions reflect different kinds of working memory representations of relations among moves. For instance, when faced with the first state in the problem space (step 7, top of the triangle, Figure 6.3) a child could simply pick up all three disks and move them to the Goal post. This infraction would be consistent with a primitive step 1 plan, representing the completion of the problem in terms of only a single move.

None of the children in the present study committed this error, however. According to straightforward skill analyses, all their rule infractions reflected some form of representational mapping, usually a one-dimensional dependency relation like that shown for step 3. For example, in Figure 6.5 a child faced with a step 7 task (requiring a representational system for solution) commits the infraction of placing a big disk on top of a little one. The simplest plan for producing this infraction is to represent a single dependency relation between two actions: move disk B to Rest in order to move disk C to Goal [$B \rule{2em}{0.4pt} C$].

Children's rule infractions thus show consistent use of simple map-

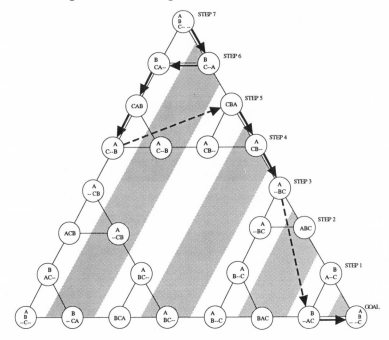

Figure 6.6   Example of a postperformance verbal plan showing tacit infractions. Dotted lines indicate tacit infractions.

ping level planning skills during their initial performance (Period 1). Since plans based on mappings can anticipate only a one-dimensional dependency relation, all the children's moves during this period were insufficient to anticipate the double dependency relations required for the step 7 tasks. As a result, all the moves either remained within the step 7 tasks or produced infractions that revealed the mapping organization of children's on-line plans.

The second assessment of the organization of children's plans was the postperformance planning condition. Of particular interest are seven children who committed a total of 14 tacit infractions—unacknowledged rule infractions, physically impossible moves, or both. In every case the tacit errors occurred when the child was describing a move originating at either step 3 or step 7, which are the steps requiring children to coordinate lower level components—mappings into systems at step 7, and single representations into mappings at step 3—to continue their progress. Children making tacit infractions described plans using a possible but nonoptimal progression of moves, then suddenly jumped to a point in the problem impossible to reach under the rule constraints— without any acknowledgment of the breach.

Figure 6.6 shows a typical pattern of infractions, by a girl who made two, which are marked by dotted lines. First she described a possible series of moves that led to a state in which disk C was on the Start post and disk A was on top of disk B on the Goal post. Then, without comment, she described placing disk B on the Rest post, a move that would involve either a rule infraction (picking up disk A to move disk B, and thus moving two at a time) or a physical impossibility (removing disk B from under disk A without moving disk A). Without acknowledging or verbally marking it, the child has effectively achieved the removal of disk B from under disk A at Goal, tacitly transferring it to the Rest post—a rule infraction that cuts out three moves. The child then described two legitimate moves, resulting in a step 3 configuration with disk A on top of disk B on the Rest post and disk C on the Goal post—just three moves away from the goal. But at this point she again committed an infraction, leaping to a new point in the problem space: she described a move of disk B to the Goal post without accounting for or even referring to the necessary move of disk A off disk B.

These two infractions again show the use of mapping plans rather than systems, one-dimensional dependencies rather than two-dimensional ones. The girl's first moves immediately after the initial infraction showed that she wanted to get disk C to the Goal post. Before the infraction she had mentally positioned disk A on disk B at the Goal post. Her plan apparently involved forming a subgoal of moving disks A and B to the Rest post so that she could move disk C to Goal, a mapping level plan (see step 6 in figure 6.2). However, carrying out this plan without an infraction required relating this subgoal to the additional subgoal of moving disk A off disk B in order to move disk B to Rest. The child seems to have been unable to hold both component mappings on line in working memory simultaneously, so she inadvertently neglected the second mapping relation. Instead she tacitly assumed the outcome of that move sequence—disk B on Rest—and continued with her plan. Now, having let one component of the double dependency slip, she found herself faced only with the mapping level problem of planning the move of disk A from Goal to Rest in order to move disk C to Goal, placing her at a step 3 configuration. From this point she committed a second tacit infraction, again consistent with a mapping level plan. Here she described a move of disk B to Goal in order to move disk A on top of it, a mapping level plan. But she ignored the fact that disk A first had to be removed from disk B in order to move B to Goal—a second mapping. Again, when confronted with a problem requiring the simultaneous control of two mappings, she inadvertently reduced the complexity to a single mapping level plan.

Finally, a comparison of performance infractions and later tacit infractions supported the hypothesis that children with lower entry level skills would not retain the systems level skills they temporarily constructed during their first trial. Children who committed rule infractions during their first trial were significantly more likely to commit tacit infractions in their verbal/gestural plans (χ^2 [1] = 10.4, $p < .001$). Of the 9 children who committed rule infractions during the first trial, 6 committed tacit infractions later, but of the 13 children who did not commit rule infractions on the first trial, only 1 committed a tacit infraction during the verbal/gestural plans. All actual rule infractions occurred during the initial phase of the children's trials, and most originated in step 7 tasks. It appears that the children who had more difficulty constructing a systems level plan in the first trial also had more difficulty sustaining it in the less supportive verbal planning assessment.

Summary: Construction of New Plans from Component Plans

Consistent with the dynamic skills model presented earlier, most of the children began Period 1 with mapping level plans that were inadequate to solve the task and at some point showed a sudden change to an effective systems level plan. How were these children able to suddenly acquire a skill that they so clearly lacked at the outset of the session? The present evidence supports the hypothesis that they constructed the new skill—at least temporarily—from component skills they brought into play during Period 1, induced by the support of particular task configurations they produced.

During Period 1 children had the opportunity to try out alternative move sequences and presumably to instantiate several versions of plans based on mappings. The high proportion of behavioral indicators— pausing, private speech, tapping the table, gesturing possible moves— during this period suggests that children were actively reflecting on the moves they were making. Also, they seldom repeated moves, which suggests that they were actively judging the efficacy of their moves and remembering previous moves to avoid repetition with present ones.

Still, as long as the children continued to represent mapping level plans *successively*, one after another, they were doomed to failure, since no single mapping plan can bring together in working memory the complex double dependency relations required for solution. Somehow the child must bring the two dependency relations into co-occurrence in working memory and organize them into the *simultaneous* system of double dependencies needed to anticipate the correct sequence of moves.

Since each mapping level plan that a child employs during Period 1 involves a single dependency relation, each is a potential component for the construction of the needed double dependency plan. The challenge is to find the correct component mapping skills and hold them on line long enough to integrate them. When the right component plans for a given step 7 task variation are brought together in working memory for comparison, the child has an opportunity to integrate the component plans into a new, more complex and inclusive plan at a new level of planning skill.

The new planning skill constructed by this componential integration is not necessarily stable across time and place, however. Although all the children succeeded in solving the problem, and therefore in integrating the component mappings at least temporarily, a number of children made tacit infractions during the postperformance planning, indicating that their newly created planning skill was not stable enough to regenerate an adequate plan in this low support situation.

Analysis of patterns of transitional behavior suggested that younger children have a harder time with integration, and the correlations between infractions across conditions indicated that children who had difficulty achieving the initial integration also tended to have a hard time reconstructing it later. These children's solutions reached their optimal level, representational systems (Rp3), in part because their behavior was supported by their actually manipulating the disks and viewing particular disk configurations that "primed" (Fischer et al., 1993) their construction by calling up co-occurrent instantiations of the component mappings. But to consistently produce the complete plan without contextual support, children must be able to sustain all the components in the skill on their own, without priming. The girl whose postperformance plan is shown in Figure 6.6 illustrates vividly how the systems level plan she used in correctly solving the task decomposed into mappings when she had no contextual support.

In sum, these findings present us with a picture of coparticipation of macro- and microdevelopmental processes in the construction of new planning skills. Even though all children in the sample displayed an optimal level of representational systems by solving the task, there was considerable variability across age in the degree of constructive activity needed to implement that level in a novel task, and in the stability of the planning skill constructed. A few of the oldest children, most likely to have already consolidated systems level skills owing to their macrodevelopmental history, were able to construct the correct solution immediately and did not show tacit errors in their later verbal plans. For these children, systems level (Rp3) tasks were automatized and could be applied in more challenging contexts to construct higher level skills, pushing their optimal potential even higher. Younger children, whose systems level skills were presumably least consolidated, approached the task with entry level skills much below their optimal potential, and many of them could not sustain their new skill in verbal planning. Their macrodevelopmental status constrained their entry level skills to mappings, and their microdevelopmental task was to extend and consolidate their current Rp3 optimal level.

FUTURE DIRECTIONS

The dynamic skills model of planning development offers a set of conceptual and methodological tools for the systemic study of developmental transitions in on-line planning skills, analysis of which has only begun in this chapter. One area where the model may be useful is in understanding the relations between planning and other developmental domains. Two such domains touched on here are brain-behavior relations and development of problem-solving strategies.

The psychological processes of co-occurrence and coordination seem to be related to neuropsychological processes in which frontal cortical functioning contributes to working memory in tasks that involve on-line planning. The model provides a potential framework for analyzing developmental relations between frontal functioning and on-line planning because it makes specific predictions about co-occurrence and coordination in the development of on-line planning (Fischer & Rose, 1993).

In the area of problem solving, the dynamic skills model may be useful in better understanding the developmental relations between the representational function of working memory and the various strategic and performance processes typically studied by problem-solving researchers. Klahr and Robinson (1981, p. 146), for example, suggested that the development of representational or encoding abilities is an important and understudied factor in accounting for developmental changes in children's strategies. They proposed that an important constraint on young children's strategy use is their limited ability to create "an internal representation upon which their general problem-solving methods could effectively operate." In this chapter we have presented a systematic framework for the study of macro- and microdevelopmental transitions in internal representations called on-line plans. We have shown that data on strategy shifts at both macro- and microdevelopmental levels parallel the predictions of the model. An important area of future work will be to apply the dynamic skills model to the elaboration of relations between strategic performance and the development of on-line planning skills.

More generally, we hope that by presenting a model of planning development that combines a general cognitive-developmental framework with a specific task-analytic methodology, we will contribute to the development of more precise and powerful analyses of planning development in its many guises. Developmental research on planning and other future-oriented processes has tended toward global generalizations about the character of planning and its acquisition. Linking the study of planning processes to established developmental theories and task- and situation-specific predictions can help move the study of planning from a peripheral topic to a central one in developmental research.

REFERENCES

Anzai, Y., & Simon, H. A. (1979). The theory of learning by doing. *Psychological Review, 86*, 124–140.

Atkinson, R. C., & Shiffrin, R. M. (1968). Human memory: A proposed system and its control processes. In K. W. Spence & J. T. Spence (Eds.), *The psychology of learning and motivation* (Vol. 2, pp. 90–195). New York: Academic Press.

Bell, M. A., & Fox, N. A. (1992). The relations between frontal brain electrical activity and cognitive development during infancy. *Child Development, 63*, 1142–1163.

Bell, M. A., & Fox, N. A. (1994). Brain development over the first year of life: Relations between EEG frequency and coherence and cognitive and affective behaviors. In G. Dawson & K. W. Fischer (Eds.), *Human behavior and the developing brain* (pp. 314–345). New York: Guilford.

Bidell, T. R. (1990). *Mechanisms of cognitive development in problem solving: A structural integration approach.* Unpublished doctoral dissertation, Harvard University.

Bidell, T. R., & Fischer, K. W. (1991). Beyond the stage debate: Action, structure, and variability in Piagetian theory and research. In R. Sternberg & C. Berg (Eds.), *Intellectual development* (pp. 100–140). New York: Cambridge University Press.

Case, R. (1980). The underlying mechanism of intellectual development. In J. Kirby & J. Biggs (Eds.), *Cognition, development, and instruction* (pp. 5–37). New York: Academic Press.

Case, R. (1985). *Intellectual development: Birth to adulthood.* New York: Academic Press.

Casey, M. B. (1990). A planning and problem-solving preschool model: The methodology of being a good learner. *Early Childhood Quarterly, 5*, 53–67.

DeLisi, R. (1987). A cognitive developmental model of planning. In S. L. Friedman, E. K. Scholnick, & R. L. Cocking (Eds.), *Blueprints for thinking: The role of planning in cognitive development.* Cambridge: Cambridge University Press.

Fischer, K. W. (1980a). Learning and problem solving as the development of organized behavior. *Journal of Structural Learning, 6*, 253–267.

Fischer, K. W. (1980b). A theory of cognitive development: The control and construction of hierarchies of skills. *Psychological Review, 87*, 477–531.

Fischer, K. W., & Bidell, T. R. (1991). Constraining nativist inferences about cognitive capacities. In S. Carey & R. Gelman (Eds.), *The epigenesis of mind: Essays on biology and knowledge* (pp. 199–235). Hillsdale, NJ: Erlbaum.

174 / Planning in Problem Solving

Fischer, K. W., Bullock, D., Rotenberg, E. J., & Raya, P. (1993). The dynamics of competence: How context contributes directly to skill. In R. Wozniak & K. Fischer (Eds.), *Development in context: Acting and thinking in specific environments* (pp. 93–117). Hillsdale, NJ: Erlbaum.

Fischer, K. W., & Elmendorf, D. (1986). Becoming a different person: Transformations in personality and social behavior. In M. Perlmutter (Ed.), *Minnesota symposium on child psychology* (vol. 18, pp. 137–178). Hillsdale, NJ: Erlbaum.

Fischer, K. W., & Farrar, M. J. (1987). Generalizations about generalization: How a theory of skill development explains both generality and specificity. *International Journal of Psychology, 22,* 643–677.

Fischer, K. W., Hand, H. H., & Russell, S. L. (1984). The development of abstractions in adolescence and adulthood. In M. Commons, F. A. Richards, & C. Armon (Eds.), *Beyond formal operations* (pp. 43–73). New York: Praeger.

Fischer, K. W., & Jennings, S. (1981). The emergence of representation in search. *Developmental Review, 1,* 18–30.

Fischer, K. W., & Pipp, S. L. (1984). Processes of cognitive development: Optimal level and skill acquisition. In R. J. Sternberg (Ed.), *Mechanisms of cognitive development* (pp. 45–80). New York: Freeman.

Fischer, K. W., & Roberts, R. J., Jr. (1991). *The development of classification skills in the preschool years: Developmental level and errors.* Cognitive Development Laboratory Report. Cambridge: Harvard University.

Fischer, K. W., & Rose, S. P. (1994). Development of coordination of components in brain and behavior: A framework for theory and research. In G. Dawson & K. W. Fischer (Eds.), *Human behavior and the developing brain* (pp. 3–66). New York: Guilford.

Friedman, S. L., Scholnick, E. K., & Cocking, R. L. (1987). Reflections on reflections: What planning is and how it develops. In S. L. Friedman, E. K. Scholnick, & R. L. Cocking (Eds.), *Blueprints for thinking: The role of planning in cognitive development.* Cambridge: Cambridge University Press.

Goldman-Rakic, P. S. (1987). Connectionist theory and the biological basis of cognitive development. *Child Development, 58,* 601–622.

Gottlieb, D. E., Taylor, S. E., & Ruderman, A. (1977). Cognitive bases of children's moral judgments. *Developmental Psychology, 13,* 547–556.

Granott, N. (1991). Puzzled minds and weird creatures: Phases in spontaneous process of knowledge construction. In I. Harel & S. Papert (Eds.), *Constructionism.* Norwood, NJ: Ablex.

Granott, N. (1993). *Microdevelopment of co-construction of knowledge during problem-solving: Puzzled minds, weird creatures, and wuggles.* Unpublished doctoral dissertation, MIT.

Karat, J. (1982). A model of problem solving with incomplete constraint knowledge. *Cognitive Psychology, 14,* 538–559.

Klahr, D. (1978). Goal formation, planning, and learning by preschool problem-solvers. In R. S. Siegler (Ed.), *Children's thinking: What develops?* Hillsdale, NJ: Erlbaum.

Klahr, D., & Robinson, M. (1981). Formal assessment of problem-solving and planning processes in preschool children. *Cognitive Psychology, 13,* 113–148.

Klahr, D., & Wallace, J. G. (1976). *Cognitive development: An information processing view.* Hillsdale, NJ: Erlbaum.

Kotovsky, K., Hayes, J. R., & Simon, H. A. (1985). Why are some problems hard? Evidence from the Tower of Hanoi. *Cognitive Psychology, 17,* 248–294.

Lashley, K. S. (1951). The problem of serial order in behavior. In L. A. Jeffress (Ed.), *Cerebral mechanisms in behavior* (pp. 112–146). New York: Wiley.

McCormick, C. B., Miller, C. B., & Pressley, M. (1989). *Cognitive strategy research: From basic research to educational applications.* New York: Springer-Verlag.

Miller, G. A. (1956). The magical number seven, plus or minus two: Some limits on our capacity for processing information. *Psychological Review, 63,* 81–97.

Miller, G. A., Galanter, E., & Pribram, K. H. (1960). *Plans and the structure of behavior.* New York: Holt, Rinehart, and Winston.

Newell, A., & Simon, H. A. (1972). *Human problem solving.* Englewood Cliffs, NJ: Prentice-Hall.

Pascual-Leone, J. (1970). A mathematical model for the transition rule in Piaget's developmental stages. *Acta Psychologica, 32,* 301–345.

Perry, M., Church, R. B., & Goldin-Meadow, S. (1988). Transitional knowledge in the acquisition of concepts. *Cognitive Development, 3,* 359–400.

Piaget, J. (1952). *The origins of intelligence in children* (M. Cook, Trans.). New York: International Universities Press. (Original work published 1936)

Piaget, J. (1976). *The grasp of consciousness* (S. Wedgewood, Trans.). Cambridge: Harvard University Press. (Original work published 1974)

Roberts, R. J., Jr. (1981). Errors and the assessment of cognitive development. In K. W. Fischer (Ed.), *Cognitive development* (pp. 69–78). New Directions for Child Development, 12. San Francisco: Jossey-Bass.

Rogoff, B. (1990). *Apprenticeship in thinking: Cognitive development in social context.* New York: Oxford University Press.

Siegler, R. S. (1976). Three aspects of cognitive development. *Cognitive Psychology, 8,* 481–520.

Siegler, R. S. (1981). Developmental sequences within and between concepts. *Monographs of the Society for Research in Child Development, 46*(2, Serial No. 189).

Siegler, R. S. (1989). Mechanisms of cognitive development. In M. R. Rosenzweig & L. W. Porter (Eds.), *Annual review of psychology.* Palo Alto, CA: Annual Reviews.

Siegler, R. S., & Crowley, K. (1991). The microgenetic method: A direct means for studying cognitive development. *American Psychologist, 46,* 606–620.

Simon, H. A., & Reed, S. K. (1976). Modeling strategy shifts in a problem-solving task. *Cognitive Psychology, 8,* 86–97.

Spitz, H. H., & Borys, S. V. (1982). Depth of search: How far can the retarded search through an internally represented problem space? In R. Sperber, C. McCauley, & P. Brooks (Eds.), *Learning, cognition, and mental retardation.* Baltimore: University Park Press.

Sternberg, R. J. (Ed.). (1984). *Mechanisms of cognitive development.* New York: Freeman.

Thatcher, R. W. (1991). Maturation of the human frontal lobes: Physiological evidence for staging. *Developmental Neuropsychology, 7,* 397–419.

Thatcher, R. W. (1994). Cyclic cortical reorganization: Origins of human cognitive development. In G. Dawson & K. W. Fischer (Eds.), *Human behavior and the developing brain* (pp. 232–266). New York: Guilford.

Uzgiris, I. C., & Hunt, J. Mc.V. (1975). *Assessment in infancy: Ordinal scales of psychological development.* Urbana: University of Illinois Press.

Van der Maas, H., & Molenaar, P. (1992). A catastrophe-theoretical approach to cognitive development. *Psychological Review, 99,* 395–417.

Van Geert, P. (1991). A dynamic systems model of cognitive and language growth. *Psychological Review, 98,* 3–53.

Wansart, W. L. (1990). Learning to solve a problem: A microanalysis of the solution strategies of children with learning disabilities. *Journal of Learning Disabilities, 23,* 164–170.

Watson, M. W., & Fischer, K. W. (1977). A developmental sequence of agent use in late infancy. *Child Development, 48,* 828–835.

Watson, M. W., & Fischer, K. W. (1980). Development of social roles in elicited and spontaneous behavior during the preschool years. *Developmental Psychology, 16,* 484–494.

Welsh, M. (1991). Rule-guided behavior and self-monitoring on the Tower of Hanoi disc-transfer task. *Cognitive Development, 6,* 59–76.

Welsh, M. C., Pennington, B. F., & Groisser, D. B. (1991). A normative-developmental study of executive function: A window on prefrontal function in children. *Developmental Neuropsychology, 7,* 131–149.

Wolf, D. (1982). Understanding others: A longitudinal case study of the concept of independent agency. In G. Forman (Ed.), *Action and thought: From sensorimotor schemes to symbolic operations.* New York: Academic Press.

Chapter Seven

Discovering the Present by Predicting the Future

David Klahr

Remember that the future is neither ours nor wholly not ours, so that we may neither count on it as sure to come nor abandon hope of it as certain not to be.

(Epicurus, 300 B.C.)

If a man carefully examine his thoughts he will be surprised to find how much he lives in the future. His well-being is always ahead. Such a creature is probably immortal.

(Ralph Waldo Emerson, 1827)

Marshall Haith solicited contributions to this volume with a claim and a challenge. His claim was that contemporary psychologists have had a "dearth of concern" with future-oriented phenomena. His challenge was for us to view our own work in such terms.

My initial response to the claim was skepticism: "Certainly people

This work was supported in part by grants from the National Institute of Child Health and Human Development (RO1-HD25211) and the Andrew W. Mellon Foundation. The chapter is based in part on work done in collaboration with Mitchell Robinson, Kevin Dunbar, and Anne L. Fay. I am indebted to the volume editors as well as to Sharon Carver, Anne L. Fay, Ken Kotovksy, David Penner, Christian Schunn, and especially Shari Ellis for their comments and suggestions on earlier drafts.

have grappled with the psychology of the future," I thought. But as the opening quotations suggest, most of what has been said on the topic has come from philosophers rather than psychologists (although one might anachronistically interpret Epicurus's statement as a comment on decision making under uncertainty and Emerson's as relevant to metacognition). And though there is an extensive literature on the psychology of time (Friedman, 1990, estimates thousands of articles in the last 100 years), little of it has addressed the psychology of thinking about the future, and much of it tends to be inconsistent and inconclusive (see Benson's summary, this volume).

Before writing this chapter, I had not thought about my own research areas—problem solving and scientific discovery—in terms of future-oriented processes. However, Haith's challenge motivated me to reflect on the extent to which the behaviors I was studying involved future-oriented thinking. In so doing, I attempted to lay out a framework for classifying future-oriented processes within which I could locate my own work (and ultimately work in other domains). Therefore my present goal is to review some of my research on the development of problem solving and scientific discovery skills and to recast that work in terms of what it suggests about how adults and children think about the future.

In the first section, I propose a framework for considering future-oriented processes. In the second, I lay the groundwork for discussing future orientation in terms of problem solving. In the next two sections I summarize two lines of research that are based on this problem-solving orientation, and I interpret the results of those studies in terms of future-oriented processing: the third section summarizes some investigations of preschool children's ability to think ahead in the context of simple, well-defined puzzles, and the fourth summarizes research on the development of scientific reasoning skills. Here the problem-solving formulation is extended to the domains of hypothesis formation and experimental design. In the final section, I return to the framework and attempt to summarize the important future-oriented attributes of the processes of problem solving and scientific discovery.

Before closing this introductory section, I must explain the somewhat cryptic title I have chosen. It derives from considering the future-oriented implications of the work on scientific discovery to be described in the fourth section. Attempts to predict the future behaviors of a complex system are successful only insofar as its underlying principles—operating in the present—have been discovered. To the extent that our predictions turn out to be incorrect, we must revise our characterization of the current situation. That is, we discover the present by predicting the future.

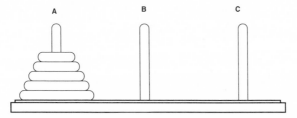

Figure 7.1   Five-disk Tower of Hanoi puzzle. The goal is to move all the disks from peg A to peg C subject to the following constraints: (a) only one disk can be moved at a time; (b) a larger disk can never be placed above a smaller disk. The minimum path requires 31 moves. (In general, an n-disk problem requires $2^n - 1$ moves.)

A FRAMEWORK FOR CONSIDERING FUTURE-ORIENTED PROCESSES

Future-oriented processes appear to differ in the following critical attributes: uncertainty, control, contingency, abstraction, social dependency, and grain of abstraction. I can best explain these attributes by example. Suppose you are thinking about making the first move in a puzzle like the well-known Tower of Hanoi (TOH), shown in Figure 7.1. One could ask the following questions about your thought processes:

Uncertainty. How certain can you be about the possible outcomes of the move? In principle, deterministic puzzles with perfect information— such as the TOH—have no uncertainty. You simply consider every possible first move you could make, all possible second moves, and so on, until you have reached the goal. Then you make the first move leading to a minimum path solution. However, even in simple puzzles the combinatorics of this approach may require considering an enormous number of moves, and such computations would overwhelm the limited human cognitive capacity. Thus, even in a formally deterministic puzzle, the degree of uncertainty depends on both the demands of the external environment and the limitations of the human system. In contrast, some situations are inherently uncertain, such as predicting the roll of dice, or the deal of a hand of cards.

Control. To what extent are you in control of the current and future situation? In two-person games like chess, control is only partial, because your opponent's possible moves must form a part of your view of the future. In contrast, in the TOH there is no adversary. Once you make a legal move, you can be sure of reaching the state that move is supposed to produce. As noted, even in the TOH, planning a full solution path involves some uncertainty, but there is no agent beyond you that will be making any of the moves.

Type of contingency. What kind of environmental response will be evoked by your move? In zero-sum games like chess and checkers, it is clear that the response will be *adversarial.* The opponent will attempt to undermine your attempt to determine the future course of events. In the TOH there is no such contingent reaction. Nothing in the context responds to whatever state you may reach. In collaborative or joint problem-solving situations, the contingency is *supportive.* There are other agents in the context who will support and guide your outcomes.

Abstraction. Is the "grain"—the level of detail—of your thinking at the same level as the grain of the relevant events? One function of a plan is to suppress detail so that a rough sketch of the solution path can be formulated. In chess one can suppress detail and make a general plan (center control, queen side attack, etc.), but each of these plans is ultimately unpacked into finer-grain units that eventuate in a legal move.

Social. Do you have to consider the future orientation of other people in your own deliberations? This is related to the contingency issue listed earlier, but it is focused entirely on the impact that other human problem solvers, and your representation of *their* decision-making and problem-solving situation is required in your own. This would involve some estimate of their own goals and priorities. (The classic Prisoner's Dilemma paradigm for studying cooperation and conflict exemplifies the issues here.)

Temporal extent. What is the order of magnitude of the temporal interval involved? Thinking about the future can be limited to very brief intervals or extend to planning one's life. It may be that the cognitive processes involved for vastly different temporal extents are quite distinct. For example, the range of future-oriented processes discussed in this chapter varies from a couple of seconds to an hour or so, and real scientific reasoning can go on for months and years.

At this point in the development of the taxonomy, it is likely that these attributes are neither mutually exclusive nor exhaustive nor independent. Nevertheless, I offer them as a useful starting point in the endeavor. I will attempt to answer the questions listed above in the context of research on the development of problem-solving and scientific reasoning skills. The projects to be described are based on the view that a wide range of higher-order cognitive processes can be viewed as different types of problem solving. Therefore I will preface the description of those projects with a few general comments on what I mean by a problem.

PROBLEM SOLVING

Newell and Simon (1972) define a problem as comprising an initial state, a goal state, and a set of operators that allow the problem solver to transform the initial state into the goal state via a series of intermediate states. Operators have constraints that must be satisfied before they can be applied. The set of states, operators, and constraints is called a "problem space," and the problem-solving process can be characterized as a search for a path that links the initial state to the goal state. (But the search need not be constrained to start with the initial state. Indeed, working backward—from goal state to initial state—is an appropriate procedure in some situations.)

Weak Methods

In all but the most trivial problems, the problem solver is faced with a very large set of alternative states and operators, so the search process can be demanding. For example, if we represent the problem space as a branching tree of m moves with b branches at each move, then there are b^m moves to consider in the full problem space. As soon as m and b get beyond very small values, exhaustive search for alternative states and operators is beyond human capacity,[1] so effective problem solving depends in large part on how well the search is constrained. Newell and Simon (1972) divided different approaches to search constraint into two broad categories: *strong methods* and *weak methods*.

Strong methods are algorithmic procedures, such as those for long division or for computing means and standard deviations. The most important aspect of strong methods is that—by definition—they guarantee a solution to the problem they are designed to solve. However, strong methods have several disadvantages for human problem solvers. First, they may require extensive computational resources. For example, a strong method for minimizing cost (or maximizing protein) of a list of grocery items subject to other dietary and budget constraints is to apply a standard linear-programming algorithm (Hadley, 1962). Of course doing this in one's head while pushing a shopping cart is hardly feasible. Second, strong methods may be difficult to learn because they may require many detailed steps (for example, the procedure for inverting a matrix, or computing a correlation coefficient by hand). Finally, strong methods, by their very nature, tend to be domain specific and thus have little generality.

---

1. For example, Newell and Simon (1972, p. 669) note that in chess "there are something like 10^{120} continuations to be explored, with much less than 10^{20} nanoseconds available in a century to explore them."

Weak methods are heuristic: they may work or they may not, but they are highly general. The trade-off for the lack of certainty associated with weak methods is that they make substantially lower computational demands, are more easily acquired (indeed, some may be innate), and are domain general. Newell and Simon (1972) describe several kinds of weak methods, used by both human problem solvers and artificial intelligence systems. I will describe only four such weak methods and comment on the differences in their "future orientedness."

Generate and Test

The generate and test method is commonly called "trial and error." It consists of simply applying some operator to the current state and then testing to determine if the goal state has been reached. If it has been, the problem is solved. If it has not, then some other operator is applied. In the most primitive generate and test methods, the evaluation function is binary: either the goal has been reached or it has not, and the next "move" does not depend on any properties of the discrepancy between the current state and the goal state or the operator that was just unsuccessfully applied. An example of a "dumb" generating process is searching in a box of keys for a key to fit a lock, and sampling with replacement: tossing failed keys back into the box without noting anything about the degree of fit, the type of key that seems to fit partially, and so forth. A slightly "smarter" generator would, at the least, sample from the key box without replacement.

It is difficult to attribute much of a future orientation to this method, beyond noting that the goal state is something that has not yet happened and that, if it does occur, it will occur in the future. Neither progress nor history is represented in the most primitive generate and test methods.

Hill Climbing

The hill climbing method gets its name from the analogy of attempting to reach the top of a hill whose peak cannot be directly perceived (imagine a foggy day with severely limited visibility). One makes a tentative step in each of several directions, then heads off in the direction that has the steepest gradient. More generally, the method computes an evaluation function whose maximum value corresponds to the goal state. Potential moves are generated, and the evaluation function is applied to each potential state. The state that maximizes the increment to the evaluation function is chosen, that move is made, and then the process iterates from the new state.

Hill climbing utilizes more information about the discrepancy between the current state and the goal state than does generate and test.

Instead of a simple all-or-none evaluation, it computes a measure of goodness of fit between the two and uses that information to constrain search in the problem space. However, its representation of the future— the evaluation function—is primitive in two regards. First, it is very local because it anticipates only the next step in the solution path. Second, it is at an aggregate level that does not include any details about the structure of future states.

Means-Ends Analysis

Of all the weak methods, perhaps the best known is means-ends analysis (Dunker, 1945; Newell & Simon, 1972). Means-ends analysis compares the current state with the goal state and describes any differences. Then it searches for operators that can reduce those differences. It selects an operator designed to reduce the most important differences and attempts to apply it to the current state. However, it may be that the operator cannot be immediately applied because the conditions for doing so are not met. Means-ends analysis then formulates a subproblem in which the goal is to reduce the difference between the current state and a state in which the desired operator can be applied. Then it recursively attempts to solve the subproblem.

As a homely example, consider the problem I faced in getting from my office at Carnegie Mellon University to the conference room in Breckenridge, Colorado, where I first presented the talk this chapter is based on. The "difference" was one of distance, and among the set of distance-reduction operators were flying, walking, biking, and so forth. Flying was the operator of choice, but I could not fly directly from my office to Breckenridge. This presented the subproblem of creating conditions for flying (getting to an airport). Getting to the airport could best be done by taxi, but there was no taxi at Carnegie Mellon. The sub-subproblem involved making a phone call to the cab company. But all the university phones were out of order for the day during a transition to a new system: only the pay phones worked. An even deeper subproblem: make a call on a pay phone. But I could not apply that operator (no pun intended) because I had no change. A Coke machine was handy, however, and it accepted dollar bills and gave change. So I bought a Coke in order to get on the solution path to transport myself to Colorado.

Means-ends analysis constructs a hierarchy of goals and subgoals, with the parent node for a state corresponding to why something is being done and the descendants of a node corresponding to how it will be done. Because means-ends analysis computes a qualitative evaluation of the difference between the current state and the goal state, and because it generates a goal tree, it requires a highly articulated representation of both the present and the future. Of the methods described thus far, means-ends analysis has the greatest future orientation.

Planning

Newell and Simon (1972) define planning[2] as another problem-solving method consisting of:

1. forming an abstract version of the problem space by omitting certain details of the original set of states and operators;

2. forming the corresponding problem in the abstract problem space;

3. solving the abstracted problem by applying any of the methods listed here (including planning);

4. using the solution of the abstract problem to provide a plan for solving the original problem;

5. translating the plan back into the original problem space and executing it.

If we apply the planning method to the problem of getting to Breckenridge, we might produce a three-step plan: (1) take taxi to airport; (2) fly to Denver; (3) drive rental car to Breckenridge. This plan contains none of the details about phone calls, change, and Coke machines. Because planning suppresses some of the detail in the original problem space, it is not always possible to implement the plan, for some of the simplifications result in planned solution paths that cannot be effected. For example, there might be no rental cars at the Denver airport.

Of the four methods described here, planning has the strongest future orientation in its broad sweep from the current state to the goal state. It actually produces a sketch of the solution before the solution itself is executed and in that sense anticipates the future.

Weak Methods and the Attributes of Future Orientation

This set of weak methods can be applied in a wide variety of contexts involving different levels of uncertainty, control, contingency, and so on. That is, the weak methods can be crossed with the future-oriented attributes listed in the previous section to form a large space of future-oriented situations. In the following sections I describe a small subset

---

2. Planning has had a very wide variety of definitions, ranging from "little computer programs that program the mind to perform certain cognitive tasks, such as long division, brushing your teeth, or generating a sentence" (Wickelgren, 1974, p. 357) to "any hierarchical process in the organism that can control the order in which a sequence of operations is to be performed" (Miller, Galanter, & Pribram, 1960, p. 16) to "the predetermination of a course of action aimed at achieving a goal" (Hayes-Roth & Hayes-Roth, 1979, p. 275). An elaboration and discussion of the many definitions can be found in Scholnick and Friedman (1987). I use the Newell and Simon (1972) version here because it is much better defined than the others and fits nicely in the set of weak methods.

of this space, based on several investigations of problem solving and scientific reasoning in children and adults.

PROBLEM-SOLVING METHODS USED BY PRESCHOOL CHILDREN

The broad generality of these four methods (as well as several others) raises the question of their developmental course. To the extent that these methods vary in their degree of future orientation, understanding their developmental trajectory might give us some insight into children's ability to anticipate and represent the future.

My interest in children's problem solving was stimulated by what I perceived to be a discrepancy between Piaget's (1976) claims about the limited problem-solving capacities of preschoolers and my observations of my own young children. Piaget (1976) used two-, three-, and four-disk TOH problems (see Figure 7.1) with children from about 5½ to 12 years old. He reported that most 5- and 6-year-old children "cannot move the three-disk tower even after trial and error. They do succeed in moving the two-disk tower, but only after all sorts of attempts to get around the instructions and without being conscious of the logical links" (p. 288). From this performance Piaget concluded that "none of these subjects make a plan or even understand how they are going to move the tower" (p. 290); and later, "There is . . . a systematic primacy of the trial-and-error procedure over any attempt at deduction, and no cognizance of any correct solution arrived at by chance" (p. 291). In contrast, I could see behavior in my children that strongly suggested a capacity to plan modestly complex action sequences, such as using one kind of object to facilitate getting another that could then be used to accomplish a goal (Klahr, 1978). In this section I will describe two studies designed to investigate the kinds of methods preschool children use when faced with novel puzzles that require them to "think ahead."

Preschoolers' Problem Solving on the Tower of Hanoi

The first task I will describe is a modification of the Tower of Hanoi shown earlier. This puzzle has been used extensively to study adults' problem solving (Simon, 1975; Anzai & Simon, 1979). It conforms to the definition of a well-defined problem given earlier in that it contains unambiguous descriptions of an initial state, a final state, and legal moves (operators). The difficulty lies in discovering the sequences of legal moves that transform the initial configuration into the desired one. To use this task with young children, we modified it in several ways that changed its superficial appearance while maintaining its basic structure (Klahr & Robinson, 1981).

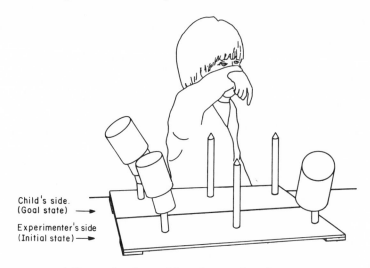

Child's side.
(Goal state) ⟶

Experimenter's side
(Initial state) ⟶

Figure 7.2 Child seated in front of "monkey cans" working on a one-move problem (state 2 to state 1: see Figure 7.3).

Materials. We reversed the size constraint and used a set of nested inverted cans that fit loosely on the pegs. When they were stacked up it was impossible to put a smaller can on top of a larger can (see Figure 7.2). Even if the child forgot the relative size constraint, the materials provided an obvious physical consequence of attempted violations: smaller cans fell off bigger cans.

Externalization of final goal. In addition to the initial configuration, the goal configuration was always physically present. We arranged the child's cans in a goal configuration and the experimenter's cans in the initial configuration. Then the child was asked to tell the experimenter what she (the experimenter) should do in order to get her (experimenter's) cans to look just like the child's. This procedure was used to elicit the child's reasoning about several future states: children were asked to describe the complete *sequence* of moves necessary to solve the problem.

Cover story. Problems were presented in the context of a story in which the cans were monkeys (large daddy, medium-size mommy, and small baby), who jump from tree to tree (peg to peg). The child's monkeys were in some good configuration, the experimenter's monkeys were "copycat" monkeys who wanted to look just like the child's monkeys. The cans were redundantly classified by size, color, and family membership for easy reference. Children found the cover story easy to comprehend and remember, and they readily agreed to consider the cans as

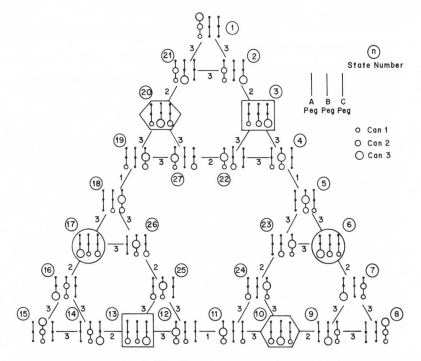

Figure 7.3 State space of all legal configurations and moves for three-can problem. States are arbitrarily numbered from 1 to 27. The can that moves between one state and the next is indicated on the line connecting the states. The minimum path solutions for all tower-to-tower problems (see text) are seven moves. Flat-to-flat problems enclosed by matching geometric shapes (e.g., state 17 to state 6) also have seven-move minimum path solutions.

monkeys. The remaining variations are best described after considering some of the formal properties of this task.

Figure 7.3 shows the state space for this problem: all possible legal states and moves. Each state is one move distant from its neighbors, and the can that is moved is indicated by the number on the line connecting adjacent states. The solution to a problem can be represented as a path through the state space. For example, the minimum solution path for the problem that starts with all three cans on peg A (state 1) and ends with them on peg C (state 8) is shown along the right-hand side of the large triangle in Figure 7.3. The first move involves shifting the largest can (can 3) from peg A to peg C, producing state 2. The next move places can 2 on peg B (state 3), followed by a move of can 3 to peg B (state 4), and so on. The "standard" TOH problems always end with all the cans stacked up on one peg. We call these "tower-ending" (T-end) problems. In the six states indicated by the large squares, circles, and hexagons in Figure 7.3, all pegs are occupied. We call any problem that ends in one of these states "flat-ending" (F-end). We used F-end as well as the more commonly used T-end problems. As we shall see, for the children in this study, F-ends were much more difficult.

Subjects

Fifty-one children attending the Carnegie Mellon University Children's School participated in the study. There were 19 children each in the 4-year and 5-year groups and 13 in the 6-year group. The children came predominantly, but not exclusively, from white, middle-class backgrounds. There were approximately equal numbers of boys and girls at each age level.

Procedure

Children were familiarized with the materials shown in Figure 7.2, in the context of the following cover story.

> Once upon a time there was a blue river (experimenter points to space between rows of pegs). On your side of the river there were three brown trees. On my side there were also . . . , etc. On your side there lived three monkeys: a big yellow daddy (present yellow can and place on peg), a medium size blue mommy (present and place), and a little red baby. The monkeys like to jump from tree to tree [according to the rules]; they live on your side of the river. (Establish legal and illegal jumps.) On my side there are also three: a daddy, [etc.] (introduce experimenter's cans). Mine are copycat monkeys. They want to be just like yours, right across the river from yours. Yours are all stacked up like so [state 1] mine are like so [state 2 or state 21]. Mine are very unhappy because they want to look like yours, but right now they are a little mixed up. Can you tell me what to do in order to get mine to look like yours? How can I get my daddy across from your daddy [etc.]?

During the initial part of the familiarization phase, the child was allowed to handle the cans but was gradually dissuaded from doing so and was instead encouraged to tell the experimenter what she should do in order to get her cans to look like the child's.

The final procedural variation we used was designed to satisfy two opposing constraints. On the one hand, in order to give a precise diagnostic of children's problem-solving strategies, we wanted to use a rule assessment procedure (Siegler, 1981), but that required a relatively long series of problems (up to 40). On the other hand, we wanted to minimize test effects that might result from children's learning about different path segments in the state space. Therefore we proceeded as follows:

for each problem the child told the experimenter the full sequence of proposed moves, and the experimenter gave supportive acknowledgment *but did not move the cans.* Then the next problem was presented.

We used a set of 40 problems: four problems having minimum path lengths of one, two, three, and four, and eight problems each with path lengths five, six, and seven. For each path length, half the problems were T-end and half were F-end. Problems were presented in two blocks with only T-end problems in one block, only F-end problems in the other. Children were randomly assigned to one of the two block orders (F-T or T-F).

Within a given block increasingly difficult problems were presented in order until the child appeared to reach his upper limit. There were several indicators of this upper limit: (a) explicit statements of confusion or inability to continue; (b) abrupt violation of rules of the game (e.g., putting monkey in the river); (c) sudden loss of motivation; (d) consistent errors in planned moves. At this point the session was terminated.

Scoring

Videotape recordings of children's behavior were transcribed and scored as shown in the two examples in Table 7.1. The child's move sequences were encoded as shown on the right side of the table. Recall that no cans were actually moved during these protocols, so all the configurations shown in the "results" column (except the initial and final ones) are imagined rather than real. The two protocols shown in Table 7.1 were scored as perfect six-move solutions.

Results

The main question of interest is how far into the future a child could "see" in describing move sequences. To avoid overestimating this capacity on the basis of a few fortuitous solutions, we used a very strict criterion. A child was scored as able to solve n-move problems only after proposing the minimum path solution for *all four* of the problems of length n. For example, to be classified as having the capacity to see five moves into the future, a child would have to produce the minimum path solution for the four five-move problems.[3]

The proportion of subjects in each age group producing correct solutions for all problems of a given length is shown in Figure 7.4a for T-end problems and Figure 7.4b for F-end problems. It is important to reemphasize that the abscissa in Figure 7.4 is not overall proportion correct, but rather a much more severe measure: the proportion of

---

3. The four five-move problems included the following initial-final states shown in Figure 7.3: 23–1, 3–8, 22–8, and 6–1.

TABLE 7.1   Two Six-Move Protocols and Their Encodings

	3/21/– Initial (state 16)	321/–/– Goal (state 1)	Move	Result 3/21/–	(Initial)
What you do is you put the daddy (3) . . .					
What you do is you move the daddy (3) over this tree (points to C).					
and move and move the baby . . .					
and then you move the mommy (2).					
Wait; where could you move the mommy (2) to?					
Well first move the mommy (2) on this tree (points to C)			2BC	3/ 1/2	
then put the daddy (3) on that tree (points to C)			3AC	–/ 1/32	
and put the baby (1) over there (points to A).			1BA	1/ –/32	
Then how would the mother? . . .					
And after you put the baby (1) over here (points to A)					
you could put the daddy (3) (points to B)			3CB	1/ 3/2	
then you could put the mommy (2) over the baby,			2CA	21/ 3/–	
and the daddy over the mommy.			3BA	321/–/–	

	3/–/21 Initial (state 7)	321/–/– Goal (state 1)		3/–/21	(Initial)
Oh, that. OK. That's easy.					
Just take the yellow one (3) and put it on there (B).					
Take the (pointing to 2[C]) . . . and take . . . , take the ba . . .					
No, take the blue one (2), put it on there (B),			2CB	3/ 2/ 1	
and the, then take the yellow (3)					
and put it on the blue (points toward C, then to B),			3AB	–/32/ 1	
and then take the red (1) one and put it on here (A).			1CA	1/32/–	
And then take the blue (2) one and . . .					
no, and then . . . and then put the yellow (3) one here (C)			3BC	1/ 2/ 3	
and then put the blue one (2) on the red one,			2BA	21/–/ 3	
and then put the yellow one on the blue one.			3CA	321/–/–	

subjects with perfect solutions on all problems of a given length. For example, 69% of the 6-year-olds were correct on all four of the five-move problems, while only 16% of the 5-year-olds and 11% of the 4-year-olds produced four flawless five-move solutions.

The absolute level of performance was striking, given the results of previous studies with children on this task (e.g., Piaget, 1976). On the T-end problems over two-thirds of the 5-year-olds and nearly all of the 6-year-olds consistently gave perfect four-move solutions, and over half of the 6-year-olds gave perfect six-move solutions. Almost half of the 4-year-olds could do the three-move problems. Recall that these solutions required that the child manipulate mental representations of future states, because the cans were not moved during or after the child's

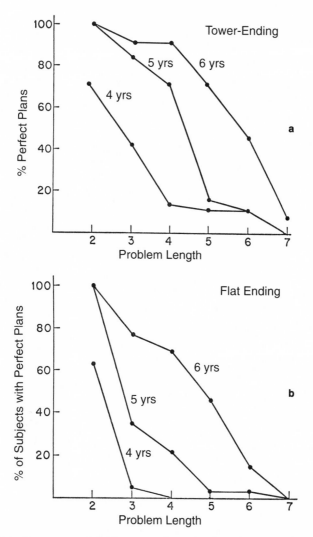

Figure 7.4   Proportion of children at each age level producing perfect solutions: (a) T-end problems; (b) F-end problems.

description of the solution sequence. Furthermore, all intermediate states were different from, but highly confusable with, the two physically present states (the initial and final configurations).

A different picture emerged with F-end problems. One-third of the youngest children could not do anything beyond a one-move problem, and barely one-third of the 5-year-olds could reliably do the three-move problems. Although the 6-year-olds did much better than the two younger groups, their F-end scores were also substantially below their T-end levels.

Summary: Future Orientation in Preschoolers' Solutions to the Tower of Hanoi

Our analysis revealed two important results—one relating to absolute performance, the other to the effects of goal configuration. First, it is clear that many 6-year-olds and some 5-year-olds are able to look ahead six moves into the future, even in a novel domain with arbitrary goals and constraints, as long as the subgoals are easily ordered. This ability appears to result from systematic application of both planning and means-ends analysis, as suggested by the typical protocols shown in Table 7.1.

Second, the relative difficulty of formally equivalent problems (same materials, rules, state space, and path length) depends on the form of the goal configuration. Consider the seven-move, F-end problem from state 15 to state 3: Which can will reach its ultimate destination first? It is not immediately apparent. In contrast, for the T-end problem that goes in the opposite direction (from state 3 to state 15), it is clear that the smallest can will have to reach the goal peg first, then the middle-size can, and so on. More generally, our results suggest that when the surface form of the problem did not suggest an unambiguous ordering of subgoals, children had a difficult time applying means-ends analysis.

How do these results bear on the attributes of future-oriented thinking listed earlier? Although there was no difference between T-end and F-end problems with respect to control, contingency, social dependency, or temporal grain, the two types of problems did differ with respect to effective uncertainty and grain of abstraction. On T-end problems, children were able to minimize the uncertainty that might have been introduced by their own inability to keep track of the future sequence of states, because they could focus on the sequence in which objects had to reach their final position in the goal state. This unambiguous subgoal ordering enabled children to apply both the planning method and means-ends analysis. They could plan to achieve the subgoal sequence (at a slightly abstracted level of analysis) and then "unpack" the plan by applying means-ends analysis in order to execute the detailed move sequence necessary to achieve that subgoal. For F-end problems, the ambiguous ordering of subgoals rendered planning difficult. This in turn made it difficult to deal with the subgoals at a slightly abstracted level (as in planning) and kept the solutions at a very low level. Given children's capacity limitations, this difficulty increased the uncertainty level of move outcomes.

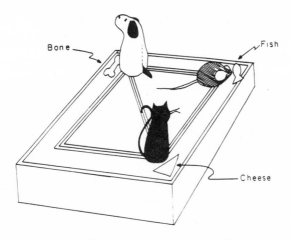

Figure 7.5 The apparatus for the Dog-Cat-Mouse problem. Each animal must be moved to its favorite food: the dog to the bone, the cat to the fish, and the mouse to the cheese. On each move, an animal must move all the way from one corner to another.

Preschoolers' Problem Solving on the Dog-Cat-Mouse Problem

In the second study to be described here, I investigated preschoolers' ability to solve problems in which both planning and means-ends analysis were difficult to apply (see Klahr, 1985, for details). By using a problem that precluded the use of subgoals, I was able to assess the extent to which children used some of the other weak methods listed above. More specifically, I sought evidence that they could use the "hill climbing" method.

The Dog-Cat-Mouse (DCM) puzzle consists of three toy animals (a dog, cat, and mouse) and three toy foods that "belong" to the animals (a bone, a fish, and a piece of cheese). The animals and the foods were arranged on the game board illustrated in Figure 7.5. The board had four grooves running parallel to each side of the square and a diagonal groove between the upper left and lower right corners of the square formed by the four outside grooves. The animals could move along the grooves, but they could not be removed from the board. The foods could be fastened to and unfastened from small patches of Velcro glued to each of the four corners. A problem consisted of an initial state—indicated by the placement of each animal in a corner of the puzzle, and a final state—indicated by some arrangement of the bone, fish, and cheese. The goal of the problem was to move each animal to its corresponding food.

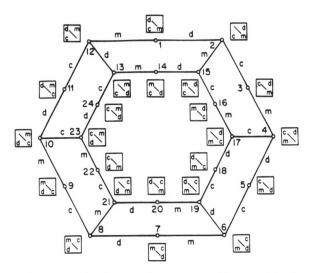

Figure 7.6   State space for the Dog-Cat-Mouse problem. Each node represents a unique configuration of the three animals. Each arc is labeled with the piece that is moved to change states.

This puzzle was chosen for several reasons. First, and most important, it has ambiguous subgoal ordering: the order in which the animals will reach their foods is not at all obvious. Second, it has easily remembered rules and a natural way to represent the goal state. Third, the puzzle has a sufficiently wide range of levels of difficulty. Finally, it is novel, so children are unlikely to have encountered similar puzzles.

The state space is illustrated in Figure 7.6. Each node represents one of the legal configurations of the three animals at the corners of the game board. Each arc label corresponds to the animal that was moved to get from one state to its neighbor. For example, traversing the state space between nodes 1 and 2 requires a move of the dog. All problems are defined in terms of their initial states (determined by the arrangement of the animals) and their final states (determined by the arrangement of the foods). For example, the problem shown in Figure 7.5 starts at node 11 and ends at node 20.

Several properties of the state space are relevant to our subsequent discussion:

Path length. The minimum number of moves required to get from the initial state to the final state. Problems vary in path length from one move to seven moves. (Example: 1–20 has a path length of seven.)

Problem type. Some problems (*rotation* problems) do not change the cyclical ordering of the three objects, while other problems (*permutation* problems) require a change in the ordering by using the diagonal link on the problem board (also represented as a change from the outer to the inner hexagon in Figure 7.6). Permutation problems start and end with different permutations of the three animals (e.g., D-C-M-D . . . versus D-M-C-D) (Examples: 1–15, 22–3). Permutation problems generally have several minimum paths. For example, the minimum path from node 1 to node 19 could cross from the outer to the inner loop at nodes 2, 4, or 6.

The effect of problems that differ along these attributes depends on the processes subjects use to solve them. If they use a lot of forward search, then on average longer problems should be more difficult, and for equal-length problems, those starting with open nodes (three possible first moves) should on average be more difficult than those with closed nodes (two possible first moves). Permutation problems should be easier for two reasons: first, they usually have several minimum paths, and if subjects are moving randomly they are more likely to find one; second, if subjects *are* able to formulate subgoals, then a very useful one would be to fix the permutation (use the diagonal) and then rotate to the goal.

Problems, Subjects, and Procedure

Eight problems varying in path length (from four to seven) and problem type (permutation or rotation) were used. They are listed in the bottom section of Table 7.2. In addition, four three-move training problems were used to familiarize the children with the rules of the game. They are shown at the top of Table 7.2. Forty children from the Carnegie Mellon University Children's School participated (mean = 4 years, 10 months, SD = 6.3 months). Children were tested individually in a small playroom, adjacent to their regular classrooms, that was equipped with videotape recording facilities. After being brought into the room, the children were presented with the DCM puzzle in the context of the following cover story.

> This is a game about three hungry animals, and your job in the game will be to make sure that each animal gets its favorite food. I have a dog here who loves to chew on bones—would you please give the dog his bone? I have a cat who loves to eat fish, and I have a mouse who loves cheese [subject distributes food]. In this game I will mix up the animals and the food, and you will have to move each animal to its favorite food. There are three important rules about how you can move the animals:
>
> First of all, the animals always sit in the corners next to these circles. They can move along these blue lines—around the outside or up the middle, backward or forward—but they always have to stop in a corner by a circle. That means they can never stop in the middle of a line like this.

TABLE 7.2 Problem Sets, Structural Variables, Subject Performance, and Model Performance for Dog-Cat-Mouse Puzzle

	STRUCTURAL VARIABLES				PERFORMANCE VARIABLES	
Problem number	Initial state[a]	Goal state[a]	Path length	Problem type	Problem difficulty[b]	Model's performance[c]
Training set						
T1	1	4	3	Rotation		
T2	7	22	3	Permutation		
T3	12	9	3	Rotation		
T4	2	17	3	Permutation		
Problem Set						
1	17	21	4	Rotation	.640	.544
2	18	8	4	Permutation	.950	.869
3	11	20	5	Permutation	.436	.510
4	10	5	5	Rotation	.179	.278
5	13	19	6	Rotation	.184	.399
6	24	18	6	Rotation	.263	.352
7	14	7	7	Permutation	.436	.740
8	15	8	7	Permutation	.590	.800

[a] See Figure 7.6.
[b] Proportion of children finding minimum path by second attempt.
[c] Probability of model's finding minimum path within two attempts.

The second rule is that only one animal can be in a corner at a time. This is because my mouse is afraid of my cat, my cat is afraid of my dog, and believe it or not, this big dog is afraid of mice. So they never sit together in one place, and you must never move an animal into a corner where another one is already sitting.

The third rule is easy to remember—they always move one at a time. While the dog moves the cat and the mouse wait, and while the mouse moves the dog and the cat wait. Let's start with a couple of easy ones, and then they will get harder. (Children were not explicitly instructed to minimize the number of moves; nevertheless here, as in many other studies, they appear to spontaneously attempt to produce efficient solutions.)

Problems were presented in the order shown in Table 7.2. Children were given two chances to produce a minimum path solution to each problem. If a problem was solved in the minimum number of moves, then the next problem in the sequence was presented. If it was solved in more than the minimum number, or if it had not been solved after twice the minimum number of moves had been made, or if the subject gave up, then the same problem was presented a second time. Regardless of whether the second trial produced the minimum path, a longer solution path, or no solution, the next problem in the sequence was then presented.

As each problem was presented, the children were reminded to re-arrange the animals so that each animal would get its favorite food. The children were allowed to make their own moves; if they attempted an illegal move, they were reminded of the rules.[4]

Scoring and Results

For each problem, subjects were assigned a 1/0 score based on whether they found a minimum path solution by the second presentation. Each subject was assigned a score based on the proportion of passes across the eight problems. Each problem was assigned a score based on the proportion of subjects passing it.

Relative subject performance. Subjects' performance varied widely: the highest-performing subject solved all but one problem, and three subjects failed all but one. Problem difficulty also varied widely, from nearly all subjects' passing the easiest problem to over 80% failing the hardest. The top-ranked subjects tended to fail only the harder problems, and the lowest-scoring subjects passed the easier rather than the harder problems. Although ages were fairly uniformly distributed between 50 and 65 months, age was not correlated with proportion correct.

Relative problem difficulty. The mean problem difficulty (defined as the proportion of subjects finding the minimum path) is shown in Table 7.2. Path length was a poor predictor of problem difficulty. The two easiest problems (1 and 2) were also the shortest, but even though they both have a path length of four, there was a 30% difference in the proportion of subjects passing them. The two next easiest problems (7 and 8) were the longest (seven moves). The four hardest problems were intermediate in path length, and within that set there was a large difference between the pairs with the same path length. Neither path length nor problem type was significantly correlated with problem difficulty.

Both path length and problem type are *structural variables:* features of the problem rather than of the problem-solving process. Even if they are good predictors of difficulty, they leave unstated the underlying processes they affect. But structural variables alone do not cause behavior directly: they are mediated by underlying processes. In situations of even modest complexity, such as the DCM puzzle, there are several plausible processes—or components of weak methods—and their interactions can

---

4. The most common illegal moves were moving an animal only halfway between two corners, moving two animals to the same corner, or attempting to rearrange the foods rather than the animals. However, illegalities occurred on fewer than 5% of trials and tended to occur only on the training problems.

best be understood by formulating an explicit process model. In the next section I consider some models that might account for these results.

Weak Methods on the DCM Puzzle

State evaluation. Each of the weak methods described earlier has the ability to evaluate the quality of a proposed move. That is, each can look to the future, but they differ in how much information they extract from it and how they use that information about the future to guide their behavior in the present. In generate and test, the evaluation is binary: a state either matches the goal or it does not. In contrast, the hill climbing method uses an evaluation function that gives some measure of how well the current state matches the goal state. For the DCM puzzle, consider an evaluation function—$EV(x, y)$—that computes how many of the pieces in state x are in the same positions in state y. For example, $EV(1, 7) = 0$ because none of the pieces are in matching positions, whereas $EV(24, 5) = 2$ because both the cat and the dog are positioned the same way in the two states (see Figure 7.6).

If children used such an evaluation function, then we would see two kinds of biases in their move patterns: one bias would show up as a tendency to favor moves that increase the function over those that leave it unchanged. For example, in problem 2 ($18 \rightarrow 8$) a first move of the cat increases the evaluation function, while moving the dog does not. (A cat move also stays on the minimum path, while a dog move does not.) Over all trials and all subjects, on this problem, the cat was moved 81% of the time. Even more revealing are the "garden path" problems, in which the evaluation function produces a local improvement for moves off the minimum path. In problem 4 ($10 \rightarrow 5$), the minimum path move is the mouse, which does not increase the evaluation function. In contrast, moving the cat does increase the partial evaluation function, and it was preferred on 66% of the trials even though it is off the minimum path. Similarly, on problem 5 ($13 \rightarrow 19$), the nonminimum path move of the dog was preferred on 61% of the trials.

Another bias would be to prefer moves that leave the evaluation function unchanged over those that reduce it. For example, on problem 3 ($11 \rightarrow 20$) the minimum path sequence requires that the dog be temporarily removed from its goal position even though this reduces the evaluation function. On 65% of all trials with problem 3, subjects preferred to move the cat rather than the dog even though this took them off the minimum path.

To determine whether subjects were using hill climbing on this problem, for each subject, I computed an *evaluation sensitivity score:* the proportion of trials on which, if such an evaluation function preferred one move to another, then the subject chose (one of) the preferred alternative(s). All subjects showed a sensitivity to partial evaluation. Evaluation sensitivity scores ranged from .60 to .90 (mean = .69, SD = .05). As noted, this sensitivity to local evaluation is not necessarily beneficial, for on garden path problems it moves subjects away from the minimum path. Indeed, evaluation sensitivity scores were *negatively* correlated with overall performance, suggesting that on this set of DCM problems excessive reliance on hill climbing was dysfunctional.

Goal detection. Instead of a multivalue evaluation function, a problem solver could use a simple binary evaluation in conjunction with the capacity to search n moves ahead for the goal. Then we should see perfect performance (no deviations from a minimum path) from n steps away. To assess how far ahead each subject could "see," I computed a *goal detection score* based on the distance from the goal reached directly 100% of the time. For example, if a subject produced minimum path solutions every time he or she was two moves from the goal state but on only 85% of the occasions from three moves away, then the subject would get a goal detection score of 2. Four subjects had goal detection scores of 0, nine had scores of 1, 11 scores of 2, 13 scores of 3, and 2 scores of 4. Overall, two-thirds of the subjects could stay on the minimum path when they were no more than two moves distant from the goal, and one-third could do it even from three moves away.

Strategic analysis. Because subjects appeared to be using a combination of methods, I attempted to capture their behavior by formulating a simple model of how they might approach problems—such as the DCM—in which subgoal ordering is ambiguous. The model has three parameters whose values were empirically determined. First I will describe the model, and then I will justify the parameter settings. The model makes each move according to the following rules:

If there is an n-move sequence that can reach the goal state, then make it, otherwise:

Generate all candidate moves. On all but p_1% of trials, delete the piece just moved from the candidate set (e.g., backup is allowed with probability p_1).

If there is more than one candidate, then compute EV between each candidate node and the goal node. Choose the move with the maximum EV on p_2% of trials. On $(1 - p_2\%)$ of the trials, or if the EVs for all candidate moves are equal, choose among them randomly.

The model is an imperfect hill climber. The imperfections are that (a) the model occasionally backs up, (b) it moves directly to the goal when

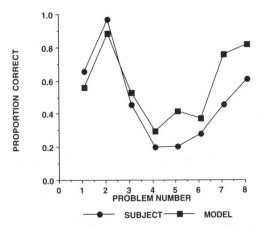

Figure 7.7 Actual versus predicted problem difficulty. Circles show proportion of all subjects passing by second trial. Squares show proportion of 400 cases that model passed by second trial.

it is near, and (c) it does not always choose the move having the maximum EV. The imperfections are captured in the model's parameters: n is the depth of goal detection, p_1 is the backup probability, and p_2 is the probability of being affected by EV. The values for these parameters were empirically derived: n was set to 2, based on the goal detection analysis, p_1 was set to .10, because 10% of all moves were double moves, and p_2 was set to .69.[5]

The model was implemented as a computer program, and each problem was presented to the program 400 times. Each solution path was scored as a 1 or 0 by the same criteria used for subjects' performance. Then the proportion of minimum path solutions (out of the 400) was computed, and this was converted to a probability of solution by the second attempt. The results are shown in the final column in Table 7.2 and Figure 7.7. The model accounts for over 70% of the variance in problem difficulty.

Summary: Future Orientation in Preschoolers' Use of Hill Climbing

Presenting preschoolers with problems having ambiguous subgoal ordering revealed what weak methods they could invoke when means-ends analysis was not useful. One extreme possibility was that they would resort to random trial and error. The other was that they would use a more appropriate weak method. The results of this study support the latter alternative.

5. This equals the mean of the partial evaluation sensitivities described earlier.

The composite model described above embodies two kinds of future orientation. When the short-term future (in this instance two moves away) is certain, fully controlled, and noncontingent, the model moves directly to the goal. Otherwise it computes the difference between the desired future and the locally available options and chooses the best of those. This sensitivity to incremental progress could degrade children's performance (as in the garden path problems). Nevertheless, it is reasonable for children to attempt to use such information.

THINKING AHEAD IN SCIENTIFIC DISCOVERY: DEVELOPMENTAL DIFFERENCES

The two problem-solving studies described so far use arbitrary tasks designed to minimize the influence of children's prior knowledge about the world. At the other extreme of both complexity and the relevance of prior knowledge lies the process of scientific discovery. Although it can be viewed as a type of problem solving, scientific discovery has several features that distinguish it from the simpler types of problems described earlier.

First, the search process takes place in two spaces: a space of hypotheses about the domain under investigation and a space of experiments in the domain. Scientific discovery requires what we have called a "dual search" in these two spaces (Klahr & Dunbar, 1988).

Second, the goal state is ill defined and complex. At the outset the goal is simply "understand the domain," and the constraints and parameters of that understanding are developed during the discovery process itself. The complexity derives from the fact that the goal state is not a static configuration like those used in TOH or DCM, but a state or rule of nature that can only be inferred from the behavior of a complex, dynamic system.

Third, there is mutuality between the states and operators in each space. Moves from one hypothesis to another in the hypothesis space are effected by "applying" experimental operators and interpreting the results of experimental outcomes. Moves from one experiment to the next in the experiment space are effected by attempts to evaluate the current hypothesis.

Fourth, prior knowledge plays an influential role in scientific discovery, because subjects always come to the task with potentially relevant knowledge about the domain. This prior knowledge influences the kinds of hypotheses that are generated, the strength with which they are held, and the experiments that are conducted to evaluate them.

These considerations led us to design a laboratory investigation of the scientific discovery process. Given this goal, we faced the problem of searching our own experiment space. In doing this search, we imposed some constraints on the kind of task we would use: (a) We wanted a domain in which prior knowledge could influence both the initial hypotheses that subjects might propose and the strength with which they held them. (b) We wanted to allow subjects to design and evaluate their own experiments rather than choose among a set of predetermined alternatives. (c) We wanted a domain in which the mapping between experimental outcomes and hypotheses was not trivial. (d) We did not want to play God with the subjects by telling them whether they had discovered a true hypothesis. Instead, we wanted subjects to decide for themselves when to terminate experimentation. (e) Finally, we wanted a task that was interesting and challenging for a wide range of ages.

Future Orientation in Discovery Microworlds

Scientific discovery requires subjects to think about the future in three senses: (a) they need to be future oriented in their specific predictions about the outcome of the next experiment; (b) they need to consider the future unfolding of the planned sequence of experiments that will be used to evaluate currently held hypotheses; (c) they need to think about the future of their own knowledge states and how they might be changed by the results of their experiments. The studies to be described below investigate the extent to which children and adults can think about the future in these senses.

Laboratory Simulation of Scientific Discovery: BigTrak

The device we used is a computer-controlled toy robot tank called Big-Trak. It is a battery-operated, programmable, self-contained vehicle approximately $13'' \times 5'' \times 8''$. The BigTrak keypad interface is depicted in Figure 7.8.[6] The basic execution cycle involves first clearing the memory with the CLR key and then entering a series of up to 16 instructions, each consisting of a function key (the command) and a one- or two-digit number (the argument). The five command keys are: ↑ (move forward), ↓ (move backward), ← (turn left), → (turn right), and FIRE. When the GO key is pressed BigTrak executes the program. For example, suppose you pressed the following series of keys:

$$\text{CLR} \uparrow 5 \leftarrow 7 \uparrow 3 \rightarrow 15 \text{ FIRE } 2 \downarrow 8 \text{ GO}.$$

When the GO key was pressed, BigTrak would move forward five feet, rotate counterclockwise 42° (corresponding to seven minutes on an ordinary clockface), move forward three feet, rotate clockwise 90°, fire (its

---

6. Figure 7.8 actually shows the keypad from the BT microworld (to be described shortly) based on the BigTrak toy.

Figure 7.8   Keypad used in BigTrak and BT studies. See text for details.

"laser cannon") twice, and back up eight feet. Our precedure had three phases.

1. Subjects were introduced to BigTrak and instructed on the use of each basic command. They were also instructed in how to generate verbal protocols. During this phase the RPT key was not visible. Subjects were trained to criterion on how to write a series of commands to accomplish a specified maneuver. This phase corresponded to a scientist's having a basic amount of knowledge about a domain but not understanding all its ramifications.

2. Subjects were shown the RPT key. They were told that it required a numeric parameter (N), and that there could be only one RPT N in a program. They were told that their task was to find out how RPT worked by writing programs and observing the results. This corresponded to a new problem in the domain: an unresolved question in an otherwise familiar context.

3. Subjects could formulate hypotheses about RPT and run experiments to test them. This required decisions about hypotheses and decisions about experiments. Subjects were never told whether they had discovered how RPT worked. They had to decide when to terminate search.

In one of our studies (Dunbar & Klahr, 1989) we used two groups of subjects: Carnegie Mellon University undergraduates and children

TABLE 7.3 Common Hypotheses (in Decreasing Order of "Popularity" or "Plausibility")

'RPT N' tells BigTrak to	Role of N
1. Repeat the entire program N times	Counter
2. Repeat the last step N times	Counter
3. Repeat the subsequent steps N times	Counter
4. Repeat the entire program once	Nil
5. Repeat the last N steps once	Selector
6. Repeat the Nth step once	Selector
7. Repeat the first N steps once	Selector
8. Repeat the entire program $f(N)$ times	Counter

between the ages of 8 and 11 years. Before I describe their performance, here is how the RPT key works. It takes the N instructions preceding the RPT N instruction, and it repeats that sequence one more time. Because this rule is somewhat counterintuitive to the common interpretation of "repeat," it was not easy to discover.

Results: BigTrak Study

Only 2 of 22 children were successful, although 12 of the unsuccessful children were sure they had discovered the correct rule and terminated their experimentation quite satisfied with their discovery. In contrast, nearly all the adults discovered the correct rule, but it was not a trivial task for them. In fact, with respect to average time, number of hypotheses, and number of experiments, the adults were not very different from the children. The explanation for these vastly different success rates must lie at a deeper level. We need to look more closely at the nature of the hypothesis space and the experiment space.

Subjects generated a variety of hypotheses during their experimental phase. The more common hypotheses are listed in Table 7.3 in order of decreasing popularity or plausibility. (Recall that the correct rule is actually number 5.) Hypotheses are classified according to the role they assign to the parameter that goes with the RPT command. In hypotheses 1, 2, 3, and 8, N *counts* the number of repetitions. We call these "counter" hypotheses. In hypotheses 5, 6, and 7, N determines which segment of the program will be *selected* to be repeated. We call these "selector" hypotheses. This distinction between counters and selectors turns out to be very useful in our subsequent experiments. Search in the BigTrak hypothesis space can involve local search among counters or among selectors, or it can involve more far-ranging search between counters and selectors.

How can we characterize the BigTrak experiment space? At one extreme it is enormous: for example, counting only commands, but not

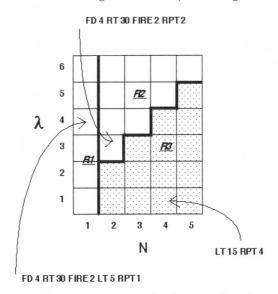

Figure 7.9   Part of the experiment space for the BigTrak studies. Each cell corresponds to a particular combination of program length (λ) and argument for the RPT key (N). Sample programs are shown for three cells: (4,1) (3,2) and (1,4).

their numerical arguments, as distinct, there are over 5^{15} distinct programs that subjects could write. However, we have found that we can adequately characterize the experiment space in terms of just two parameters. The first is λ, the length of the program preceding the RPT. The second is the value of N, the argument that RPT takes. Because both parameters must have values less than 16, there are 225 "cells" in the $\lambda - N$ space. Within that space, we identify three distinct regions: region 1 includes all programs with $N = 1$; region 2 includes all programs in which $1 < N < \lambda$; region 3 includes all programs in which $N \geq \lambda$. A segment of the experiment space, showing the different regions, is depicted in Figure 7.9, together with illustrative programs from each region. Programs from different regions of the experiment space vary in their effectiveness. Note that programs from region 2, where there are more steps than the value of N, are particularly informative.

This analysis of the hypothesis space and the experiment space enabled us to discover a couple of interesting things about how subjects approached this task. By examining the pattern of experiments, we could determine how much of the experiment space subjects searched, and by analyzing their verbal protocols we could classify experiments in terms of where they were in the hypothesis space at the time of each experiment.

We found there were two distinct types of subjects, with fundamen-

TABLE 7.4 Differences between Theorists and Experimenters in BigTrak Study

Defining property	THEORISTS State selector frame *without* sufficient evidence	EXPERIMENTERS State selector frame only *after* sufficient evidence
Time (minutes)	11	25
Total experiments	9.3	18.4
Experiments without hypotheses	0.8	6.1
Comments about experiment space	5.9	0.9
Experiment space cells used	5.7	9.9

tally different strategies. We distinguished the two groups by how much information they had when they changed from a counter frame to a selector frame. If they made the switch without having seen the result of a region 2 experiment, then we called them theorists, because they could not have based their decision on conclusive experimental evidence. On the other hand, if they made the switch from counters to selectors only after running region 2 experiments, we called them experimenters. (This analysis makes sense only for the adults, since so few children discovered the correct rule.)

The two strategies were accompanied by other differences, as shown in Table 7.4. Experimenters took twice as long to discover how RPT worked; they explored much more of the experiment space; and they conducted many more experiments without any active hypothesis. That is, they ran experiments in order to generate a data pattern over which they could induce a frame.

Development of Search Constraints in the Experiment Space

This tendency to suspend the hypothesis-testing mode while attempting to discover some kind of regularity in the data is very common and an extremely important aspect of scientific reasoning. In terms of future-oriented processes, subjects realized they had little control over the outcome of an experiment because they were unable to produce any hypotheses at this point. By switching from hypothesis space search to experiment space search, they were attempting to discover some regularities that would enable them to gain control and certainty over their predictions. This behavior suggested that we needed to find out a lot more about how subjects searched the experiment space and about how different goals might influence that search.

To study these issues, we decided to use the BigTrak paradigm in such a way that we could focus on developmental differences in the heuristics used to constrain search in the experiment space. We knew that subjects at all ages shared *domain-specific* knowledge that biased them in the same direction with respect to the plausibility of different hypotheses. We expected both age and scientific training to reveal differences in the *domain-general* heuristics used to constrain search in the experiment space.

One consequence of domain-specific knowledge is that some hypotheses about the domain are more plausible than others. We explored the effect of domain-specific knowledge by manipulating the role of plausible and implausible hypotheses. Our goal was to investigate the extent to which prior knowledge—as manifested in hypothesis plausibility— influenced how people designed experiments and how they interpreted the results of those experiments.

For this study (Klahr, Fay & Dunbar, 1993) we moved from the original BigTrak toy to a computer microworld called BT, in which a simulated "spaceship" moved around on a computer screen according to instructions entered on a BT keypad (also displayed on the screen).

The study had three phases. The first and third phases were the same as in the previous study. Subjects learned about all the normal keys and were trained to criterion on getting BT to move around the screen. In the second phase, the RPT key was introduced as before. Subjects were told that their task was to find out how RPT worked by writing at least three programs and observing the results. But then we changed the procedure a bit, by suggesting one way that RPT might work. The experimenter said:

> "One way that RPT might work is": [and then we stated one of four hypotheses listed below]. Then we continued with the instructions: "Write down three good programs that will allow you to see if the repeat key really does work this way. . . ."

When subjects had written, run, and evaluated three experiments, they were given the option of either terminating or writing additional experiments if they were still uncertain about how RPT worked. The entire session lasted approximately 45 minutes.

Throughout the study, we used only four rules for BT. Recall that our earlier studies with adults and grade-school children revealed two very "popular" hypotheses about the effect of RPT N in a program. The two popular, or plausible hypotheses were counters:

A: Repeat the entire program N times,
B: Repeat the last step N times.

TABLE 7.5 Design of BT Experiment: Specific Hypotheses for Each Given-Actual Condition

	ACTUAL RULE	
Given hypothesis	Counter	Selector
Counter	B: Repeat last step N times ↓ A: Repeat entire program N times *Theory refinement*	A: Repeat entire program N times ↓ D: Repeat last N steps once *Theory replacement*
Selector	D: Repeat last N steps once ↓ A: Repeat entire program N times *Theory replacement*	C: Repeat step N once ↓ D: Repeat last N steps once *Theory refinement*

In contrast, there were two hypotheses (selectors) that subjects were unlikely to propose:

C: Repeat the Nth step once,
D: Repeat the last N steps once.

We provided each subject with an initial hypothesis about how RPT might work. *The Given hypothesis was always wrong,* but depending on the condition, subjects regarded it as either plausible or implausible. BT was always set to work according to some other rule. We called that the Actual rule. Both the Given and Actual could be either plausible or implausible. In some conditions the Given hypothesis was only "somewhat" wrong, in that it was from the same frame as the way RPT actually worked. In other conditions the Given was "very" wrong, in that it came from a different frame than the Actual rule.

The BT simulator was programmed so that each subject worked with a RPT command obeying one of the two counter rules or two selector rules described above. We used a between-subjects design, depicted in Table 7.5. The Given hypothesis is the one suggested by the experimenter, and the Actual rule is the way BT was programmed to work for a particular condition. Remember, the key feature of this design is that *RPT never worked in the way that was suggested.*

Changing from a hypothesis within a frame to another hypothesis from the *same* frame (from one counter to another counter) requires only a single slot value change. In our microworld, this corresponds to *theory refinement.* In contrast, changing from a hypothesis from one frame to another hypothesis from a *different* frame (from a counter to a selector) requires a simultaneous change in more than one attribute, because the values of some attributes are linked to the values of others. This corresponds to *theory replacement.*

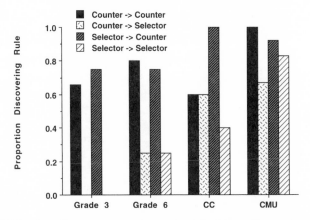

Figure 7.10 Overall success rates: proportion of subjects discovering the rule as a function of grade level and Given-Actual condition.

Subjects

We used four groups of subjects: Carnegie Mellon University (CMU) undergraduates, community college (CC) students, "sixth" graders (a mixed class of fifth to seventh graders, mean age 11 years), and third graders (mean age 9 years).

CMUs were mainly science or engineering majors, whereas the CCs had little training in mathematics or physical sciences. Children came primarily from academic and professional families. Most of the third graders had about six months of LOGO instruction (all had at least one month of LOGO). Note that CCs had less programming experience than the third graders.

Results of the BT Microworld Study

As we expected, domain-specific knowledge—as manifested in expectations about what "repeat" might mean in this context—played an important role. Regardless of what the Given hypothesis was, subjects found it easier to discover counters (81%) than selectors (35%). There was also a main effect for group: the correct rule was discovered by 83% of the CMUs, 65% of the CCs, 53% of the sixth graders, and 33% of the third graders. This group effect is attributable to the Actual = selector conditions, in which 56% of the adults but only 13% of the children were successful. In fact, none of the third graders discovered selectors. For counters, adults and children were not so different in their success rates (88% versus 75%).

What about subjects' reactions to the Given hypothesis? Recall that we presented subjects with either plausible or implausible hypotheses

TABLE 7.6 Subjects' Responses to the Given Hypothesis

	ADULTS		CHILDREN	
Category	Counter	Selector	Counter	Selector
1. Accept Given	.70	.60	.71	.33
2. Accept Given *and* propose alternative	.30	.40	.06	.06
3. Reject Given, propose alternative	0	0	.23	.61

in order to determine the extent to which search in the hypothesis space was influenced by plausibility. This is one of the points at which *domain-specific* knowledge (which determines plausibility) might affect *domain-general* knowledge about experimental strategies.

Before running the first experiment, subjects were asked to predict what would happen. Their predictions indicated how well they understood and accepted the Given hypothesis. Each subject's response to the Given hypothesis was assigned to one of three categories: 1, accept the Given hypothesis; 2, accept the Given, but also propose an alternative; 3, reject the Given and propose an alternative.

The proportion of subjects in each category is shown in Table 7.6 as a function of grade level and type of Given hypothesis. In both conditions the adults always accepted the Given hypothesis, either on its own (category 1) or in conjunction with an alternative that they proposed (category 2). Adults never rejected the Given hypothesis. In contrast, no third grader and only two sixth graders ever proposed an alternative to compare with the Given (category 2). Instead, children considered only one hypothesis at a time. When given counters they mainly accepted them, but when given selectors they mainly rejected them and proposed an alternative, which was usually a counter of their own design.

This propensity to consider multiple versus single hypotheses affected the type of experimental goals the subjects set. These goals, in turn, were used to impose constraints on search in the experiment space. We looked at these goals more closely by analyzing both what subjects said about experiments and the features of the experiments they actually wrote.

Subjects' verbal protocols contained many statements indicating both explicit understanding of the experiment space dimensions and a general notion of "good instrumentation": designing interpretable programs containing easily identifiable markers. Subjects made explicit statements about both kinds of knowledge. Here are some typical adult statements:

TABLE 7.7 Proportion of Self-Generated Constraints

	CMU	CC	Sixth grade	Third grade
Explicit $\lambda - N$ comments	.83	.60	.53	.20
Standard turn units	.92	.95	.71	.53
Small arguments	.92	.85	.65	.47
Proportion of programs in small experiment-space region	.50	.63	.26	.31

> I don't want to have two of the same move in there yet, I might not be able to tell if it was repeating the first one or if it was doing the next part of my sequence;

> I'm going to use a series of commands that will . . . *that are easily distinguished from one another*, and won't run it off the screen;

> so I'm going to pick two [commands] that are the direct opposite of each other, to see if they don't really have to be direct opposites but I'm just going to write a program that consists of two steps, *that I could see easily*. (emphasis added)

Sixth graders were somewhat less articulate but still showed a concern for both experiment space dimensions and program interpretability. In contrast, third graders rarely made such comments. The proportion of subjects making such comments is shown in the top row of Table 7.7.

At a finer level of detail, good instrumentation was assessed by how well subjects observed three pragmatic constraints: (a) using standard units of rotation, such as 15 or 30 "minutes" (90° and 180°), for turn commands; (b) using small numeric arguments (values <5) on move commands, so that the actions of BT are not distorted by having it hit the boundaries of the screen; and (c) using distinct commands in a program where possible. Programs constrained in these ways produce behavior that is easier to observe, encode, and remember. For both turns and moves, there was a strong effect of grade level.

Yet another interesting difference between the children and the adults was the way adults limited their search to a small "corner" of the experiment space. We looked at the section of the experiment space with λ between 1 and 4, and N between 1 and 3. This corresponds to only 5% of the full experiment space. But we discovered that over half of the adults' experiments occurred within this small area. On the other hand, children's experiments were much more scattered throughout the space. Both what subjects *said* and what they *did* support the conclusion that older subjects—even those with weak technical backgrounds—were better able than children to constrain their search in the experiment space and to design interpretable experiments.

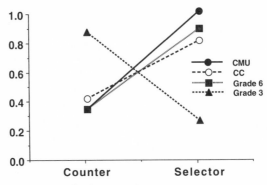

Figure 7.11   Proportion of subjects with λ > N on first experiment, by grade level and Given condition.

So what were subjects trying to do here? What were their experimental goals? How can we infer these goals from the kinds of experiments they ran? We reasoned as follows: If the experimental goal is to *determine* which of the program steps are repeated for selector hypotheses, or to discriminate between selectors and counters, then subjects should write programs having more than N steps (i.e., with λ > N). (In programs where λ is several steps greater than N, it is easy to distinguish among repeats of all steps, first step, last step, and N steps.) On the other hand, if the goal is to *demonstrate* the effect of a counter, then subjects should use larger values of N and (for pragmatic reasons) relatively short programs (programs with λ ≤ N). Figure 7.11 shows the proportion of subjects in each condition whose first programs had λ > N. Both of the adult groups' responses and sixth graders' responses were consistent with the normative account I just gave. Third graders showed the opposite pattern. More detailed results can be found in Klahr, Fay, and Dunbar (1993).

Heuristics for Constraining Search

We believe that these patterns of constrained search in the experiment space result from a set of domain-general heuristics that are differentially available to children and adults. Based on the present study, we have proposed the following four heuristics:

1. *Use the plausibility of a hypothesis to choose experimental strategy.* In this study we found that both children and adults varied their approach to confirmation and disconfirmation according to the plausibility of the currently held hypothesis. When hypotheses were plausible, subjects at all levels tended to set an experimental goal of *demonstrating* key features of the given hypothesis rather than conducting experiments that could discriminate between rival hypotheses.

For implausible hypotheses, adults and young children used different strategies. Adults' response to implausibility was to propose hypotheses from frames other than the Given frame and to conduct experiments that could *discriminate* between them. Our youngest children's response was to propose a hypothesis from a different, but plausible, frame and then to ignore the initial, and implausible, hypothesis while attempting to demonstrate the correctness of the plausible one. Third graders were particularly susceptible to this strategy.

2. *Focus on one dimension of an experiment or hypothesis.* An incremental, conservative approach has been found to be effective in both concept attainment and hypothesis testing. This suggests that in moving from one experiment or hypothesis to the next, or in moving between experiments and hypotheses, one should decide on the most important features of each and focus on just those features. Here the CMU adults stood apart from the other three groups. They were much more likely than any of the others to make conservative moves—that is, to minimize differences in program content between one program and the next.

3. *Maintain observability.* As BT moved along the screen it left no permanent record of its behavior. Subjects had to remember what BT actually did. Thus, one way to implement this heuristic is to write short programs. Adults almost always used it, whereas the youngest children often wrote programs that were very difficult to encode. This heuristic depends on knowledge of one's own information-processing limitations as well as knowledge of the device. Our finding that the third graders did not attempt to maintain observability, whereas the sixth graders and adults did, may be a manifestation, in the realm of experimental design, of the more general findings about the development of self-awareness of cognitive limitations (Wellman, 1990).

4. *Design experiments giving characteristic results.* This heuristic maximizes the interpretability of experimental outcomes. Physicians look for "markers" for diseases, and physicists design experiments in which suspected particles will leave "signatures." In the BT domain, this heuristic is instantiated as "use many distinct commands." On average, about half of all programs in each group did not contain any repeated commands, although because third graders were more likely to use long programs, they were more likely to use repeated commands, which reduced the possibility of generating characteristic behavior.

These, then, are the four heuristics our subjects used to constrain search in the experiment space. As I noted in describing each one, adults and children differed in their use. Adults not only appeared to use each of them, but also they seemed able to deal with their inherent contradictions. In contrast, children either failed to use these heuristics at all or else let one of them dominate. This is not simply a matter of children being unable to understand the *logic* of the discriminating experiment or the difference between testing hypotheses and generating effects. Indeed, Sodian, Zaitchik, and Carey (1991) have shown that even first graders understand these distinctions in simple, two-alternative situations. The problem for young children is how to constrain search in a very large space of hypotheses and experiments.

Thinking About the Future in Discovery Tasks

In these discovery tasks, the subjects' goal is to discover something about the world. The only way they can gather information about the current workings of that world is to enter a program and predict its outcome. The subjects evaluate their understanding about how RPT works by assessing the accuracy of that prediction. Thus, attempts to predict the future behavior of a complex system lead to the discovery of its underlying principles.

Recall the three senses in which scientific discovery invokes future-oriented thinking: (a) predictions about specific experiments, (b) planning an experimental sequence, and (c) understanding that experimental outcomes may, in the future, change current knowledge states. Adults were able to maintain this future orientation in all three senses. Children of middle-school age and beyond appeared to be able to deal with the first sense but had difficulty with the other two. For example, even our youngest children understood that their experiments would be played out in the future, and that their predictions were about things yet to come. However, children were less able than adults to understand that they would be engaged in a series of experiments and that the experimental series itself required an overall plan in which the outcome of one experiment was related to the outcomes of prior and subsequent experiments. Instead, our youngest children were satisfied with demonstrating that they could maintain their current hypotheses by obtaining a particular effect. Finally, although we have only indirect evidence from the studies reported here, it seems that adults were much more aware than children that their own knowledge states would be changed by the results of experimentation.

CONSIDERING THE FUTURE IN PROBLEM SOLVING AND SCIENTIFIC DISCOVERY

In this final section, I return to the framework (see Table 7.8) and apply it to the domains discussed earlier. The rows correspond to various situations in which an individual may have to think about the future, and the columns correspond to the attributes of the framework. The cell

TABLE 7.8 Framework for Future-Oriented Thinking Processes

Domain	Subject of thinking	Uncertainty	Control	Contingency	Abstraction	Social	Temporal extent
Game playing and problem solving	Move in chess or checkers	In principle, no; capacity limits, yes	Partial	Adversarial	No	No	minutes
	T-end problems in TOH	No	Full	None	Probably	No	seconds
	F-end problems in TOH	Yes	Full	None	No	No	seconds–minutes
	Solution path in DCM	Near goal, no; distant from goal, yes	Full	None	No	No	minutes
Scientific reasoning	BT discovery	Yes	Partial	Informational	Several levels	No	minutes–hours
	Collaborative discovery tasks	Yes	Partial	Supportive	Several levels	Yes	minutes–hours

entries indicate the value of the attribute for the situation (at least according to my best guess; this is, after all, a pretty informal process).

Future Orientation in Problem Solving

The entries at the top of Table 7.8 summarize the earlier analyses. For many problem-solving and game-playing situations, the formal properties of the task interact with the limited capacity of the problem solver in ways indicated earlier. For example, for the Dog-Cat-Mouse problem, the level of uncertainty depends on the distance remaining to the goal and the subject's depth of search capacity.

Future Orientation in Scientific Discovery

These attributes can also be considered with respect to the cognitive processes involved in scientific discovery. Scientific reasoning is inherently uncertain, since nature responds to "moves" in ways still unknown (else there would be no discovery to be made). The contingencies are benign, because the physical world does not attempt to deceive or "hide its secrets." In our studies, control over the design of an experiment is complete, but the outcome is not fully determined by the problem solver. The degree of abstraction varies widely and is one of the distinctions between effective and ineffective problem solvers in discovery tasks. Our most effective subjects suppressed much of the detail in experimental variation and thought only in terms of λ and N. Indeed, in most areas of real-world science, skilled performance rests in no small measure on the scientist's ability to work at just the right grain size, neither ignoring relevant detail nor being overwhelmed by irrelevancies. In the tasks reported here, there is no social aspect, but others have used the BT paradigm to study the effects of collaboration on scientific discovery (Teasley, 1992), and the real scientific enterprise has very influential social components.

Other Varieties of Future-Oriented Thinking

All the tasks discussed in this chapter, from the Tower of Hanoi and the Dog-Cat-Mouse to the BigTrak discovery tasks, involve problem solving. But there are other kinds of future-oriented processes that are not easily characterized in those terms. In these concluding paragraphs I will mention a few extreme departures from the set of tasks I have just described. I leave it as an exercise for the reader to extend the framework listed in Table 7.8 to accommodate these situations, as well as the many others described in this volume.

Consider first the kind of tasks presented to infants by Haith, Hazan, and Goodman (1988)[7] in their demonstration that 3.5-month-old infants developed expectations for patterns of alternating visual events. Because the infants were responding to events that were not contingent on the infants' behavior, Haith et al. characterized their future orientation in terms of "expectancies" and "anticipations" about perceptual events. In this most rudimentary form of future orienation, it appears that infants' default assumption is to expect the future to be pretty much like the past: static objects are expected to remain in place, moving objects are expected to continue along their trajectories, and simple systematic patterns of perceptual activity are expected to repeat indefinitely. Can this kind of future orientation be cast as a type of problem solving? Perhaps. Haith et al. imply that infants do have a goal in such situations: "to detect regularities in dynamic events and to develop expectations partly in order to bring their behavior under self-control" (1988, p. 477). Another example of discovering the present by predicting the future? Perhaps.

There are other variations. One can think about the future with no particular goal in mind: consider weather forecasting. One can construct representations for nonexistent states (as in planning) but still lack a future orientation (dreams, reminiscences, musings about missed opportunities and "the road not taken"). For example, consider the following: I am thinking about the feasibility of skiing tomorrow from the top of one mountain (A) to the bottom of a nearby mountain (B). I have a good memory of the network of trails, and I mentally work my way down the

7. These tasks are also described in Haith's chapter in this volume.

slopes, planning tomorrow's day. Now consider a different situation. As I reflect on today's skiing, I recall all the paths I took and think about whether I *could have gone* from the top of A to the bottom of B. What is the difference in these two mental processes? How does the future-oriented plan differ from the memory-oriented reflection? What are the processes and representations that differentiate these situations? In constructing models of the psychological processes involved in future-oriented thinking, it will be important to clarify these issues. I believe that we do not know how to do this at present. Perhaps we will, in the future.

REFERENCES

Anzai, Y., & Simon, H. A. (1979). The theory of learning by doing. *Psychological Review, 86,* 124–140.

Dunbar, K., & Klahr, D. (1989). Developmental differences in scientific discovery strategies. In D. Klahr & K. Kotovsky (Eds.), *Complex information processing: The impact of Herbert A. Simon* (pp. 109–143). Hillsdale, NJ: Erlbaum.

Dunker, K. (1945). On problem solving, *Psychological Monographs, 58* (270).

Friedman, W. J. (1990). *About time: Inventing the fourth dimension.* Cambridge: MIT Press.

Hadley, G. (1962). *Linear programming.* Reading, MA: Addison-Wesley.

Haith, M. M., Hazan, C., & Goodman, G. S. (1988). Expectation and anticipation of dynamic visual events by 3.5-month-old babies. *Child Development, 59,* 467–479.

Hayes-Roth, B., & Hayes-Roth, F. (1979). A cognitive model of planning. *Cognitive Science, 3,* 275–310.

Klahr, D. (1978). Goal formation, planning, and learning by pre-school problem solvers, or "My socks are in the dryer." In R. S. Siegler (Ed.), *Children's thinking: What develops?* (pp. 181–212). Hillsdale, NJ: Erlbaum.

Klahr, D. (1985). Solving problems with ambiguous subgoal ordering: Preschoolers' performance. *Child Development, 56,* 940–952.

Klahr, D., & Dunbar, K. (1988). Dual space search during scientific reasoning. *Cognitive Science, 12*(1), 1–55.

Klahr, D., Fay, A. L., & Dunbar, K. (1993). Heuristics for scientific experimentation: A developmental study. *Cognitive Psychology, 24*(1), 111–146.

Klahr, D., & Robinson, M. (1981). Formal assessment of problem solving and planning processes in preschool children. *Cognitive Psychology, 13,* 113–148.

Miller, G. A., Galanter, E., & Pribram, K. (1960). *Plans and the structure of behavior.* New York: Holt, Rinehart and Winston.

Newell, A., & Simon, H. A. (1972). *Human problem solving.* Englewood, NJ: Prentice-Hall.

Piaget, J. (1976). *The grasp of consciousness.* Cambridge: Harvard University Press.

Scholnick, E. K., & Friedman, S. L. (1987). The planning construct in the psychological literature. In S. L. Friedman, E. K. Scholnick, & R. R. Cocking (Eds.), *Blueprints for thinking* (pp. 3–38). Cambridge: Cambridge University Press.

Siegler, R. S. (1981). Developmental sequences within and between concepts. *Monographs of the Society for Research in Child Development, 46* (Whole No. 189).

Simon, H. A. (1975). The functional equivalence of problem-solving skills. *Cognitive Psychology, 7,* 268–288.

Sodian, B., Zaitchik, D., & Carey, S. (1991). Young children's differentiation of hypothetical beliefs from evidence. *Child Development, 62,* 753–766.

Teasley, S. D. (1992, April). Children's collaborations and talk. Paper presented at symposium on Learning through peer collaboration: Conceptual and methodological issues (E. Forman, Chair), conducted at the annual meeting of the American Education Research Association, San Francisco.

Wellman, H. M. (1990). *The child's theory of mind.* Cambridge: MIT Press.

Wickelgren, W. A. (1974). *How to solve problems.* San Francisco: Freeman.

NEURAL BASES

Chapter Eight

Neural Mechanisms of Future-Oriented Processes
In Vivo Physiological Studies of Humans

Daniel R. Weinberger, Karen Faith Berman,
James Gold, and Terry Goldberg

If the capacity to think ahead—to consciously plan for and anticipate complex future events—is particularly characteristic of human cognitive ability, it follows that the neurobiological substrate of this capacity is likely to be an evolutionarily advanced neural system, perhaps one uniquely well developed in the human brain. Although this may seem to be a logical and intuitively appealing conclusion, it is supported by remarkably few scientific data that bear directly on this issue. There are only a few investigations in humans that have attempted to identify the neural systems related to this manner of mental activity. Indeed, if "future-oriented processing" has been the subject of relatively limited scientific discussion in the cognitive psychology literature, it has received even less attention in the neurobiological literature. This may represent in part the unavailability until recently of the experimental tools necessary to explore this question.

In this chapter we will summarize the results of several recent studies that have measured brain physiology in humans while they were engaged in complex mental tasks involving elements of future-oriented cognition. These studies have directly implicated highly evolved neural systems as subserving such processes. First we will review some clinical observations about brain lesions that impair future-oriented types of cognition. These case studies have tended to implicate disruption of neural functions attributed to the prefrontal cortex as being responsible for such defects. These studies also represent the basis of efforts by numerous investigators to characterize the cognitive functions of the prefrontal cortex of the human brain. In reviewing what have been proposed as the fundamental functions of the prefrontal cortex, we will emphasize overlap with concepts relevant to future-oriented processes. In this regard, the literature on clinical lesions has set the stage for studies using functional imaging methods in normal subjects. Before considering the functional imaging data, we will present a brief review of clinical neuropsychological tests of putative prefrontal function. These tests involve several aspects of future-oriented processes, especially the executive control of memory functions. Next we will review studies of neuroimaging during performance of such tasks. Most of these studies have assessed regional cerebral blood flow because it is a sensitive measure of brain activity. Finally, we will consider a uniquely human illness where future-oriented processing appears to be impaired. The illness is schizophrenia, and the brain imaging data suggest that the reason for this impairment has to do with a defect in the underlying neural mechanisms responsible for it.

NEUROPSYCHOLOGICAL LOCALIZATION BASED ON HUMAN LESIONS

To the extent that neuropsychological investigators and theoreticians have argued for a cerebral localization of the cognitive functions involved in planning and anticipation, they have emphasized a link with the frontal lobes. This linkage has been based primarily on clinical studies of people who have suffered injury to the frontal lobes and who have seemed as a result to lose the capacity to plan, to anticipate, and to utilize past experience in the service of predicting or preparing for future events. The classical neuropsychology literature contains numerous references to planning and anticipation as fundamental functions of the frontal lobes, in particular the association cortex of the prefrontal region. Luria's (1966) detailed clinical studies of patients with various focal cerebral lesions led to a theory of frontal lobe function that emphasized executive control of purposeful behavior and the role of the prefrontal cortex in anticipation, planning, and following through on a sequential course of action.

Other investigators emphasized different aspects of frontal functions based on similar studies of patients with focal lesions. For example, Pribram (1969) proposed that appreciation of context, which among other things could be temporal, was an important frontal lobe function. More recently, Fuster (1989) has singled out temporal context as a critical prefrontal function and argued that the prefrontal cortex is responsible for the overall temporal organization of behavior and for the coordination of temporally discontinuous elements of cognition. The future seems virtually by definition to be the most temporally discontinuous aspect of human experience. That it could be anticipated at all or prepared for even in a probabilistic sense requires integration of past experiences that logically prepare for possible future occurrences. Fuster has argued in this regard that maintaining a so-called preparatory mental set is an essential prefrontal function. It involves priming cognitive resources and holding them on line in anticipation of processing expected sensory and/or cognitive information. It is analogous to Luria's notion that prefrontal cortex sets a "cortical tone" and to Teuber's (1972) proposal of a corollary discharge from prefrontal cortex to prime other cortical zones.

Other conceptualizations of prefrontal neuropsychological function have also emphasized the control of memory processes in the service of purposeful and future-oriented behavior. Goldman-Rakic (1987) maintains that working memory—the capacity to guide behavior by the memory of past stimuli (i.e., "internal representations") and their relevance rather than by the stimuli themselves—is the prefrontal cognitive function. Working memory as she describes it seems to be an essential aspect of future-oriented processing. To stay on a goal-directed course, one must have the capacity to compare current sensory information with a prior concept or rule about the goal and to modify behavior or update the rule or concept based on this comparison. In this sense the capacity to act based on anticipation of the future cannot exist without access to relevant past experience. Although it may not have been stated in precisely these terms, the use of memory to guide behavior that is future oriented seems to be the centerpiece of many current views of prefrontal function. An additional example is the hypothesis of Ingvar (1985), who proposed that the prefrontal cortex is involved in "memory for the future," a form of cognitive "fortune-telling" based on past experience. These various conceptualizations of prefrontal function, which emphasize the use of memory to guide goal-directed behavior and to plan and anticipate, seem isomorphic with many aspects of future-oriented processing as discussed in the cognitive psychology literature.

That the prefrontal cortex is the most highly evolved and phylogenetically distinct part of the human brain (Fuster, 1989) is consistent with

TABLE 8.1 Examples of Clinical Tests Used to Assess Prefrontal
Cognitive Functions

Wisconsin Card Sorting Test
Porteus Maze
Delayed response
Stroop Color-Word Interference Test
Verbal fluency tests
Memory tests of recency and frequency
Trails B test
Halstead Category Test
Tower of Hanoi type tasks

---

the assumption about the neural substrate of future-oriented processing stated above. However, neural localization based on lesion studies is inconclusive and potentially flawed. Such studies show only that a particular normal function cannot be performed without the damaged brain part; they do not tell what brain part or parts normally perform the particular function. To address how the normal brain approaches a cognitive activity, one must have tools that can localize normal brain function as it is taking place. This has become possible with the advent of brain-imaging techniques. Before turning to this literature, however, we must first consider how prefrontal cognition is assessed. This is accomplished with a variety of neuropsychological tasks, most of which, interestingly enough, had originally been validated in patients with focal brain lesions. As these tasks have become utilized along with brain-imaging methods, it has become possible not only to map the neural activity associated with doing the tasks but also to test conclusions about the tasks themselves based on lesion models.

NEUROPSYCHOLOGICAL TESTS

A variety of clinical neuropsychological tests of prefrontal function have been described, and many of them are routinely used to examine prefrontal function (see Table 8.1). Although most patients with prefrontal damage will show impairments on at least some of these tests, none are absolutely specific in the sense that only patients with prefrontal injury do poorly on them, and none are absolutely sensitive in that every patient with prefrontal injury will show impairment. This may mean that the right test has not yet been developed or that prefrontal function is ultimately not reducible to an absolute standard of performance that characterizes every human being. In general these tests address a variety of cognitive functions that have been loosely described as "executive." They tend to involve the purposeful control of information—that is, how information is used—not what the information is or how it is acquired.

Some of these tests can be interpreted as involving cognitive processing that is future oriented. The prototypical prefrontal test is the delayed-response test. As originally described by Jacobsen (1931) in studies of monkeys with lesions of the dorsolateral prefrontal cortex, the test requires a subject to consciously hold in mind past information that will become critical for making an appropriate response in the near future. In Jacobsen's classic experiments, animals had to remember over a delay period the spatial location of a past reward in order to receive it again in the future. The reward itself was covered so that sensory stimuli could not inform the animal of where the reward was when the chance arose to secure it again. It could be found only by remembering where it was in the past. A variation on the test might superimpose an additional response rule that also had to be applied to the future. For instance, in the delayed-alternation variation, the animal had to remember not only the past location of the reward but also the rule that each future response had to select an alternate location from its immediate predecessor. Monkeys with damage to the principal sulcus region of the dorsolateral prefrontal cortex have difficulty with these tasks. Recent studies suggest that some human subjects with prefrontal disease or dysfunction are impaired on such tasks as well (Oscar-Berman, McNamara, & Freedman, 1991).

Another prefrontal-type neuropsychological task that involves future-oriented processing is the Tower of Hanoi task. In this task subjects must "look ahead" and plan in their minds how to move a pile of disks from one post to another while respecting rules that restrict how the disks can be piled on top of each other. Although there are a number of variations on this tower puzzle task, studies in patients with diseases of various brain regions suggest that the simple three-disk version involves the clearest example of purposeful, conscious planning ahead and is the one where performance is most often impaired in patients with prefrontal dysfunction (Goldberg, Saint-Cyr, & Weinberger, 1990). This conclusion may seem counterintuitive, since more difficult versions of this task exist. One interpretation, however, is that versions with more than three disks are too complex and require too many moves for anticipation mechanisms to be the primary approach to reaching the goal. The longer versions seem to depend more on trial and error—on learning by doing (procedural or habit learning)—and as such are probably less directly related to the prefrontal cortex.

The Wisconsin Card Sorting Test (WCST) is perhaps the most familiar test referable to the prefrontal cortex. Based on a paradigm originally developed by Weigl (1941), the task in its current form requires planning and anticipation as well as abstract problem solving (Robinson, Heaton, Lehman, & Stilson 1980). It involves sorting cards that differ by the color, shape, and number of geometric objects displayed on their faces. To sort correctly, the subject must learn an arbitrary and abstract sorting principle or rule (either the number or color or shape of objects). This rule can be learned because the examiner informs the subject after each attempt at sorting whether the decision was right or wrong. By holding on line the memory of whether the immediate past sort was correct and by using this information to guide the next attempt (while at the same time inhibiting tendencies to repeat past errors), the subject can arrive at and maintain the correct sorting principle. Compared with other neuropsychological tests, the WCST has proved to be a relatively sensitive and specific clinical test of prefrontal damage. The term "relative" cannot be overemphasized, however, since it is also clear that some patients with extrafrontal lesions have difficulty with this task and some patients with prefrontal injury have no apparent difficulty (Anderson, Damasio, Jones, & Tranel, 1991).

That poor performance on the WCST is not categorically associated with damage to the prefrontal cortex has led to debate about whether it is a good prefrontal task (Anderson et al., 1991). On theoretical grounds, it appears to be an excellent one, since it involves most, if not all, of the elements of putative prefrontal cognitive function described above. However, lesion studies have suggested otherwise. This apparent inconsistency may be explainable in terms of the uncertainty of conclusions about functional localization based solely on lesion data, as mentioned above. Alternatively, the WCST may not be understandable in neural terms at the level of only the prefrontal cortex. These issues have begun to be addressed through the application of brain-imaging techniques. In particular, using these methods, it has been possible to map the neural activity that corresponds in the normal brain to the performance of future-oriented processing type of tasks such as the WCST and the Tower of Hanoi and to address the validity of conclusions about localization based on lesion data.

IN VIVO CEREBRAL PHYSIOLOGICAL STUDIES: GENERAL ISSUES

Although studies of deficits associated with prefrontal lesions have implicated the prefrontal cortex in certain future-oriented processes, the possibility of identifying the neural substrates normally subserving such processes is increasing because of the development of neuroscience technologies such as positron emission tomography (PET), single photon emission computed tomography (SPECT), and other functional neuroimaging techniques. These methods permit relatively high-resolution mapping of functional brain activity. Brain function is measured in terms of regional cerebral blood flow (rCBF) or the regional cerebral metabolic rate of glucose utilization. Glucose is the principal substrate of neuronal metabolism and energy production, the fuel of brain activity. Regional blood flow is closely coupled with glucose utilization and directly proportional to it. Because the methods of rCBF measurement have much better time resolution than do those that measure glucose metabolism (less than 1 min as compared with approximately 30 min), the former have become the methods of choice for mapping the regional physiological correlates of mental activity.

All the rCBF techniques to be discussed are nuclear medicine scanning methods. They involve administration, usually by inhalation or intravenous injection, of trace quantities of a radioactive substance that serves as a tracer of rCBF. As such, the tracer is carried in the blood to the brain, where its passage through the brain is monitored and interpreted using mathematical models that describe the kinetic behavior of the tracer in terms of flow parameters. The ability to monitor the passage of the tracer through the brain depends on emission of gamma rays, which are counted and localized by detectors that surround the head. PET and SPECT differ in terms of the type of radioactive substances used to emit the gamma rays, the types of tracers used to map rCBF, and the resolution and sensitivity of the detector systems that measure the emitted radioactivity (gamma rays) and reconstruct images of rCBF. PET has a distinct advantage in each of these areas, but it is much more expensive, slightly more invasive and uncomfortable, and less widely available. It is also not clear to what degree the technical advantages of PET translate into meaningful research advantages in terms of mapping cognitive activity.

Over the past decade there have been numerous reports of rCBF measured during the performance of cognitive tasks. Many of these studies have been interpreted as revealing the functional landscape underlying the task, that is, as localizing the neural systems responsible for doing the task. In general the approach taken in most of these studies is to average across individuals the rCBF maps from two yoked cognitive conditions and to compare the averages. The two tasks are usually designed so that they vary only in terms of a selective element. The difference between the maps is taken to represent the neural activity that is specific for the selective element that differs between the two conditions. For example, in a landmark series of studies by Raichle and colleagues, semantic processing was examined by having subjects perform a carefully graded series of stepwise language tasks (Petersen, Fox, Posner, Mintun, & Raichle, 1988, 1991). In this manner the functional neural map corresponding specifically to the motor components of reading words aloud was deduced by subtracting the functional map generated while subjects read words silently from the maps generated when they read words out loud.

Unfortunately, there are a number of pitfalls in performing these studies, and none of them have been methodologically perfect. The design of the cognitive conditions is obviously critical, but important additional issues include how one determines the precise anatomical location of an activation signal, how one assesses the statistical significance of activation, and even how one converts information about the distribution of radioactivity into quantitative data about brain activity. Each of these issues is the subject of heated debate and discussion in the literature. Because there is no perfect solution to any of these problems, each adds error to the rCBF method.

Even notwithstanding these potential errors, the validity of the yoked task approach to neural localization with PET is open to challenge. For one thing, the assumption that cognition occurs in stepwise, decomposable fashion can be challenged. The brain may not process complex mental activities in terms of physiological building blocks. Doing two things at once, such as reading and speaking, may involve a qualitatively unique pattern of neural activity rather than an arithmetic summation of the two isolated activities. Moreover, the assumption that cognition is a serial process and that retroactive effects do not occur also has been challenged (Sergent, Zuck, Lévesque, & MacDonald, 1992). The specific nature of what one selects as the "subtraction" task also may affect the experimental results (Sergent et al., 1992). More important, a PET scan of rCBF provides a number corresponding to the amount of activity occurring during a particular period in a particular part of the brain. This number is itself the summation of numerous physiological processes, many of which may be related to neural functions that may be only indirectly related to the cognitive process under study. For example, approximately 60% of the magnitude of this number represents the neural activity related to wakefulness and alertness. When people are asleep and dreaming, the rCBF numbers from many regions of the brain are of the same magnitude as found during normal wakefulness. Yet clearly such data do not correspond to normal waking mental activity. Attention and concentration are also probably major components of the physiological signals recorded during a waking PET scan. These components may change slightly or significantly from one cognitive condition to another and may, unknown to the investigator, dominate the PET data. Other cognitively nonspecific signals, such as signals related to maintaining so-called preparatory sets, also may be critical, and they have received little attention in the PET literature.

These uncertainties should be borne in mind when interpreting the results of PET studies of cognition. They may account for a number of inconsistencies in the PET literature, including the variations in rCBF maps that have been described by independent groups examining the same or similar cognitive tasks (even simple word association; Wise et al., 1991), the apparent differences that are found when the same subject repeats the same task (Raichle et al., 1991; Warach et al., 1992), and the general tendency to find little relation between how well a subject performs a task and how much physiological activation occurs. In fact, with more demanding tasks brain activation tends to vary inversely with performance, suggesting that the activation signals reflect something about processing efficiency (Parks et al., 1989).

The prefrontal cortex has been reported to show activation during a wide variety of cognitive conditions. Few studies, regardless of the paradigm employed, have failed to observe activation in some region of the prefrontal cortex. It has been reported to activate with word generation, focused attention, shifting attention, calculations, problem solving, and so on (Berman & Weinberger, 1991a). This broad spectrum of activation suggests that the prefrontal cortex plays, among other things, a superordinate function that probably is a necessary but not sufficient component of such tasks. This may correspond to the preparatory set function mentioned above. Teasing out prefrontal activity that is cognitively generic from that which relates to specific cognitive processes (e.g., future-oriented processes) is a major challenge.

IN VIVO PHYSIOLOGICAL STUDIES OF FUTURE-ORIENTED PROCESSES

Gevins et al. (1987) used an electrophysiological mapping technique to study the distribution and so-called cross-cortical coherence of evoked potential signals related to simple anticipatory sensorimotor processes. Subjects were required to make graded fine motor responses to numeric visual stimuli with either the right or left hand. The investigators identified a pattern of coactivation of prefrontal and sensorimotor cortices that occurred in anticipation of a correct response. Moreover, the appropriate "network" was not seen when incorrect responses were made. Gevins et al. proposed that the network is the neurophysiological substrate of maintaining a preparatory set that must be recruited if the task is to be performed without error. They assigned the executive (the recruitment function), to the prefrontal component.

Our group has looked at a variety of working memory tasks that involve using memory to anticipate a correct response to a future question. We have studied the Wisconsin Card Sorting Test (WCST) most extensively. Our early studies of the WCST involved having normal subjects take an automated version of the task while regional cerebral blood flow was determined by the so-called surface probe, xenon-133 inhalation method (Weinberger, Berman, & Illowsky, 1988; Weinberger, Berman, & Zec, 1986). This method uses radioactive xenon gas inhaled through a snorkel mouthpiece as a tracer of rCBF. Because the gas is metabolically inert (it is not consumed or transformed by the brain) and because it readily crosses the blood/brain barrier, its transport to the brain and washout from the brain are determined by rCBF. The rate of transport and washout is monitored by an array of scintillation detectors that literally rest on the scalp. This method is relatively inexpensive and noninvasive, but it suffers from limited spatial resolution and can measure rCBF only in the cerebral cortex. In addition to measuring rCBF during the WCST, we also measured it during a simple visual matching-to-sample number task that in theory controlled for the sensorimotor and cognitively nonspecific physiological correlates of the WCST. This study represented the first application of the yoked task subtraction approach and the use of intersubject averaging to enhance signal localization with functional brain imaging.

In a sample of 25 normal subjects, we found that when the rCBF data during the WCST were compared with the data during the matching-to-sample task, significant changes occurred exclusively in the dorsolateral prefrontal cortex (Weinberger et al., 1986) (see Figure 8.1). No significant lateralization was seen, but the method itself is relatively insensitive to laterality effects (Berman & Weinberger, 1990).

We recently looked again at the WCST, this time using a computerized version and a variation of the xenon-133 inhalation method involving single photon emission computed tomography (SPECT), a more sophisticated nuclear medicine technique that has improved spatial resolution and the potential for measuring rCBF throughout the brain. Again, activation was primarily within the dorsolateral prefrontal cortex, greater in the right hemisphere (Marenco, Coppola, Daniel, Zigun, & Weinberger, 1993).

The measurement of rCBF using oxygen-15 water injected intravenously as the radioactive tracer and PET is currently the most sensitive and reliable method for the in vivo assessment of brain perfusion. It provides spatial resolution of approximately 6 mm, almost twice that of other nuclear medicine methods, at all anatomical levels of the brain. In our studies of the WCST with the oxygen-15 water PET technique, we have confirmed and extended the results found with the xenon approaches (Berman et al., 1991).

Berman et al. (1991) studied normal subjects who performed the WCST twice, first in the standard format and then after repeated admin-

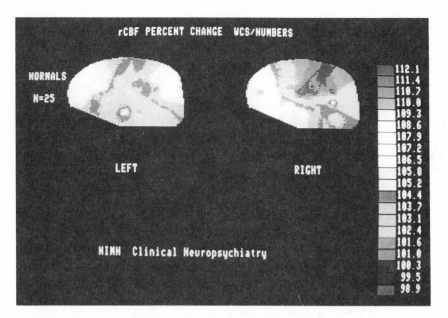

Figure 8.1 Maps of cortical activation associated with doing the Wisconsin Card Sort Test. Images show mean distribution of the change in cortical rCBF for left and right hemispheres during performance of the WCST in 25 normal subjects as compared with a simple sensorimotor matching-to-sample control task. Scale is percentage of activation. Frontal pole is to the left of each image.

istration so that they performed it without difficulty. The latter condition was aimed at controlling for the novelty and uncertainty involved in taking the WCST for the first time. In principle, the second condition emphasized the purely cognitive aspects of the test. Once again, the results indicated that the dorsolateral prefrontal cortex is activated during performance of this task, and the degree of activation is the same even after repeated administrations. This finding strongly suggests that the pattern of activation reflects the underlying neural substrate of doing the test. It can be argued that while subjects are doing the WCST, numerous cognitive functions are recruited, including those involving achieving abstract sets, coping with novelty and uncertainty, responding to feedback, and searching through a lexicon of problem-solving strategies, as well as working memory. The cognitive component that probably survives as least attenuated after repeated administration is the working memory component: no matter how many times one has performed the test, it is still possible to respond correctly only by keeping in mind the current sorting principle and continually updating it. To the extent that the dorsolateral prefrontal signal is the only rCBF activation that remains unattenuated with repeated administration, this signal likely corresponds to prefrontally linked working memory.

In contrast to our earlier results with SPECT and perhaps because of the greater sensitivity and resolution of the PET (with oxygen-15) method, bilateral activation was observed. It is interesting that in none of our studies of normal subjects performing the WCST did we find a relation between how well subjects did on the test and their degree of prefrontal activation. This lack of a direct correlation between the magnitude of the physiological response and the behavior, despite the consistent finding that the behavior activates this region, raises a number of questions. Is this simply an artifact of the WCST's being too easy and normal subjects' not having sufficient variance in performance? Or does it mean there is too much physiological redundancy (too many ways to physiologically compensate) for a consistent relationship to emerge? Perhaps the activation signal corresponds primarily to summoning the necessary neural circuits into action and not to how well they do their job. These possibilities will need to be addressed in subsequent studies.

In an effort to further define the cognitive correlates of the prefrontal activation during the WCST, Gold, Berman, Randolph, Goldberg, and Weinberger (1991) developed a novel working memory task that shares certain cognitive elements with the WCST but few of the primary sensory components. The task is a variant of the delayed-response test used to assess prefrontal function in the nonhuman primate. Subjects must select one of two squares that appear on a computer terminal after having seen a similar image a few seconds earlier, except that one of the squares in the earlier image was colored. Each selection is followed by feedback ("right" choice or "wrong") and then by a new set of yoked images. The subject learns from the feedback that a simple rule defines the correct choice. If the previous correct choice was the square that was colored a few seconds earlier, the next correct choice is the square that corresponded to the uncolored square, and so on. The working memory features of the task involve continually updating one's status with respect to the rule (whether choosing the same or the alternate square) and continuously keeping in mind which square was colored in the previous image. The rCBF results with PET in a sample of 12 normal subjects were remarkably similar to those from studies of the WCST.

In a preliminary analysis of the PET rCBF data using a method for mapping cerebral activation in three-dimensional space throughout the brain developed by Friston et al. (1989), we found that the physiological correlates of doing the WCST and of doing the delayed-alternation task are widespread and extend outside the dorsolateral prefrontal cortex. Both tasks seem to activate a network of cortical sites, which include the dorsolateral and orbital prefrontal cortices, parietal cortex, and probably limbic temporal cortex, though the precise location of the sites within each of these cortical regions varies slightly from task to task. This system of coactivated cortical sites is analogous to that observed by Gevins et al. (1987) and is also similar to the assembly described by Goldman-Rakic and Friedman (1991) as subserving working memory in the nonhuman primate.

In a related study, Andreasen et al. (1992) recently reported rCBF data while normal subjects performed a computerized version of a variant of the three-disk Tower of Hanoi task. The method used was a xenon-133 SPECT procedure. They reported that normal subjects tended to activate the prefrontal cortex during this task, especially the mesial prefrontal cortex. Although these findings are consistent with the lesion data on the three-disk tower task, the study suffered from serious methodological limitations that compromise its interpretation. In addition to uncertain anatomical referencing of the physiological data and weak statistical results, the control task was not designed to include motor responding as the tower task did. Thus the results of this study might simply reflect activation of the mesial supplemental and lateral primary motor cortices.

The observation that doing working memory tasks such as the WCST involves activation of a distributed network of interrelated cortical sites is consistent with current models of distributed parallel processing of cognitive information. It illustrates, moreover, the anatomical complexity involved in such models and the explanatory weakness of serial processing models, and it provides a possible explanation for why extraprefrontal damage can impair performance on "prefrontal" tasks. Future studies will address whether this network is the neural substrate of working memory or a more generic neural assembly involved in certain aspects of cognitive set preparation.

SCHIZOPHRENIA: AN EXAMPLE OF A DISORDER OF BEHAVIOR-LINKED PREFRONTAL DYSFUNCTION

In addition to the familiar symptoms of psychosis, patients suffering from schizophrenia often have profound difficulty adapting to the social and occupational exigencies of day-to-day existence. They have long been observed to manifest difficulties with planning their activities, with anticipating future events, and with using past experience to guide their behavior ("learning from experience"). These difficulties are especially apparent when patients are expected to function autonomously with minimal environmental structure and support—that is, when they must resort to internal resources to achieve goals. It has become increasingly popular to view these adaptational difficulties as secondary to fundamental cognitive deficits, and in view of the foregoing discussion, these deficits suggest impaired working memory and to that extent implicate specific neural system dysfunction (Goldberg, Gold, & Braff, 1991). This view is consistent with numerous studies showing that patients tend to perform poorly on a variety of cognitive tasks involving primary memory functions, and they also perform poorly on tests involving working memory, such as the WCST (Goldberg et al., 1991). The degree to which they manifest deficits on these tests has been shown to have prognostic importance and to predict the severity of social and occupational adaptation (Brier, Schrieber, Dyer, & Pickar, 1991; Goldberg, Ragland, et al., 1990). Moreover, the degree of cognitive dysfunction is not related to ongoing psychotic symptoms (Goldberg et al., 1993), which are not consistently predictive of outcome or disability, and is generally not improved with conventional treatment. Because impaired control of memory function appears to be a consistent finding in most studies of schizophrenic cognitive deficits, dysfunction of the limbic cortex of the medial temporal lobe and of the dorsolateral prefrontal cortex has been assumed to be the neural fingerprint of the deficits. Anatomical studies of the brains of patients with schizophrenia, both from in vivo anatomical neuroimaging techniques and from postmortem tissue examinations (Hyde, Casanova, Kleinman, & Weinberger, 1991), also suggest that these brain regions are morphologically deviant in this illness.

There have been a series of rCBF studies of patients with schizophrenia performing working memory tasks that appear to further support this assumption about prefrontal cortical dysfunction. Most of these studies involve measuring rCBF while patients and normal subjects used as controls perform the WCST. In every report, less activation of dorsolateral prefrontal cortex was observed in the patients with schizophrenia than in the normal controls (Berman & Weinberger 1991b).

We initially employed the xenon-133 technique to examine a sample of young (mean age = 29) but relatively chronic patients ($N = 20$) and normal controls ($N = 25$) (Weinberger et al., 1986). The patients had been medication free for at least four weeks. Although no differences in rCBF were found during the resting state or during the sensorimotor control task, highly significant hypoactivity of the dorsolateral prefrontal cortex during the WCST was found in the patients as a group. Moreover, subtracting the control task rCBF data from the WCST rCBF data for each group revealed significantly reduced WCST-related activation of the dorsolateral prefrontal cortex in the patients. The patients did not perform the task as well as did the controls. A second study in an independent sample ($N = 15$) of similar patients using the identical methodology replicated these results (Weinberger et al., 1988).

These initial studies raised several questions that were important in interpreting the implications of the findings. First, since the patient had been free of antipsychotic medications, they tended to manifest florid psychotic symptoms. Was it possible that their rCBF differences reflected this epiphenomenon? To address this possibility, we studied an additional sample of patients who were maintained on standard doses of standard antipsychotic medications and were generally less floridly symptomatic (Berman, Zec, & Weinberger, 1986). The results were the same as in the medication-free patients, indicating that acute symptomatic and medication status did not explain the findings. Second, since the patients performed more poorly than the normal subjects on the test, was it possible that the rCBF differences simply reflected poorer performance on a test, per se? Several studies addressed this point. We examined a sample of patients with schizophrenia performing a difficult, dynamically paced visual continuous performance task on which they also performed very poorly (Berman et al., 1986). Prefrontal rCBF did not differ significantly between patients and controls with this paradigm, perhaps because prefrontal activation was not required in the normals. In any case, simply doing poorly on a demanding cognitive task did not appear to explain prefrontal hypofunction during the WCST. This conclusion was confirmed in another study comparing patients and normal subjects during Raven's Progressive Matrices (RPM), a nonverbal reasoning and intelligence task that has traditionally been linked primarily to posterior cortical function (Berman, Illowsky, & Weinberger, 1988). Again, even though RPM is a difficult reasoning task and patients did not perform as well on it as the controls, prefrontal hypofunction was not seen. We suggested that the neural localization differences between RPM and the WCST may have something to do with the working memory demands of the latter, which tend not to be inherent in the former. To the extent that the WCST, in contrast to RPM, can be conceived of as requiring future-oriented processing, and to the extent that this processing correlates with prefrontal activation, such activation is defective in patients with schizophrenia.

The results of these studies left open three additional questions. First, although differences in prefrontal hypofunction were observed between groups of patients and normal controls, the likelihood that an individual patient had defective prefrontal function was not known. The issue is especially unclear because it is improbable that there is an absolutely normal quantitative value for prefrontal rCBF during the WCST. It is likely that this would vary across a broad range for a variety of reasons (see below) in any given individual. Second, what was the relation of the rCBF abnormality to other aspects of the neurobiology of schizophrenia, such as genetic predisposition and anatomical changes in the medial temporal lobe? And third, although acute medication status did not adequately explain the rCBF findings, was it possible that prior chronic treatment did?

These additional questions were addressed to some degree by a study of monozygotic twin pairs, some discordant ($N = 10$ pairs) and some concordant ($N = 8$ pairs) for schizophrenia (Berman, Torrey, Daniel, & Weinberger, 1992). The twin paradigm controls for many of the factors that are likely to account for interindividual variability in cognitive and physiological performance. In every discordant pair, the affected twin had less relative prefrontal rCBF during the WCST than did the unaffected twin, even if the pair did not differ in performance on the test. This indicated that prefrontal hypoactivity was a seemingly characteristic feature of schizophrenia that might be observable in every affected individual if there was some way of controlling for other factors that contribute to variance in the range of normal values. The data also indicated that this could not be accounted for by genetic predisposition, since genetic endowment was absolutely controlled. In other words, the failure of prefrontal function in the patients with schizophrenia had to be environmentally influenced. That absolute discrimination of affected from unaffected twin occurred only during the WCST and not during either the resting or control conditions suggested that this was a cognitively relevant deficit and that working memory was the relevant process (Figure 8.2).

In support of this conclusion was the finding that differences within pairs in prefrontal rCBF during the WCST strongly correlated (rho = .80, $p < .01$) with intrapair differences in the size of the hippocampus determined from anatomical scanning with magnetic resonance imaging (MRI) (Figure 8.3) (Weinberger, Berman, Suddath, & Torrey, 1992). Hippocampal size also had proved to be a reliable discriminator of affected from unaffected twin (Suddath, Christison, Torrey, & Weinberger, 1990). The anatomical parameter correlated with prefrontal rCBF only during the WCST, suggesting that when it was necessary to recruit the prefrontal-limbic network implicated in performance of the WCST (see below), the defect in this network (anatomical on the limbic side, physiological prefrontally) becomes apparent. Since the anatomical data also implicated a pathological process that had to be at least in part environmentally based, the results suggested that damage to the hippocampal formation represented a primary brain abnormality with far-reaching physiological implications for patients with this illness.

Finally, examination of the concordant twins addressed the question

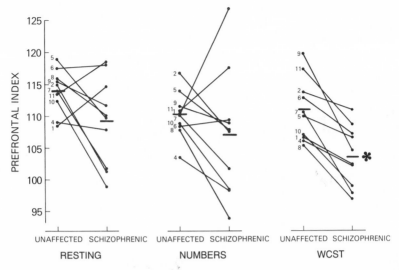

Figure 8.2   Comparison of relative prefrontal blood flow in monozygotic twins discordant for schizophrenia during three different conditions: a resting state, a sensorimotor matching to sample task, and the WCST. Each dot corresponds to an individual who is connected to his or her twin. The horizontal line indicates the group means. The asterisk indicates statistical significance by matched-pair t test of means ($p < .001$).

of prior long-term antipsychotic drug treatment. Concordant twins shared not just genetic and other similarities but also the experience of chronic schizophrenia. These pairs differed in little else but variance in amount of chronic drug therapy. In almost all cases the twin with the greater medication history had relatively greater prefrontal rCBF during the WCST, suggesting that this factor does not explain the basic finding in schizophrenia. This conclusion is further supported by a recent study of rCBF during the WCST in never-medicated, first-episode patients with schizophrenia, which also found them to be prefrontally hypofunctional relative to controls (Rubin et al., 1991).

Note that the rCBF data in schizophrenia, interpretable in terms of future-oriented processing, is not confined to the WCST. Andreasen et al. (1992) recently reported that prefrontal hypofunction was also seen during performance of a three-"ball" version of the Tower of Hanoi task. This study, however, must be considered in light of the methodological problems mentioned above.

CONCLUSIONS

A variety of human neuropsychological tasks thought to involve neural functions of the prefrontal cortex require cognitive processing that has

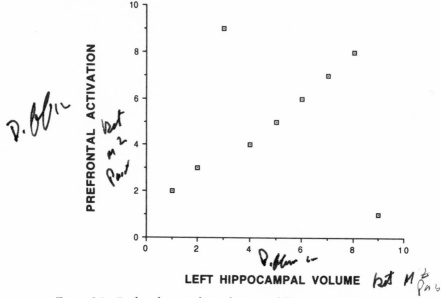

Figure 8.3   Rank order correlation between differences within monozygotic twin pairs discordant for schizophrenia on MRI based measurement of volume of left anterior hippocampal formation and rCBF activation associated with the WCST (Spearman rho = .80, $p < .01$).

future-oriented elements. Most of these use memory to anticipate events and guide future actions. Studies of patients with diseases or lesions of prefrontal cortex suggest that the prefrontal cortex subserves these cognitive functions. Recently the advent of methods for in vivo assessment of cerebral activity during performance of such tasks has made it possible to test these notions about anatomical localization. In a series of studies using several methods for determining rCBF, we and others have found that prefrontal cortex is activated during tasks such as the Wisconsin Card Sorting Test and during delayed-response tests. It appears, however, that the prefrontal cortex is one node in a network of interconnected and coactivated cortical regions that includes parietal and temporal cortices as well. This network may represent a neural assembly that provides the cognitive machinery for future-oriented processes. In the disease schizophrenia, where anatomical studies have implicated damage to the hippocampal region of the medial temporal lobe and functional brain imaging studies implicate prefrontal hypofunction, abnormalities of future-oriented cognitive processes have frequently been reported. Recent studies suggest that physiological hypofunction of the prefrontal cortex during tasks such as the WCST, perhaps because of a breakdown of the mechanisms of distributed function of prefrontal-limbic cortical networks, may account for these deficits.

REFERENCES

Anderson, S. W., Damasio, H., Jones, R. D., & Tranel, D. (1991). Wisconsin Card Sorting Test performance as a measure of frontal lobe damage. *Journal of Clinical and Experimental Neuropsychology, 13,* 909–922.

Andreasen, N. C., Rezai, K., Alliger, R., Swayze, V. W., Flaum, M., Kirchner, P., Cohen, G., & O'Leary, D. S. (1992). Hypofrontality in neuroleptic-naive patients and in patients with chronic schizophrenia: Assessment with xenon 133 single-photon emission computed tomography and the Tower of London. *Archives of General Psychiatry, 49,* 943–958.

Berman, K. F., Illowsky, B., & Weinberger, D. R. (1988). Physiological dysfunction of dorsolateral prefrontal cortex in schizophrenia: 4. Further evidence for regional and behavioral specificity. *Archives of General Psychiatry, 45,* 616–622.

Berman, K. F., Randolph, C., Gold, J., Holt, D., Jones, D. W., Goldberg, T. E., Carson, R. E., Herscovitch, P., & Weinberger, D. R. (1991). Physiological activation of frontal lobe studied with positron emission tomography and oxygen-15 water during working memory tasks. *Journal of Cerebral Blood Flow and Metabolism, 11,* S851.

Berman, K. F., Torrey, E. F., Daniel, D. G., & Weinberger, D. R. (1992). Regional cerebral blood flow in monozygotic twins discordant and concordant for schizophrenia. *Archives of General Psychiatry, 49,* 927–934.

Berman, K. F., & Weinberger, D. R. (1990). Lateralization of cortical function during cognition: Studies in normals and patients with schizophrenia. *Journal of Neurology, Neurosurgery, and Psychiatry, 53,* 150–160.

Berman, K. F., & Weinberger, D. R. (1991a). Cognitive and physiological factors that affect regional cerebral blood flow and other measures of brain function. In M. Piksic & R. C. Reba (Eds.), *Radiopharmaceuticals and brain pathology studied with PET and SPECT* (pp. 427–442). Boca Raton, FL: CRC Press.

Berman, K. F., & Weinberger, D. R. (1991b). Functional localization in the brain in schizophrenia. In A. Tasman & S. M. Goldfinger (Eds.), *American Psychiatric Press review of psychiatry* (vol. 10, pp. 24–59). Washington, DC: American Psychiatric Press.

Berman, K. F., Zec, R. F., & Weinberger, D. R. (1986). Physiological dysfunction of dorsolateral prefrontal cortex in schizophrenia: 2. Role of medication, attention, and mental effort. *Archives of General Psychiatry, 43,* 126–135.

Brier, A., Schreiber, J. L., Dyer, J., and Pickar, D. (1991). National Institute of Mental Health longitudinal study of chronic schizophrenia. *Archives of General Psychiatry, 48,* 239–246.

Friston, K. J., Passingham, R. E., Nutt, J. G., Heather, J. D., Sawle, G. V., & Frackowiak, R. S. J. (1989). Localisation in PET images: Direct fitting of the intercommissural (AC-PC) line. *Journal of Cerebral Blood Flow and Metabolism, 9,* 690–695.

Fuster, J. M. (1989). *The prefrontal cortex.* New York: Raven Press.

Gevins, A. S., Morgan, N. H., Bressler, S. L., Cutillo, B. A., White, R. M., Illes, J., Greer, D. S., Doyle, J. C., & Zeitlin, G. M. (1987). Human neuroelectric patterns predict performance accuracy. *Science, 235,* 580–586.

Gold, J., Berman, K., Randolph, C., Goldberg, T., & Weinberger, D. R. (1991). PET validation and clinical application of a novel prefrontal task. *Neuropsychology, 13,* 81.

Goldberg, T. E., Gold, J. M., & Braff, D. L. (1991). Neuropsychological functioning and time-linked information processing in schizophrenia. In A. Tasman & S. M. Goldfinger (Eds.), *American Psychiatric Press review of psychiatry* (vol. 10, pp. 60–78). Washington, DC: American Psychiatric Press.

Goldberg, T. E., Greenberg, R., Griffin, S., Gold, J. M., Pickar, D., Kleinman, J. E., & Weinberger, D. R. (1993). The impact of clozapine on cognitive impairment and psychiatric symptomatology in patients with schizophrenia. *British Journal of Psychiatry, 162,* 43–48.

Goldberg, T. E., Ragland, J. D., Gold, J., Bigelow, L. B., Torrey, E. F., & Weinberger, D. R. (1990). Neuropsychological assessment of monozygotic twins discordant for schizophrenia. *Archives of General Psychiatry, 47,* 1066–1072.

Goldberg, T. E., Saint-Cyr, J. A., & Weinberger, D. R. (1990). Assessment of procedural learning and problem solving in schizophrenic patients by Tower of Hanoi type tasks. *Journal of Neuropsychiatry, 2,* 165–173.

Goldman-Rakic, P. S. (1987). Circuitry of primate prefrontal cortex and regulation of behavior by representational memory. In F. Plum (Ed.), *The handbook of physiology: Section 1. The nervous system: Vol. 5. Higher functions of the brain* (pp. 373–417). Bethesda, MD: American Physiological Society.

Goldman-Rakic, P. S., & Friedman, H. R. (1991). The circuitry of working memory revealed by anatomy and metabolic imaging. In H. S. Levin, H. M. Eisenberg, & A. L. Benton (Eds.), *Frontal lobe function and dysfunction* (pp. 72–91). New York: Oxford University Press.

Hyde, T., Casanova, M., Kleinman, J. E., & Weinberger, D. R. (1991). Neuroanatomical and neurochemical pathology in schizophrenia. In A. Tasman & S. M. Goldfinger (Eds.), *American Psychiatric Press review of Psychiatry* (vol. 10, pp. 7–23). Washington, DC: American Psychiatric Press.

Ingvar, P. H. (1985). Memory of the future: An essay on the temporal organization of conscious awareness. *Human Neurobiology, 4,* 127–136.

Jacobsen, C. F. (1931). A study of cerebral function in learning: The frontal lobes. *Journal of Comparative Neurology, 52,* 271–340.

Luria, A. R. (1966). *Higher cortical functions in man.* New York: Basic Books.

Marenco, S., Coppola, R., Daniel, D. G., Zigun, J. R., & Weinberger, D. R. (1993). Regional cerebral blood flow activation with the Wisconsin Card Sort Test in normal subjects studied by Xe-133 dynamic SPECT: Comparison of absolute values, percent distribution values, and covariance analysis. *Psychiatry Research: Neuroimaging, 50,* 177–192.

Oscar-Berman, M., McNamara, P., & Freedman, M. (1991). Delayed-response tasks: Parallels between experimental ablation studies and findings in patients with frontal lesions. In H. S. Levin, H. M. Eisenberg, & A. L. Benton (Eds.), *Frontal lobe function and dysfunction* (pp. 230–255). New York: Oxford University Press.

Parks, R. W., Crockett, D. J., Tuokko, H., Beattie, B. L., Ashford, J. W., Coburn, K. L., Zec, R. F., Becker, R. E., McGeer, P. L., & McGeer, E. G. (1989). Neuropsychological "systems efficiency" and positron emission tomography. *Journal of Neuropsychiatry, 1,* 269–282.

Petersen, S. E., Fox, P. T., Posner, M. I., Mintun, M., & Raichle, M. E. (1988). Positron emission tomographic studies of the cortical anatomy of single-word processing. *Nature, 331,* 585–589.

Petersen, S. E., Fox, P. T., Posner, M. I., Mintun, M., & Raichle, M. E. (1991). Positron emission tomographic studies of the processing of single words. *Journal of Cognitive Neuroscience, 1,* 153–170.

Pribram, K. H. (1969). The primate frontal cortex. *Neuropsychologia, 7,* 259–266.

Raichle, M. E., Fiez, J., Videen, T. O., Fox, P. T., Vardo, J. V., & Petersen, S. E. (1991). Practice-related changes in human brain functional anatomy. *Society for Neuroscience, Abstracts, 17,* 21.

Robinson, A. L, Heaton, R. K., Lehman, R. A. W., & Stilson, D. W. (1980). The utility of the Wisconsin Card Sorting Test in detecting and localizing frontal lobe lesions. *Journal of Consulting and Clinical Psychology, 48,* 605–614.

Rubin, P., Holm, S., Friberg, L., Videbeck, P., Andersen, H. S., Bendsen, B. B., Strømsø, N., Larsen, J. K., Lassen, N. A., & Hemmingsen, R. (1991). Altered modulation of prefrontal and subcortical brain activity in newly diagnosed schizophrenia and schizophreniform disorder: A regional cerebral blood flow study. *Archives of General Psychiatry, 48,* 987–995.

Sergent, J., Zuck, E., Lévesque, M., & MacDonald, B. (1992). Positron emission tomography study of letter and object processing: Empirical findings and methodological considerations. *Cerebral Cortex, 2,* 68–80.

Suddath, R. L., Christison, G. W., Torrey, E. F., & Weinberger, D. R. (1990). Cerebral anatomical abnormalities in monozygotic twins discordant for schizophrenia. *New England Journal of Medicine, 322,* 789–794.

Teuber, H.-L. (1972). Unity and diversity of frontal lobe functions. *Acta Neurobiologiae Experimentalis, 32,* 625–656.

Warach, S., Gur, R. C., Gur, R. E., Skolnick, B. E., Obrist, W., & Reivich, M. (1992). Decreases in frontal and parietal lobe regional cerebral blood flow related to habituation. *Journal of Cerebral Blood Flow and Metabolism, 12,* 546–553.

Weigl, E. (1941). On the psychology of so-called processes of abstraction. *Journal of Abnormal and Social Psychology, 36,* 3–33.

Weinberger, D. R., Berman, K. F., & Illowsky, B. (1988). Physiological dysfunction of dorsolateral prefrontal cortex in schizophrenia: 3. A new cohort and evidence for a monoaminergic mechanism. *Archives of General Psychiatry, 45,* 609–615.

Weinberger, D. R., Berman, K. F., Suddath, R., & Torrey, E. F. (1992). Evidence for dysfunction of a prefrontal-limbic network in schizophrenia: An MRI and rCBF study of discordant monozygotic twins. *American Journal of Psychiatry, 149,* 890–897.

Weinberger, D. R., Berman, K. F., & Zec, R. F. (1986). Physiological dysfunction of dorsolateral prefrontal cortex in schizophrenia: 1. Regional cerebral blood flow (rCBF) evidence. *Archives of General Psychiatry, 43,* 114–125.

Wise, R., Chollet, F., Hadar, U., Friston, K., Hoffner, E., & Frackowiak, R. (1991). Distribution of cortical neural networks involved in word comprehension and word retrieval. *Brain, 114,* 1803–1817.

Chapter Nine

The Working Memory Function of the Prefrontal Cortices

Implications for Developmental and Individual Differences in Cognition

Bruce F. Pennington

By virtue of the singular process of working memory, the prefrontal cortex maintains access to internalized representations for the time necessary to complete a response or response sequence. The emergence of this capacity in postnatal life could accomplish the dual purpose of initiating and guiding correct responses and per force disallowing or inhibiting incorrect ones that would be mediated by centers of associative conditioning.

P. S. Goldman-Rakic (1987a)

Thus, working memory is a computational arena or workspace. . . . When working memory is viewed as a computational arena, it becomes clear that its capacity should be construed not just as a storage capacity (perhaps measured in chunks), but as operational capacity or throughput.

P. A. Carpenter and M. A. Just (1989)

In spite of all similarities every living situation has, like a newborn child, a new face, that has never been before and will never come again. It demands of you a reaction which cannot be prepared beforehand. It demands nothing of what

The work reported in this chapter was supported by National Institute of Mental Health grants MH00419 (RSDA), MH38870 (MERIT award), and MH45916, as well as by National Institute of Child Health and Human Development Center Grant HD27802. I thank Janette Benson, Loisa Bennetto, Geraldine Dawson, Frank Dempster, Kurt Fischer, Patricia Goldman-Rakic, Marshall Haith, Dan Levine, Sally Ozonoff, Ralph Roberts, Sally Rogers, Jim Russell, and Lise and Michael Wallach for their helpful comments.

> is past. It demands presence, responsibility, it demands you. I call a great
> character one who by his actions and attitudes satisfies the claim of situations
> out of deep readiness to respond with his whole life, and in such a way that
> the sum of his actions and attitudes expresses at the same time the unity of his
> being in its willingness to accept responsibility.
>
> M. Buber (1955)

This chapter integrates research on cognitive differences from several disparate areas—developmental neuropsychology, cognitive development in both youth and age, cognitive aging, and intelligence—by means of a working memory theory of the functions of the prefrontal cortices. The general argument will be that one very important mechanism underlying cognitive differences—whether between species or between children of different ages, individuals at a given age, or older adults of different ages—is the working memory function of the prefrontal cortices. Thus this chapter is a beginning attempt at an integration that has been sorely lacking across the various research traditions concerned with cognitive differences.

To support my general argument, I will (1) define working memory more precisely, distinguish it from both short- and long-term memory, and use this construct to provide an integrated account of the diversity of executive function deficits observed after prefrontal damage; (2) present data from our studies indicating that executive functions, and by inference working memory, are especially vulnerable in various developmental disorders, suggesting that working memory is an important basis of both individual and developmental cognitive differences; (3) review other data indicating a key role for working memory in individual differences in intelligence; (4) examine the role of working memory in cognitive development in childhood; (5) argue that declines in prefrontally mediated working memory play a key role in cognitive aging; (6) place working memory within a new integrated theory of individual and developmental differences in cognition and intelligence; and (7) end with a consideration of the implications and problems of my account. Hence the chapter is divided into these seven sections. The first and longest section comprises five subsections, concerned with a brief historical overview of theories of prefrontal functions; a definition of working memory; the computational dynamics of working memory; relations among working, short-term, and long-term memory; and how to account for the diversity of executive deficits.

A WORKING MEMORY ACCOUNT OF
PREFRONTAL FUNCTIONS

Historical Overview of Theories of Prefrontal Functions

One of the general themes of this chapter is that the prefrontal cortices (PFCs) have a much more central and pervasive role in human cognition than is usually recognized. Early accounts did accord the PFCs a special place in human cognition—one consistent with their large relative size, unique interconnectivity to the rest of the brain, and rapid expansion in primate brain evolution. For instance, Burdach (1819/1939) called the frontal lobes "the special workshop of the thinking process," and both Harlow (1868) and Bianchi (1922) emphasized the planning deficits that follow frontal injury, clearly linking the frontal lobes to future-oriented processes. However, through much of this century the PFCs have been viewed as either silent or a mystery. Contributing to this negative view was the finding that PFC lesions acquired in adulthood had relatively minor effects on IQ tests (Hebb, 1945) and on other standardized tests of language, memory, and spatial cognition. So difficulties in the cognitive characterization and measurement of functions mediated by the PFCs have led to an underestimation of their importance, even as much more detailed cognitive models and measures of other domains such as memory, vision, and language were developing rapidly. More recent work by Goldman-Rakic (1987a,b, 1988, 1992, this volume), Shallice (1982, 1988), Weinberger (1992, this volume), and others has helped clarify the nature of prefrontal functions and reemphasized their important role in both normal and abnormal cognition. Nonetheless, a clear, coherent cognitive theory of their functions remains elusive.

Thus the first question to be addressed is, Can we provide a more coherent and parsimonious cognitive account of the diversity of functions, tasks, and symptoms attributed to the PFCs? These diverse functions, often termed "executive functions," include such things as planning, set shifting, inhibition, selective attention, and initiation.

With regard to tasks, unlike the situation in Hebb's time, we now have several tests on which patients with PFC lesions are selectively and sometimes dramatically impaired. These tests include the Wisconsin Card Sorting Test (WCST), the Tower of Hanoi disk-transfer task (TOH), the Stroop Color-Word Interference Test, the delayed-response (DR) and delayed-alternation (DA) tasks, the antisaccade task (AST), and others. The trouble is that a given patient with PFC damage is rarely impaired on all these tasks, and some such patients are not impaired on any of them (Damasio, Tranel, & Damasio, 1991; Shallice & Burgess, 1991). Nonetheless, such patients exhibit striking impairments in the planning activities of everyday life. Moreover, factor analytic investigations of batteries of executive function tasks (Levin, Culhane, Mendel-sohn, et al., 1991; Welsh, Pennington, & Groisser, 1991) have failed to find one common "prefrontal" factor.

Third, with regard to symptoms, patients with PFC lesions exhibit a somewhat baffling array of behavioral alterations. Their symptoms include incontinence and other socially inappropriate and impulsive behaviors, but also withdrawal and lack of initiative; perseveration but also lack of persistence; distractibility but also overfocusing of attention. Such patients also have difficulty planning and organizing everyday activities, programming sequential movements (including voluntary eye movements), processing text, and maintaining narrative coherence.

To understand this diversity of functions, tasks, and behavioral symptoms associated with the PFCs, we need a better understanding of their cognitive function, which the next three sections attempt to provide.

Definition of Working Memory

I propose that the construct of working memory, properly defined, begins to provide a unified explanation for this diversity of functions, tasks, and symptoms associated with the frontal lobes, one that makes much better contact with recent cognitive theories than an executive function account and that permits an integration across the various areas concerned with cognitive differences. There are several key aspects to the definition of working memory proposed here. The opening quotations from Goldman-Rakic (1987a) and Carpenter and Just (1989) contain most of these ideas, and my conception of working memory has been heavily influenced by their work. So working memory is a computational arena, in which information relevant to a current task is both maintained on line and subjected to further processing. Because it is a limited-capacity system, inhibition or interference control is intrinsic to its operation (see also Cohen & Servan-Schreiber, 1992; Dempster, 1991). So the same mechanism both maintains some information on line *and* inhibits other information.

In addition, since the overall function of working memory is to decide what to do next, this competitive dynamic extends to action selection. Action selection is an important bottleneck in the cognitive system (analogous to the famous von Neumann bottleneck in computer architecture). It appears that a limited-capacity central resource is involved in most action selection, even on very simple tasks, across stimuli of different modalities, and after considerable practice (see Pashler, 1992, for a review). This conclusion is based on studies of response time (RT) in dual task situations, where both tasks involve response uncertainty and therefore response selection; in contrast, no interference is produced if the secondary task does not require response selection, as is the case in a repetitive motor or sensory attention task. Thus nervous systems can undoubtedly process much information in parallel, but in a very important sense can do only one thing at a time. Consequently, under the conditions detailed below, adaptive action selection requires working memory. Working memory integrates information from many brain systems so as to select actions that maximize the organism's adaptive success. The integration and action selection occurs through a dynamic, competitive process in which inhibition of many other candidate actions is an inevitable by-product.

Second, we can think of the computational problem solved by working memory as a constraint satisfaction problem in the sense discussed in McClelland and Rumelhart (1987). Such a problem is one whose solution requires the simultaneous satisfaction of a large number of constraints, of which some may be "hard" or obligatory and others "weak" or desirable. Solution of such a problem involves satisfying as many of the most important constraints as possible. Such problems can be very difficult to solve, partly because the search space of possible solutions is very large. Connectionist networks solve such problems in a very natural way, however. Constraints are represented by units, the importance of a given constraint is represented by the strength of its unit's connections, and the relation among constraints is represented by the sign $(+$ or $-)$ of the connection between units. From this formulation, a global goodness of fit function can be defined; solution of the constraint satisfaction problem involves maximizing this global goodness function.

Returning to working memory and the prefrontal cortices, we can think of each of the multiple inputs into the PFCs as providing a separate constraint. The more constraints an organism can represent, the better the fit of the selected action to a particular (and often unique) adaptive environment. Natural selection has led to an often exquisite match between an animal's behavioral repertoire and its environmental niche through a protracted, gradual optimization process. Learning permits similar behavioral optimization to occur within an animal's life span, but prefrontal cortex allows the fastest adaptation of all, often to a unique context. (See Calvin, 1989, for a similar, Darwinian account of action selection.)

Third, an important corollary of the previous point is that the processing of prefrontally mediated working memory is context specific and transient. Multiple sources of constraint, each with many possible values, quickly lead to many unique or novel combinations of constraints—hence context specificity. The opening quotation from the famous theologian Martin Buber (1955) strikingly captures this context specificity. The transience of working memory follows from the fact that it must deal with unique or novel contexts.

So just as it is important to have some parts of a nervous system learn in a fairly permanent, archival fashion, it is likewise important to have other parts that are uncommitted; otherwise the organism could never deal with novelty. This consideration leads to a nontrivial, testable prediction: Synaptic strengths in at least some parts of prefrontal cortex should not be modified by long-term potentiation, for instance, in the same way as the synapses in posterior cortex involved in the storage of long-term memories.

For clarity, I will now summarize this definition of working memory and explicitly address its relation to two other constructs, inhibition and short-term memory. Working memory, as defined here, is a limited-capacity computational arena. Its key characteristics are *action selection,* which operates through a dynamic process of *constraint satisfaction,* which must necessarily be *context specific* and *transient.* Just as selection logically implies deselection, activation of some things in this limited-capacity system necessarily implies *inhibition* of other things. So instead of reifying inhibition as a separate cognitive process, this account views inhibition as intrinsic to the competitive dynamics of the working memory system, just as the opening quotation from Goldman-Rakic (1987a) suggests. I will be more specific about possible mechanisms for these competitive dynamics shortly.

With regard to short-term memory (STM), the relation proposed here is similar to that proposed by Baddeley (1986), but with one key difference. In Baddeley's account the working memory system has three components: a central executive plus two modality specific short-term memories, the articulatory loop and the visuospatial scratch pad. So in his account, separate verbal and visual STMs are subsystems within working memory. In contrast, my notion of working memory corresponds only to the central executive portion of Baddeley's model; so neither verbal or visual STM is a subsystem within what I am calling working memory. As does Baddeley, I view these STMs as serving working memory, but since the two constructs are empirically dissociable in both normal and abnormal populations, I think it is more useful to treat them as distinct.

Finally, it is worth addressing a third confusion that may arise from the use of the term "working memory," especially in a book on future-oriented processes. Specifically, How can a cognitive system whose cardinal function, action selection, is future oriented have a past-oriented cognitive process, "memory," in its name? I believe this is a superficial problem. The computational arena that I am labeling working memory (WM) holds representations of past, present, and future on line, all to act as constraints on action selection. This process is undoubtedly future oriented. It is a memory process in that these various representations are all maintained briefly over time, in a common system so they can interact. Hence WM is transient. The main reason for choosing "working memory" as the name for the cognitive system I am describing is that the current use of this term in cognitive psychology and neuropsychology comes closest to the concept I am trying to elaborate. Moreover, this term, used with a similar meaning, is also found in several of the literatures I wish to integrate: cognitive development, cognitive aging, and intelligence. I could have picked another label, such as "computational arena," "on-line processing," "central executive," or even "future-oriented processes" for the theoretical construct I am elaborating here, but any of these terms would have caused even more confusion. I hope that by the end of this section my construct of working memory will be clear enough so that both its overlap with and its differences from other uses of the term will be clear.

In what follows, I will give a more specific account of the *cognitive* mechanisms operating in the working memory system proposed here and more fully characterize the relation between working memory and both short-term memory and long-term memory. I will then use my account of WM to integrate results across various traditions concerned with cognitive differences.

Computational Dynamics of Working Memory: Avoiding the Homunculus Problem

The reader may be wondering at this point how this account avoids the homunculus problem implicit in the metaphor of a central executive or a supervisory attentional system (Shallice, 1988). How can we have planning without a planner, future-oriented behavior without an agent who is oriented to the future, intentionality without an intender, reference without an Intender (in the philosophical sense of Intention), or consciousness without a central observer? This is a difficult issue because our everyday psychological language is inextricably tied to the metaphor of a single conscious agent who receives information and decides what to do next. How to think about consciousness and agency without using this metaphor is discussed at length by Dennett (1991), who replaces what he calls "the central witness" in the "Cartesian theater" with a "multiple drafts" theory of consciousness. In his theory there is no one place where it all comes together, but instead there are varying distributed coalitions of "specialists" evoked by different circumstances.

I think the account of WM given here is compatible with Dennett's (1991) view, as long as we do not slip into thinking of working memory or the prefrontal cortices as the single seat of consciousness or the place where decisions are made. The unique connectivity of the prefrontal cortex allows a widely distributed ensemble of activated brain regions to dynamically interact at the same time (Goldman-Rakic, 1988). We could say that this distributed ensemble is the momentary "localization" of consciousness or planning, but in the next moment the distribution of activated regions would shift.

The real test of whether we have avoided the homunculus problem, however, is to make these ideas about prefrontally mediated working memory more formal and computational and then see if the resulting model can perform executive function tasks without needing an executive. As I mentioned earlier, I think the key idea here will turn out to be that of constraint satisfaction, which resembles Darwinian natural selection except on a time scale of seconds and minutes instead of eons (cf. Calvin, 1989; Edelman, 1987). Both organisms and plans can be thought of as intentional systems that evolve through a process of generation and selection. Both are dynamic configurations and reconfigurations of simpler elements, none of which contains an executive or "intender." Instead, intentionality is derived (from genes, ultimately) and emergent (Dennett, 1987). There is nothing miraculous or discontinuous about the mechanisms of human thought, including future-oriented thought. Brains have evolved just as other organs (and organisms) have evolved. Within a brain, the computational mechanisms or dynamics should be similar from the lowest to highest levels of processing; moreover, these mechanisms should have a deep formal similarity to the mechanisms or dynamics found in various biological systems.

Both brains and other biological systems are nonlinear, dynamic systems. (Their operation can at times be chaotic, in the formal mathematical sense of that term; that is, they can exhibit extreme sensitivity to slight variations in initial conditions—the "butterfly effect.") The various states that a nonlinear dynamic system can take on are described by an attractor topology, and the evolution of the system over time can be described as movement through attractor space. Connectionist networks, which simulate the function of actual neuronal networks with varying degrees of realism, are likewise nonlinear dynamic systems whose behavior can be described using attractors. One appealing characteristic of connectionist networks that is highly relevant for this construct of WM is that they allow for both rulelike and context-specific processing within the same mechanism (Van Orden, Pennington, & Stone, 1990). Highly covariant mappings between input and output lead to deep attractors, whereas more context-specific mappings lead to shallow attractors.

How can we apply these connectionist concepts to understanding the computational dynamics of prefrontally mediated WM? Since we have already argued that the problem solved by PFC draws on the broadest context available to the organism, the problem it faces is how to guide action selection by some of the shallowest attractors of all and to simultaneously avoid deep attractors. Why do I say "shallowest"? Because sometimes the combination of constraints specifying a context is unique. As a result, such contexts for action selection are completely novel; no attractor already exists. How does WM accomplish this seemingly impossible task? In some sense, it must temporarily alter the prevailing attractor topology. One way it could do this is by detecting covariation among the constellation of constraints currently available to it; this covariation would temporarily lead to a new attractor topology.

If we think about tasks that have been found to be sensitive to PFC lesions, they generally require the subject to use a broader and sometimes novel context to guide action selection, simultaneously inhibiting an action based on an established and deep attractor. Another way of putting this is to say that such tasks require the subject to override an old "meaning" of an input and to base action selection on a new "meaning." For example, the Stroop test requires subjects to name ink colors instead of printed words; the delayed-alternation task requires subjects to look in the location opposite from where they saw the reward hidden; and the Wisconsin Card Sorting Test requires subjects to sort by a different dimension than the one that was just reinforced.

So I am proposing that the computational principles that operate in the neural networks of the PFC and related structures are fundamentally the same as those that operate in other parts of the brain. All the brain's networks are nonlinear dynamic systems that are sensitive to both covariant relations and context-specific ones. What is different about PFC is that its unique connectivity makes available the broadest range of contextual constraints.

If we examine the input and output connections of PFC, it is clear that this pattern of connectivity is consistent with this computational function. A given area of PFC has recurrent (two-way) connections with much of the rest of the brain, as well as with other areas of PFC. For example, there are recurrent connections with posterior neocortex, basal ganglia, thalamus, hippocampus, and brain stem nuclei. Goldman-Rakic (1987a,b, 1988) has described this connectivity in detail and argued that it is consistent with parallel distributed processing.

Several previous cognitive models of prefrontal functions have been proposed, some more formal than others. All can be seen as embodying processes of pooling, competition, and selection. Norman and Shallice (1980) made an early attempt. An appealing feature of their model was that action selection was ordinarily handled by "contention scheduling" among competing productions. In situations where contention scheduling did not work, a supervisory attentional system (SAS) was called into play. The main drawbacks of their model are that it is not computational and that it includes an unanalyzed "executive" processor (the SAS). More recently, connectionist modelers have tackled this problem and have provided models in which there is no executive and action selection is accomplished through a dynamic competitive process. Dehaene and Changeux (1989, 1991) and Levine, Leven, and Prueitt (1992) have each provided simulations of classic frontal tasks, such as the delayed-response and alternation tasks, and the Wisconsin Card Sorting Test. These models also involve competition but contain no executive; they simulate frontal performance by weakening the effect of reinforcement from recent trials, allowing overlearned responses to predominate. These models also contain processes that may be interpreted as working memory.

Cohen and Servan-Schreiber (1992) have further elaborated how inhibition falls naturally out of the dynamics of a connectionist WM system. In their simulations of three frontal tasks, whether a prepotent response is chosen or inhibited is a result of dynamic competition among pooled activation vectors. One activation vector arises from context units that maintain an internal representation of the problem context.

Using a network that simulates performance on the Stroop test, their model receives inputs about the current ink color and word name, which project onto hidden units. Ordinarily the strength of the word connections are stronger, because of greater word-naming experience relative to color naming experience. Hence, word connections would dominate action selection unless opposed by something else. In this model the "something else" is provided by the "task demand" units, which are really WM units that maintain a representation of the current problem context. If this context is color naming, than the task demand input helps to override the otherwise prepotent word naming response, although generating the correct response takes longer because of the increased competition (hence the Stroop effect).

Cohen and Servan-Schreiber (1992) suggest that the extent to which a task taps prefrontal function is a joint product of how strong the prepotent response is and how difficult it is to maintain the internal representation of context in working memory. My colleague Ralph Roberts has used these two dimensions, prepotency and WM load, to provide an integrated account of a wide range of executive tasks (Roberts, Hager, & Heron, in press).

Although it is impressive that these various connectionist models simulate both normal and abnormal performance on tasks previously shown to be sensitive to PFC lesions, nonetheless there are aspects of the general computational account given earlier that are not fully captured in these models. For instance, in the Cohen and Servan-Schreiber (1992) models, context sensitivity is not an intrinsic property of the whole network. Instead, it is "built in" by adding special context units. As I implied earlier, connectionist networks without special context units can nonetheless exhibit context specificity, so it would be desirable to have the context specificity of a model of the PFCs arise out of the intrinsic dynamics rather than being localized in special context units. Second, their model does not use a recurrent architecture or satisfy multiple constraints, whereas the actual connectivity of the PFCs involves recurrent connections between the PFCs and several other brain regions.

In summary, I am arguing that a recurrent, connectionist network could conceivably simulate the computational dynamics of the PFCs, and solve PFCs' constraint satisfaction problem. Such a network would avoid the homunculus problem in much the same way that connectionist models of other domains of performance avoid discrete representations of roles or symbols—by using distributed representations and competition resulting in a system that is sensitive to both covariation and context specificity. I now turn to how the WM system relates to other memory systems.

Relations among Working Memory, Short-Term Memory, and Long-Term Memory

The distinction between short-term memory and long-term memory (LTM), as well as the idea that short-term memory differences relate to intellectual differences, dates from the 19th century. William James (1890) distinguished primary and secondary memory, and his distinction continues to be used in modern cognitive psychology. Primary memory refers to holding information in conscious awareness, whereas secondary memory refers to the retrieval of information no longer in conscious awareness. It seems intuitively obvious that the capacity of primary memory, how much information one can "hold in mind" at one time, should be related to intelligence. Several 19th-century authorities made this connection, including Jacobs (1887), Galton (1887), and Binet and Simon (1905), who included a digit-span measure in the first IQ test. Even earlier, Oliver Wendell Holmes (1871) called span "a very simple mental dynamometer which may yet find its place in education" (cited in Dempster, 1985, p. 215).

In retrospect, the operationalization of primary or short-term memory by the digit-span task is unfortunate because this task encourages a simplistic, capacity view of primary memory. In fact, digit span is frequently normal in various neurological disorders that severely impair higher cognitive functions; examples include various dementias, limbic amnesia, and some of the developmental disorders discussed later. Moreover, digit span is less closely related to normal intellectual differences than other measures of primary memory that tap its processing function. For instance, in a dual task experiment, Baddeley and Hitch (1974) found that a concurrent digit-span task with a near span load of six digits interfered with a reasoning task much less than would be expected if both tasks depended on the same STM capacity or resource. This result, among others, led to Baddeley's WM model (1986, 1992) in which digit span would be handled by the articulatory loop, whereas reasoning tasks would depend more on the central executive.

To emphasize the active processing functions of primary or short-term memory, many cognitive researchers have adopted the term "working memory" (e.g., Anderson, 1974, 1983; Daneman & Carpenter, 1980; Schneider & Shiffrin, 1977), either using this term to replace "short-term memory" or redefining STM as a system distinct and functionally separate from working memory (Brainerd & Kingma, 1984; Case, 1978; Greeno, 1973). This redefined STM is now seen as a passive storage system. As discussed earlier, this is essentially the theoretical position taken here.

In terms of tasks, verbal STM as defined here can be operationalized by a simple digit-span task. Working memory is frequently operationalized by tasks that require concurrent storage and processing, such as the Sentence Span task (Daneman & Carpenter, 1980) or the Counting Span task (Case, Kurland, & Goldberg, 1982). Tasks such as these exhibit greater changes in development (in both youth and age) and a stronger relation to individual differences in intellectual performance than span tasks (see Craik & Jennings, 1992, and Dempster, 1985, for reviews). Although these traditional WM tasks include some of the aspects of the WM construct developed here, they do not capture other aspects as well, such as action selection and multiple constraint satisfaction. Moreover, because of their storage component, WM tasks such as Sentence Span or Counting Span may show moderate correlations with simple digit span, which is inconsistent with the position taken here that WM and STM are distinct systems.

The relation between WM and STM has been tested in several studies. Klapp and colleagues (Klapp, Marshburn, & Lester, 1983) documented the ubiquity of the confusion between WM and verbal STM in cognitive psychology. They then conducted systematic experiments demonstrating the independence of WM and verbal STM in normal adults. Brainerd and Kingma (1985) documented that within the same task there was stochastic independence in young children between verbal STM for background facts and WM-related, reasoning performance. In two other experiments they found that measures of each construct were affected by separate manipulations in young children. These authors also argued that WM changes are more important than STM changes in cognitive development.

Cantor, Engle, and Hamilton (1991) recently explored the relations among verbal STM, WM, and verbal intelligence (as measured by the verbal Scholastic Aptitude Test [SAT]) among young adults. Working

	Transient	Archival
Prospective	WM	HPM?
Retrospective	STM	LTM

Figure 9.1   Relation of working memory to short-term memory and long-term memory.

memory and verbal STM loaded on separate factors and accounted for separate variances in verbal intelligence. Moreover, the relation between verbal STM and verbal SAT was strongest for verbal STM items and tasks that afforded the *least* opportunity for rehearsal, consistent with Baddeley's (1986) conception of verbal STM as a simple, passive storage buffer. Morris and Jones (1990) have also provided experimental evidence for the separation between WM and STM. They found that manipulations that affect STM, such as irrelevant speech and articulatory suppression, do not affect an important component of WM—memory updating.

Let me now detail the theoretical rationale for why working memory should be distinct from other kinds of memory. There are two useful distinctions here, both relating to time, but in different ways. The first distinction concerns how permanent a given memory is. This is the distinction between "transient" memory and relatively permanent or "archival" memory. The second distinction pertains to future versus past orientation. Memory, as we usually use the term, is oriented toward the past. Yet we also remember things we will do in the future. I will use the terms "retrospective" and "prospective" to refer to the past and future orientations of memory. Since our memories of our future plans can be either transient or fairly permanent, this second distinction is orthogonal to the first, thus yielding four cells (Figure 9.1). We see that WM, STM, and LTM fall into different cells in this matrix: WM is prospective, unlike STM, and transient, unlike LTM. The fourth cell is occupied by "habitual prospective memory" (HPM), which constitutes learned scripts for carrying out routine actions.

We will now explore these two distinctions further. Earlier workers in psychology have cited examples relevant to the first distinction, that between transient memory and archival memory, though its full significance is only now being grasped. For instance, Kurt Lewin's student Bliuma Zeigarnik investigated the so-called Zeigarnik effect, in which memory for interrupted tasks is about twice as accurate as memory for completed ones (Denmark, 1984). According to the story, Kurt Lewin enjoyed talking science with his students in the cafés of Vienna. His student, Zeigarnik, noticed that the waiters in the café had impressive memories for orders yet to be filled, but almost no memory for completed orders, and she went on to explore this phenomenon experimentally.

Likewise, Miller, Galanter, and Pribram (1960, p. 65), in their classic book on planning, distinguished a memory system important for keeping intended actions on line: "The memory we use for the execution of our Plans [is] a kind of quick access 'working memory.'"

More recently, Goldman-Rakic (1992) has emphasized that the working memory function of the prefrontal cortex is transient and time dependent, whereas long-term memory is permanent and archival. Similarly, Levine and colleagues (Levine, Leven, & Prueitt, 1992, p. 322) state: "Indeed the difference between time-dependent and time-independent pattern processing is one of the two most cogent functional distinctions between the prefrontal cortex and other multimodal association areas like the temporal and parietal cortices." The other distinction they cite is "the prefrontal area's greater ability to process emotional inputs." These authors have incorporated both distinctions in connectionist simulations of prefrontal tasks.

Turning now to the second distinction, our common language for memory respects in a subtle way the distinction between retrospective and prospective memory. Consider the distinction we make between forgetting a fact (such as a person's name) and forgetting to do something (such as picking up some milk on the way home from work). Munstadt (1966) pointed out that if one fails at the former, we consider that one's memory is unreliable, whereas if one fails at the latter, we consider the possibility that the *person* is unreliable. So memory for intended actions is more tightly tied to our commonsense notions of an agent and an agent's responsibilities.

Does research on human memory provide support for the distinction between WM and LTM? I would argue the answer is yes, based on recent research on memory functions in adult patients with frontal versus limbic lesions. Frontal patients demonstrate a pattern of memory problems that contrasts interestingly with those found in classic amnesia due to limbic (amygdalohippocampal) lesions. In particular, frontal patients were found to be impaired on source memory, metamemory, and temporal-order memory, as well as on free recall and some measures of verbal STM (presumably because some verbal STM tasks, like free recall, also require rehearsal and retrieval strategies). In contrast, classic amnesics were *not* impaired on source memory, metamemory, or temporal-order memory. An opposite contrast was found on various measures of recognition and long-term memory; classic limbic amnesics were impaired on these measures, whereas frontal patients were not (Shimamura, Janowsky, & Squire, 1991).

In summary, limbic lesions impair the ability to form new long-term memories; hence the failures exhibited by patients with such lesions on tests of LTM and recognition memory, whereas frontal lesions appear to affect operations *on* memory but leave the ability to form new long-term memories essentially intact. Shimamura and colleagues (1991, p. 191) describe frontal patients as being impaired in *prospective* memory, which they define as including not only remembering to perform and monitor future actions, but also "processes and strategies involved in planning, monitoring, and organizing *memory,* not just actions." They relate this prospective memory deficit to the so called "dysexecutive" syndrome found in frontal patients. They also relate working memory to prospective memory. So frontal lesions may affect organizational and strategic processes important in both encoding into and retrieval from LTM. In contrast, I am arguing that they do not affect the transfer or storage process itself, which is mediated by the limbic memory structures.

The relation between WM and LTM gets particularly interesting for episodic memory. Computational analyses of episodic memory point to the need for some kind of interference control in the network that stores episodic long-term memories; otherwise there would be too much "cross-talk" between the elements of distinct episodes. Anyone who has attended a busy conference or who tries to keep up with a number of similar psychotherapy or assessment patients can attest to this problem. Sloman and Rumelhart (1992) have proposed and modeled a means of dealing with this interference problem in a connectionist LTM network. Their solution has two components: sparse coding and episodic gating. Episodic gating is accomplished by a set of hidden units, one per episode. Let us suppose that these episode units are in the hippocampus and that they bind together distributed cortical representations that are the components of a complex episodic memory. In classic amnesia, new episodic memories cannot be stored because these hippocampal episode units are impaired and the particular ensemble of distributed representations that constitute a new episodic memory cannot be bound together. Note, however, that implicit memory for constituents of the episode, which are handled by single cortical or subcortical networks, would *not* be impaired by a hippocampal lesion. This account provides a neural explanation for the functional dissociability of implicit memory from episodic memory.

Now the question naturally arises of how episodes are constructed. This can hardly be a function of the hippocampus alone. Although it is in a good position anatomically to detect correlated activity across distributed cortical networks and send out a binding signal that holds together "pieces" of an episode, it can hardly decide what constitutes a memorable episode. We can think of a memorable episode as a coherent "story" or "narrative" that is relevant or adaptive for the organism at that time. Episodes must be constructed as they are experienced, and it is that construction that is stored into LTM. The construction of a coherent episode, I would argue, calls for WM, in much the same way that both discourse comprehension and narrative planning do. So we expect prefrontal cortex to play an important role in selecting, constructing, and eventually retrieving episodes.

If this hypothesis is correct, there should be both appropriate anatomic connections between prefrontal cortex and the hippocampus and correlated activation during the time it is reasonable to expect that an episode is being formed.

Goldman-Rakic and colleagues have identified both structural and functional relations that are consistent with this hypothesis (Goldman-Rakic, Seleman, & Schwartz, 1984; Goldman-Rakic & Friedman, 1991). Specifically, in terms of structure, the prefrontal cortex has both input and output connections with the hippocampal circuit. As Weinberger (1992) has pointed out, the placement of these connections is consistent with the idea that prefrontal cortex performs a gating function on information flow into and out of the hippocampus. We can think of information flow into the hippocampus as all the concurrent activation vectors from various networks that are candidates for binding together into an episode. The prefrontal cortices also receive independent projections from these various networks. Thus, on the input side, the PFCs can gate which constituents will be considered for binding by the hippocampus. The outflow from the hippocampus is presumably some kind of binding signal (possibly long-term potentiation [LTP]) that is sent back to the same distributed networks. The prefrontal cortex connections on the output side of the hippocampal circuit could thus function as a final check on the relevance and coherence of the new episode that is about to be stored. In terms of function, monkeys performing prefrontal WM tasks, such as DR and DA, also exhibit elevated metabolic activity in parts of the hippocampal circuit, specifically in the dentate gyrus and Ammon's horn (Friedman & Goldman-Rakic, 1988). Moreover, if the delay interval in DR and DA is too long (greater than about 18 s), then task performance on DR and DA is no longer insensitive to hippocampal lesions. We might say that lengthening the delay interval too much begins to turn a WM task into an LTM task; instead of requiring transient storage, the memory for the location of the food reward in the DR task now depends on storage that is beginning to be archival.

In summary, working memory is distinct from both STM and LTM in that it is a transient, prospective memory system that handles the constraint satisfaction problem posed by novel, context-specific problems. Working memory selectively accesses the content of other memory systems. But most important, WM is a mental work space for on-line problem solving and action selection, in which the current problem context, partial products of relevant computation, and memory representations are all held on line until the problem is solved and the appropriate action is selected and executed. In other words, WM is a locus of active processing that pools information from various sources relevant to a current problem and operates on it. Working memory reconfigures the various contents it has access to into a novel, integrated representation to guide action selection. Because it is a limited-capacity system, this pooling must be selective; keeping activated memory items out of WM may be at least as important as maintaining some few memory items in WM. Allocation of attention among the content of WM is also crucial.

Accounting for the Diversity of Executive Deficits

We now return to the question we started with: How can we provide an integrated theoretical account of the diversity of functions, tasks, and symptoms attributed to the PFCs?

The various executive functions, such as planning, set shifting, inhibition, selective attention, and initiation, are not separate functions, but just descriptions (most in everyday language) of behaviors that the WM system described here would permit. Similarly, the various executive function tasks all require holding context-specific information on line and using it to select some actions and inhibit others. Although tasks vary in how much they stress each of these two dimensions, representing context and inhibition, the two dimensions are not separate functions. Roberts, Hager, and Heron (in press) have discussed various executive function tasks in terms of these two dimensions. Moreover, they have demonstrated that increasing WM load on a seemingly pure inhibition task, the antisaccade task, impairs normal adult performance so that it resembles the performance of patients with prefrontal lesions.

Finally, in terms of symptoms, a WM impairment could account for the confusing, and seemingly opposite, symptoms exhibited by patients with PFC lesions. Failure to maintain the current social context in WM could lead to the expression of inappropriate impulses that would otherwise be inhibited, but without an input that elicited an impulse, little or no behavior would result, resulting in the symptoms of withdrawal or lack of initiative. Similarly, the apparent opposites of perseveration and lack of persistence, as well as those of distractibility and overfocusing of attention, can be seen as manifestations of an underlying WM problem. Perseveration or overfocusing would occur when there was a prepotent stimulus present; otherwise, without WM guidance, action selection and attention would "drift." Planning at various time scales involves selecting and sequencing some actions and inhibiting others and hence requires WM. Finally, narrative comprehension and reproduction both require WM to hold to a particular "path" of meaning and to inhibit others that are activated at every "turn" of a story.

A WM impairment would also account for the failure to plan and organize everyday activities found even in frontal patients with preserved high IQs and normal performance on classic frontal tasks such as the WCST. Shallice and Burgess (1991) recently studied three such patients and demonstrated that they were impaired on two new tests of open-ended, multiple-subgoal situations. These new tests clearly tax WM and require inhibition of prepotent responses, since the subject must strategically shift among subgoals; thus these new frontal tasks would also fit into our theoretical framework.

PREFRONTAL FUNCTIONS ARE VULNERABLE IN MANY DEVELOPMENTAL DISORDERS

Developmental disorders hold a special place in this account for two reasons, one merely historical and the other deeper and substantive. Unlike the brain changes acquired in adulthood, those caused by developmental disorders are especially instructive for attempting an integrated account of individual and developmental cognitive differences. Although brain changes acquired in adulthood may inform us about the mature and relatively invariant cognitive architecture, they tell us little about either the ontogeny of that architecture or individual cognitive differences. In contrast, developmental disorders can be particularly informative about the ontogeny of the cognitive architecture, and they are clearly one cause of individual cognitive differences. The more common ones, such as dyslexia and attention deficit hyperactivity disorder (ADHD), probably account for appreciable "normal" variation in cognition. The data I will review here indicate that WM appears to be a cognitive component that is particularly vulnerable in a variety of developmental disorders, and hence an important reason for failures on classic developmental tasks and an important source of individual cognitive differences.

Turning now to history, our research on the role of the PFC in normal and abnormal development began with the serendipitous discovery that some children with early-treated phenylketonuria (PKU) had pronounced deficits on the Wisconsin Card Sorting Test (Pennington, Van Doornick, & McCabe, 1985). This discovery led to the hypothesis that high phenylalanine levels in children caused dopamine depletion, which in turn disrupted the functions of the PFCs. To test this hypothesis, we needed to deal with several difficult issues: What is a cognitive definition of the functions of the PFCs? What is the normal developmental trajectory of these functions? and What behavioral tasks are appropriate for measuring them at different ages? (Welsh & Pennington, 1988; Welsh, Pennington, & Groisser, 1991). In many ways the first issue was the most difficult. Following other writers in both cognitive psychology and neuropsychology, we chose the term "executive functions" (EFs) to describe the functions of the PFCs. Our umbrella definition of this term was an attempt to cover all the behaviors attributable to the PFCs (Welsh & Pennington, 1988, pp. 201–202): "Executive function is defined as the ability to maintain an appropriate problem-solving set for attainment of a future goal (Bianchi, 1922; Luria, 1966). This set can involve one or more of the following: (a) an intention to inhibit a response or to defer it to a later more appropriate time, (b) a strategic plan of action sequences, and (c) a mental representation of the task, including the relevant stimulus information encoded in memory and the desired future goal-state."

This definition captured the important ideas that EFs serve future-oriented problem solving and depend on mental representation and inhibition, yet it did not really say how a single cognitive system might perform all these functions. But as discussed at length above, this kind of definition was unsatisfactory because it was not parsimonious, said little about underlying cognitive mechanisms, could be considered to invoke a homunculus, and left us open to the question, Do all complex and demanding tasks require EFs? The current working memory account of prefrontal functions developed in the last section avoids many of these problems. For our initial task of examining presumably prefrontal functions in developmental disorders, however, our initial, provisional definition was sufficient to lead to some interesting empirical results.

We have found striking and fairly specific deficits on EF tasks in several developmental disorders, two of which—early-treated PKU and fragile X in females—have discrete genetic etiologies (Mazzocco, Hagerman, Cronister-Silverman, & Pennington, 1992; Mazzocco, Pennington, & Hagerman, 1993; Welsh, Pennington, Ozonoff, Rouse, & McCabe, 1990). (See Figures 9.2 and 9.3.) In each study, the discriminant measures included measures of LTM. Neither the PKU nor the fragile X group was impaired on these tasks. I should add that verbal STM, as measured by digit span, also was not impaired in these two populations.

Three issues are worth discussing in thinking about these results. One is that since we did not measure WM directly in these populations, the evidence that they are impaired on WM is indirect and is based on the argument presented above that EF tasks all require WM. There is, however, evidence from other studies that at least some of our EF tasks, such as the Wisconsin Card Sorting Test and the Tower of Hanoi, do

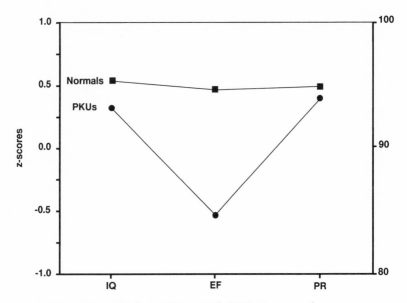

Figure 9.2   Test results from subjects with PKU. Executive function composite: visual search, Tower of Hanoi, verbal fluency, motor planning. Picture recognition (PR): Continuous Picture Recognition task (Brown & Scott, 1971).

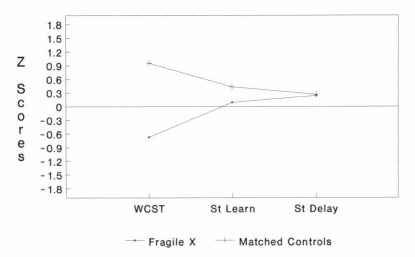

Figure 9.3   WCST and verbal memory in fragile X females.

require WM (see Weinberger, this volume, and Carpenter, Just, & Shell, 1990). Likewise, without validating neurological evidence, the argument that the EF deficits in these populations reflect dysfunction in the PFCs is by inference only. However, in the PKU group there was a significant inverse correlation with FSIQ partialed out ($-.88$) between phenylalanine (Phe) levels and an EF composite score, supporting our dopamine depletion hypothesis. Diamond, Ciaramitaro, Donner, Djali, and Robinson (in review) have recently used an animal model to demonstrate that high Phe levels deplete dopamine in the PFCs somewhat selectively; these same animals are impaired on delayed-response tasks that require WM. In a companion longitudinal study of children with PKU, Diamond and colleagues have demonstrated deficits on classic PFC tasks, whereas their performance on various tasks sensitive to parietal function is intact (Diamond, Hurwitz, Lee, Bockes, Grover, & Minarcik, in review). So now the evidence of prefrontal dysfunction in PKU is quite strong. Moreover, in two other groups with EF deficits discussed in this section, ADHD and autism, there is also some more direct evidence of PFC involvment (Piven et al., 1990; Zametkin et al., 1990).

A third issue concerns the relation between EF and IQ. In these studies, the effects of overall IQ were controlled by matching the control group on this variable. Thus, IQ differences did not account for EF deficits. However, I would not wish to argue that IQ and EF and completely independent constructs. Indeed, I believe that the IQ deficits found in these populations are due in large part to EF deficits. But since traditional IQ tests measure other things besides EF, we were still able to detect EF deficits after controlling for IQ. I will return later to the relation between IQ and EF.

Another group, high-functioning autistics, was just as impaired on an LTM task as on EF (the EF tasks in this study included the TOH and the WCST). This result presented a puzzle (Ozonoff, Pennington, & Rogers, 1991). We used a different memory task than the ones we employed in the PKU and fragile X studies, namely the Bushke Selective Reminding Task (SRT), which is a verbal list learning task in which only incorrect items are repeated over trials. So the subject must utilize an effective rehearsal strategy to retain previously correct items while at the same time processing the repeated items. That is, the Bushke SRT appears to require concurrent storage and processing, which is one operational definition of working memory. So, without realizing it, we may have picked as a discriminant memory measure a WM task! A recent, more extensive study of memory functions in high-functioning autistics (HFAs), found few differences between autistics and IQ matched controls on the California Verbal Learning Test (Minshew & Goldstein, 1993), arguing against more widespread LTM deficits in autism.

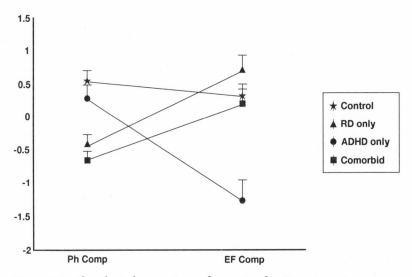

Figure 9.4   Phonological processing and executive function composite scores (full-scale IQ covaried) for each group (ADHD = attention-deficit hyperactivity disorder; RD = reading disability [dyslexia]).

In more recent work on HFAs, we have found they have deficits on standard WM tasks (Counting Span and Sentence Span) relative to IQ-matched controls (Pennington, Rogers, Bennetto, & Ozonoff, 1993). These deficits remained even after performance on verbal STM (as measured by digit span) was covaried out. Moreover, there was a significant relation between performance on these WM tasks and the WCST in the HFA group, even after partialing out age, full-scale IQ, and digit span. These results provide more direct evidence for a WM deficit in autism.

One might ask two other discriminant validity questions at this point: Are EF deficits just a general feature of all developmental disorders? and How can symptomatically different developmental disorders, such as autism and PKU, have the same underlying cognitive deficit?

Fortunately, the answer to the first question is no. We have also studied another developmental disorder, dyslexia, that does not exhibit EF deficits, but in which there are clear deficits in phonological processes, such as phoneme segmentation and awareness. Interestingly, we found that the cognitive profile in dyslexia is *opposite* to that found in another developmental disorder often characterized by EF deficits— ADHD, without dyslexia (Pennington, Groisser, & Welsh, 1993). (See Figure 9.4). Other evidence argues for the view that dyslexia is a disorder of posterior neural networks important for phonological representations and word recognition in reading. In the terminology used to distinguish various memory systems, these posterior networks would be involved in implicit memory and perhaps verbal STM, but not in working memory. So not all developmental disorders are EF disorders.

Among those that are, how can different symptom profiles be produced by the same underlying deficit? This is our second question. Several straightforward answers come to mind. One is that EF deficits can be produced by brain lesions in a variety of prefrontal and associated structures; different lesion loci would produce different associated symptoms in addition to similar EF deficits. A second possibility is that PFC dysfunction is common to these various disorders but that what differentiates them is dysfunction in a second locus, *outside* the PFC and its associated structures (e.g., dysfunction in PFCs and cerebellum in one disorder, dysfunction in PFCs and middle temporal gyrus in another). A third answer is that severity differences in EF deficits could produce different symptom profiles. A fourth possibility is that differences in age of onset of PFC dysfunction could produce very different symptoms; for instance, both autism and schizophrenia may involve PFC dysfunction, but they differ considerably in age of onset.

It is worth elaborating the first possibility, since it is clearly true of adult neurological diseases that disrupt performance on EF tasks. Weinberger (1992) has divided these diseases into two categories, intrinsic and extrinsic. Those in the first category involve neuropathology within the PFCs themselves, an example of which is Pick's disease. In Pick's disease there is degeneration of PFC neurons, diminished PFC metabolism in imaging studies (hypofrontality), and personality changes and neuropsychological deficits similar to those seen in patients with other PFC lesions. Those in the second category involve neuropathology outside the PFCs but in closely connected structures. Examples of this latter category would include Huntington's disease and Parkinson's disease, both of which affect the basal ganglia, but in different ways. Both of these diseases have EF deficits in common but show other clinical features that are specific to the particular disease. So we could propose that there are both intrinsic and extrinsic developmental disorders that affect EFs. At the extreme, a completely diffuse neurological disease might qualify as extrinsic, since the WM function of the PFCs may be more vulnerable than other functional systems, just because the PFCs have such widespread connectivity. So it is possible that some developmental disorders with greater executive than nonexecutive impairment might have underlying diffuse changes in brain structure or function.

To conclude this section, we have found fairly specific EF deficits in several developmental disorders with different etiologies and have begun to relate these deficits to WM. These deficits are not simply due to deficits in overall IQ, although there is a relation between EF and IQ development. Nor are they due to deficits in verbal STM or LTM, consistent with evidence reviewed earlier that WM is dissociable from both of these other kinds of memory. In addition, the EF deficits found here are doubly dissociable from deficits in reading, demonstrating the neuropsychological separability of these two domains.

These results have implications for both individual and developmental differences in cognition. With regard to individual differences, I hypothesize both that there is wide variation in human populations in prefrontally mediated WM skills and that many etiologies contribute to this variation. With regard to developmental differences in cognition, the developmental failures in these developmentally disabled groups (excluding dyslexics) appear due, at least in part, to EF deficits, indicating that developmental differences in prefrontally mediated WM may underlie cognitive development in an important way.

WORKING MEMORY AND INDIVIDUAL COGNITIVE DIFFERENCES

There are three key empirical findings in the study of cognitive differences that any adequate theory must address: a wide range of individual differences among individuals at a given age; a wide range of developmental differences across ages; and the positive correlation ("positive manifold") found among virtually all mental tests. I am suggesting that we can account for an important part of both individual *and* developmental differences in intelligence with the same cognitive mechanism—prefrontally mediated WM. Moreover, if WM is an important cognitive component of many IQ measures, then we could account for the positive manifold as well. Thus we could conceivably produce a theory of intelligence that integrates the cognitive, developmental, and psychometric research traditions and has ready links to the biological bases of cognition, at the level of both brain systems and genetic etiologies.

I will argue that WM corresponds most closely to what is called fluid intelligence in the psychometric tradition. In contrast, crystallized intelligence appears to depend more on LTM than on WM. This distinction actually has a long history in psychological theories of intelligence (Table 9.1).

There have been recent demonstrations that most of the variance of fluid intelligence (as measured by reasoning tasks or by the Raven's matrices) is accounted for by individual differences in working memory. In the psychometric tradition, the Raven's is a central measure of fluid intelligence, so identifying which cognitive mechanisms underlie individual differences on this IQ test would be a very important integrative step. Larson and Sacuzzo (1989) found a correlation in the range of .50

TABLE 9.1   Two Kinds of Intelligence

	WM related	LTM related
Wertheimer, 1945	Productive	Reproductive
Hebb, 1949	Problem solving	Accumulated knowledge
Wechsler, 1955	Don't hold	Hold
Cattell, 1943 and Horn, 1985	Fluid	Crystallized
Sternberg, 1985	Nonroutine	Routine

to .59 between a WM task (Mental Counters) and the Raven's, which is impressively high, given that the reliability of the Mental Counters task was only .64. They argue that "g appears related to the ability to flexibly and consistently reconfigure the contents of working memory" (p. 5). Kyllonen and Christal (1991) found correlations in the range of .80 and .88 between working memory and reasoning factors in four studies with a total N of over 2,000 subjects.

Carpenter, Just, and Shell (1990) performed a detailed cognitive task analysis of the Raven's matrices, using verbal reports, eye movement, error patterns, and a computer simulation. They found that individual differences were mainly attributable to two component processes, "the ability to induce abstract relations and the ability to dynamically manage a large set of problem-solving goals in working memory" (p. 404). Moreover, they tested the importance of goal management in working memory by comparing Raven's performance with performance on the Tower of Hanoi puzzle, a well-studied cognitive task that is known to tax goal management in working memory. The Tower of Hanoi is also of interest because it appears to be sensitive to prefrontal dysfunction in adults (Shallice, 1982) and children (Levin, Culhane, Mendelsohn, et al., 1991), and because it has been a very discriminating measure in our four studies of executive function deficits in developmental disorders reviewed earlier. They found a correlation of .77 between the Raven's and Tower of Hanoi performances. Taken together, these results indicate a close relation between WM and fluid intelligence, and by inference, between both constructs and executive functions.

So we have begun to answer our first question about cognitive mechanisms underlying individual differences in intelligence. Working memory is clearly one very important mechanism that appears to account for considerable variance in what is called fluid intelligence. Incidentally, WM also accounts for individual differences in a variety of complex language processing tasks, including reading comprehension (Daneman & Carpenter, 1980), drawing inferences from text (Hasher & Zacks, 1988), avoiding "garden paths," parsing embedded reduced clauses, and discourse planning (Dennis, 1991). As I mentioned earlier, frontal patients appear to be impaired in such complex language processes. There are also wide individual and developmental differences on such tasks, including deficits in cognitive aging.

In summary, there is emerging evidence that relates individual differences in WM to individual differences on reasoning tasks, including tasks such as the Raven's matrices, which is a central measure of what is called fluid intelligence in the psychometric tradition. However, although there is overlap, there is no identity relation between WM as defined in the first section, currently available WM tasks (such as Sentence Span, Counting Span, or Mental Counters), and the Raven's matrices.

One problem is that a complex task like the Raven's is open to a variety of strategies, and some of them may minimize its WM demands. On the Raven's, all the necessary stimuli are continuously available to the subject, so information does not have to be held "on line" over a delay interval. Likewise, there are no obvious prepotent responses, even though it is a multiple-choice test. So the Raven's does not have some of the key characteristics of other tasks that tap WM, though it requires novel problem solving and considerable on-line processing on the harder items. In their task analysis of the Raven's Carpenter et al. (1990) noted that some subjects immediately look at the six choices at the bottom of the page before trying to figure out what the missing piece in the matrix should look like. This strategy is less optimal and is characteristic of subjects with lower scores, but it would considerably reduce the WM demands of the task. Perhaps the use of such a strategy would explain why autistics, who are impaired on EF and WM tasks, perform somewhat better on the Raven's than other IQ measures would predict. (A similar argument could explain autistics' preserved performance on the Block Design subtest of the Wechsler, which also has a high loading on the fluid intelligence factor.)

WORKING MEMORY AND DEVELOPMENTAL COGNITIVE DIFFERENCES

The next question is whether WM also is a significant contributor to developmental differences in intelligence. First of all, it is interesting that at a very general level, the key Piagetian concepts of assimilation and accommodation fit well into our framework for classifying prefrontal tasks. Assimilation can be thought of as the domination of behavior by established memory or by prepotent responses. Accommodation occurs when such prepotency is resisted and a new schema is developed in working memory, then stored in LTM.

A number of neo-Piagetian theorists have proposed that maturational changes in a central processing resource underlie the statelike progression observed in normal cognitive development across a broad range of tasks (e.g., Case, 1978, 1985, 1991; Fischer, 1980; Pascual-Leone, 1970, 1973). One goal of these process theories was to overcome the weaknesses of Piaget's structuralist approach (Case, 1985). Both Case and Pascual-Leone identified something very much like WM as the central processing resource that increases with development.

In his theory, Pascual-Leone called this resource "M-space," which refers to the number of schemes that can be coordinated at one time under executive control. He proposed that M-space increased steadily across development, and he identified M-space with the functions of the PFC (J. Pascual-Leone, personal communication, 1993). Although there are the predicted age increases on measures of M-space, it is unclear whether these reflect changes in capacity or processing speed (see Dempster, 1985, for a review).

Case (1978, 1985, 1991) has developed a detailed theoretical account of the role of WM in cognitive development. Case followed up Herbert Simon's (1962) insight that "Piaget's structures can be interpreted as sequences of increasingly complex and powerful executive structures" (Case, 1978, p. 48). Case explained a child's relative progression through substages within each Piagetian stage as being due to two factors, experience with the strategy and an increase in the size of WM within each stage. The WM increase in turn is due to increasing automaticity of basic operations, so that there is decreasing need for attentional control. In his article he cited a number of studies documenting developmental increases in WM.

While Case (1978, 1985) postulates a developmental increase in WM, this increase is not due to an expanding central resource, as in Pascual-Leone's theory. Instead, he views total processing space as constant across development. What changes in development is the relative allocation of processing space to cognitive operations and storage. Thus the developmental increase in WM is due to increasing automaticity of basic operations, so that they have a decreasing need for attentional control, freeing up processing resources for WM storage.

In his later work Case (1985, 1991, 1992) has further elaborated this basic theory and conducted an extensive program of research to test it. Of particular interest here is his finding of a close correspondence between the development of working memory, as indexed by a Counting and Spatial Span task, and level of strategy exhibited on several tasks, including Piaget's Balance Beam Task, the Raven's Matrices, and a standard concept acquisition task, in which cards can be sorted along several possible dimensions, similar to the WCST (Case, 1985, 1992).

As Case (1978, 1992) points out, children's difficulties on these tasks and classic Piagetian tasks involve both attending to new or multiple dimensions and inhibiting a response to a previously rewarded dimension. Piagetian tasks are both novel and misleading because they evoke a simpler strategy that will "constantly interfere" with efforts to solve the task. So, in theorizing about Piagetian cognitive development, Case identified the same two task dimensions that we mentioned earlier as being central for thinking about EF tasks: WM load and prepotency of irrelevant responses. Thus Case's work indicates that WM performance predicts cognitive developmental level and that classic cognitive developmental tasks have an important structural similarity to EF tasks. Consistent with the latter point, Shute and Huertas (1990) found that a test of Piagetian formal operations, the Shadows task, and various executive function tasks, including the WCST, loaded on a common factor in a study of normal young adults.

Case (1992) has recently linked his WM theory of cognitive development to neuropsychology. He has proposed that these developmental changes in WM are prefrontally mediated, noting the strong similarity between the developmental trajectories of increases in WM (on tasks such as Counting and Spatial Span) and increases in frontal-posterior EEG coherence in Thatcher's (1991) data. He also points out that Segalowitz, Wagner, and Menna (1992) recently provided more direct evidence of frontal mediation of these WM tasks (Counting and Spatial Span) in an evoked potential study in which the frontally mediated contingent negative variation (CNV) was measured. In that study the correlations between CNV and the span tasks were in the range of .40 to .44.

Another recent developmental theory that is explicitly neuropsychological and that focuses on inhibition has been provided by Dempster (1992). Dempster has reviewed evidence indicating that young children, older adults, and patients with frontal lesions perform similarly on what he calls "interference-sensitive" tasks. The tasks he reviews include the WCST, the Stroop test, measures of field dependence, classic Piagetian tasks (conservation and class inclusion), the Brown-Peterson task, text processing, and selective attention tasks (including the "negative" priming task). All these tasks can be conceptualized in the framework elaborated earlier; each requires maintenance of a WM representation to inhibit a competing but incorrect response. Dempster (1992) makes a proposal similar to that contained in this chapter; that is, he argues that developmental increases and aging declines in prefrontally mediated inhibitory processes provide a unified explanation for life-span cognitive development. His proposal differs from the one here in that it is not concerned with individual cognitive differences and it is focused more exclusively on inhibition, rather than seeing inhibition as intrinsic to WM.

The best evidence that some cognitive developmental tasks are prefrontally mediated has been provided by the careful systematic cross-species comparisons conducted by Diamond and Goldman-Rakic (1989). They have demonstrated that the classic A not B task is prefrontally mediated in young monkeys, just as are the DR and DA tasks, and that the developmental ontogeny of these tasks is very similar in young monkeys and human infants.

Dealing with a later age, Shute and Huertas (1990) recently found that a test of Piagetian formal operations, the Shadows task, and various executive function tasks, including the WCST, loaded on a common factor in a study of normal young adults.

Finally, if the WM function of the PFC underlies cognitive development, we ought to find protracted development of its structures and physiologic functions. The evidence here is complicated. Although many developmental writers assume this point to be true, partly based on older evidence (e.g., Huttenlocher, 1979), some markers of prefrontal function appear early, such as synaptogenesis and regional blood flow (see Welsh & Pennington, 1988, for a review). Without some evidence for early functional activity, the infant data on frontal involvement in A not B (and possibly joint attention) would not make sense. So instead of conceptualizing the frontal lobes as "turning on" at some late point in development, it is better to think of them as undergoing continuous protracted development, a large part of which consists of coordinating their activity with the distributed ensemble of other brain regions to which they are connected. Consistent with this view, Thatcher's (1991) cross-sectional study of EEG coherence indicates that most of the developmental changes in coherence relations between brain regions involves the frontal lobes, with these frontal coherence changes continuing to maturity.

In summary, we have a fairly strong pattern of suggestive evidence for the proposed central role of prefrontally mediated WM in cognitive development. It would be very desirable to have more direct evidence from studies of brain structure and function. In addition, direct experimental tests of whether manipulating WM affects performance on classic cognitive developmental tasks would provide a critical test of this theory.

WORKING MEMORY AND COGNITIVE AGING

If a WM perspective is promising for understanding cognitive developmental differences in youth, is it similarly helpful for understanding such differences across the life span? To answer this question, we will review, (1) long-standing evidence for differential cognitive declines in aging, such that measures related to fluid intelligence, (measures that require novel, on-line processing) are more impaired by age than are measures related to crystallized intelligence; (2) experimental evidence that this cognitive aging profile is mediated by declines in WM and the WM-related process of inhibition; (3) evidence for a pattern in aging of memory impairments (on measures of recency, source, and working memory) and relative strengths (on measures of cued recall and recognition memory) that is similar to what is found in patients with frontal lesions and contrasts with what is found in classic amnesia; and (4) evidence for differential vulnerability of the prefrontal cortices in aging. These four converging lines of evidence provide fairly strong support for our hypothesis that declines in prefrontally mediated WM are a central mechanism in cognitive aging.

With regard to the first point, evidence is drawn from Salthouse (1991), an excellent recent book on cognitive aging. Several of Salthouse's points are pertinent to my argument here. One is that there is a very well documented pattern in aging of contrasting decline on some IQ subtests and maintenance on others that cannot be explained as an artifact of some kind. Tests like Block Design or the Raven's matrices, which require active, on-line processing, are much more vulnerable to aging than are measures like Vocabulary or Information, which tap previously stored verbal knowledge. The median correlations between adult age and the former two tests are $-.37$ and $-.55$ respectively. In contrast, the median age correlations for Vocabulary and Information are $-.05$ and $-.09$.

It has long been hypothesized that there is a WM deficit in aging. Welford (1958) first made this suggestion. Baddeley (1986) reviews evidence from studies conducted since then using a variety of paradigms that support this view. Working memory tasks also have been found to have high negative age correlations (e.g., $-.46$ for computational span) whereas the median age correlation for Digit Span, a verbal STM task, is lower, $-.19$ (all correlations from Salthouse, 1991). Craik and Jennings (1992, p. 61), in a review of memory changes in aging, state that "in general, there is now good argument that older people do less well on WM tasks, and that such age differences underlie a variety of age related deficits in cognitive performance."

Moreover, the magnitude of correlations between age and various EF tasks is in the same range as that found for fluid intelligence and WM tasks (e.g., .63 for the interference condition on the Stroop test; Cohn, Dustman, & Bradford, 1984). Although these correlations do not provide direct evidence that a common mechanism underlies aging declines on measures of fluid intelligence, WM, and EF, they are consistent with this hypothesis.

Attempts to characterize this differentiated pattern of aging effects

TABLE 9.2 Cognition: Large Versus Small Age Effects

Greatest age effects	Smallest age effects	Source
Flexibility and elasticity	Routine or accustomed work	Proctor, 1873
Adaptability and rapid adjustment	Accumulated experience	Foster & Taylor, 1920
Capacity to develop new patterns of response	Functioning of already developed patterns of response	Hebb, 1942
Fluid ability, capacity to discriminate and perceive relations	Crystallized ability, long-established habits	Cattell, 1943
Capacity to acquire a new way of thinking	Ability to recall acquired information	Raven, 1948
Ability to acquire information	Previously learned or stored information	Birren, 1952
Abstract intelligence	Accumulated experience	Jones, 1959
Mental agility	Ordered knowledge	Welford, 1962
Immediate problem-solving ability	Previously accumulated experience	Fitzhugh, Fitzhugh, and Reitan, 1967
Current processing efficiency	Accumulated products of prior processing	Salthouse, 1988

Source. Salthouse (1991).

(Table 9.2) point to a theoretical distinction that is similar both to the one developed here between WM and other memory systems and to that contained in Table 9.1 between two kinds of intelligence. Although these distinctions are informal and descriptive, it is clear that it has long been recognized that the cognitive effects of aging take their greatest toll on novel problem-solving ability, flexibility of thinking, and on-line processing capacity, all of which can be seen as depending on prefrontally mediated WM and related to fluid intelligence. Is there likewise experimental evidence (point 2) that WM is central to the cognitive declines in aging?

Salthouse and colleagues (Salthouse, Mitchell, Skovronek, & Babcock, 1989) found a very similar pattern of age declines for a WM task (computational span) and both a verbal reasoning and spatial visualization task, on each of which they systematically manipulated complexity by increasing WM load. As complexity increased, older subjects exhibited greater impairment, and these age-by-complexity interaction effects were highly correlated between the verbal and spatial tasks. Moreover, statistical control of variance associated with the separate WM task significantly and similarly attenuated the age effects on each complex task, both verbal *and* spatial. These results are consistent with the view that the ubiquitous age-by-complexity interaction effect is due, at least in part, to a decline in a central, modality-independent resource, in this case WM.

In another study of WM in normal aging, Salthouse and Babcock (1991) again found large negative correlations between age ($-.39$ to $-.52$) and two different WM measures, computation span and listening span, which were themselves moderately correlated (.49 to .62). Using path analysis, they tested which hypothesized components of WM—processing efficiency, storage capacity, or coordination effectiveness—best accounted for the age declines in WM. In a result reminiscent of Case's work reviewed earlier, processing efficiency for simple operations accounted for the greatest portion of age declines in WM.

Another line of experimental evidence also points to WM dysfunction in cognitive aging. Hasher and colleagues have been pursuing the hypothesis that inhibitory deficits underlie cognitive aging. Their original goal was to analyze the discourse- and text-comprehension deficits prominent in aging within a WM framework (Hasher & Zacks, 1988). Somewhat surprisingly, they found that instead of being forgetful, older subjects kept too many candidate interpretations of a text active in WM while processing it (Hamm & Hasher, 1992), suggesting a deficit in the inhibitory processes of WM.

Subsequent studies have utilized several experimental paradigms to probe this inhibitory deficit in cognitive aging, including the "negative priming" task, the addition of irrelevant text, memory for previously relevant but now irrelevant information, and the fan effect paradigm of Anderson (1974). Aging deficits in inhibition have been found across all four paradigms (Hasher, Stoltzfus, Zacks, & Rypma, 1991; Connelly, Hasher, & Zacks, 1991; Hartman & Hasher, 1991; Gerard, Zacks, Hasher, & Radvansky, 1991). Moreover, in some of their studies, lack of inhibition in the elderly correlates with the size of the Stroop effect (e.g., Hartman & Hasher, 1991). As I noted earlier, the Stroop test appears to require prefrontally mediated WM, and performance on it demonstrates the steep age decline also found on both WM and fluid intelligence tasks.

In summary, Hasher and colleagues point out that the deficit in inhibition they have discovered would lead to a fundamental and pervasive WM problem, difficulty "maintaining a coherent line of thought" (Stoltzfus, Hasher, Zacks, Ulivi, & Goldstein, 1994). This problem in maintaining the coherence of the line, or path, of thought would in turn impair performance on a broad range of tasks, including narrative production, discourse comprehension, memory coding and retrieval, and reasoning. All these tasks are potentially WM intensive, insofar as they require active construction of a coherent and possibly novel representation.

I now turn to the third point, that there is a differential pattern of memory impairment in aging that is consistent with an underlying frontal impairment. Since the popular conception is that aging takes its greatest toll on memory, it is important to review here what is known about aging effects on STM and LTM and how these might relate to a decline in WM. There is a general consensus (Salthouse, 1991) that remote memory is least impaired in aging, that the formation of new LTMs is most impaired, and that STM lies somewhere between. Performance on various implicit memory tasks, including repetition and semantic priming, is found to be preserved with age. Within the most impaired domain of memory, LTM, aging deficits are less on tests of both cued recall and recognition than on tests of free recall; these differences may be due to the reduced processing requirements of cued recall and recognition memory tasks relative to free recall. As discussed earlier, patients with PFC lesions are likewise more impaired on free recall than on cued recall or recognition memory, whereas classic amnesics have clear deficits on all three; thus frontal patients do not appear to be impaired in storing or consolidating information, but they exhibit problems in retrieving it because of their deficits in "fluency, problem solving, and planning" (Shimamura et al., 1991, p. 182).

Several investigators have in fact postulated an important frontal component to the memory deficits in aging. For instance, MacIntyre and Craik (1987) found greater aging effects on source memory than on item memory. Older subjects made four times as many source errors as younger subjects, even though source errors were scored only on correctly recalled fact information. As these authors point out, memory for source is part of the context-specific information pertinent to an episode. Faulty episodic gating by the prefrontal cortex at either encoding or retrieval would differentially impair source memory relative to fact memory. As noted above, deficits in source memory are part of the constellation of memory deficits observed in frontal patients, but not in classic limbic amnesia. In a later study, Craik and colleagues (Craik, Morris, Morris, & Loewen, 1990) demonstrated that source amnesia in the elderly was correlated with frontal behavioral measures.

Parkin and Walter (1991) examined aging effects in both the Brown-Peterson (BP) task and a test of recognition memory. The BP task combines short-term storage with intervening interference by a secondary task, such as counting backward. Thus the BP task involves concurrent storage and processing and might qualify as a WM task, though it is not usually classified under this rubric (but see Dempster, 1992). Parkin and Walter (1991) found aging declines on both recognition memory and the BP task. In their older group, BP performance correlated with performance on both frontal measures (the WCST and a verbal fluency measure) and recognition memory scores, but recognition memory was unrelated to the frontal measures. These results could be interpreted as suggesting both a hippocampal and a frontal component to aging effects on memory, a point I will return to later.

If the hypothesis of a strong WM contribution to cognitive aging is correct, we ought to find corresponding brain changes with age in the PFCs and related structures. This is point four in my argument. Several authors have argued that the prefrontal regions are the most vulnerable parts of the brain in normal aging (Albert & Kaplan, 1980; Braun & Lalonde, 1990; Fuster, 1989; Hochnadel & Kaplan, 1984). A variety of neurological evidence supports this view. The greatest cell loss with normal aging occurs in the frontal lobes and the associated neostriatum, where the degree of loss has reached 15%–20% by the eighth decade. In contrast, cell loss in posterior cortex is less marked (Brizzee, Ordy, & Bartus, 1980; Haug et al., 1983; Terry, DeTeresa, & Hansen, 1987). There are also documented decreases with age in PFC neurochemistry and physiology, specifically in dopamine receptors (Mesco, Joseph, Blake, & Roth, 1991; Wong et al., 1984), concentrations of the catecholamines, dopamine, and norepinephrine (Carlsson, 1981; Goldman-Rakic & Brown, 1981; McEntee & Crook, 1990), and frontal blood flow (Gur et al., 1987; Shaw et al., 1984; Warren, Butler, Katholi, & Halsey, 1985). Thus the prefrontal cortices and striatum appear to suffer disproportionate losses with aging in terms of structure, neurochemistry, and metabolism. Moreover, there are brain changes extrinsic to the PFCs that occur with age that might be expected to have a disproportionate effect on the integrative functions of the prefrontal cortices, such as demyelination of the periventricular white matter, especially around the anterior frontal horns of the lateral ventricles (Mittenberg, Seidenberg, O'Leary, & Di Giulio, 1989). These same authors have documented that the most prominent aging effects on neuropsychological measures occur on frontal measures. For instance, they found the greatest aging effects on a measure of recency memory, a test on which performance has been shown to be impaired by frontal lesions but not by temporal-limbic lesions (Petrides & Milner, 1982). More recently, Daigneault, Braun, and Whitaker (1992) have documented aging declines before age 65 on various prefrontal neuropsychological measures (including the WCST and the Stroop test).

It would be simplistic, however, to assert that the brain changes in normal aging are exclusively in the PFCs and related structures. Obviously, any general metabolic or circulatory change with age will affect the whole brain. Moreover, there is evidence that the hippocampus is also differentially vulnerable to age. Squire (1987) cites evidence of both cell loss and pathologic changes (neurofibrillary tangles and plaques) in the hippocampus with normal aging (although there is other evidence suggesting *increased* dendritic branching in the hippocampus in normal

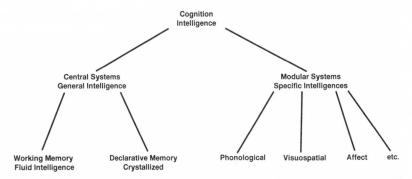

An Integrated Theory of Cognition and Intelligence

Figure 9.5   An integrated theory of cognition and intelligence.

humans from age 50 to 80; Buell & Coleman, 1979). Overall, Squire argues that the memory losses observed in normal aging are both frontal and hippocampal in origin.

In summary, although the brain changes in aging are not exclusively prefrontal, there is a fairly strong pattern of converging evidence for our hypothesis that declines in prefrontally mediated WM are central in cognitive aging.

AN INTEGRATED THEORY OF INTELLIGENCE

Given the evidence reviewed in the previous sections for the important role of WM in both life-span developmental and individual cognitive differences, it appears reasonable to attempt some theoretical intregration. I will now sketch out what an integrated theory of intelligence might look like (Figure 9.5).

This theory, like other modern hierarchical theories of intelligence (e.g., those of Vernon, 1950, and Horn, 1985), views overall intelligence, as measured by IQ tests, as a composite of different, more specific abilities. Unlike those theories, it attempts to provide an integrated account of both individual and developmental differences and uses neuropsychological data and theory to provide constraints.

At the second level of the hierarchy in Figure 9.5, the division is between central and modular systems, following Fodor's (1983) terminology. Many of the specializations exhibited by humans and other organisms meet many, but not all, of Fodor's criteria for a module: a dedicated and encapsulated processor that has evolved to quickly accomplish a certain input-output mapping. Phoneme perception and face recognition in humans, echolocation in bats, and aspects of navigation in many animals (see Gallistel, 1990) qualify as modular processes. In humans, many of these modules are mediated by posterior cortical networks, such as those found in the parietal lobes for dealing with spatial information, or those in perisylvian areas specialized for phonological processing. Such processes are species typical; they very efficiently handle information processing that is critical to the survival of that species. With a few interesting exceptions (e.g., phonological processing in humans), we would expect fewer human individual differences in modular processes (Pennington, 1991).

In contrast to modular processes, central processes are *not* specialized for a given content domain. Instead they operate across content domains and integrate information from various sources. In my theory, variation in the efficiency of central processes is the main source of variation on IQ tests, which is often called general intelligence, or "g." I identify two central systems that are important for individual differences—a hippocampally mediated LTM system and a frontally mediated WM system. As I argued earlier, this WM system underlies much of what is termed fluid intelligence in the psychometric tradition, although the openness of complex fluid measures, like the Raven's matrices, to strategy differences means they are not always sensitive or specific measures of WM. In constrast, I argue that what is called crystallized intelligence depends mainly on the declarative LTM system.

With regard to domain general, developmental cognitive differences, my theory postulates that these are mainly due to developmental differences in prefrontally mediated WM. As discussed earlier, it appears that the functional maturation of the prefrontal system is more protracted than the maturation of the hippocampal system. Thus developmental disorders are more likely to disrupt WM than either LTM or the various modular systems; as was demonstrated above, deficits in executive function are found in a variety of developmental disorders. In each of the disorders we discussed, early-treated PKU, ADHD, fragile X in females, and autism, there is also some loss of overall IQ. I argue that this loss is mainly caused by the underlying deficits in WM.

Moveover, since the development of the different neural systems underlying the modular and central cognitive systems is partially independent, and both competitive and compensatory, early damage or dysfunction in one system may lead to overdevelopment of another system. Since overall IQ is a composite measure of the functioning of all those neural systems, the drop in IQ will *not* be proportional to the loss in WM. Therefore overall IQ is more "buffered" than its components. Strikingly different "portfolios" of components can lead to the same measured overall IQ. Thus, IQ-independent deficits in WM can be found, even though WM is an important component of fluid intelligence. In addition, the overdevelopment of other systems will lead to unexpected strengths in either LTM or modular processes. Hence the finding of splinter skills, or even savant performances, in developmental disorders.

IMPLICATION AND PROBLEMS

I have sketched out an integrative theory of individual and developmental differences in intelligence in which the construct of WM plays a pivotal but not exclusive role. The theory is neuropsychological in that WM is presumed to be mediated by the PFC and associated structures. This theory has several testable implications.

1. WM tasks should correlate with both EF and fluid intelligence (FI) tasks, and EF tasks should correlate with FI tasks.

2. All three constructs (WM, EF, and FI) should load on the same factor and be more closely related to each other than to measures of STM and LTM.

3. All three constructs should respond similarly to manipulations, either experimental (load, delay, prepotency) or quasi-experimental (age or developmental disorder).

4. The relation between all three constructs and measures of STM and LTM should vary with the strategic processing requirements of the memory task.

5. The relation between all three constructs should hold across modalities (verbal vs. nonverbal). Some verbal tasks (e.g., letter series) have high WM demand, whereas others have low ones. Similarly, some spatial tasks (e.g., Block Design) have high WM demands whereas others have low ones.

6. Therefore, just as was predicted for memory, the relations between all three constructs and verbal or spatial tasks should vary with the strategic processing requirements of those tasks.

7. A negligible relation should be found between all three constructs and modular processes (e.g., face recognition, phoneme perception, implicit memory).

Obviously, much remains to be done to test the broad theory proposed here. There are also some important issues remaining. Chief among these issues is how to prevent WM from becoming a theoretical "soup stone" (Navon, 1984). Is the account of WM presented here another vague construct, like "processing resources," that somehow does all the work in explaining cognitive performance or differences? It is true that once one starts thinking about WM, it is easy to see it as ubiquitous. Indeed, I have argued that many complex cognitive processes, from planning to reasoning to discourse comprehension, require WM. But I have also argued that some processes do not—specifically STM and the storage function of LTM. To this list, we can add implicit memory, sensation, perception, and practiced motor skills. So there is a lot of cognition that does not involve WM. The current proposal does have the advantage of providing a computational and neurological account of WM, so that predictions can be made about which tasks, manipulations, and populations should demonstrate WM effects and which should not. I also argue that this account of WM is more clearly specified theoretically than WM constructs found in mainstream developmental and cognitive psychology. It differs from those constructs in its emphasis on constraint satisfaction, competitive dynamics, and inhibition. But clearly this account of WM currently lacks tasks that operationalize all its features, which is certainly a weakness.

Another key issue concerns the generality of WM. Is there one highly interdependent WM system that is a common bottleneck for action selection across many tasks? Or are there content-specific WMs in the PFCs, as suggested by Goldman-Rakic (1987)? The latter proposal enjoys some neuroanatomical and behavioral support, but it faces the problem that integration across content-specific WMs must occur in some tasks; these various WMs cannot select action completely in parallel. Dual task studies, utilizing WM tasks with different contents, could begin to address this important theoretical issue.

A third issue concerns the relation between the WM construct proposed here and processing speed or operational efficiency. Work by Case (1985), Salthouse (1991), and Kail (1991) suggests that declines and then decreases in processing speed partly account for life-span development across a very broad range of tasks. Is the g of development a change in processing speed? Is processing speed necessarily distinct from WM? The efficiency of WM, particularly its inhibitory aspect, would definitely affect speed of processing. Moreover, recent work in the psychometric tradition by Larson and Sacuzzo (1989) examined the relations among processing speed, WM, and individual differences in intelligence. Although there is a robust, moderate relation between simple RT measures (both mean and SD) and psychometric g, they found that this relation appeared to be driven by individual differences in WM. Even a simple RT task requires action selection; hence the efficiency of WM will affect both the latency and the consistency (SD) of RT.

A final theoretical issue concerns the feasibility of a neuropsychology of central cognition or thought. Fodor (1983), working in the symbolic tradition, was pessimistic that central processes could ever be analyzed because, unlike modular processes, they are not encapsulated or domain specific. Confirmation of any given belief is sensitive to "global properties of the field of beliefs taken collectively." Therefore central "systems are unlikely to exhibit articulated neuro-architecture" (p. 127), and hence, brain-behavior relations for central systems will be hard to find (essentially, Lashley's equipotentiality problem). More important, such a system, because it is holistic or global, will not be computationally tractable. Thus, in sum, central systems will be neither localizable to particular neural circuits nor computationally tractable in a cognitive theory.

How can we answer these proposed limits? Ironically enough, the answers lie in the connectionist aspect of our theory. Notice that our proposal for the computations performed by prefrontally mediated WM allows for a global system that is computationally tractable and does have a specific neuroarchitecture. WM solves the constraint satisfaction problem; everything an organism "knows" is available as a constraint on current action selection as mediated by WM. The computational model employed is a distributed, connectionist network in which a global best fit is worked out through a dynamic, competitive process. So just as a connectionist approach has proved useful for analyzing cognitive processes such as perception, which appear more modular, it may likewise prove useful for understanding central processes, thus providing a neuropsychology of thought.

REFERENCES

Albert, M. S., & Kaplan, E. (1980). Organic implications of neuropsychologic deficits in the elderly. In L. W. Poon, J. L. Fozard, L. S. Cermak, D. Arenberg, & L. W. Thompson (Eds.), *New directions in memory and aging* (pp. 403–429). Hillsdale, NJ: Erlbaum.

Anderson, J. R. (1974). Retrieval of propositional information from long-term memory. *Cognitive Psychology, 6,* 451–474.

Anderson, J. R. (1983). *The architecture of cognition.* Cambridge: Harvard University Press.

Baddeley, A. D. (1986). *Working memory.* Oxford: Clarendon Press.

Baddeley, A. D. (1992). Working memory. *Science, 255,* 556–559.

Baddeley, A. D., & Hitch, G. J. (1974). Working memory. In G. Bower (Ed.), *Recent advances in learning and motivation* (Vol. 3). New York: Academic Press.

Bianchi, L. (1922). *The mechanism of the brain and the function of the frontal lobes.* Edinburgh: Livingstone.

Binet, A., & Simon, T. (1905). Méthodes nouvelles pour le diagnostic du niveau intellectual des anormaux. *Année Psychologique, 11,* 191–244.

Birren, J. E. (1952). A factorial analysis of the Wechsler-Bellevue scale given to an elderly population. *Journal of Consulting Psychology, 16,* 399–405.

Brainerd, C. J., & Kingma, J. (1984). *Memory and cognitive development: Are short-term memory and working memory separate systems?* Research Report, Department of Psychology, University of Alberta.

Brainerd, C. J., & Kingma, J. (1985). On the independence of short term memory and working memory in cognitive development. *Cognitive Neuropsychology, 17,* 210–247.

Braun, C. M. J., & Lalonde, R. (1990). Decline of cognitive functions in the aged: A neuropsychological perspective. *Revue Canadienne du Viellissement, 9,* 135–158.

Brizzee, K. R., Ordy, J. M., & Bartus, R. T. (1980). Localization of cellular changes within multi-modal sensory regions in aged monkey brain: Possible implications for age-related cognitive loss. *Neurobiological Aging, 1,* 45–52.

Brown, A. L., & Scott, S. S. (1971). Recognition memory of pictures in preschool children. *Journal of Experimental Child Psychology, 11,* 401–412.

Buber, M. (1955). *Between man and men.* Boston: Beacon Press.

Buell, S. J., & Coleman, P. D. (1979). Dendritic growth in the aged human brain and failure of growth in senile dementia. *Science, 206,* 854–856.

Burdach, K. F. (1939). In G. Rylander, Personality changes after operations of the frontal lobes. *Acta Psychiatrica et Neurologica Scandanavia* (Suppl. 20). (Original work published 1819)

Calvin, W. H. (1989). *The cerebral symphony.* New York: Bantam Books.

Cantor, J., Engle, R. W., & Hamilton, G. (1991). Short-term memory, working memory, and verbal abilities: How do they relate? *Intelligence, 15,* 229–246.

Carlsson, A. (1981). Aging and brain neurotransmitters. In T. Crook & S. Gershon (Eds.), *Strategies for the development of an effective treatment of senile dementia* (pp. 93–104). New Canaan, CT: Mark Powley.

Carpenter, P. A., Just, M. A. (1989). The role of working memory in language comprehension. In D. Klahr & K. Kotovsky (Eds.), *Complex information processing: The impact of Herbert A. Simon* (pp. 31–68). Hillsdale, NJ: Erlbaum.

Carpenter, P. A., Just, M. A., & Shell, P. (1990). What one intelligence test measures: A theoretical account of the processing in the Raven Progressive Matrices Test. *Psychological Review, 97,* 404–431.

Case, R. (1978). Intellectual development from birth to adulthood: A neo-Piagetian interpretation. In R. S. Siegler (Ed.), *Children's thinking: What develops?* (pp. 37–71). Hillsdale, NJ: Erlbaum.

Case, R. (1985). *Intellectual development.* New York: Academic Press.

Case, R. (1991). *The mind's staircase.* Hillsdale, NJ: Erlbaum.

Case, R. (1992). The role of the frontal lobes in the regulation of cognitive development. *Brain and Cognition, 20,* 51–73.

Case, R., Kurland, M., & Goldberg, J. (1982). Operational efficiency and the growth of short-term memory span. *Journal of Experimental Child Psychology, 33,* 386–404.

Cattell, R. B. (1943). The measurement of adult intelligence. *Psychological Bulletin, 40,* 153–193.

Cohen, J. D., & Servan-Schreiber, D. (1992). Context, cortex, and dopamine: A connectionist approach to behavior and biology in schizophrenia. *Psychological Review, 99,* 45–77.

Cohn, N. B., Dustman, R. E., & Bradford, D. C. (1984). Age-related decrements in Stroop Color Test performance. *Journal of Clinical Psychology, 40,* 1244–1250.

Connelly, S. L., Hasher, L., & Zacks, R. T. (1991). Aging and the inhibition of spatial location. *Journal of Experimental Psychology: Human Perception, 19*(6), 1238–1249.

Craik, F. I., & Jennings, J. M. (1992). Human memory. In F. I. Craik and T. A. Salthouse (Eds.), *The handbook of aging and cognition.* Hillsdale, NJ: Erlbaum.

Craik, F. I., Morris, L. W., Morris, R. G., & Loewen, E. R. (1990). Relation between source amnesia and frontal lobe functioning in older adults. *Psychological Aging, 5*(1), 148–151.

Daigneault, S., Braun, C. M. J., & Whitaker, H. A. (1992). Early effects of normal aging on perseverative and non-perseverative prefrontal measures. *Developmental Neuropsychology, 8*(1), 99–114.

Damasio, A. R., Tranel, D., & Damasio, H. C. (1991). Somatic markers and the guidance of behavior: Theory and preliminary testing. In H. S. Levin, H. M. Eisenberg, & A. L. Benton (Eds.), *Frontal lobe function and dysfunction* (pp. 217–229). New York: Oxford University Press.

Daneman, M., & Carpenter, P. A. (1980). Individual differences in working memory and reading. *Journal of Verbal Learning and Verbal Behavior, 19,* 450–466.

Dehaene, S., & Changeux, J. P. (1989). A simple model of prefrontal cortex function in delayed-response tasks. *Journal of Cognitive Neuroscience, 1,* 244–261.

Dehaene, S., & Changeux, J. P. (1991). The Wisconsin Card Sorting Test: Theoretical analysis and modeling in a neuronal network. *Cerebral Cortex, 1,* 62–79.

Dempster, F. N. (1985). Short-term memory development in childhood and adolescence. In C. J. Brainerd and M. Pressley (Eds.), *Basic processes in memory development.* New York: Springer-Verlag.

Dempster, F. N. (1991). Inhibitory processes: A neglected dimension of intelligence. *Intelligence, 15,* 157–173.

Dempster, F. N. (1992). The rise and fall of the inhibitory mechanism: Toward a unified theory of cognitive development and aging. *Developmental Review, 12,* 45–75.

Denmark, F. L. (1984). Zeigarnik effect. In R. J. Corsiri & B. D. Ozaki (Eds.), *Encyclopedia of psychology.* New York: Wiley.

Dennett, D. C. (1987). *The intentional stance.* Cambridge: MIT Press.

Dennett, D. C. (1991). *Consciousness explained.* Boston: Little, Brown.

Dennis, M. (1991). Frontal lobe function in childhood and adolescence: A heuristic for assessing attention regulation, executive control, and the intentional states important for social discourse. *Developmental Neuropsychology, 7,* 327–358.

Diamond, A., Ciaramitaro, V., Donner, E., Djali, S., & Robinson, M. (in review). An animal model of early-treated PKU.

Diamond, A., & Goldman-Rakic, P. S. (1989). Comparison of human infants and rhesus monkeys on Piaget's AB task: Evidence for dependence on dorsolateral prefrontal cortex. *Experimental Brain Research, 74,* 24–40.

Diamond, A., Hurwitz, W., Lee, E. Y., Bockes, T., Grover, W., & Minarcik, C. (in review). Cognitive deficits on frontal cortex tasks in children with early-treated PKU: Results of two years of longitudinal study.

Edelman, G. M. (1987). *Neural Darwinism.* New York: Basic Books.

Fischer, K. W. (1980). A theory of cognitive development: The control and construction of hierarchies of skills. *Psychological Review, 87,* 477–531.

Fitzhugh, K., Fitzhugh, L., & Reitan, R. (1967). Influence of age on measures of problem solving and experimental background in subjects with long-standing cerebral dysfunction. *Journal of Gerontology, 19,* 132–134.

Fodor, J. A. (1983). *The modularity of mind.* Cambridge: MIT Press.

Foster, J. C., & Taylor, G. A. (1920). The applicability of mental tests to persons over 50. *Journal of Applied Psychology, 4,* 39–58.

Friedman, H. R., & Goldman-Rakic, P. S. (1988). Activation of the hippocampus by working memory: A 2-deoxyglucose study of behaving rhesus monkeys. *Journal of Neuroscience, 8,* 4693–4706.

Fuster, J. M. (1989). *The prefrontal cortex: Anatomy, physiology, and neuropsychology of the frontal lobe* (2nd ed.). New York: Raven Press.

Gallistel, C. R. (1990). *The organization of learning.* Cambridge: MIT Press.

Galton, F. (1887). Notes on prehension in idiots. *Mind, 12,* 79–82.

Gerard, L., Zacks, R. T., Hasher, L., & Radvansky, G. A. (1991). Age deficits in retrieval: The fan effect. *Journal of Gerontology: Psychological Sciences, 46,* P131–136.

Goldman-Rakic, P. S. (1987a). Development of cortical circuitry and cognitive function. *Child Development, 58,* 601–622.

Goldman-Rakic, P. S. (1987b). Circuitry of primate prefrontal cortex and regulation of behavior by representational memory. In F. Plum, (Ed.), *Handbook of physiology: Section 1. The nervous system: Vol. 5. Higher functions of the brain.* Bethesda, MD: American Physiological Society.

Goldman-Rakic, P. S. (1988). Topography of cognition: Parallel distributed networks in primate association cortex. *Annual Review of Neuroscience, 11,* 137.

Goldman-Rakic, P. S. (1992). Prefrontal cortical dysfunction in schizophrenia: The relevance of working memory. In B. Carroll (Ed.), *Psychopathology and the brain.* New York: Raven Press.

Goldman-Rakic, P. S., & Brown, R. B. (1981). Regional changes of monoamines in cerebral cortex and subcortical structures of aging rhesus monkeys. *Neuroscience, 6,* 177–187.

Goldman-Rakic, P. S., & Friedman, H. R. (1991). The circuitry of working memory revealed by anatomy and metabolic imaging. In H. S. Levin, H. M. Eisenberg, & A. L. Benton (Eds.), *Frontal lobe function and dysfunction* (pp. 72–91). New York: Oxford University Press.

Goldman-Rakic, P. S., Seleman, L. D., & Schwartz, M. L. (1984). Dual pathways connecting the dorsolateral prefrontal cortex with the hippocampal formation and parahippocampal cortex in the rhesus monkey. *Neuroscience, 12,* 719–743.

Greeno, J. G. (1973). The structure of memory and the process of solving problems. In R. C. Solso (Ed.), *Contemporary issues in cognitive psychology.* Washington, DC: Winston.

Gur, R. C., Gur, R. E., Obrist, W. D., Skolnick, B. E., & Reivich, M. (1987). Age and regional cerebral blood flow at rest and during cognitive activity. *Archives of General Psychiatry, 44,* 617–621.

Hamm, V. P., & Hasher, L. (1992). Age and the availability of inferences. *Psychology and Aging, 7,* 1–9.

Harlow, J. M. (1868). Recovery from the passage of an iron bar through the head. *Publications of the Massachusetts Medical Society, 2,* 327–346.

Hartman, M., & Hasher, L. (1991). Aging and suppression: Memory for previously relevant information. *Psychology and Aging, 6,* 587–594.

Hasher, L., Stoltzfus, E. R., Zacks, R. T., & Rypma, B. (1991). Age and inhibition. *Journal of Experimental Psychology: Learning, Memory, and Cognition, 17,* 163–169.

Hasher, L., & Zacks, R. T. (1988). Working memory, comprehension, and aging: A review and a new view. In G. H. Bower (Ed.), *The psychology of learning and motivation* (Vol. 22, pp. 193–225). San Diego, CA: Academic Press.

Haug, H., Barmwater, U., Eggers, R., Fischer, D., Kuhl, S., & Sass, N. L. (1983). Anatomical changes in aging brain: Morphometric analysis of the human prosencephalon. In J. Cervos-Navarro & H. I. Sarkander (Eds.), *Brain aging: Neuropathology and neuropharmacology (Aging, Vol. 21),* pp. 1–12. New York: Raven Press.

Hebb, D. O. (1942). The effect of early and late brain injury upon test scores, and the nature of normal adult intelligence. *Proceedings of the American Philosophical Society, 85,* 275–292.

Hebb, D. O. (1945). Man's frontal lobes: A critical review. *Archives of Neurology and Psychology, 54,* 10–24.

Hebb, D. O. (1949). *The organization of behavior.* New York: Wiley.

Hochnadel, G., & Kaplan, E. (1984). Neuropsychology of normal aging. In M. Albert (Ed.), *Clinical neurology of aging* (pp. 231–244). New York: Oxford University Press.

Holmes, O. W. (1871). *Mechanism in thought and morals.* Boston: Osgood.

Horn, J. L. (1985). Remodeling old models of intelligence. In B. Wolman (Ed.), *Handbook of intelligence* (pp. 267–300). New York: Wiley.

Huttenlocher, P. R. (1979). Synaptic density in human frontal cortex: Developmental change and effects of aging. *Brain Research, 163,* 195–205.

Jacobs, J. (1887). Experiments in prehension. *Mind, 12,* 75–79.

James, W. (1890). *Principles of psychology* (Vol. 1). New York: Holt, Rinehart and Winston.

Jones, H. E. (1959). Intelligence and problem solving. In J. E. Birren (Ed.), *Handbook of aging and the individual* (pp. 700–738). Chicago: University of Chicago Press.

Kail, R. (1991). Developmental change in speed of processing during childhood and adolescence. *Psychological Bulletin, 109,* 490–501.

Klapp, S. T., Marshburn, E. A., & Lester, P. T. (1983). Short term memory does not involve the "working memory" of intellectual processing: The demise of a common assumption. *Journal of Experimental Psychology: General, 112,* 240–264.

Kyllonen, P. C., & Christal, R. E. (1991). Reasoning ability is (little more than) working memory capacity?! *Intelligence, 14,* 389–433.

Larson, G. E., & Sacuzzo, D. P. (1989). Cognitive correlates of general intelligence: Toward a process theory of g. *Intelligence, 13,* 5–31.

Levin, H. S., Culhane, K. A., Hartmann, J., Evankovich, K., & Mattson, A. J. (1991). Developmental changes in performance on tests of purported frontal lobe functioning. *Developmental Neuropsychology, 7*(3), 377–395.

Levin, H. S., Culhane, K., Mendelsohn, D., Chapman, S., Harward, H., Hartmann, J., Bruce, D., Fletcher, J., & Ewing-Cobbs, L. (February, 1991). *Effects of frontal versus extrafrontal lesions on planning ability in head-injured children.* Paper presented at the annual meeting of the International Neuropsychological Society, San Antonio, TX.

Levine, D. S., Leven, S. J., & Prueitt, P. S. (1992). Integration, disintegration, and the frontal lobes. In D. S. Levine and S. J. Leven (Eds.), *Motivation, emotion, and goal direction in neural networks* (pp. 301–335). New York: Erlbaum.

Luria, A. (1966). *Higher cortical functions in man.* New York: Basic Books.

MacIntyre, J. S., & Craik, F. I. M. (1987). Age differences in memory for item and source information. *Canadian Journal of Psychology, 41*(2), 175–192.

Mazzocco, M. M. M., Hagerman, R. J., Cronister-Silverman, A., & Pennington, B. F. (1992). Specific frontal lobe deficits among women with the fragile X gene. *American Academy of Child and Adolescent Psychiatry, 31,* 1141–1148.

Mazzocco, M. M. M., Pennington, B. F., & Hagerman, R. J. (1993). The neurocognitive phenotype of female carriers of fragile X: Additional evidence for specificity. *Journal of Developmental and Behavioral Pediatrics, 29,* 328–335.

McClelland, J. L., & Rumelhart, D. E. (1987). *Explorations in parallel distributed processing.* Cambridge: MIT Press.

McEntee, W. J., & Crook, T. H. (1990). Age-associated memory impairment: A role for catecholamines. *Neurology, 40,* 526–530.

Mesco, E. R., Joseph, J. A., Blake, M. J., & Roth, G. S. (1991). Loss of D^2 receptors during aging is partially due to decreased levels of MRNA. *Brain Research, 545,* 355–357.

Miller, G. A., Galanter, E., & Pribram, K. H. (1960). *Plans and the structure of behavior.* New York: McGraw-Hill.

Minshew, N. J., & Goldstein, G. (1993). Is autism an amnesic disorder? Evidence from the California Verbal Learning Test. *Neuropsychology, 7,* 209–216.

Mittenberg, W., Seidenberg, M., O'Leary, D. S., & Di Giulio, D. V. (1989). Changes in cerebral functioning associated with normal aging. *Journal of Clinical and Experimental Neuropsychology, 11,* 918–932.

Morris, N., & Jones, D. M. (1990). Memory updating in working memory: The role of the central executive. *British Journal of Psychology, 81,* 111–121.

Munstadt, S. (1966). *The concept of memory.* New York: Random House.

Navon, D. (1984). Resources—a theoretical soup stone? *Psychological Review, 91,* 216–234.

Norman, D. A., & Shallice, T. (1980). *Attention to action: Willed and automatic control of behavior* (Tech. Rep. No. 99). San Diego: University of California, Center for Human Information Processing. (Reprinted in revised form in R. J. Davidson, G. E. Schwartz, & D. Shapiro [Eds.] [1986]. *Consciousness and self-regulation* [vol. 4]. New York: Plenum Press.)

Ozonoff, S., Pennington, B. F., & Rogers, S. (1991). Executive function deficits in high functioning autistic children: Relationship to theory of mind. *Journal of Child Psychology and Psychiatry, 32*(7), 1081–1105.

Parkin, A. J., & Walter, B. M. (1991). Aging, short-term memory, and frontal dysfunction. *Psychobiology, 19*(2), 175–179.

Pascual-Leone, J. (1970). A mathematical model for the transition rule in Piaget's developmental stages. *Acta Psychologia, 63,* 301–345.

Pascual-Leone, J. (1973). *A theory of constructive operators, a neo-Piagetian model of conservation, and the problem of horizontal decalages.* Unpublished manuscript, York University.

Pashler, H. (1992). Attentional limitations in doing two tasks at the same time. *Current Directions in Psychological Science, 1,* 44–52.

Pennington, B. F., Groisser, D., & Welsh, M. C. (1993). Contrasting deficits in attention deficit hyperactivity disorder versus reading disability. *Developmental Psychology, 29,* 511–523.

Pennington, B. F., Rogers, S., Bennetto, L., & Ozonoff, S. (1993, March). *Executive functions and imitation skill in autistic children.* Paper presented at the meeting of the Society for Research in Child Development, New Orleans.

Pennington, B. F., Van Doorninck, W. J., & McCabe, E. R. B. (1985). Neuropsychological deficits in early treated phenylketonuria. *American Journal of Mental Deficiency, 89,* 467–474.

Petrides, M., Milner, B. (1982). Deficits on subject-ordered tasks after frontal- and temporal-lobe lesions in man. *Neuropsychologia, 20,* 249–262.

Piven, J., Berthier, M. L., Starkstein, S. E., Nehme, E., Pearlson, G., & Folstein, S. (1990). Magnetic resonance imaging evidence for a defect of cerebral cortical development in autism. *American Journal of Psychiatry, 147,* 734–739.

Proctor, R. A. (1873). Growth and decay of mind. *Cornhill Magazine, 28,* 541–555.

Raven, J. C. (1948). The comparative assessment of intellectual ability. *British Journal of Psychology, 39,* 12–19.

Roberts, R. J., Hager, L. D., and Heron, C. (in press). Prefrontal cognitive processes: Working memory and inhibition in the antisaccade task. *Journal of Experimental Psychology: General.*

Salthouse, T. A. (1988). Initializing the formalization of theories of cognitive aging. *Psychology and Aging, 3,* 1–16.

Salthouse, T. A. (1991). *Theoretical perspectives on cognitive aging.* Hillsdale, NJ: Erlbaum.

Salthouse, T. A., & Babcock, R. L. (1991). Decomposing adult age differences in working memory. *Developmental Psychology, 27,* 763–776.

Salthouse, T. A., Mitchell, D. R. D., Skovronek, E., & Babcock, R. L. (1989). Effects of adult age and working memory on reasoning and spatial abilities. *Journal of Experimental Psychology, 15,* 507–516.

Schneider, W., & Shiffrin, R. M. (1977). Controlled and automatic human information processing: I. Detection, search and attention. *Psychological Review*, *84*, 1–66.

Segalowitz, S. J., Wagner, W. J., and Menna, R. (1992). Lateral versus frontal ERP predictors of reading skill. *Brain and Cognition, 20*, 85–103.

Shallice, T. (1982). Specific impairments in planning. In D. E. Broadbent & L. Wieskrantz (Eds.), *The neuropsychology of cognitive function*. London: Royal Society.

Shallice, T. (1988). *From neuropsychology to mental structure*. Cambridge: Cambridge University Press.

Shallice, T., & Burgess, P. (1991). Higher-order cognitive impairments and frontal lobe lesions in man. In H. S. Levin, H. M. Eisenberg, & A. L. Benton (Eds.), *Frontal lobe function and dysfunction*. New York: Oxford University Press.

Shaw, T. G., Mortel, K. F., Meyer, J. S., Rogers, R. L., Hardenberg, J., & Cutaia, M. M. (1984). Cerebral blood flow changes in benign and cerebrovascular disease. *Neurology, 34*, 855–862.

Shimamura, A. P., Janowsky, A. P., & Squire, L. R. (1991). What is the role of frontal lobe damage in memory disorders? In H. S. Levin, H. M. Eisenberg, & A. L. Benton (Eds.), *Frontal lobe function and dysfunction*. New York: Oxford University Press.

Shute, G. E., & Huertas, V. (1990). Developmental variability in frontal lobe function. *Developmental Neuropsychology, 6*, 1–11.

Simon, H. (1962). An information processing theory of intellectual development. In W. Kessen & C. Kohlman (Eds.), Thought in the young child. *Monographs of the Society for Research in Child Development, 27*(2), 150–155.

Sloman, S. A., & Rumelhart, D. E. (1992). Reducing interference in distributed memories through episodic gating. In A. F. Healy, S. M. Kosslyn, & R. M. Shiffrin (Eds.), *Essays in Honor of W. K. Estes*. Hillsdale, NJ: Erlbaum.

Sternberg, R. J. (1985). *Beyond IQ: A triarchic theory of human intelligence*. Cambridge: Cambridge University Press.

Stoltzfus, E. R., Hasher, L., Zacks, R. T., Ulivi, M. S., & Goldstein, D. (1994). Investigations of inhibition and interference in younger and older adults. Manuscript submitted for publication.

Squire, L. (1987). *Memory and brain*. New York: Oxford University Press.

Terry, R. D., DeTeresa, R., & Hansen, L. A. (1987). Neocortical cell counts in normal human adult aging. *Annals of Neurology, 21*, 530–539.

Thatcher, R. W. (1991). Maturation of the human frontal lobes: Physiological evidence for staging. *Developmental Neuropsychology, 7*, 397–419.

Van Orden, G. C., Pennington, B. F., & Stone, G. O. (1990). Word identification in reading and the promise of subsymbolic psycholinguistics. *Psychological Review, 97*, 488–522.

Vernon, P. E. (1950). *The structure of human abilities*. New York: Wiley.

Warren, L. R., Butler, R W., Katholi, C. R., & Halsey, R. M. (1985). Neurological effects of occupational exposure to cadmium. *Journal of Clinical and Experimental Neuropsychology, 11*, 933–943.

Wechsler, D. (1955). *Manual for the Wechsler scale.* New York: Psychological Corporation.

Weinberger, D. R. (1992). *A neural systems approach to the frontal lobes.* Paper presented at the American Academy of Neurology meeting, San Diego.

Welford, A. (1958). *Aging and human skill.* London: Oxford University Press.

Welford, A. (1962) On changes of performance with age. *Lancet, 17,* 335–339.

Welsh, M. C., & Pennington, B. F. (1988). Assessing frontal lobe functioning in children: Views from developmental psychology. *Developmental Neuropsychology, 4,* 199–230.

Welsh, M. C., Pennington, B. F., & Groisser, D. B. (1991). A normative-developmental study of executive function: A window on prefrontal function in children? *Developmental Neuropsychology, 7*(2), 131–149.

Welsh, M. C., Pennington, B. F., Ozonoff, S., Rouse, B., & McCabe, E. R. B. (1990). Neuropsychology of early-treated phenylketonuria: Specific executive function deficits. *Child Development, 61,* 1697–1713. (Reprinted in *Annual Progress in Child Psychiatry and Child Development,* 1991, *24*)

Wertheimer, M. (1945). *Productive thinking.* New York: Harper.

Wong, D. F., Wagner, H. N., Dannals, R. F., Links, J. M., Frost, J. J., Ravert, H. T., Wilson, A. A., et al. (1984). Effects of age on dopamine and serotonin receptors measured by positron tomography in the living human brain. *Science, 21,* 1393–1396.

Zametkin, A. J., Nordahl, T. E., Gross, M., King, A. C., Semple, W. E., Rumsey, J., Hamberger, S., & Cohen, R. (1990). Cerebral glucose metabolism in adults with hyperactivity of childhood onset. *New England Journal of Medicine, 323,* 1361–1415.

LANGUAGE AND NARRATIVE

Chapter Ten

Language in, on, and about Time

Elizabeth Bates, Jeffrey Elman, and Ping Li

Language is a system that lives in time—perhaps more so than any other aspect of mind and behavior. Literate individuals can write down their thoughts and leave them lying about for a while in some atemporal paper space. But these written forms are frozen and lifeless until someone picks them up and turns them back into a temporal stream. Spoken language can be used to talk about the past, and it lives in a rapidly changing present. But it always faces forward, rushing toward a future that is (more often than not) charted only a few words or syllables in advance. These forward-facing, temporally constrained properties have some important implications for the way language is acquired by children, implications that we will review in this chapter from three points of view: language *in* time, language *on* time, and language *about* time.

In the first section (*in* time), we deal with the central role of prediction (i.e., guessing what comes next) in language learning. In particular, we will review some recent simulations of language learning in recurrent nets, a kind of neural network architecture that also lives in time, using information about the present and the past to guess what word (or other linguistic element) is going to come next. Results suggest that a future-

Partial support for the writing of this chapter was provided by the Human Frontier Science Program Organization.

oriented system of this kind has enormous potential for capturing realistic aspects of language learning in children.

In the second section (*on* time), we view language as a complex skill that must be carried out under serious temporal constraints. In particular, we compare and contrast the effect of temporal constraints on comprehension (i.e., strategies for optimizing information before it fades away) and on production (strategies for the rapid access of words and sentence frames, and the problems of choice and commitment in sentence planning). This framework helps us to understand aspects of language development that go beyond the "acquisition" of words and grammatical rules, with an emphasis on developmental changes in the efficiency of real-time language use.

In the third and final section (*about* time), we look at how children learn to talk about time. This involves a brief review of cross-linguistic evidence on the development of time words (e.g., "tomorrow," "now"), verb tense (e.g., past, present, future), and verb aspect (e.g., complete vs. incomplete events; continuous, punctate and/or iterative events). Emphasis will be placed on cognitive and conceptual prerequisites for the development of "time talk."

LANGUAGE IN TIME

Time is clearly important to human behavior, if only because many activities are necessarily expressed as temporal sequences. We understand causality because causes precede effects; we learn that the coherent motion over time of points on the retinal array is a good indicator of objecthood; and it is difficult even to think about phenomena such as language, goal-directed behavior, or planning without some way of representing time. So it is particularly curious that most theories of human behavior completely neglect time.

To be sure, there are notable exceptions. Some theorists have seen that the processing of serially ordered events and the abstract representation of those events pose serious challenges. For example, an important issue in models of motor activity is whether the action plan is a literal specification of the output sequence or represents serial order in a more abstract manner (e.g., Fowler, 1977, 1980; Jordan & Rosenbaum, 1988; Kelso, Saltzman, & Tuller, 1986; Lashley, 1951; MacNeilage, 1970; Saltzman & Kelso, 1987). Linguistic theoreticians, on the other hand, have tended to be less concerned with the representation of time (typically assuming, for instance, that all the information in a sentence is somehow made available simultaneously in a syntactic tree); but the research in natural language processing suggests that the problem is not trivially solved (e.g., Frazier & Fodor, 1978; Marcus, 1980). Thus one of the most elementary facts about human activity—that it has temporal extent—is sometimes ignored and is often problematic.

Connectionist Models

In the past decade there has been renewed interest in computational models of behavior that have "brainlike" properties. The guiding principle underlying this approach (sometimes called "connectionism," or "parallel distributed processing," or "neural network models") is that many important aspects of human behavior may be explained by understanding the constraints and properties of the hardware (neural tissue) that supports it. Although it is undoubtedly true that we know far less about brain function than remains to be discovered, there are nonetheless a number of ways the brain is clearly different from the standard digital computer. On one hand, memory access time is dramatically slower in the brain (tens of milliseconds, compared with nanoseconds for the computer); on the other hand, digital computers execute instructions serially, one at a time, whereas processing in the brain is distributed over millions of units that may be active simultaneously. Programs in the computer consist of lists of instructions; "programs" in the brain are probably stored as modifications in synaptic strengths.

Connectionist models attempt to capture these basic properties by using a large number of simple processing units (each with roughly the computational power of a neuron), in which processing elements may display a graded range of outputs (but with nonlinearities in their output function), with massive interconnections between units. An important feature of this approach is the existence of relatively simple learning algorithms that allow networks of this sort to learn behaviors based on example rather than explicit instructions or rules.

Although one of the early attractions of such systems was their ability to carry out processing in parallel (in a way similar to what is believed true of humans), more recent developments have opened up a new way of dealing with serial processing. A variety of approaches have been studied (e.g., Elman, 1990; Jordan, 1986; Stornetta, Hogg, & Huberman, 1987; Tank and Hopfield, 1987; Waibel, Hanazawa, Hinton, Shikano, & Lang, 1987; Watrous & Shastri, 1987; Williams & Zipser, 1988). The most intriguing are those that treat the processor as a dynamic system (that is, a system in which the current state depends to some degree on its prior state). These systems are deceptively simple in appearance but have yielded surprising results.

One of the key insights that has emerged from simulations involving these models is that an enormous amount of information can be gleaned merely by attending to serially ordered input and attempting to predict what will come next. In some sense, of course, this is hardly surprising.

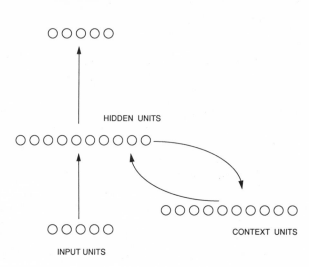

OUTPUT UNITS

HIDDEN UNITS

CONTEXT UNITS

INPUT UNITS

Figure 10.1   Simple recurrent network. Hidden-unit activations are copied into the context units on cycle t, then fed back to the hidden units on cycle $t + 1$.

The order of events in the world (for example, of words in utterances) is rarely either random or lacking structure, but it reflects a rich and complex interaction of constraints. It makes sense that a system that can predict which events will follow other events must be sensitive (if only implicitly) to those constraints. What is less clear is how much prior knowledge must be possessed in order to learn these constraints. The simulations we describe below suggest that rather less prior knowledge is required than one might think.

Learning about Lexical Categories

For instance, consider the problem of lexical semantics: How do children learn the meanings of words? Clearly there are multiple sources of information that allow children to learn word meanings. But what about the primitive semantic and grammatical categories themselves: animate, human, breakable, noun, transitive verb, and so on? Are these innately specified, or can they be induced from the input alone?

Elman (1990) attempted to answer this question by presenting a neural network with a simple problem. The network (shown in Figure 10.1) consisted of three layers. The nodes in the input and output layers were used to represent words (each word was represented by turning on a different node). The intermediate ("hidden") layer was used to allow the network to form intermediate or internal representations of the words it received as input. A context layer was used to recycle hidden-layer activation patterns. This recurrent, or feedback, layer provided the network with internal memory. The network was given a sequence of words as input, one at a time, and asked to produce on its output layer a prediction of which word would follow. The words formed simple sentences and were concatenated so there were approximately 27,000 words in all (a sample fragment is shown below:

    input: dog chase woman woman smash plate   boy eat sandwich . . .
    output: chase woman woman smash plate boy   eat sandwich girl . . .

The network itself was initially configured with random weights along the connections between layers, so that the predictions at the outset were random (typically all output units would receive some small random activation). As the training proceeded, the network prediction after each new input was compared with the next word that was actually received and the discrepancy between predicted and actual word was used to adjust the weights in the network (using the back-propagation of error-learning algorithm; Rumelhart, Hinton, & Williams, 1986). This procedure allows the network weights to gradually converge on a set of values such that the correct output can be produced in response to any reasonable input.

In fact, at the conclusion of training, the network's performance was quite good. Interestingly, the network was not able to predict the exact word that would follow in any given context. Short of memorizing the sentences, this would not have been possible. A sentence beginning "The woman . . ." might continue in a variety of ways. What the network learned instead was to predict all of the words that might occur in a given context, in proportion to their likelihood of occurrence.

At this point it is worth asking how the network solved the problem. Recall that each word was represented by a vector of 30 ones and zeros in which a single bit—arbitrarily chosen—was turned on. As a result, there is no built-in information about a word's grammatical category or about its meaning. (More precisely, the words are represented by basis vectors, which are orthogonal to each other and lie at the corners of a 30-dimensional hypercube). Indeed, the very notions of grammatical category and semantic feature are not part of the representations made available to the network.

However, grammatical categories and semantic features clearly play a role in the order of words in these sentences. Although it is true that many words might occur in any given context, not just any word was acceptable. Only words that "fit" by virtue of the grammar or semantics of that sentence could be predicted. So we might expect that to solve the prediction problem the network might have to learn something about grammatical and semantic categories. If so, where would this information be situated?

The most likely location would be in the hidden layer. As the network processes a sentence, each new word activates the nodes in the hidden layer. The hidden-layer activations then cause the output nodes to be activated (in order to predict the next word). Although the encoding for words is set in advance, the activation patterns in the hidden units are learned over time by the network, and the network is free to develop internal representations of words that reflect their properties in a way that allows the network to do the prediction task. Thus it is instructive to look at these internal representations.

This can be done by allowing the trained network to process additional sentences. As each word is presented, we save the hidden unit activation pattern it evokes (in the process of producing a prediction). Metaphorically, we might imagine that we are recording event-related potentials (ERPs) from the network as it processes the stimuli, much as we might collect scalp potentials from human subjects as they listen to sentences. Eventually we end up with hidden unit activation patterns corresponding to each of the possible input words. These patterns are vectors in 150-dimensional space (because there are 150 hidden units). It is not feasible to visualize such high-dimensional patterns directly, but we can see how they are distributed in space by looking at the similarity relations between them. A hierarchical clustering tree represents this information by joining vectors that are close in space low in the tree; vectors or groups of vectors that are more distant are joined higher up.

In Figure 10.2 we see a hierarchical cluster diagram of a trained network's hidden unit activations for the words used in this simulation. Remarkably, it appears that the network has discovered a great deal about both the grammatical and the semantic characteristics of the words. The hidden unit activation space is divided into two major regions: verbs (shown on the top of the tree) lie within one region, and nouns (shown on the bottom) within the other. Transitive, intransitive, and optionally transitive verbs are grouped separately within the verb space. And nouns are partitioned into regions corresponding to animate and inanimate, with further divisions marking human, nonhuman, breakable, large versus small animal, and so forth.

These groupings are not part of the input in any overt sense, but they do reflect the temporal structure of the sentences. The noun/verb distinction underlies the basic word order; the argument structure of different verbs and the semantic features of different nouns account for other ways word order is constrained. So while the task of the network was not to extract these distinctions explicitly, it is clear that the

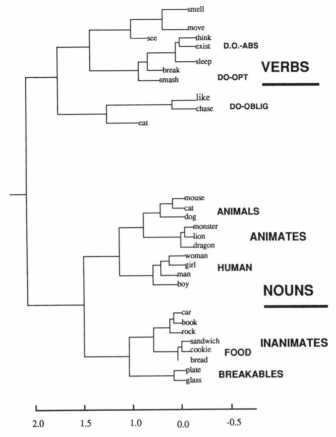

Figure 10.2   Hierarchical cluster of hidden unit activation patterns from network described in simulation 1. The input patterns are orthogonal vectors, but the hidden unit activations encode a similarity structure that reflects the semantic and grammatical characteristics of the lexicon.

(apparently simple) task of prediction provides a powerful motivation for inducing much more structure than we might have supposed at the outset.

Rules as Trajectories through State Space

In the last simulation we saw that the network was able to make useful inferences about the lexical category structure of words, based on distributional facts. The representation of the lexicon in this system looks very different from the standard lexicon we are familiar with in psycholinguistics. Rather than being a table of dictionarylike entries, the lexicon here is a region in state space, embodied in the activation patterns on the

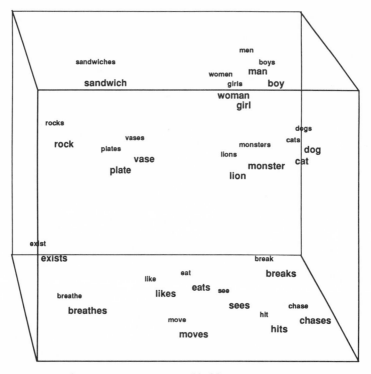

Figure 10.3   Schematic representation of hidden-unit activation patterns as vectors in an N-dimensional state space. Lexical items are points in space; different regions correspond to grammatical categories or semantic features.

hidden unit layer. The network learns to organize this space into regions that represent grammatical and semantic information. Thus the lexicon is simply the region of space into which the network moves when it "hears" a word. Figure 10.3 depicts how this might look in three dimensions. What is missing from this picture is a sense of how grammar itself is represented in such a scheme. That is, the lexicon is an important part of language, but we also need a way to represent the constraints on how words may be combined to form interpretable sentences. In traditional schemes, of course, this is accomplished through rules. We might wonder how such constraints could be represented in a system with dynamical properties, such as a recurrent network.

To explore this question, let us consider a somewhat more complex language than the one used in the first simulation, where sentences consisted of only two or three words. Obviously, natural language typically involves utterances that are not only longer, but more complex. For example, consider a sentence such as "The cat the dogs chase climbs up the fence." In some sense, there are really two sentences here: "The cat climbs up the fence," and "The dogs chase the cat." The sentences are combined here using relative-clause formation (as opposed to simply conjoining them with "and"). As a result, there is a part-whole relation between the subordinated sentence ("The dogs chase the cat") and the noun it modifies ("the cat"). There are not only conceptual consequences to this relation, but grammatical consequences as well (e.g., the first noun, "cat," is in the singular and agrees in number with the last verb, "climbs," whereas the second noun, "dogs," is in the plural and agrees with the first verb). An important question, thus, is how a network such as the one used in the first simulation might represent the structure of such complex sentences. The problem is that the significant structure of the sentence departs from the simple linear order of the words.

This problem was addressed in Elman (1991). A simple recurrent network, similar to the one shown in Figure 10.1, was trained on a prediction task involving complex sentences. The following sample illustrates the sort of sentences used:

> boys who chase dogs see girls.
> girl who boys who feed cats walk.
> cats chase dogs.
> mary feeds john.
> dogs see boys who cats who mary feeds chase.

The prediction task was complicated by the many long-distance dependencies (e.g., between main clause subject nouns and their verbs, often separated by several embedded clauses; or verbs whose direct objects preceded, rather than followed, the verbs). The network was able to learn the grammar only when it began the task with limited resources and a narrow attentional window and then "matured" slowly over time (Elman, 1993). At the conclusion of this training regime, the network not only mastered the training data but was able to generalize its performance to novel sentences that contained new lexical items and structures it had not seen before. At least from its performance, it appears that the network learned the complex grammar underlying the data. How was the grammar encoded?

One can answer this question in much the same way as for the first simulation, by looking at the hidden unit patterns as the network processes the sentences. This time, however, it is instructive to study these patterns as they change over time (and so our network ERPs are really more analogous to the time-varying traces recorded with human subjects than the static traces recorded in the first simulation). Figure 10.4 shows the trajectory of the network's "mental state" as it processes two sentences: "boy who boys chase chases boy" (bottom trace) and "boys who

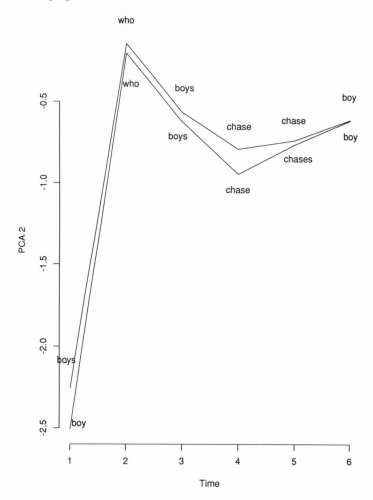

Figure 10.4 Trajectory through (hidden unit) state space as a network processes the sentences "boy who boys chase chases boy" and "boys who boys chase chase boy." The horizontal axis represents time; the vertical axis represents position in state space. The difference in the number of the initial noun (singular vs. plural) is encoded by a displacement in state space.

boys chase chase boy" (top trace). The two sentences are identical except for the embedded relative clauses, which have a singular subject in one case and a plural subject in the other. What Figure 10.4 shows is how the network marks the number of the main clause subject. This is encoded as an upward displacement (for plurals) in the plane of state space.

Figure 10.5 shows state space trajectories for the three sentences "boy chases boy," "boy sees boy," and "boy walks." The verbs in these

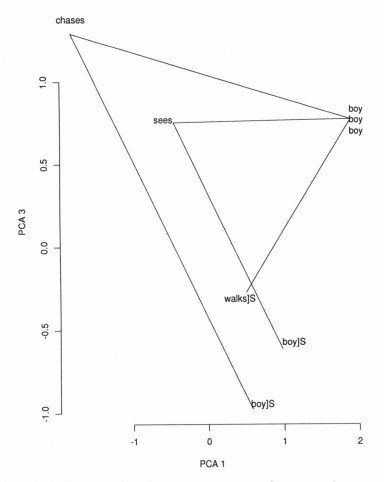

Figure 10.5 Trajectory through state space as a network processes the sentences "boy chases boy," "boy sees boy," and "boy walks." The horizontal and vertical axes represent different dimensions in the state space (see Elman, 1991, for details). The three verbs differ in their verb argument structure: in this grammar, "chases" is obligatorily transitive, "sees" is optionally transitive, and "walks" is obligatorily intransitive. The network represents verb argument expectations along an axis running from the upper left to lower right in state space.

sentences differ with regard to their verb argument structure. In this grammar, "chases" is obligatorily transitive and so always requires a direct object; "sees" is optionally transitive (in this example it is followed by a direct object, but it need not be); and "walks" is intransitive. The network learns to encode this difference in argument structure along an

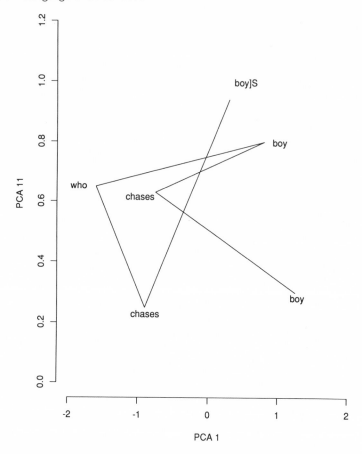

Figure 10.6 Trajectory through state space as a network processes the complex sentence "boy chases boy who chases boy." The horizontal and vertical axes represent different dimensions in the state space (see Elman, 1991, for details). The canonical pattern for a simple sentence is represented in embedded causes as a displacement (to the lower left) in state space.

axis that runs from upper left (for transitive verbs) to lower right regions of state space (for intransitive verbs).

Finally, in Figure 10.6 we see how the network represents levels of embedding. The first part of the trajectory (corresponding to the main clause, "boy chases boy") turns out to be the canonical pattern for all simple transitive sentences (the pattern looks different from that in Figure 10.5 simply because we have changed our viewing perspective and are looking at a different plane in the high-dimensional state space of the network's "brain"). In this figure we see that as the network processes additional relative clauses it replicates the basic canonical pattern, displacing it to the left and downward in state space. This spiraling pattern is typical for embedded clauses and is the way the network represents the hierarchical organization of complex sentences.

Let us now try to summarize what we have learned from these simulations. First, it is clear that there is a great deal of information to be gleaned from the linguistic input. The network starts off with minimal a priori information but is nonetheless able to discover the lexical category structure and grammatical structures implicit in the input. We do not imagine that children are tabulae rasae in the extreme sense that these networks are; yet these results suggest caution about exactly how much prior innate knowledge must be attributed to account for language acquisition.

Second, although the prediction task used in these simulations is elementary and children obviously do more than simply predict, it is also apparent that anticipating how the world will change over time is a powerful driving force for induction and leads to results that are not obviously related to the task itself. We find it plausible to believe that, particularly at early stages of development, children (and other organisms) might use prediction as a way to impose basic order on the world and to bootstrap further learning.

Finally, these networks give us new ways of thinking about the lexicon and about rules. The view that words are simply sensory stimuli that (through convention) move our brains into particular regions of mental space is appealing and is more consistent with the way we might view other sensory inputs. Sentences are not phrase structure trees, but rather trajectories through this mental space. The trajectories are constrained, of course. The dynamics of the system permit certain sequences to be processed; these are grammatically well-formed sentences. Ungrammatical sentences are sequences of words that move against the dynamics. Thus, rules are simply the sets of attractor and repeller regions contained within the system.

In short, we obtain a very different view of linguistic representations and language learning if both are viewed within the framework on temporal dynamics. Now we can turn to another approach to language and time: learning to use language under the severe temporal constraints imposed by the limits of information processing.

LANGUAGE ON TIME

There is a widespread tendency to think of linguistic knowledge as a relatively static set of meanings and rules, like the dictionaries and grammar books that gather dust on library shelves. Indeed, it is common to talk about the dynamic process of language learning as "language acquisition," a metaphor that brings to mind visions of consumers standing in checkout lines to pay for groceries, or squirrels storing nuts for the winter. We would like to argue instead that the state of "knowing a language" is better viewed as an extremely complex skill, one that must be executed rapidly and efficiently, under a number of very serious constraints on the way information can be received, stored, maintained, retrieved, transformed, and output in real time. From this point of view language development involves "learning how" as well as "learning that." If we take this straightforward and yet uncommon perspective on the nature of language learning, then a number of otherwise mysterious facts fall into place.

Under the developmental account that is implied by the term "language acquisition," words or rules have to make an abrupt transition from *outside* the child to *inside*. If this is correct, then we should also observe a large number of abrupt and discontinuous changes in behavior, reflecting the presence of linguistic knowledge that was absent just a short time before. In fact, such abrupt behavioral changes are rare (although they are occasionally observed). New words may appear quite suddenly (Carey, 1982), but their meaning and range of use are shaped gradually across months or years. And as Roger Brown (1973) has observed, grammatical regularities tend to come gradually, "like ivy growing between the bricks" (for extended discussions of this point, with corroborating evidence, see Maratsos, 1983; Marchman & Bates, 1994; Marcus et al., in press; Pizzuto & Caselli, 1992).

The usual move that linguists make to deal with such discrepancies between theory and data is the distinction between competence (linguistic knowledge) and performance (language use). On this argument, linguistic knowledge is indeed a discrete and discontinuous matter, but our view of it is often clouded by psychological factors that are independent of language proper (e.g., fading memory, changes of mind, momentary lapses of attention). This move does serve its primary purpose: It salvages abstract theories of linguistic knowledge from the vicissitudes of imperfect behavioral data. But it leaves the developmental psycholinguist with a number of difficult problems. In particular, to determine when a rule is "really there," the researcher has to develop complex criteria to separate the behavioral wheat from the chaff.

Within the field of child language, these criteria are usually treated together under the rubric of "productivity": a rule is productive when its usage can be demonstrated over some specified number or range of situations or contexts. Productivity criteria are supposed to help us eliminate situations in which the child imitates an application of a rule without any understanding, including repeated uses in well-practiced but poorly analyzed routines like "Whatchadoin?" (for "What are you doing") or

"Don't!" (uttered by a child who does not understand or use the separate elements "Do" and "not"). However, the distinction between rote usage and "true" application of a rule is not easy to make. This is particularly true for morphological markings that appear gradually—"Now you see it, now you don't"—moving from zero to 100% application across a period that may last as long as ten years. Typically, researchers compromise by establishing an arbitrary border, like Brown's criterion of "90% use in obligatory contexts" or Bloom's criterion of "use with at least five different word types in one session" (Bloom, 1970; Brown, 1973; for a comparison of these and several other criteria for productivity, see Bates, Bretherton, & Snyder, 1988). The problem with these criteria is that they are so arbitrary, assigning a sharp border to a gradual phenomenon in order to preserve a theory that does not fit the data very well. Other researchers are willing to give credit for productivity only when the child uses the rule in a novel and creative manner, with nonsense words provided by the experimenter (e.g. "Here is a wug . . . here is another wug. . . . Now I have two wugs"), or in creative errors that could not possibly have occurred in the child's linguistic input (e.g., "The cereal spilled on the floor, so I broomed it"). The problem here is that such errors or novel uses are rare in observations of spontaneous speech, so that investigators who use such criteria are likely to underestimate the child's control over the grammar.

The contrast between linguistic knowledge and linguistic use emerged quite clearly in a recent study on the "acquisition" of the English passive. Passive sentences occur roughly 1% of the time in informal English speech, yet they have been studied extensively in the psycholinguistic literature—perhaps more extensively than they deserve. The popularity of passives in psycholinguistic research is due in part to their complexity, requiring coordination of several aspects of grammar and meaning. For example, the two sentences "John hit the ball" and "The ball was hit by John" differ in word order ("John" in preverbal position vs. "the ball" in preverbal position), grammatical morphology ("hit" vs. "was hit by"), and meaning (the active form focuses on John as topic, while the passive form focuses on the ball as topic). Marchman, Bates, Burkhardt, and Good (1991) conducted a study of production of the passive in more than 170 children and adults ranging in age from 3 to 21 years. Subjects were shown a series of short black-and-white cartoons in which one character acted on another (e.g., a horse biting a goat). At the end of each cartoon, the subject was asked to describe what happened from one of two points of view; for example, "Tell me about the horse" versus "Tell me about the goat." The latter situation (focus on the patient or receiver of the action) can be viewed as the ideal context or "ecological niche" for a passive form (e.g., "The goat was bitten by the horse"), although it would of course be technically correct for the speaker to describe the situation in some other way. In this study mastery of the passive form was measured in two ways: (1) Was the speaker able to produce at least one well-formed passive sentence in response to a discourse probe that focused on the receiver of the action? (2) How often did the speaker use the passive form in its ecological niche (i.e., in response to items in which the experimenter focused on the patient)? These two measures gave very different views of the process by which passives are "acquired." All of the subjects aged 9–21 produced at least one well-formed passive; furthermore, production of at least one passive was observed in 67% of the 3-year-old children. From this point of view, we should conclude that passives are acquired (on average) before the age of 3. However, 3-year-old children produced the passive only 11% of the time on patient-focus items, compared with an average of 85% in adults. Between the ages of 3 and 21 years there was a monotonic increase in rate of passive production. From this point of view, when should we conclude that the passive is "acquired"? Based on traditional competence theories, it is acquired before the age of 3. And yet there is a very large and continuous change in the ability to produce passive forms that does not level off until at least 21 years of age. Three-year-olds "have" the requisite knowledge of passive forms. They also "have" the requisite knowledge of what passives are for, because they clearly know that an active form like "The horse bit the goat" is really not a good answer to "Tell me about the goat." Indeed, they find all kinds of direct or indirect ways to obey the discourse probe (e.g., "The goat just stood there and the horse bit him!"). So what is changing from 3 to 21 years of age? Marchman et al. (1991) conclude that there are slow and continuous developmental changes in the *accessibility* of linguistic forms. The requisite knowledge is there very early (in some rudimentary form), but speakers must learn to retrieve that knowledge efficiently and rapidly for use in conversation. Because passives are so rare (occurring less than 1% of the time in the child's input), children have relatively little experience with this complex form. They *have* it, but they cannot *do* it easily in real time.

There are many aspects of linguistic development that display these characteristics. For example, in the domain of phonology we find a phenomenon called "coarticulation," which refers to alterations in the pronunciation of one phoneme in preparation for a phoneme that is coming up shortly. Thus the sound *b* in the word "bee" is pronounced differently from the sound *b* in the word "boot." Skilled speakers make these adjustments rapidly and unconsciously. Furthermore, skilled listeners exploit these coarticulatory cues in order to predict the sounds they are going to hear next (see above). There is relatively little research on the development of coarticulation in children, but there is some reason to believe it is yet another very gradual process, in both comprehension and production, and constitutes one of the reasons little children sound the way they do.

In the domain of grammar, many more examples can be found. Bates and MacWhinney (1989) have reviewed a number of relatively late changes in sentence comprehension, reorganizations in the way preexisting knowledge is used to interpret sentences in real time. For example, Italian children "know" the rules that govern subject-verb agreement in their language by 2½ to 3 years of age (Pizzuto and Caselli, 1992) but they do not "use" that knowledge extensively to decide "who did what to whom" in sentence interpretation before 6–7 years of age (Devescovi, D'Amico, Smith, Mimica, & Bates, 1993). Given a sentence like "The dog are kicking the cows" (which would be quite grammatical in Italian), Italian adults respond by saying that "The cows did it" (i.e., they assign the actor role to the noun that agrees with the verb in number). But Italian children below age 6 are more likely to respond by choosing the dog as the actor (using word order instead of subject-verb agreement to make their decision). Devescovi et al. suggest that use of agreement cues comes in relatively late, presumably because they require the child to hold several elements in memory before a decision can be made (comparing agreement marking on the first noun, the verb, and the second noun). Thus even though very young Italians "know" the principles that govern agreement in their language (using them productively in free speech), they do not "trust" or "like" to use those rules in real time because the costs of crowding up memory are too high.

There are many other ways languages differ in how they are used in real time. From the perspective of speech production, they differ in the point at which certain *commitments* have to be made in real time. Consider, for example, the production of articles, modifiers, and nouns. Imagine an English speaker extemporizing happily about some topic, hoping to hold the floor for precious milliseconds while he figures out the word he wants to use to describe a particular object. This speaker can stall for time by saying something like the following: "The uhmmmm the little . . . knob there on the left . . ." By using the word "the," the English speaker has committed himself to nothing more specific than production of an English noun. By the time he arrives at the word "little," things have gotten a bit more precise—but not much. Consider how different things are for a speaker of Italian: "Il uhmmmm il piccolo . . . la piccola maniglia alla sinistra . . ." This speaker may have stalled for time, but at the expense of making a grammatical mistake or (at best) a false start that has to be retracted before he can go on. The reason is quite simple: The article in Italian is marked for number and gender, which means that production of the article commits the speaker to a particular number and gender. In the example above, the speaker did not know what word he would eventually use to describe "the little knob." He started out with the masculine article "il," compounded his problem by using the masculine adjective "piccolo" (for "little"), and then had to switch to the feminine form for each of these words before he could go on to produce the right target noun. The problem is even worse for a native speaker of German, because the article must be marked not only for number and gender, but for case (i.e., a marking on the article that indicates whether the noun that follows will be nominative, genitive, dative, accusative, etc.). In essence, German speakers have to have most of the sentence planned (grammatical forms as well as word selection) before they can start out.

On the other hand, these "disadvantages" in the timing of word and sentence planning end up as advantages from the listener's point of view. Assuming that the speaker does not make a mistake and does not have to retract the opening lines, German or Italian listeners can start to zero in on the identity of the noun that is coming several precious tenths of a second before English counterparts. Indeed, Kilborn (1987) has shown that German listeners have a slight but measurable advantage in word recognition experiments, owing perhaps to the exploitation of these early cues to noun identity. Like everything else in the evolution of natural languages, there appears to be a trade-off: lose something here, gain something there. All languages represent an imperfect, constantly changing, but reasonably workable set of solutions to the problem of communicating lots of information in a short time, under very serious constraints of perception, memory, and production. Each language represents a somewhat different configuration of skills, maximizing the timing and utility of information during comprehension while holding the costs of production and the likelihood of error down to some acceptable minimum. From this perspective the process of language learning has more in common with learning to walk, to dance, or to type than we might expect if we restricted ourselves entirely to the "acquisition of competence" view that has dominated the developmental literature to date. Language takes place *in time,* and the child has to learn to comprehend and produce it *on time.* This brings us to the final issue in our review: learning how to use language to talk *about time.*

LANGUAGE ABOUT TIME

The expression of time constitutes an indispensable part of language use. We describe situations as being in the past, present, or future and talk about events as ongoing or completed. Languages differ in the resources they offer for expressing time concepts, for example, whether they use grammatical devices such as tense and aspect markers or lexical items such as temporal adverbials. But they can all express basic notions concerning time.

Two of the most important devices for expressing time concepts in the world's languages are *tense* and *aspect*. Tense is typically used to locate the *event time* (the time of the event being talked about) with respect to the *speech time* (the time when the speaker utters the sentence). The event time can also be specified with reference to some time other than the speech time—the *reference time*. When the event time is before the speech time, we use the *past* tense; when speech time is before the event time, we use the *future* tense; and when the two overlap, we use the *present* tense. Note that in all these cases the speech time and the reference time overlap. When they do not, we use tense markings such as the *pluperfect* (event time before reference time and reference time before speech time) or the *future perfect* (speech time before event time and event time before reference time).

In contrast to tense, which is concerned with the relation between situations at different time points, aspect is the way speakers view the internal temporal constituency of a single situation, for example, as beginning, continuation, or completion. Traditionally, aspect is divided into two basic perspectives: *perfective* versus *imperfective* (cf. Comrie, 1976). Perfective aspect presents a situation in its entirety as a single whole (often with emphasis on the completion of the action), while imperfective aspect presents a situation with emphasis on its internal structure (focusing on the event as ongoing). As a grammatical category, aspect is expressed by inflectional morphology (e.g., "is doing" vs. "has done" in English), derivational morphology (e.g., in Russian), and other grammatical devices such as particles (e.g., in Chinese).

Clearly, children grow up speaking language in time, and they necessarily learn to use the language about time. In what follows, we will review two important theories originating from crosslinguistic studies of children's acquisition of time talk and present a general view on the relation between cognitive prerequisites and the development of temporal expressions. A first important theory (or "working hypothesis") about the acquisition of temporal expressions is Richard Weist's four-stage model. Weist (1986, 1989) proposes that children proceed through a sequence of four systems of time talk in the framework of speech time, event time, and reference time as discussed above.

The first system is the *speech time system* (about 1;0 to 1;6),[1] under

---

1. For consistency, all ages are given in the format "years;months" (e.g., 1;6 is 1 year, 6 months).

which both the event time and the reference time are frozen at the speech time. At this stage children can talk only about here and now, that is, visible objects in the immediate perceptual field. This system is characterized as having no tense, aspect, modality, and so on (cf. Brown, 1973). Weist presents crosslinguistic evidence from studies of a number of languages to support this system, including English, Polish, Hebrew, Japanese, and Mandarin Chinese. For example, Chinese has aspect but not tense markings; however, according to Erbaugh (1982), child Mandarin is not marked even for aspect at this initial phase.

The second system is the *event time system* (about 1;6 to 2;6), under which the event time has been separated from the speech time. This system is characterized by children's ability to talk about event time relative to speech time. At this stage children get out of the here and now constraints of the speech time system, and now can express both an ongoing event at the time of speech and an event at a past time, that is, before the speech time. According to Weist, they can also express their intentions and desires concerning potential subsequent events at this stage. For example, in Mandarin Chinese, children often use the modal verbs *hui* 'can' and *yao* 'want' to express their intentions (cf. Erbaugh, 1982), which prepares for the occurrence of future marking.

The third system is the *restricted reference time system* (about 2;6 to 3;0), under which the event time is now "anchored" within a framework of the reference time. The emergence of the concept of reference time is characterized by the occurrence of temporal adverbs and temporal adverbial clauses in children's utterances. At this stage children begin to use adverbs denoting reference time such as "today," "tomorrow," and "yesterday" and adverbial clauses that indicate the framework within which an event takes place, such as "when Mama was little . . ." In this case children have learned to use temporal adverbs and adverbial clauses to set up the reference time. However, it appears that the use of reference time is still restricted at this stage, because the event children talk about takes place only within the reference time; that is, children can relate only two points in time at this stage.

Only at the last stage, when the *free reference time system* about 3;0 to 4;6) is established, can they set up a reference time before or after the speech time and relate the event time to it at a third point in time. At this stage all three time concepts can be manipulated independently, and children can freely relate events to one another in time. This system is characterized by the emergence of words like *before* and *after* that allow the establishment of temporal sequencing at different time points in children's time talk. Weist also points out that although there is evidence the children can coordinate three temporal locations as early as 3 years of age, most research indicates that it is not until about 4;0 to 4;6 that children can freely express the concepts of speech time, event time, and reference time.

It has long been recognized that there is a close relation between children's expression of modality and their acquisition of the future tense. Weist (1989) points out that though researchers accept that children can express modality relatively early, they are nevertheless reluctant to credit them with the ability to express future. He suggests it is possible that all references to the future have some modal value, that is, some sense of possibility or necessity (intention, desire, obligation, permission, etc.), and therefore the expression of future is also relatively early in child language. As early as 1;7 years of age, Polish children can say things like "Mommy will take it out" as a request, and "will turn (it) over" as a statement. These kinds of requests or statements, whatever their modal value might be, surely express the deictic relation of the event time's being subsequent to the speech time.

The four-stage development of the temporal system is a very interesting phenomenon in children's expression of time. What is more interesting is that these stages correspond nicely to the cognitive and conceptual development of time. Weist suggests that children's linguistic coding of events and situations allows us to infer their conceptual development, and that crosslinguistic evidence is crucial in this respect because different languages encode time concepts in a variety of ways. When the linguistic devices used to encode a time concept are the same across languages (e.g., temporal adverbs), the emergence of the time concept into the evolving temporal systems is stable across those languages. In contrast, when the linguistic devices are different (e.g., tense and aspect markers), the emergence of the time concept will be variable. Weist suggests that each time the child makes a transition from one temporal system to another, a corresponding conceptual development is established. For example, there is evidence that children's conceptual development is no longer restricted to the here and now when they proceed to the event time system, because at this stage they have achieved the capacity for displacement—that is, they now can talk about objects outside the immediate perceptual field. Conceptually, they are now able to retrieve prior experience from memory, knowing that these experiences happened before the present time. When children have developed the reference time system at the last stages of temporal development, they can separate time points and express them either in a serial order or in reversible orders. Initially they may be restricted to expressing things only in the natural order in which things happen, such as "After John had his breakfast, he went to work," and only later can they say "Before John went to work he had his breakfast."

A second important line of theorizing about the development of children's language about time is Slobin's "Basic Child Grammar" (Slobin, 1985). Although this model is more general and not specifically designed for temporal development like Weist's four-stage model, it bears important relevance to the issue of the expression of time. The "Basic Child Grammar" assumes that children come to the language acquisition task with a prestructured "semantic space" containing a universal, uniform set of semantic notions that are at first neutral with respect to language-specific categories. According to Slobin, these semantic notions are "privileged" to be mapped onto grammatical forms of individual languages in the process of language acquisition. That is, before children's experience with specific properties of the grammar, these notions strongly attract grammatical forms of the input language in the form-meaning mapping processes. Slobin proposes two universal "temporal perspectives" in the semantic space: *process* vs. *result*. These temporal perspectives function early to define a semantic contrast in children's learning of tense and aspect systems. Slobin emphasizes that *result* is a particularly salient perspective to children and provides an early mapping point for speech segments associated with content words referring to actions. Specifically, whenever a language has an acoustically salient past tense or perfective marker on the verb, its first use by the child seems to be to comment on an immediately completed event that results in a visible change of state, such as situations denoted by the verbs "drop," "fall," "break," and "spill."

Slobin's hypothesis has been supported by crosslinguistic studies in a number of languages, including English, French, Italian, Turkish, Greek, and Chinese. In English, Bloom, Lifter, and Hafitz (1980) found that the distribution of children's tense and aspect markers was correlated with different semantic categories. In particular, between ages 1;10 and 2;4, "-ing" occurred in children's utterances almost exclusively with action verbs that named durative, noncompletive events, for example, "play", "ride," and "write," whereas "-ed" and irregular past-tense forms occurred overwhelmingly with verbs that named nondurative, completive events, that is, events "with a relatively clear result," such as "find," "fall," and "break."

Bronckart and Sinclair (1973) found that before age 6, the French children in their study used the *passé composé* (past perfective) forms significantly more often than the *présent* (present) for "perfective events" that had a clear end result and, conversely, used the *présent* significantly more often than the *passé composé* for "imperfective events" that did not lead to any observable result. These authors conclude that the distinction between process and result is the predominant and perhaps the only aspectual feature in the language of French children below 6 years old.

In Italian, Antinucci and Miller (1976) showed that their subjects first restricted their use of the past tense (*passato prossimo*) to "change of state" verbs that specified actions with a clear result, such as "fall," "find," and "break." The children did not combine activity and stative verbs with the past tense but rather used the *imperfetto* (imperfect). They also found that children made the inflectional endings of past participles agree with the number and gender of the *object* of the verb. In the adult language the participle agrees only with the subject—with one interesting exception. When there is a clitic (unstressed) object pronoun before the verb, the participle must agree with the object pronoun. Thus, the English sentence "The horse has pushed the cow" should be translated as "Il cavallo ha spinto la mucca," where the only agreement marking (indicated with underlining) occurs between subject, *cavallo* and the verb auxiliary *ha*. However, things change with the addition of an emphatic object pronoun before the verb, as in "The horse (it) has kicked the cow" (where the pronoun "it" refers to the cow). This emphatic form requires an additional agreement between participle and object, as in "Il cavallo la ha spinta la mucca," which is usually reduced further by rules of vowel elision to "Il cavallo l'ha spinta la mucca."

This is a very subtle rule in Italian, one we might not expect children to notice until they are fairly far along in development. However, it looks as though Italian children find this pattern very early and overgeneralize it to all past-participle forms, producing impossible sentences like "Il cavallo ha spinta la mucca." This "invention" or overextension of a syntactic agreement rule suggests that they tend to focus intently on the result of the event.

In Turkish, Aksu (1978) reported similar findings. Turkish children before age 4;6 tend to use the past-tense form -*di* with "change of state" verbs to mark punctual, resultative events, but use the progressive form -*iyor* with activity verbs that do not indicate any result.

In Modern Greek, Stephany (1981) found that perfective aspect occurred more frequently with resultative verbs than with nonresultative verbs in young Greek children's utterances, whereas the reverse was true for imperfective aspect. Furthermore, past tense occurred only with perfective aspect, and present tense only with imperfective aspect.

Finally, in Mandarin Chinese, Li (1990, 1991) conducted three experiments to test the process/result distinction in children's speech between ages 3 and 6. The comprehension experiment revealed that children understood the perfective marker -*le* better with resultative verbs and the imperfective marker *zai* better with process verbs. The production experiment also showed that there was a strong association between perfective aspect and resultative verbs and between imperfective aspect and process verbs in children's productive speech. The imitation experiment indicated that children repeated sentences with the perfective marker -*le* significantly better than those with the imperfective marker *zai* when the verb was resultative. Taken together, the results from cross-linguistic studies of tense and aspect systems are consistent with Slobin's hypothesis about the "temporal perspectives" in the time talk of early child language, with special emphasis on the child's interest in "getting results."

The temporal perspectives in Slobin's "Basic Child Grammar" assign a significant role to the child's cognitive predisposition, since Slobin hypothesizes that children are sensitive to the semantic distinction between *result* and *process* before their experience with specific properties of the target grammar. However, the extent to which the meaning-form associations in children's time talk conform to the distribution patterns in the adult language, together with evidence from studies of early child-mother interactions, suggests another equally plausible explanation without invoking prestructured semantic categories as Slobin does. There is now good evidence that children are influenced at a very early age by the input they are exposed to (see Snow, 1977, for discussion). In the domain of children's expression of time, we also have strong evidence that children's speech reflects adult language patterns and that mother-child interactions at an early stage promote certain temporal perspectives (see Li, 1990, for a summary). Brown (1973) noticed that children's use of past tense begins with a small set of verbs that refer to instantaneous events, such as "fell," "dropped," "crashed," and "broke," and he reasoned that these verbs may have always or almost always occurred in the past tense in mothers' speech at early stages of child language. Stephany (1981) specifically explored the correlation between children's use of tense and aspect markers and mothers' use of these markers. Her analysis indicated that the distribution of tense and aspect markers with different types of verbs in young Greek children's speech conforms surprisingly well to the patterns mothers use in speaking directly to children. In addition, Stephany also compared the mothers' speech to children and mothers' speech to adults and found that mothers modify their speech to children with respect to the use of temporal forms and the frequency of these forms. More important, in an investigation of the acquisition of Brazilian Portuguese, de Lemos (1981) showed how mothers model temporal markers in special contexts designed to direct the child's attention to certain situational properties, in particular, to the result of an event. De Lemos's (1981) detailed analyses of the patterns inherent in child-mother interactions suggest that the child's sensitivity to the contrast between process and result is strongly promoted and encouraged by the mother. Each time the child plays a game and the game leads to some observable results, the mother emphasizes the completed result by using a perfective marker with relevant verbs, and at one stage the child could also imitate the mother's speech. This kind of routine is very characteristic of child-mother interactions between ages 1;6 and 2;2, according to de Lemos. Results seem to be a very salient property of situations, especially in child play (e.g., the child builds a toy tower and knocks it down), and the world's languages place special emphasis on it (see Li, 1990, on the properties of Chinese, and Nedjalkov, 1988, for a discussion of resultative constructions of the world's languages). It is therefore not surprising that mothers intentionally direct children's attention to it at a very early stage in their acquisition of time talk.

Bowerman (1985, 1989) argues that children are sensitive to the characteristics of input patterns from early on and that their speech reflects their efforts in the analysis of the distributions of form-meaning mappings. With crosslinguistic evidence of the described kind, it is reasonable to propose that input patterns and child-mother interactions play an important role in the early stages of children's expression of time, and that young children attend to the temporal perspectives from early on as a result of the child's analysis of the learning environment, not because of prestructured semantic categories.

In this section we discussed some features inherent in children's learning of the language *about time*, that is, the development of time talk. Two theoretical hypotheses about children's expression of time were reviewed. First, Weist (1986, 1989) hypothesizes that in learning to talk about time, children proceed through four stages of the temporal system: the speech time, the event time, the restricted reference time, and the free reference time. The progress from one stage to another reflects corresponding cognitive and conceptual development. Second, Slobin (1985) proposes two temporal perspectives, process and result, to which children are sensitive from a very early stage in their acquisition of temporal expressions. Slobin hypothesizes that these perspectives are prestructured and "privileged" to be mapped to corresponding grammatical forms. However, crosslinguistic evidence suggests that the patterns observed with children's acquisition of time talk can be better accounted for by reference to the properties of the input and to child-mother interactions than by invoking predisposed semantic structures.

CONCLUSION

We have now come full circle. In the first section we stressed the extent to which a simple neural network that lives *in time* can succeed in learning very complex aspects of language, simply by trying to "guess what comes next." In the second section we pointed out that much of grammatical learning can usefully be viewed as a form of skill acquisition, as children learn to produce and understand speech as efficiently as possible, that is, *on time*. In the third section we reviewed current theories of the process by which children learn to talk *about time*. To a great extent, these theories have presupposed that learning to talk about time reflects strong innate constraints (whether they are linguistic or cognitive in nature). However, we end by concluding that these biases can (to some extent) be induced from exposure to a well-structured environment. In other words, a system that lives *in time* can learn to talk *about time*, by attending closely to the way language is used in the world around it. In other words, much of the exquisite organization that we see in language learning can be explained by temporal constraints.

REFERENCES

Aksu, A. (1978). *Aspect and modality in the child's acquisition of the Turkish past tense*. Ph.D. dissertation, University of California, Berkeley.

Antinucci, F., & Miller, R. (1976). How children talk about what happened. *Journal of Child Language, 3*, 167–189.

Bates, E., Bretherton, I., & Snyder, L. (1988). *From first words to grammar: Individual differences and dissociable mechanisms*. New York: Cambridge University Press.

Bates, E., & MacWhinney, B. (1989). Functionalism and the competition model. In B. MacWhinney & E. Bates (Eds.), *The crosslinguistic study of sentence processing*. New York: Cambridge University Press.

Bloom, L. (1970). *Language development: Form and function in emerging grammars*. Cambridge: MIT Press.

Bloom, L., Lifter, K., & Hafitz, J. (1980). Semantics of verbs and the development of verb inflection in child language. *Language, 56*, 386–412.

Bowerman, M. (1985). What shapes children's grammars? In D. Slobin (Ed.), *The crosslinguistic study of language acquisition: Vol. 2. Theoretical issues*. Hillsdale, NJ: Erlbaum.

Bowerman, M. (1989). Learning a semantic system: What role do cognitive predispositions play? In M. Rice & R. L. Schiefelbusch (Eds.), *The teachability of language*. Baltimore: Brookes.

Bronckart, J., & Sinclair, H. (1973). Time, tense and aspect. *Cognition, 2*, 107–130.

Brown, R. (1973). *A first language*. Cambridge: Harvard University Press.

Carey, S. (1982). Semantic development: The state of the art. In E. Wanner & L. Gleitman (Eds.), *Language acquisition: The state of the art.* Cambridge: Cambridge University Press.

Comrie, B. (1976). *Aspect: An introduction to the study of verbal aspect and related problems.* Cambridge: Cambridge University Press.

de Lemos, C. (1981). Interactional processes in the child's construction of language. In W. Deutsch (Ed.), *The child's construction of language.* New York: Academic Press.

Devescovi, A., D'Amico, S., Smith, S., Mimica, I., & Bates, E. 1993). *The development of sentence comprehension in Italian and Serbo-Croation: Local versus distributed cues.* Manuscript, University of Rome "La Sapienza," submitted for review.

Elman, J. L. (1990). Finding structure in time. *Cognitive Science, 14,* 179–211.

Elman, J. L. (1991). Distributed representations, simple recurrent networks, and grammatical structure. *Machine Learning, 7,* 195–225.

Elman, J. L. (1993). Learning and development in neural networks: The importance of starting small. *Cognition, 48,* 71–99.

Erbaugh, M. (1982). *Coming to order: Natural selection and the origin of syntax in the Mandarin-speaking child.* Ph.D. dissertation, University of California, Berkeley.

Fowler, C. (1977). *Timing control in speech production.* Bloomington: Indiana University Linguistics Club.

Fowler, C. (1980). Coarticulation and theories of extrinsic timing control. *Journal of Phonetics, 8,* 113–133.

Frazier, L., & Fodor, J. D. (1978). The sausage machine: A new two-stage parsing model. *Cognition, 6,* 291–325.

Jordan, M. I. (1986). *Serial order: A parallel distributed processing approach.* Institute for Cognitive Science Report 8604. University of California, San Diego.

Jordan, M. I., & Rosenbaum, D. A. (1988). *Action.* Technical Report 88-26. Department of Computer Science, University of Massachusetts at Amherst.

Kelso, J. A. S., Saltzman, E., & Tuller, B. (1986). The dynamical theory of speech production: Data and theory. *Journal of Phonetics, 14,* 29–60.

Kilborn, K. (1987). *Sentence processing in a second language: Seeking a performance definition of fluency.* Ph.D. dissertation, University of California, San Diego.

Lashley, K. S. (1951). The problem of serial order in behavior. In L. A. Jeffress (Ed.), *Cerebral mechanisms in behavior.* New York: Wiley.

Li, P. (1990). *Aspect and aktionsart in child Mandarin.* Ph.D. dissertation, Leiden University.

Li, P. (1991). *Zai* and *ba* constructions in child Mandarin. *Center for Research in Language Newsletter* 5(5) (University of California, San Diego).

MacNeilage, P. F. (1970). Motor control of serial ordering of speech. *Psychological Review, 77,* 182–196.

Maratsos, M. (1983). Some current issues in the study of the acquisition of grammar. In J. Flavell & E. Markman (Eds.), *Handbook of child psychology* (Vol. 3). New York: Wiley.

Marchman, V., & Bates, E. (1994). Continuity in lexical and morphological development: A test of the critical-mass hypothesis. *Journal of Child Language, 21:2,* 339–366.

Marchman, V., Bates, E., Burkhardt, A., & Good, A. (1991). Functional constraints on the acquisition of the passive: Toward a model of the competence to perform. *First Language, 11,* 65–92.

Marcus, G. F., Pinker, S., Ullman, M., Hollander, M., Rosen, T. J., & Xu, F. (in press). Overregularization in language acquisition. *Monographs of the Society for Research in Child Development.*

Marcus, M. (1980). *A theory of syntactic recognition for natural language.* Cambridge: MIT Press.

Nedjalkov, V. (Ed.). (1988). *Typology of resultative constructions.* (Translation ed. B. Comrie). Amsterdam: John Benjamins.

Pizzuto, E., & Caselli, M. (1992). Acquisition of Italian morphology: Implications for models of language development. *Journal of Child Language. 19,* 3, 491–557.

Rumelhart, D. E., Hinton, G. E., & Williams, R. J. (1986). Learning internal representations by error propagation. In D. E. Rumelhart and J. L. McClelland (Eds.), *Parallel distributed processing: Explorations in the microstructure of cognition* (Vol. 1). Cambridge: MIT Press.

Saltzman, E., & Kelso, J. A. S. (1987). Skilled action: A task dynamic approach. *Psychological Review, 94,* 84–106.

Slobin, D. (1985). Crosslinguistic evidence for the language-making capacity. In D. Slobin (Ed.), *The crosslinguistic study of language acquisition: Vol. 2. Theoretical issues.* Hillsdale, NJ: Erlbaum.

Snow, C. (1977). The development of conversation between mothers and babies. *Journal of Child Language, 4,* 1–22.

Stephany, U. (1981). Verbal grammar in Modern Greek early child language. In P. S. Dale & D. Ingram (Eds.), *Child language: An international perspective.* Baltimore: University Park Press.

Stornetta, W. S., Hogg, T., & Huberman, B. A. (1987). *A dynamical approach to temporal pattern processing.* Paper presented at the IEEE Conference on Neural Information Processing Systems, Denver.

Tank, D. W., & Hopfield, J. J. (1987). *Neural computation by concentrating information in time.* Paper presented at the IEEE International Conference on Neural Networks, San Diego.

Waibel, A., Hanazawa, T., Hinton, G., Shikano, K., & Lang, K. (1987). *Phoneme recognition using time-delay neural networks.* ATR Technical Report TR-I-00006; Japan: ATR Interpreting Telephony Research Laboratories.

Watrous, R. L., & Shastri, L. (1987). *Learning phonetic features using connectionist networks: An experiment in speech recognition.* Paper presented at the IEEE International Conference on Neural Networks, San Diego.

Weist, R. (1986). Tense and aspect: Temporal systems in child language. In P. Fletcher & M. Garman (Eds.), *Language acquisition.* Cambridge: Cambridge University Press.

Weist, R. (1989). Time concepts in language and thought: Filling the Piagetian void from two to five years. In I. Levin & D. Zakay (Eds.), *Time and human cognition: A life-span perspective.* Amsterdam: Elsevier.

Williams, R. J., & Zipser, D. (1988). *A learning algorithm for continually running fully recurrent neural networks.* Institute for Cognitive Science Report 8805. University of California, San Diego.

Chapter Eleven

Using Goal-Plan Knowledge to Merge the Past with the Present and the Future in Narrating Events on Line

Tom Trabasso and Nancy L. Stein

GOALS AND PLANS: GUIDES TO FUTURE-ORIENTED BEHAVIOR

An infant reaches out toward an object. A teenager takes an examination. What do these two activities have in common? In each instance, a person is carrying out an action. An observer could infer that these acts are voluntary and that they are purposeful. What is inferred about these goal-directed actions would depend on the circumstances in which they occur and on the observer's use of knowledge about these circumstances

This research was supported by grants to Tom Trabasso from the Smart Foundation on Early Learning, the National Institute of Child Health and Human Development, grant HD17431, and the Spencer Foundation. Support was also provided by grant HD25742 to Tom Trabasso and Nancy Stein from the National Institute of Child Health and Human Development.

We are grateful to Dan Slobin and Virginia Marchman for providing us with the 58 protocols of the American English sample of the Berman et al. (1986) study and granting us permission to analyze them, and to Judy DeLoache for providing us with the protocols of 14 mother-child dyads on the *Frog, Where Are You?* story from the DeLoache, Cassidy, and Carpenter (1987) study.

We are particularly indebted to Camille Baughn, Margret Park Munger, Margaret Nickels, and Philip C. Rodkin for their several contributions to the research summarized in this chapter. We also wish to thank Mark Lepper and Gordon Bower of the Department of Psychology, Stanford University, and Shirley Feldman of the Family Studies Center, Stanford University, who generously lent us their facilities during the writing of this chapter while we were on a sabbatical leave from the University of Chicago.

and acts. In the first instance, the act may be seen as directed overtly toward an object such as a rattle. Based on knowledge of rattles, the kind of reaching the infant makes toward objects, the proximity and accessibility of the object, the object's familiarity to the infant, and beliefs about the infant's developmental competence, one could infer that the infant wanted the object and tried to get it. In the second instance, based on our knowledge of students and examinations in educational contexts, one could infer that the student wanted to pass or do well on the examination.

It is possible that attaining the goal in each instance serves yet other purposes. The infant may want to obtain the rattle so as to make a noise by shaking it. The student may wish to pass the examination in order to complete a course. Each action would thus be directed toward a goal subordinate to the achievement of other superordinate goals. These hierarchical actions and goals are future oriented: they are aimed at achieving particular ends or outcomes that do not exist at the time the action is initiated. In many cases, the attainment of the goals that are being served by a subordinate goal and an attempt to reach them are removed in time and space.

Goals and purposes are desired states, actions, and activities that, once initiated, exist in the past. They become states of being that are assumed to be causally prior to the actions. If the goal exists as a purpose before the action, and if the action is carried out in order to achieve the goal, we have the main ingredients of a plan. Plans require that an agent desire to obtain something and believe that a series of goals and actions can be carried out to achieve that desire. When carried out, the plan unites the past (a desired state) with the present (an attempt) and the future (the attainment of that state).

To understand and anticipate the actions of self and others, it is adaptive to acquire and use naive theories of intentional action. These theories constitute the basis for generating goals and plans when problems arise, anticipating possible obstacles to the execution of a plan, understanding and dealing with personal and interpersonal conflict, and defending oneself against another person's plan (cf. Schank, 1986; Suchman, 1987; Wilensky, 1978). With knowledge of plans, we can anticipate future events and possible courses of action. We can predict how things might turn out. When they do not turn out as expected, we can explain what went wrong so that we can repair the plans for future actions (Hammond, 1989; Hilton, Mathes, & Trabasso, 1992). According to Schank (1986), these attempts to understand are explanatory in nature. Explanations can be predictive and oriented toward preventing a harmful recurrence in the future. They can be made post hoc and be used to infer intent from the behavior of self and others that has already occurred. They can be pattern based and involve the use of knowledge of past events to recognize and retrieve analogous or similar events in order to understand past and present and to forecast future events.

SOURCES OF PLANS

Plans can be learned from the success and failure of one's own actions carried out to attain goals, or they can be induced as ad hoc categories from the experiences of others. Models for learning plans can be depicted in real life or in hearing about real or fictional experiences from others in conversation, storytelling, books, pictures, movies, or television. There are thus many cultural sources that portray and socialize planning, personal problem solving, or interpersonal conflict and conflict resolution. These are often of magical and moral significance in the world of young children (Applewood, 1991). In developing a concept of self and in learning about life experiences, these observational, vicarious, and fictional experiences build on what children already know and are motivated to acquire at different points in development. They serve as means for learning about life through the examples of others. In watching a series of events unfold over time, children have an opportunity to learn, to seek explanatory coherence in understanding self and others, and to develop knowledge of plans in complex personal and interpersonal problem-solving and conflict situations.

Children can seek meaning in these experiences by trying to figure out why the events occurred and using this interpretation to predict, bring about, or prevent similar occurrences. In witnessing a series of events, they can infer goals and plans central to the understanding of the events. If they do so, the events that are interpreted and coded into language are guided and constrained in a forward-going manner by the goal plan that is accessed. As witnesses and narrators to a sequence of events, children can selectively interpret and encode what occurs in the events in order to form a coherent, functional memory representation for future use.

USING PLANS IN THE NARRATION OF EVENTS:
AN INVESTIGATION

This chapter describes an approach to the study of how young children come to understand and use goal plans of action. It draws primarily on two recent studies (Trabasso & Nickels, 1992; Trabasso, Stein, Rodkin, Munger, & Baughn, 1992) that investigated the development of knowledge and use of goals and plans in understanding events by children as young as 3 years of age. In the basic study children witness the experiences and actions of another person over time in a picture book. The children have the responsibility of narrating what happens, scene by scene. The central question is, How do the children do this? Do they use knowledge of plans to infer the goals and purposes that unite the actions to attain them? If so, then one would expect them to encode actions selectively as attempts relevant to a plan, to mark these attempts with purposes, to indicate when the attempts fail or succeed, and to exhibit strategies of dealing with success and failure.

The basic corpus of narration come from an ambitious crosslinguistic study organized by Berman and Slobin (1987). In this study, children and adults in several different linguistic communities around the world were asked to narrate a picture sequence about a boy who engages in a sustained search for his lost pet frog (Mayer, 1969). In the American English–speaking sample whose narrations were analyzed by our approach, there were 12 children in each of four age groups (3, 4, 5, and 9 years) and 10 adults. The children came from the community in Berkeley, California, were upper middle class, and were white. The picture stories provided an opportunity for children to demonstrate their knowledge of tense and aspect properties of verbs, and the particular ages chosen were thought to be most sensitive, especially in the 3–5 year range, to changes in the development of these properties of verbs. The adults in the study were undergraduates at the University of California, Berkeley. There were equal numbers of males and females in each group. We were fortunate to obtain this corpus of 58 narrations by speakers of American English from Virginia Marchman and Dan Slobin, with permission to analyze them. The corpus is available in Berman et al. (1986).

NARRATION STUDY

Method

Each child and adult narrated a sequence of 24 scenes in a picture storybook called *Frog, Where Are You?* that was drawn by Mayer (1969). The children were asked to tell the story that was contained in the picture book after they first looked through the book one picture at a time. On the second pass through the book, the child told the story as the experimenter turned the pages. If the child did not say anything spontaneously, the experimenter prompted responses by asking, "What is happening?" Adults were told to tell the story after looking at each picture in the book, and since the book was drawn for young children, to imagine that they were telling it to a child.

Model of Analysis and Assumptions

Since the pictures were very explicit and coherent with respect to actions and situations, they contained sufficient information to let the child infer a hierarchical goal plan of action executed over time with several repeated, unexpected failures followed by a final goal success. Our aim was to analyze whether the young narrators inferred this plan and whether they used it to interpret and narrate the pictorial events. How the narrators encoded states and actions of the central protagonist in the picture story provided the main evidence for the use of knowledge about a goal plan.

Inferring goals and plans involves considerable social and personal knowledge and places heavy demands on a narrator's working memory (Trabasso & Suh, 1993). The child who narrates events needs to attend to and maintain the current event in working memory; to activate and retrieve prior knowledge relevant to the events, either in general or from earlier parts of the story, in order to interpret and explain the current event; and to integrate these interpretations into a context within a plan, all within the limitations of knowledge and working memory. In effect, over time the child is engaged in dynamic thinking, actively constructing and evaluating models and hypotheses about what is occurring. In so doing, the child creates a changing mental model that results in a long-term memory representation of what has occurred (Collins, Brown, & Larkin, 1975; Rumelhart, 1991).

The child has to infer another person's goal and the formation of a plan to attain it from the initial events or actions that are observed, or else infer goals from later actions and outcomes. In either case, once a goal is inferred, a plan of action must be accessed and its execution anticipated. Then the sequence of actions that occurs over time must be monitored selectively to assess whether the actions fit or are consistent within the context of the plan (cf. Scholnick & Friedman, 1987). The child must also evaluate whether an action leads to success or failure in goal attainment. If a failure occurs, the child must determine which strategy is followed: goal reinstatement or continuation, goal substitution, or goal abandonment (Stein, 1988; Wilensky, 1978). If the attempt is successful then the child must infer whether the goal will be maintained or whether other goals can now be attained. Evaluation of goal success and failure are very important to planning. Successes and outcomes are what lead to plan modification, emotional understanding, further planning and coping, and new goal strategies.

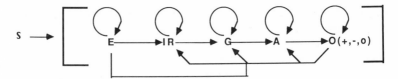

Figure 11.1   Causal network for representing episodic narrative structures (adapted from Trabasso, van den Broek, & Suh, 1989).

Plans, then, have content and structures that unfold over time. They are future oriented in that they function to anticipate, guide, interpret, monitor, and evaluate actions and outcomes. A plan, when carried out, has an episodic structure that reflects these functions. Figure 11.1 shows a general model for depicting the content and structure for narratives. The diagram is based on a discourse model of Trabasso, van den Broek, & Suh (1989) that has been used to analyze the causal network structure of narratives (Trabasso & Nickels, 1992; Trabasso, Secco, & van den Broek, 1984; Trabasso & Sperry, 1985, Trabasso et al., 1992; Trabasso & Suh, 1993, Trabasso & van den Broek, 1985). The categories of information, denoted by letters, are based on the story grammar of Stein and Glenn (1979). The arrows that connect the letters are causal relations between the categorized events and satisfied logical criteria of necessity in the circumstances of the story (cf. Mackie, 1980).

Events always occur in space and time, and they involve animate beings who must be introduced and set in context. This information is mainly captured in setting (S) statements early on in narration. Setting information is important, since it orients listeners and provides the space-time circumstances in which action can occur. Settings also give the background information on the persons or animate beings in stories (Stein & Glenn, 1979). The basic episode of a narrative contains five main categories of information that are interrelated. First among these are events (E)—changes in the state of the main protagonist that are significant to the being who experiences them. These changes initiate and affect goal states. Events are often problems that arise and create needs, lacks, or wants. Events have to be perceived, assessed, and evaluated internally before goals are established. These internal responses (IR) take on the form of perceptions, cognitions, thoughts, wishes, and emotions. The interpretation of the events and the reactions to them give rise to goals (G)—desired future states, objects, or activities. Once inferred, a plan to achieve the goal may be accessed as a set of beliefs about other goals and actions that can be carried out to achieve them. Plans may be stored and retrieved, or they may be constructed opportunistically as one proceeds through the plan, carrying out actions and failing or succeeding (Hayes-Roth & Hayes-Roth, 1979). Opportunistic

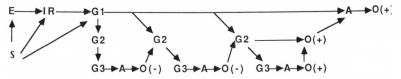

Figure 11.2   Goal plan hierarchy for the *Frog, Where Are You?* story.

planning is more likely to occur when a prestored plan is not available or when one tries to follow a prestored plan but meets with unexpected obstacles or failures. Goals motivate subordinate goals and attempts (A) to achieve them. Attempts enable other attempts and cause outcomes (O), which index goal success and failure. Outcomes are like events: they can cause or enable other outcomes; they can enable attempts; and they can also cause psychological reactions and goals.

Application of Discourse Analysis of Plans to Narrations

We now apply Figure 11.1 to the *Frog, Where Are You?* story of Mayer (1969) that was used in the Berman et al. (1986) study. The story can be characterized as a hierarchical goal plan with unanticipated failure and success. The causal network for main parts of the story is shown in Figure 11.2. In the picture story, a little boy and his dog are first seen looking at a frog in a glass jar in the boy's room at night (setting). In the next scene the boy and dog are asleep on the bed, and the frog crawls out of the jar. In the third scene, which takes place in the morning, the boy finds the empty jar (event) and looks upset (internal response). The boy then begins a search (attempts) by looking for the frog (goal) in the room, then calls out the window and goes out to look for the frog (goal reinstatement). Each new attempt is preceded by an implied or explicit failure (outcomes), such as the dog's falling out the window or a gopher's coming out of his hole and biting the boy's nose. Finally, the sequence of attempts and failed outcomes leads the boy to a swamp in which he finds his frog (successful outcome). Since the frog has a family, a new conflict arises and is resolved by the boy's taking home a baby frog (goal substitution and attempt).

Goals may or may not be materially present. The frog is absent, and the child must infer that the frog is the desired object when the boy acts. This is facilitated by knowing that there is a relationship between the boy and the frog (probably one of owner-pet) and that the boy values the frog. The frog's escape and the empty jar change the boy's state from having something he wants to not having it. This state is the basis for inferring the superordinate goal G1 that the boy wants to have the frog back, and the actions of looking, calling, and searching are the basis for inferring the plan to search for the frog, embodied in subordinate goal G2 and its execution of searching in particular locations motivated by another subordinate goal, G3. The relations among the three goals and their associated attempts and outcomes are what define the hierarchical, episodic structure of the *Frog, Where Are You?* story. The relations are hierarchical in that to have the frog back home, the boy must find it, and to find the frog, he must search in particular ways in particular locations. The success of searching in a particular location brings about the finding of the frog. This outcome enables the frog to be returned to the original state of being at home with the boy and his dog.

Examples of Narrations

Let us now look at how some children and adults narrated the pictures of the *Frog, Where Are You?* story. These examples were selected because they indicated clear cross-age differences in how the narrators interpreted and linguistically encoded the events, whether or not they inferred a goal and interpreted actions as attempts to carry out the inferred goal plan. Table 11.1 gives one complete narration example for a person at each age level.

In discussing Table 11.1, we shall focus primarily on the narrating of the first five pictures of the story, since the age-related differences shown there capture the main differences throughout the narrations. Reading the narration of the 3-year-old child, one has the impression that children of this age are deictic (identifying, naming, or pointing) and descriptive. She names, identifies, and describes primarily objects and actions. She does not introduce the characters and their relationships. She does not orient listeners or provide a sufficient context in which one can infer goals and plans. Most important, she does not describe actions that are relevant to the search. The key to the 3-year-old's understanding of events lies in her communicative ability to identify and describe.

The 4-year-old child shows four major changes in narration compared with that of the 3-year-old. The 4-year-old introduces the boy, dog, and frog characters and includes a possessive relationship. There is a temporal sequencing of the events. Actions rather than end states are encoded. Three of the encoded actions (looking) are relevant to the plan of searching for the frog. A cognition (found) is also encoded for the initiating event.

The 5-year-old child is more advanced in narrating events. She introduces the characters *and their relationships* and explicitly mentions that the boy loves the frog. She brings in emotional reactions (a rare occurrence in the children's narrations, regardless of age). She explicitly marks a search attempt (yelling) with a purpose (for the frog).

The 9-year-old child does what the 5-year-old does. In general, 9-year-olds encode and mark more relevant purposes, actions, and outcomes in relation to the boy's plan of finding the frog. The adult narration, although richer in detail and emotional reactions, by and large resembles the basic story told by the 9-year-old.

Thus the major changes in narrating events occurred during early childhood. The age-related changes moved from recognizing and describing to narrating relevant actions, and then to explaining why the actions took place by making them with purposes. This general age-related change from description to action to explanation was also found by Stein and Policastro (1984) and by Stein (1988) in storytelling by children 5 years of age and older. In these studies the children were given minimal settings and were asked to tell stories under less common and restrictive conditions than in the present situation.

With respect to integration of the past, present, and future, the 3-year-old in Table 11.1 shows no evidence of inferring and using a goal plan. Her narration stays at the level of describing and identifying objects and end states. The 4-year-old, however, is beginning to show evidence of knowing about plans by focusing on action that is relevant. The absence of purposes for the actions renders this narration present oriented. The 5-year-old shows the best evidence for integration of the past with the present and the future: the missing frog becomes the reason for searching, and this search continues in the face of failure.

Structuring the Narration as a Hierarchical Goal Plan

In the adult narration of Table 11.1, one can most clearly see a hierarchical goal plan with unanticipated goal failure, goal reinstatement, and goal success. The narrator includes a setting (S) that introduces the characters of the boy, dog, and frog, the relationships among them, and the time and space of the story. Events (E) occur where the frog escapes and the boy finds the jar empty. The internal response (IR) is the boy's emotional reaction to the loss. The goals of wanting the frog back and searching for the frog are implicit. The action takes place at the next level in a series of goal-attempt-outcome episodes. In the first episode, the boy looks for the frog in the room and fails. In the second, he calls out the window and fails. In the third, he goes outside and calls, but no frog appears. In a fourth, he looks in a hole in the ground and fails: instead, a gopher bites him on the nose. In a fifth, he climbs a tree and looks in a hole but fails as an owl comes flying out and knocks him out of the tree. In a sixth, he climbs a rock and calls but becomes entangled on the antlers of a deer that throws him into a pond. In a seventh, he crawls over a log and finally finds the frog and its family. In the last scene, he is carrying a frog and waiving to the rest of the frogs.

To discern whether children use knowledge of goal plans to interpret and narrate events, Trabasso and Nickels (1992) used the Trabasso et

TABLE 11.1   Narration Example for Each Age Group

In each narration, the narration is parsed into clauses identified by Berman et al. (1986). The clauses are separated by slashes (/).

3-Year-Old Subject 3C

There's a frog there / He's in there dusty / Here's a moon / Those are boots / Dog is going to fall over / He cry / and it fall down / He hold dog / He see / Them fall down / Dog fall down / Here's some bees / A owl in there / You owl in there / Fall him down / He don't like that / He's standing up here / He like this / He fall down / Him gonna fall down / and him hurt / He splashing in water / can't get out right here / go in here (pointing to hollow log) / go in here / He does have a penis (referring to dog) / He has a penis / He's getting out / He floating off / Frogs sitting down / He carrying a frog / Frogs /

4-Year-Old Subject 4B

There was a frog, a boy, and his dog / The boy and the dog slept / while the frog quietly go out of his jar / When they woke up / they found no frog in the jar / The boy looked / both of his shoes / both of his boots / The dog looked in the jar / They looked out the window / The dog fell / and broke the dish / They walked / and then the dog smelled something sweet / And he smelled some bees / Boy looked / and there was a hole from a squirrel / The dog made honey / It's a hive / The dog made the hive fall / The bees got angry / and the boy climbed a tree / Owl pushed the boy / while the dog was being chased by the bees / The boy was chased by the owl / Boy went on a rock / and the dog was not on the rock / He slipped onto a deer / and the deer took boy / And the dog was behind the deer/ He pushed them both off the cliff / And they landed in some water / They been very quiet / They see there is lots of frogs / playing / He took one of the frogs for a swim / That's the end /

5-Year-Old Subject 5E

There was a boy / He had a dog and a frog / When he always goes to sleep / the dog goes to sleep on his bed with him / And when they're asleep / the frog sneaks out / And then they both wake up / and then the frog is gone / So he gets dressed / and the dog gets dressed / and then he put his boot on his head / and then he put the other boot on his foot / And after went out calling for the frog / And then the dog fell out / And the boy jumped out / Then the boy had to jump out with his other boot on his foot / and get the dog / The glass broke open / Then they walked down the path / and there's lots of bees coming / and they're walking down some more of the path / And the dog found the beehive / and then the boy was looking down a hole / And a little animal came up / and poked his nose / And then the honey beehive fell down / And the dog was scared / cause all the bees were coming to get the dog / And the boy was looking through the tree / when an owl came out and / bammed him on the ground / while the dog was running away from the bees / And then the boy got up / and the owl's trying to get him / And he climbed up on a rock / and the owl went on a tree / And then he got caught by a deer / And then the deer ran off a cliff / And the dog was running before they both fell off the cliff / and the deer didn't / And they fell in the water / And the deer was happy / that they fell in the water / Then they got out of the water / Then got on a log / Then the dog jumped over / and fell on the frog / And then they didn't know which one to pick / cause they're all the same / except they picked the right one /

9-Year-Old Subject 9C

Well there was a boy / and he had a frog and a dog / He loved his frog very much / and maybe his dog did too / One night when he was asleep / the frog climbed out of his jar / The boy woke up / The next morning the frog was gone / The dog looked concerned / The boy quickly got dressed / and the dog put his head in a jar / He got stuck there / but the boy did not pull it off / Instead he opened the window / and yelled for his frog / The dog fell off of the windowsill / And

TABLE 11.1 *(Continued)*

broke the jar into pieces / The boy and the dog went looking for the frog / They yelled for the frog / They found a beehive and a gopher hole / They asked the gopher and the bees / if they had seen the frog / The gopher had not seen the frog / The bees got mad / The boy climbed a tree / and looked inside the tree / The frog was not there / The bees started chasing the dog / The owl came out of its tree / and scared the little boy / The boy fell / and the bees went right by him and after the dog / The owl swooped down / The boy climbed on a rock / The owl landed in a tree / The boy yelled for the frog / But instead a deer caught him between his horns / He was stuck there / The dog tried running after the deer / and barked / but the deer kept running ahead / with the boy on his head / He dumped them off a cliff / They fell into the water / They heard something / The little boy cupped his hand to his ear / The little boy smiled / The dog looked excited / Shh said the little boy / The dog / the little boy / climbed up to a hollow log / They looked over / There was the frog with another little lady frog / And little frogs of his own / The boy smiled / The other frog gave one of his little frogs to the boy / The boy thanked them / waved goodbye / The puppy was excited / They went home with the boy / They went home /

Adult Subject 20B

This is a story of a little kid / before he goes to bed one night / He looks in this jar / and he's checking out his frog / and his dog is there / and they both check out the frog / Then they both go to sleep / Unbeknownst to the two sleeping people in the bed / the frog crawls out of the jar / The next morning, the boy and the dog wake up / and find the empty jar / The boy looks in his boots / while the dog looks in the jar for the frog / They look out the window for the frog / The dog falls out the window / and breaks the jar / The kid goes down out the window as well / and picks up the dog / The dog is happily rescued from / having his head stuck in the jar / But the kid's a little angry / probably cause he's lost his jar and his frog / The little boy and the dog go outside / looking for the frog / The boy is calling for the frog / and the dog is sniffing for the frog / But actually the dog is sniffing at a trail of bees / coming out of a beehive / The boy is looking down a hole / to see / if the frog is in the hole / and the dog is intrigued by this beehive / The boy gets his nose either bitten or sniffed at / by some little animal living in the hole / and the dog is still intrigued with the beehive / Now, the beehive has been knocked down out of the tree by the dog / and the bees are intrigued with the dog / while the boy is sitting in a tree / looking in the hole in the tree / thinking / maybe the lost frog is there / At this point / an owl pops out of the hole in the tree / and a bunch of bees start following the dog / probably angry / that the dog has knocked their hive out of the tree / Suddenly the owl / oh no / now the boy is running away from the owl / and the boy is climbing up on a rock / and now the owl is gone for some reason / and the dog is coming back / Looks like he's either stunned / or is just very frightened and ashamed / that he was outdone by the bees / The owl is looking at the boy / and the boy is calling for the frog / Now the boy has been picked up by some antlered beast / that looks like a deer / The deer is running to a cliff / and the dog is barking at the deer / This dog is pretty useless / all he does / is cause trouble and bark at things / Now the deer has thrown the dog, no, the boy over the cliff into / it looks like they're heading for a pond / and the dog goes too / as the dog has throughout the story / And they both fall in the water / And they sit up in the water / And it seems like they both hear something coming from behind the log / And the boy tells the dog to be very quiet / and they crawl over the log / And they find on the other side of the log two happy frogs / one of which was the frog in the jar / And then they see that there was not only two happy frogs / but there is an entire family of little frogs there / and one would wonder how long / what the gestation period is for frogs / and how come they're so big / when they know / they have to go through a tadpole stage first / However, it seems that they've raised this happy family / and maybe the boy was looking for these frogs for an entire six months to a year / Who knows / Now the boy grabs one of the frogs / and leaves with his frog / leaving the two big frogs and all the tiny frogs / So it looks like he has not taken away his big frog / that was in the jar / but he has taken away one of the sibling frogs perhaps / one really can't tell / The end /

al. (1989) model, summarized in Figure 11.1, and the Warren, Nicholas, and Trabasso (1979) event chain representation to classify each clause and to identify causal relationships among the clauses from the point of view of each character (for details, see Trabasso & Nickels, 1992). This analysis yielded a set of interacting causal networks for all the characters in the story. Then the longest causal network was extracted from the multiperspective representation. In this case it is the causal network representation for the perspective of the main protagonist, the boy.

Representation of the Narration as a Hierarchical Goal Plan with Unanticipated Goal Failures, Goal Reinstatement, and Goal Success

Figure 11.3 shows a partial network for representing the narration of the adult subjects in Table 11.1 (subject 20B). Table 11.2 shows the corresponding narration. Note that Table 11.2 also includes inferred categories (in brackets).

One can see a very close correspondence between the theory and the data by comparing the bottom network in Figure 11.2 with that in Figure 11.3. Most of the content in the narrations occurs at the level of searching for the frog in particular places (goal G3). The higher-order goals of finding the frog (G2) and bringing it back home (G3) must be inferred from what is explicit in the narration. Goal G2 had to be inferred from reinstated attempts and purposes. Goal G3 had to be inferred from two or more goal G2s as well as a positive outcome for this goal at the end of the story.

Structuring the Narration Episodically

The important cross-age analysis centers on the number of episodes that occur at level 3 in the hierarchy. A connected, goal-attempt-outcome (GAO) sequence indicates that the narrator included enough explicit information for us to classify the events into these categories, to infer missing goals (or outcomes), and to relate the categories causally. Thus the occurrence of a GAO episode is a strong indication that the child interpreted the information according to the goal plan of searching for the frog in order to reinstate it as a pet at home. Figure 11.4 shows the average number of these GAO episodes per person for each age group. In addition, Figure 11.4 plots the number of events (typically unrelated settings, attempts, and neutral outcomes) that were not integrated into GAO sequences, called non-GAO units. The total number of both kinds of units is also included in Figure 11.4.

In Figure 11.4, the number of GAO units increased sharply between the fourth and fifth years. This means that at about age 5 the children became more explicit in marking attempts with purposes and in including obstacles as failed outcomes in their narrations. Five-year-olds used

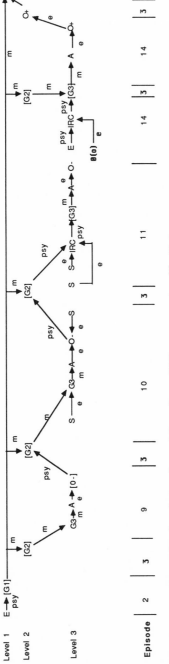

Figure 11.3   Hierarchical goal plan derived for subject 20B's narration in table 11.1.

TABLE 11.2 Selected Episodes (Boy's Perspective) of
Subject 20B's Narration

2	The boy finds the frog's jar empty. (E)
	He wants his pet frog back home. [G1]
3	The boy decides to search for his frog. [G2]
8	He wants to search for his frog outside. [G3]
	So he called for the frog. (A)
	But the frog did not come. [O −]
3	The boy decides to search for his frog. [G2]
10	There is a hole in the ground. (S)
	The boy wants to see if the frog is in there. (G3)
	The boy is looking in the hole. (A)
	Some little animal is living in the hole. (S)
	The boy gets his nose bitten by the animal. (O −)
3	The boy decides to search for his frog. [G2]
11	The boy is sitting in a tree. (S)
	There is a hole in the tree. (S)
	The boy thinks that maybe the lost frog is in there. (IRC)
	He wants to see if the frog is in the hole. [G3]
	So he looks into the hole. (A)
	But at this point an owl pops out of the hole in the tree. (O −)
3	The boy decides to search for his frog. [G2]
13	A deer threw the boy over a cliff. (O)
	The boy fell into a pond. (O)
14	The boy sits up in the water. (O)
	Some sound is coming from behind the log. (E)
	The boy can hear the sound. (IRC)
3	The boy decides to search for his frog. [G2]
	He wants to check if there are frogs behind the log. [G3]
14	So he crawls over the log. (A)
	And he finds on the other side of the log two happy frogs. (O +)
	One of which was the frog in the jar. (O +)
2	Now the boy leaves with his frog (A)

Note. The letters correspond to the content categories of the general causal transition network. The numbers on the goals refer to their level in the hierarchy. The positive and negative signs for outcomes indicate goal success or failure. The bracketed goals and outcomes are inferred.

planning knowledge to integrate information more fully into episodes. The episodes are, in turn, causally and temporally related and are organized hierarchically into an overall plan. This organization of the narration increased at age 9 and continued to increase slightly into adulthood.

The ability to use planning knowledge to interpret and narrate actions as attempts to attain the goal, and to evaluate the outcomes of the attempts in terms of goal success or failure, allowed the child to "chunk" greater amounts of information about the world. Of interest in Figure 11.4 is the relative constancy of the mean total number of units per child per age group. If one thinks of each GAO or non-GAO unit as a chunk

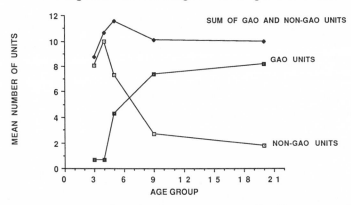

Figure 11.4   Mean number of goal-attempt-outcome (GAO) units, non-GAO units, and their sum for each age group (adapted from Trabasso & Nickels, 1992).

of information (Chi, 1978), then the children encode approximately the same total number of chunks per story. For 5-year-old children, who begin to evince the clearest use of planning knowledge, this means that they should also encode more categories per episode and more relations between episodes. Trabasso and Nickels (1992) found that the number of categories per episode and the number of causal relationships, both within and between the episodes, increased substantially after 5 years of age (Trabasso et al., 1992). These increases, then, correlated with the emergence of interpreting and structuring events into episodes by goal plans. The episodic structuring served as a kind of chunking device for organizing other categories of information within the episode and for inferring causal relations between goals and subgoals across episodes. The operations gave rise to coherent explanations of these events. The younger children, however, narrated isolated states, acts, or objects. They do not integrate these units into episodic chunks by applying knowledge of goal plans to their interpretations of what is happening. Their narrations thus lack coherence.

This analysis, then, reveals that between 4 and 5 years of age children use planning knowledge, based on past occurrences, to interpret present actions in terms of future purposes and outcomes and that their use of this knowledge provides them with a powerful way to organize and retain information about real-world events.

In the American-English–speaking sample of the Berkeley study, Trabasso and Nickels (1992) found strong evidence that 5-year-olds were able to apply planning knowledge to the actions of another when the goal object was not present. These data are consistent with a variety of findings on the developing "theory of mind" wherein children can infer the internal states of knowledge of others and use these inferences to predict future behavior (Astington, Harris, & Olson, 1988; Leslie, 1987; Perner, 1991; Wellman, 1991; Wimmer & Perner, 1983).

UNFOLDING EPISODES INTO COMPONENT PARTS OF PLANNING

The study by Trabasso and Nickels (1992) used stringent criteria to infer goals and outcomes from what was explicitly narrated by the children. The analysis required that antecedent and consequent information be explicitly encoded in order to infer goals or outcomes from the narration. There are, however, other ways children could manifest knowledge of plans that would not be assessed by the more formal analysis of Trabasso et al. (1989), employed by Trabasso and Nickels (1992). One way is to unfold the planning episodes into components (cf. Scholnick & Friedman, 1987) and perform a content analysis. The main components of planning involve goal detection, action monitoring, and evaluation of actions and outcomes. These planning components, coupled with episodic narrative analysis, can be translated into a series of specific, answerable questions: Did the child, in telling the frog story, provide setting information that introduced the characters and established a valued relationship between the frog and the boy, so that one can understand why the boy might want to have the frog back? Did the child encode the initiating events as a causal chain that resulted in the boy's generating a goal to find the frog and reinstate it as a pet? Did the child encode each action of the boy as part of a plan to find the frog, so that he could take it back home? Were the encoded attempts marked with purposes, so that one knows why the boy is doing what he is doing and can anticipate outcomes? Did the child encode the finding and the returning of the frog at the end of the story? This series of questions led Trabasso et al. (1992) to carry out a content analysis on the narrations. The answers to these questions provided a more sensitive measure of the child's use of goal-plan knowledge to interpret and encode events.

Relationship between Protagonists and Valued Objects

On the question whether the children narrated a valued relationship between a potential goal object and the protagonist, Trabasso et al. (1992) found that all the 9-year-olds encoded the relationship. Over the 3–5 age range, the proportions of children who did so increased substantially, from .17 to .25 to .58. This is an important ability in that it orients the listener to what is valued. It establishes a basis for detecting a goal in the future when the valued object is discovered to be missing. In fact, the inclusion of the relationship between the boy and his pets forecasts the narrator's subsequent use of goal-plan knowledge to narrate goals, attempts, and outcomes. There was a high positive correlation between narrating the possessive relationship between the boy and the frog in the first picture and narrating attempts and purposes related to the theme of finding the frog.

Narrating Initiating Events That Give Rise to Goals

On the question of narrating the causal sequence of events that allow goal inferences, six events were identified as possible situations for narrating attempts. Adults included the six events in their narrations at better than 90%. All the children, including the 3-year-olds, focused primarily on two observable events—the frog's leaving, and its being absent from the jar. However, from age 4 onward, there was an increased inclusion of the experiences, cognitions, and perceptions of the main protagonist (boy asleep, boy wakes, boy finds jar empty). What was missing on the part of all the children is an emotional evaluation of the event by the boy. Very few children mentioned that the boy was upset or sad, whereas all the adults mentioned an emotional reaction. The important ability developing here is taking the perspective of the main character and narrating that perception of the events. This narrating of the initiating event communicates awareness of the causes of the boy's goals of wanting to find the frog and bring it back home (the higher-order goals G2 and G1). The more of these events included in the narration, the more likely it was the child would use a goal plan to interpret action and explain it purposefully ($r = .44$, $p < .05$).

Do the Children Encode Actions as Part of a Plan, and Do They Sustain This Use of a Plan by Reinstating a Goal and Renewed Attempts?

The pictures showed seven occasions where the boy attempted to find the frog. The narration of each of these seven pictures can reveal whether a child inferred a goal and whether the child reinstated the goal plan after a failed attempt by narrating a new attempt with or without a purpose. Trabasso et al. (1992) analyzed the narrations as to narrating attempts at these seven locations. What was remarkable in these data was the constancy of the proportions of attempts narrated across the seven opportunities, independent of age. Adults did so at a rate of 90% or better; 9-year-olds averaged about 78%; 5-year-olds averaged 50%; 4-year-olds averaged 30%; and 3-year-olds narrated nearly no relevant attempts. The differences between the percentages for successive pairs of age groups were significant.

Given that attempts were encoded from age 4 onward, they were marked purposefully 21, 35, 47, and 55% of the time, respectively. These differences were significant for the two younger groups versus the two older groups.

Resolution of Story

The last planning component is on the final success in attaining the two higher-order goals of finding the frog and bringing it back home. The data showed that the children increasingly narrated explicitly whether the boy found and took home a frog. The respective proportions of subjects doing this were .16, .42, .42, .75, and 1.00. The 3-year-olds were less likely to resolve the story than 4- and 5-year-old children. The 9-year-olds performed better than any of the younger children, but adults were perfect in resolving the problem of finding and taking home the frog.

Conclusions from Analyzing Planning Components

Overall, the content analysis of the planning components indicates that even a substantial minority of the 4-year-olds showed the use of goal plans to interpret and forecast future events. The content analysis of Trabasso et al. (1992) proved to be more sensitive to the abilities of the 4-year-olds than did the formal, causal network analysis of Trabasso and Nickels (1992), which used more stringent, observable content categories and relations.

QUESTIONS OF INDIVIDUAL DIFFERENCES, ORIGINS, AND UNDERESTIMATION OF THE USE OF PLANS

The age-related data indicated that there are individual and age differences in how well children encode events linguistically according to inferred goal plans. It is possible that young children have goal-plan knowledge but do not use it spontaneously in narrating events. In this sense the data reported above may underestimate actual knowledge of plans, but not necessarily the use of plans. To study other sources of children's knowledge or use of plans within a storytelling context, Trabasso et al. (1992) carried out two other studies. These studies addressed questions on some of the reasons the 3- and 4-year-olds narrated the events the way they did.

FOSTERING INTEGRATION OF THE PAST WITH THE PRESENT AND FUTURE: HOW MOTHERS TALK WITH VERY YOUNG CHILDREN ABOUT EVENTS

Recall that in both the content and the structural analyses above, the 3-year-old children exhibited little use of knowledge of plans in narrating the action in the picture story. Rather, their narrations were focused on identifying objects and animate beings and on describing states and actions unrelated to the theme of finding the frog. The 3-year-olds required a lot of intervention and prompting by the experimenter in the Berman et al. (1986) study, and they seemed to treat the picture book task as one of communicative interaction rather than cooperative storytelling. The 3-year-olds may have reflected their assumptions about the communicative roles of adults and children in interaction with experiences such as "reading" books.

Mother-Child Conversation about Picture Books

DeLoache, Cassidy, and Carpenter (1987) had used the *Frog, Where Are You?* book to study how mothers labeled animals' genders while interacting with their children in this kind of communicative context. Trabasso et al. (1992) received permission from Judy DeLoache to analyze 13 protocols of the DeLoache et al. (1987) corpus of interactions. The children in their study ranged in age from 18 to 38 months (median age 30 months). The mothers were asked "to act naturally" in their interaction with their children over the book. Our analyses of the transcripts showed that the mothers told the child the story as background. In the foreground were the mothers' attempts through questioning to engage and maintain their children's attention throughout the telling. Each mother asked her child an average of slightly more than 30 questions over the course of the conversational interaction.

Of interest is that the mothers reduced what they told as a story to approximately the level of the 5-year-olds of the Berman et al. (1986) study. This shows a sensitivity to the competencies of the child, but it occurred at a more advanced level than the child's narration and thus served as a kind of scaffolding experience (Vygotsky, 1934). Most of the mothers' questions asked the children to identify or locate objects and to describe or elaborate actions. A minority of questions focused on what happened, why what happened did happen, and the consequences of what happened. However, these questions, central to learning about causes, consequences, and plans of action and to integrating the past with the present and the future, increased with age, indicating that the mothers also adjusted and scaffolded their questions. The mothers' adjustments occurred as the children became more conceptually and linguistically adept at answering and at asking questions. The mothers' questions began to focus more on agents and actions, to tell what was happening and why some event happened, and to speculate on what might happen in the future. The mother clearly fostered future-oriented behavior in asking the children, 30 months or older, to relate the past to the present and future.

The children's answers and questions, in turn, showed an increase as they grew older in goals and outcomes and in taking on the role of the animals in speech. The children in this study were learning to describe and identify events dynamically by narrating actions and state changes, and to relate and explain events with the aid of the mothers' scaffolding. What mothers asked for and what their children answered corresponded well with the way the 3-year-olds in the Berkeley study narrated the picture stories. The mothers' questions took into account the linguistic and cognitive skills of their children and fostered the children's descriptive and identification skills. In their attempts to tell the picture story, then, the 3-year-olds in the Berkeley study may well have reflected a history of similar interactive, communicative contexts with adults.

UNDERESTIMATION OF PLANNING KNOWLEDGE: QUESTIONING FOLLOWING NARRATION

One question of concern was why the 4-year-olds narrated relatively as many attempts relevant to the goal plan as the 5-year-olds but did not narrate purposes and outcomes to the same degree. One answer lies in the developing awareness of the need to orient and explain new actions of another to a listener. The 5-year-olds apparently had acquired this ability quite well by the time they were tested on the picture books. The other answer may lie in the relation between actions and outcomes. In the *Frog, Where Are You?* story the goal object is absent for all the attempts. Children may learn to interpret attempts purposefully earlier when they are directed at observable goal objects than when the object of the attempt is absent. By observing the results of their own and others' actions on objects, and seeing how the actions effect state changes in the world, children may learn the "means-end" correlation (Piaget, 1930, 1952) necessary for plans. That is, if they believe they can effect an outcome through action, then they can form a plan that a particular outcome can be achieved in this manner. The presence of the goal object makes the purpose of an action obvious; the absence forces one to make inferences under greater uncertainty.

Trabasso et al. (1992) carried out a second picture book, narration study on 4-year-olds, in which the goal was absent (the *Frog, Where Are You?* story) or present (*A Boy, a Dog and a Frog;* Mayer, 1967). In the latter story the boy tries repeatedly, but fails, to catch the frog in a pond. In addition to having the children narrate the story, the experimenters intervened and asked questions contingent on what the child narrated. If the child spontaneously narrated a relevant attempt with a purpose, no intervention occurred. If the child omitted a purpose but spontaneously narrated a relevant attempt, the experimenter prompted with a why question on the attempt. If the child failed to narrate an attempt, the child was prompted with a "what is the boy doing" question. If the child failed to narrate an attempt in response to the prompt, the experimenter did so.

The data showed that the 4-year-olds had sophisticated knowledge of the boy's plans in both kinds of stories but did not use it to communicate reasons why an attempt occurred when the goal object was absent. Attempts were narrated 65% of the time when the object was present and 70% when it was absent. Questioning what was happening increased these percentages to 86% and 82%. When the goal object was present, however, relevant attempts were spontaneously narrated 64% of the time, in sharp contrast to only 20% when it was absent. Prompting reasons through why questions increased the total number of purposes to 77% and 73%. Thus these young children could, spontaneously or when asked for reasons through why questions, provide purposes as explanations of attempts 89% of the time. It is clear from these data that the 4-year-olds were more likely to join attempts with purposes when the goal toward which the action was directed was materially present. It is equally clear that the 4-year-olds were capable of explaining an attempt in terms of its goal even though the goal object was not present. What differentiates the 4- from the 5-year-old children lay in the older children's ability to spontaneously provide reasons for actions when scenes shifted, thereby orienting listeners and helping them understand that the same goal plan was being maintained in changing circumstances.

CONCLUSIONS

Taken together, these three studies indicate that between 3 and 5 years of age children begin to use knowledge of goal plans to interpret and communicate about the actions and experiences of others. The age-related changes that are observed move from description to explanation of events. The 3-year-olds' narrations and communicative interactions were primarily concerned with identification and description of persons, animate beings, objects, and actions. The 4-year-olds, however, learned to orient listeners by providing background information relevant to allowing and inferring present and future events. They encoded actions relevant to a plan and indicated their purpose more when the goal toward which the action was directed was present. Five-year-olds showed a clearer use of planning knowledge; they narrated attempts with purposes when the goal was not present. Nine-year-olds and adults were quantitatively more skilled at the use of planning knowledge, but they did not differ qualitatively from the 5-year-olds except for the adults' inclusion of emotional reactions. Thus, with respect to future-oriented behavior, preschool children at about 4 years of age begin to show considerable skill in anticipating and communicating their anticipation of action and outcomes of another person by the use of planning knowledge. They understand that goal objects are valued and that their loss results in desires to reinstate them.

This knowledge about goals and changes in their status is crucial to children's understanding of the basic antecedents of emotional experience as well as to goal-plan inferences and formation (Stein & Levine, 1987, 1989). In a sense, all emotional reactions are future oriented. We feel negative emotions when an evaluation of our goals leads us to realize that a positively valued object, state, or activity is not attained or maintained or when a negatively valued object, state, or activity is not avoided or escaped. We feel positive emotions when positively valued goals are attained or maintained or when negatively valued goals are escaped or avoided. Once such an appraisal of a situation occurs, we experience a positive or negative emotion. Although appraisal is concerned with antecedents of emotion, assessment of the consequences of what has occurred follows, as well as coping with these consequences (Lazarus, 1991). Coping is definitely future oriented. To cope entails formulating and carrying out goal plans that are adaptive and deal with the changes in goal states. The appraisal of changes in goal states is a developing future-oriented behavior. The loss, or failure to attain, a goal such as having a pet results in sadness or frustration. Attempting to find or attain the pet again represents coping with the change. Although the children in the studies reported here did not explicitly tell us how the character in the story felt, they certainly told us how he coped with negative states. When asked, they also are very capable of elaborating on feeling states, thoughts, wishes, and plans (Stein & Trabasso, 1989). In this sense, the present studies on narration may have focused on actions and outcomes and may have underestimated what the children understood about emotional reactions. The data, however, show strong evidence for comprehension and narration of future-oriented coping by 4- and 5-year-old children.

The age-related progression of description to explanation found in these studies of storytelling to pictures is consistent with that found by Stein and Policastro (1984) and Stein (1988) in cross-sectional studies of children's story concept and open-ended storytelling by older children. Apparently, to understand the causal relations between changes in states and objects that are brought about by transformations through action, one has to know about the properties of these states, objects, and actions as they exist and occur in the real world. Description and identification represent knowledge that is prerequisite to developing naive theories of psychological and physical causation and intentionality.

The dramatic changes in the narrations over the three-to-five-year period corresponds to those frequently found on tasks used to assess the child's developing theory of mind (Astington et al., 1988; Perner, 1991; Wellman, 1991). The ability to take the perspective of others, to infer their perceptions, cognitions, knowledge, and motivational states, to predict their actions and reactions, and to understand the continuation of a plan of action found in these narration studies is clearly consistent with the development of naive theories of intentionality (Trabasso, Stein, & Johnson, 1981; Wellman, 1991). It is also of interest that the children who showed knowledge of goal plans in their narrations also apparently showed an understanding of false beliefs in these contexts (cf. Wimmer & Perner, 1983). That is, before telling the story, the children had seen the entire set of pictures. They therefore had the opportunity to know that the frog was missing and that it was in the swamp and not in the hole in the ground, in the tree, near the rock, and so on. Yet they often spontaneously said that the boy was looking for his frog in these places. In effect the children knew that the boy was acting on a false belief in that they described his search in locations where they knew the frog was absent, marked these searches with purposes or reasons, and told what was found instead. Knowledge of plans, then, enables one to understand, interpret, and predict actions that arise from beliefs, false or otherwise. Children can reveal much of what they know about the mind by observing and narrating what others experience. As such, the development of knowledge of intentions, plans, and actions appears to be general and basic to understanding much about the mind.

The studies reported in this chapter relied heavily on children's use of language to talk about what they witnessed in the events portrayed in picture books. Relying on the use of language in this way can, as we showed in the question-intervention study of 4-year-olds, underestimate what children know about plans of action. Since there is a heavy communicative demand, they may not demonstrate what they do when they observe others act in important, real-life situations. We can distinguish tacitly understanding plans and acting on these understandings from narrating what one understands. The former is likely to develop earlier than age 4 or 5 and to occur earliest in personally meaningful situations. Planning and using this knowledge to achieve one's own goals, and to defend oneself against the potential harms and threats of others, may occur before the development of linguistic skills in narration and the ability to reflect on these plans. The present studies center on children's ability to reflect on a series of events that are witnessed and to communicate their understanding. In real social interaction, where the stakes are higher, we would expect to see more sophisticated instances of using planning knowledge for goal attainment or in defense of one's goals. It is possible that less restricted storytelling or allowing children to act out experiences, personally or with puppets, might reveal a greater understanding of goal plans than did the narration of a commercial picture storybook. However, the methods of analysis developed here are not restricted to the techniques or conditions used to collect such qualitative data. The kind of analysis employed extends to the analysis of real-life contexts, or at least of personal narratives about important real-life experiences. Chapter 14 in this volume, by Stein and Trabasso, represents one of our first efforts to make such an extension. In this work, children who enact experience show greater recall and associations of emotional events than those who merely narrate. Reenactment techniques may thus be superior to retelling or narrating procedures for retrieving what look like state-dependent memories.

Despite the problems of estimating what one knows from linguistic or narrative data, we should recognize that talk about the past is the main way a person can represent what occurred, reflect on these experiences, and make plans for the future. Linguistic and narrative representations may well serve as the basic instances from which goals and plans are constructed, since they could preserve the conditions of the past that created problems to be resolved. Again, the data in Stein and Trabasso (this volume) attest to the importance of children's narrative understanding of what happened to them in emotional episodes. Problems and emotional states exist in the past, may go unresolved, and continue into the present. These memories motivate efforts to understand the past and to formulate means of dealing with such events in the future.

The causal analysis of what happened, why it happened, who was responsible, what followed as consequences, and what one can do about it in the future is a general human way of achieving explanatory coherence and survival. These are the processes we see humans go through when they experience untoward events such as those that occurred in the *Challenger* and Chernobyl disasters (Hilton, Mathes, & Trabasso (1992). Likewise, these processes of causal appraisal and coping underlie emotional appraisal and coping in everyday life (Lazarus, 1991; Trabasso & Stein, 1993). That we find them occurring in narrations of a picture book character's events, actions, and outcomes is not surprising. What is of interest here, however, is the age-related evolution of these skills in making these appraisals and using plans to interpret and narrate events.

We have tried to show that future-oriented behavior is dependent on causal thinking and knowledge about human intentionality. All planning and the following of plans, successful or not, is future oriented, but the plans are grounded in experiences in the past. We have demonstrated how one can analyze the components of plans in narratives and thus see how they are used to interpret, organize, guide, and anticipate behavior in terms of what happened in the past, what caused these events to happen, what goals and plans resulted from them, how current action in the present is motivated by future outcomes as purposes, and how one might deal with failures and success. Causality and planning provide the medium through which the past is glued to the present and future.

REFERENCES

Applewood, J. A. (1991). *Becoming a reader: The experience of fiction from childhood to adulthood.* Cambridge: Cambridge University Press.

Astington, J. W., Harris, P. L., & Olson, D. R. (1988). *Developing theories of mind.* New York: Cambridge University Press.

Berman, R. A., and Slobin, D. I. (1987). *Five ways of learning to talk about events: A cross-linguistic study of children's narratives* (Berkeley Cognitive Science Report No. 46). Berkeley: University of California.

Berman, R. A., Slobin, D. I., Bamberg, M., Dromi, E., Marchman, V., Neeman, Y., Renner, T., & Sebastian, E. (1986). *Coding manual: Temporality in discourse* (rev. ed.). Berkeley: Cognitive Science Program, University of California.

Chi, M. (1978). Knowledge structures and memory development. In R. S. Siegler (Ed.), *Children's thinking: What develops?* Hillsdle, NJ: Erlbaum.

Collins, A., Brown, J. S., & Larkin, K. M. (1980). Inference in text understanding. In R. J. Spiro, B. C. Bruce, & W. F. Brewer (Eds.), *Theoretical issues in reading comprehension* (pp. 385–407). Hillsdale, NJ: Erlbaum.

DeLoache, J. S., Cassidy, D. J., & Carpenter, C. J. (1987). The three bears are all boys: Mothers' gender labeling of neutral picture book characters. *Sex Roles, 17,* 163–178.

Hammond, K. J. (1989). *Case-based planning.* New York: Academic Press.

Hayes-Roth, B., & Hayes-Roth, F. (1979). A cognitive model of planning. *Cognitive Science, 3,* 275–310.

Hilton, D. J., Mathes, R. H., & Trabasso, T. (1992). The study of causal explanation in natural language: Analyzing reports of the Challenger disaster in the *New York Times.* In M. L. McLaughlin, M. J. Cody, & S. J. Read (Eds.), *Explaining one's self to others* (pp. 41–60). Hillsdale, NJ: Erlbaum.

Lazarus, R. S. (1991). *Emotion and adaptation.* New York: Oxford University Press.

Leslie, A. (1987). Pretense and representation: The origins of "theory of mind." *Psychological Review, 94,* 411–426.

Mackie, J. L. (1980). *The cement of the universe: A study of causation.* Oxford: Clarendon Press.

Mayer, M. (1967). *A boy, a dog and a frog.* New York: Dial Press.

Mayer, M. (1969). *Frog, where are you?* New York: Dial Press.

Perner, J. (1991). *Understanding the representational mind.* Cambridge: MIT Press.

Piaget, J. (1930). *The child's conception of physical causality*. New York: Harcourt Brace.

Piaget, J. (1952). *The origins of intelligence in children*. New York: International Universities Press.

Rumelhart, D. E. (1991). Understanding understanding. In W. Kessen, A. Ortony, & F. Craig (Eds.), *Memories, thoughts, and emotions: Essays in honor of George Mandler*. Hillsdale, NJ: Erlbaum.

Schank, R. C. (1986). *Explanation patterns: Understanding mechanically and creatively*. Hillsdale, NJ: Erlbaum.

Scholnick, E. K., & Friedman, S. L. (1987). The planning construct in the psychological literature. In S. L. Friedman, E. K. Scholnick, & R. R. Cocking (Eds.), *Blueprints for thinking*. New York: Cambridge University Press.

Stein, N. L. (1988). The development of children's storytelling skill. In M. B. Franklin & S. Barten (Eds.), *Child language: A reader*. New York: Oxford University Press.

Stein, N. L., & Glenn, C. G. (1979). An analysis of story comprehension in elementary school children. In R. O. Freedle (Ed.), *New directions in discourse processing: Vol. 2. Advances in discourse processes*. Norwood, NJ: Ablex.

Stein, N. L., & Levine, L. (1987). Thinking about feelings: The development and organization of emotional knowledge. In R. E. Snow & M. Farr (Eds.), *Aptitude, learning, and instruction: Vol. 3. Cognition, conation, and affect*, Hillsdale, NJ: Erlbaum.

Stein, N. L., & Levine, L. (1989). The causal organization of emotion knowledge: A developmental study. *Cognition and Emotion, 3*, 343–378.

Stein, N. L., & Policastro, M. (1984). The concept of a story: A comparison between children's and teachers' perspectives. In H. Mandl, N. L. Stein, & T. Trabasso (Eds.), *Learning and comprehension of text*. Hillsdale, NJ: Erlbaum.

Stein, N. L., & Trabasso, T. (1989). Children's understanding of changing emotional states. In P. Harris & C. Saarni (Eds.), *The development of emotional understanding*. New York: Cambridge University Press.

Suchman, L. A. (1987). *Plans and situated actions: The problem of human-machine communication*. New York: Cambridge University Press.

Trabasso, T., & Nickels, M. (1992). The development of goal plans of action in narration of a picture story. *Discourse Processes, 15*, 249–275.

Trabasso, T., Secco, T., & van den Broek, P. (1984). Causal cohesion and story coherence. In H. Mandl, N. L. Stein, & T. Trabasso (Eds.), *Learning and comprehension of text*. Hillsdale, NJ: Erlbaum.

Trabasso, T., & Sperry, L. L. (1985). Causal relatedness and importance of story events. *Journal of Memory and Language, 24*, 595–611.

Trabasso, T., & Stein, N. L. (1993). [Review of *Emotion and adaptation*, by Richard S. Lazarus]. *Psychological Inquiry, 4*, 326–333.

Trabasso, T., Stein, N. L., & Johnson, L. R. (1981). Children's knowledge of events: A causal analysis of story structure. In G. Bower (Ed.), *Learning and motivation* (Vol. 15). New York: Academic Press.

Trabasso, T., Stein, N. L., Rodkin, P. C., Munger, M. P., & Baughn, C. (1992).

Knowledge of goals and plans in the on-line narration of events. *Cognitive Development, 7,* 133–170.

Trabasso, T., & Suh, S. (1993). Understanding text: Achieving explanatory coherence through on-line inferences and mental operations in working memory. *Discourse Processes, 16,* 3–34.

Trabasso, T., & van den Broek, P. (1985). Causal thinking and the representation of narrative events. *Journal of Memory and Language, 24,* 612–630.

Trabasso, T., van den Broek, P., & Suh, S. (1989). Logical necessity and transitivity of causal relations in stories. *Discourse Processes, 12,* 1–25.

Vygotsky, L. S. (1934). *Mind in society: The development of higher psychological processes.* Cambridge: Harvard University Press.

Warren, W. H., Nicholas, D. W., & Trabasso, T. (1979). Event chains and inferences in understanding narratives. In R. Freedle (Ed.), *New directions in discourse processing* (Vol. 2). Hillsdale, NJ: Erlbaum.

Wellman, H. M. (1991). *The child's theory of mind.* Cambridge: Bradford Books/ MIT Press.

Wilensky, R. (1978). *Understanding goal-based stories.* Ph.D. dissertation, Yale University.

Wimmer, H., & Perner, J. (1983). Beliefs about beliefs: Representation and constraining function of wrong beliefs in young children's understanding of deception. *Cognition, 12,* 103–128.

SOCIAL CONTEXT

Chapter Twelve

Considering the Concept of Planning

Barbara Rogoff, Jacquelyn Baker-Sennett, and Eugene Matusov

Our goal in this chapter is to discuss planning as process, focusing on the dynamic and evolving nature of planning as it unfolds during activity in individual, social, and historical time frames. Our emphasis on planning as process rather than as the acquisition of stored objects has developed from a sociocultural perspective, which extends the notion of thinking to include mental activities of individuals and groups participating in cultural activities; however, it is consistent with research in other lines of work as well.

The basic shift is from one that assumes that cognition involves operations performed on static concepts and skills (stored in the brain) to one that suspends the use of the metaphor of representations stored in the brain to focus (more parsimoniously, we argue) on the ongoing thinking processes of people involved in actual endeavors. Traditionally, the study of planning has focused on the possession of plans rather than the processes of their development. The development of skill in planning has been regarded as a cumulative acquisition of plans along with an increase

Research reported in this chapter has been supported by grants from the National Institute of Child Health and Human Development (HD16973) and the Spencer Foundation. We appreciate the helpful comments of Nancy Bell, Cindy Berg, Pablo Chavajay, Batya Elbaum, Denise Goldsmith, Claes von Hofsten, Paul Klaczinski, Christine Mosier, and Ralph Roberts, Bruce Pennington, Janette Benson, and especially Marshall Haith.

in planning in advance of action. We argue for the importance of viewing planning as a process of transforming opportunities for anticipated events, with development involving learning to plan opportunistically—planning in advance of action or during action according to the circumstances, flexibly anticipating constraints and opportunities, and adapting to circumstances.

Our contrast between the cranial storage metaphor and the ongoing process approach to planning has grown out of our own efforts to study planning as a sociocultural activity. But we have noted in discussions with many colleagues that the contrast is deep and does not correspond to a split in topic of inquiry; rather it involves contrasting assumptions regarding basic units of analysis. Roughly half the scholars working in areas quite different from our own, such as neurological functioning, perception, animal learning, and cognition (with whom we have interacted in a number of invited addresses, symposia, and classes and in informal discussion) seem to find our perspective an intuitively clear and commonsense approach; the other half have found it to be counterintuitive and difficult to imagine. At the same time, we have noted that a sizable number of researchers studying social and cultural phenomena argue with us as vehemently as anyone else.

The contrast we focus on in this chapter relates to questions of paradigm or worldview, in the sense that Pepper (1942) and Dewey and Bentley (1949) have described. In considering the implications of a contextualist worldview for understanding cognitive development, Rogoff (1982) contrasted an *interactional* approach—in which elements of human functioning are assumed to have independent standing and the question is how they interact—with a *contextual event* (or *transactional*) approach—in which events are conceived as meaningful and coherent as a unit of analysis. For example, in an interactional approach to the relation of people and context, characteristics of the person and characteristics of the environment are assessed independent of each other and then related; in a contextual event approach, on the other hand, "neither the context nor the person's activity can ultimately be defined independently, as their meanings derive from their integration in the psychological event. The contextual event approach assumes that events are structured such that no constituent can be adequately specified apart from the specification of the other constituents" (Rogoff, 1982, p. 132).

In this chapter we build our argument on observations and assumptions of a sociocultural approach, since this is the conceptual and empirical domain in which we work, and in this area we argue that reconsidering how planning is conceived is crucial (see Rogoff, 1982, for other psychological approaches consistent with a contextual event approach). Our aim in this chapter is broader, however. We feel that the area of cognitive development would be well served by examining the cranial storage metaphor rather than treating it as a fact. If it is understood to be a metaphor, scholars can examine whether it advances their understanding in dealing with a particular question or whether it decreases parsimony in trying to understand a particular cognitive phenomenon.

We begin by explicating our contrast between planning as a process of emergence as opposed to planning as selection and application of stored plans. This approach involves an associated conceptualization of change and time. Then we argue for the necessity of this view in a sociocultural approach, in which individual, social, and cultural processes are mutually constituting. The next section describes work from this perspective that points to the importance of flexibility in planning. Finally, we turn to a discussion of how the essential questions for cognitive development are changed by this shift in the assumption system.

PLANNING AS *PROCESS*

Our view of planning focuses on the processes involved in developing ways of preparing for anticipated events, rather than treating planning as the passive possession of plans as cranially stored objects. Although researchers' references to processes as objects and to mental functioning as the operation of a storage space may serve as a shorthand to communicate about what they are studying, we regard it as a mistake to assume that metaphors for reference to an object of study are necessarily useful ways of conceptualizing what goes on when *people plan*. It appears to us that researchers often unknowingly treat the metaphors by which they communicate with each other as facts regarding the phenomena they seek to explain.

Gellatly (1989) expressed a similar concern in pointing out that it is common for cognitive researchers to develop a careful description of reasoning (e.g., children's understanding of the functioning of a balance beam) in terms of rules and to make the illegitimate jump from using these descriptions to represent what children do to assuming that the rules are possessed by the children and guide their behavior.

Roediger (1980; see also Hoffman, Cochran, & Nead, 1990) provided an extensive analysis of spatial storage and search metaphors for memory (ranging from Plato's aviary to Atkinson and Shiffrin's stores to Broadbent's library) and expressed the concern that "the theoretical controversy has been about what type of search process occurs, not whether or not the phenomena are best explained by the search metaphor in the first place" (p. 238). Although Roediger noted that several scholars have questioned the spatial storage and search assumptions (and Bartlett provided an early alternative to them), he warned that the assumptions are so ingrained in our language that the enterprise of examining alternative theories may be difficult. But he called for an examination of the assumptions, because "they add nothing new to the observations under study and simply involve circular reasoning. For example, if an experimental manipulation increases recall over some other set of conditions, why say that the manipulation encouraged better storage or search for the stimuli?" (p. 243).

In an incisive chapter, Kvale (1977, p. 177) went beyond questioning the cranial storage metaphor in traditional research on remembering and outlined an alternative:

> In a dialectical conception of remembering as a relationship there are no memory traces, no things or copies stored in an inner bank. Rather, a person's behavioral repertoire and possibilities have been altered by his past experiences. This involves, of course, physiological changes in the organism, but these need not be in the form of a library or picture album the remembering person is inspecting. The person has been changed through his experience so that he may re-produce, re-construct, re-cognize more or less vivid and accurate earlier experiences and also communicate them to others. By systematic investigations of remembering as a subject's interaction with the world, applying phenomenological descriptions and experimental studies, the recourse to an inner bureaucracy as explanation of observable remembering activity may become superfluous.

We want to draw attention to the use of the cranial storage metaphor for characterizing mental functioning in order to allow critical examination of its utility. We argue that what goes on when people plan can be studied directly as an inherently developmental *process* of planning, without resorting to intermediary constructs involving the possession or acquisition of plans. In our view, the intermediary constructs often obscure the examination of planning and other processes that can be studied through close analysis of ongoing processes when an event or activity is employed as the unit of analysis. In our experience, a more satisfying account is given when a colleague describes how people went about planning something to accomplish this or that than when the direct description of what occurred is translated into an account based on acquisition, storage, and retrieval of plans in the brain.

This does not mean the cranial storage metaphor is never useful; some researchers may find it very revealing. Rather, our argument is against the practice of treating it as a premise not to be questioned. And we note that when we remove it from accounts of planning and remembering, the resulting explanation seems to us to be just as complete and more parsimonious. Sometimes colleagues who rely on the cranial storage metaphor ask us for evidence that it is unnecessary;

rather, we propose that researchers examine it and consider when it *is* necessary or useful.

Processes of Ongoing Activity versus Black Boxes with Homunculi

Models of planning that attribute explanatory strength to assumptions of cranial storage of mental representations seem to us to promote static views of cognitive processes presumed to be collected inside individuals' heads. This statement may seem puzzling since many lines of research refer to the study of *process*. We argue that approaches that seek basic elements (such as cranially stored objects) and view process as the change of state of these elements make processes themselves difficult to specify (instead, mechanisms of change in state are sought). In contrast, approaches that truly study process focus on the ongoing events as they change and do not seek static elements on which to rest analysis.

The traditional view portrays planning as the shuffling of cranially stored mental representations (Fabricius, 1988; Klahr & Robinson, 1981), with most attention devoted to characterizing potential mental representations and little devoted to how the shuffling occurs. The use of latencies in reaction time studies to infer planning processes seems to be the way the traditional approach examines the shuffling of the stored representations. Such an approach treats planning as a black box, with inputs and outputs specified and observed and internal working assumed to involve objects labeled with the terms researchers use to classify and discuss the tasks given to the subjects ("memory," "perception," etc.). The research focuses on identifying the locations and relations between these assumed mental objects; their actual use is not observed and usually requires the assumption of a homunculus or an executive process to make decisions regarding how to use the cranially stored representations. Since the cranial storage metaphor makes it difficult to observe the processes as they occur, researchers in this tradition seem to be satisfied with treating reaction time as an indicator of how long the mysterious processes take to change from state 1 to state 2. At least for some research endeavors, the application of this metaphor leads to a less parsimonious approach than does studying planning activities directly.

Guba and Lincoln (1982, p. 251) have similarly argued that the black box approach is unable to deal with process considerations, whereas other research perspectives focus directly on the processes involved in events:

> In the early decades of this century, for example, physicists were obsessed with modeling the atom, and a variety of models were proposed. . . . But all of these models proved unsatisfactory. Moreover, means were not (nor

are) available to "see" inside the atom in any event. Atoms came to be regarded as "black boxes" which could be manipulated from the outside and which would produce reactions, but the process by which the stimuli were reacted to (inside the black box) remained a mystery. The inability of physicists to deal with process and the invention of the "black box" idea came to be viewed, in an interesting reversal, as the proper way to do research—stimulate, wait for reaction, observe reactions, and never mind how stimulus came to be translated into reaction. . . . But what physicist would forego looking inside the atom if able to do so? And if, in other areas, process can be examined, . . . why persist in the use of a model that ignores that possibility?

In the black box approach, processes are often attributed to an "executive" function that coordinates the other parts (memories, percepts, motives, and so on), but the functioning of the executive (a homunculus) must also be explained. The problem can be illustrated with an anecdote about an absentminded Russian professor of mathematics. To keep his promises to other people he used a traditional Russian memory strategy—tying knots in his pocket handkerchief. This usually worked well for the professor. But once he missed an appointment with his student despite making a knot. As his excuse, he told the student, "There are three problems that everyone experiences with this technique of making knots. First, it is necessary *to remember when* it is appropriate to think of the handkerchief. Second, it is necessary *to remember where* one put the handkerchief. Third, it is necessary *to remember what* one meant when making the knot." From the perspective of the cranial storage metaphor, explanation is in terms of the encoding and retrieval of the representation of the mental note (remembering what), and where it is stored (remembering where). The homunculus itself, which performs these activities and determines when the information is needed (implementing the plan to remember what and where, and remembering when to), eludes explanation. A sociocultural approach calls for focus directly on the *person* (not black boxes within the person) remembering, planning, perceiving, and thinking. In our view, focusing on the activity itself is a more direct and parsimonious way to go about understanding planning than having to explain both the boxes and the homunculus. After all, the efforts of people *can* be observed.

We are not arguing against mental representation *as an activity*. In fact, planning is a process that often involves representing one situation in terms of another, with or without material support. The acts of re-presenting ideas at another time and of transforming ideas to other forms are essential to human thinking. The use of material representations such as maps or schedules is a central feature of human cultural activity, and shuffling papers in metal file cabinets can usefully be seen as working with material mental representations. An imagined map, like a physical map, becomes a tool in the actual process of planning; the imagined map does not exist outside the planning process (C. von Hofsten, personal communication, 1993).

The point of our argument is to question the assumption that planning is an operation carried out on mental representations *stored* in the brain. The questions of how people represent and transform ideas, imagine, think, solve problems, remember, plan, and so on, remain very much a focus of interest in our approach. We argue for studying what people actually *do* to re-present ideas, imagine, plan, remember, and so on.

Consistent with our stress on planning as an active process is an integration of cognitive processes that in other views have often been separated. We aim to understand how people manage their endeavors; it is not our aim to separate planning from remembering, feeling, thinking, wanting, creating. Indeed, we do not regard these as separate processes (Rogoff, 1982, 1990). Their treatment as separate processes derives from the view that thinking consists of activating stored cranial objects such as plans, concepts, thoughts, emotions, and motivations, with a need to separately define each of these assumed elements.

If we view thinking as the inherently integrated and dynamic transformations in people's management of their endeavors, we must recognize that our concept of change and time is also different from the conception involved in the activation of mental objects.

Conceptions of Time and Change

We consider events and activities to be inherently dynamic rather than consisting of static conditions with time added to them as a separate element. Change and development, rather than static characteristics or elements, are basic (Kvale, 1977; Michaels & Carello, 1981; Pepper, 1942; Rogoff, 1982). Time is an inherent aspect of events and is not divided into separate units of past, present, and future. Any event in the present extends previous events and is directed toward goals that have not yet been accomplished. As such, the present contains past and future and cannot be separated from them.

When people act in the present based on their previous involvements, their past is present. The past is not merely a cranially stored memory called up in the present; it contributes to the event at hand by having prepared it. The present event is different than it would have been had previous events not occurred, but this fact does not require a storage model of past events.

Rogoff (in press a) provided a physical example: "The size, shape, and strength of a child's leg at age 6 are a function of growth and use that have occurred previously; the child's leg has *changed* over development—it is not a summation of stored units of growth or of exercise. The past is not *stored* in the leg; the leg has developed, changed, to be as it is currently. There is no need to separate past and present or future or to conceive of the development in terms of the acquisition of stored units. Development is clearly a process spanning time, dynamic, with change throughout rather than accumulation of new items" (p. 37 of manuscript). Similar examples could be drawn from social processes of change—for example, the development of a company is conceived of as change, not as an accumulation of stored units of some sort.

Not only is the past present, but the future is also present in each moment. Children's physical growth, and human activity in general, moves in particular directions (which are usually not explicit or precise). Little doubt exists when a child is 6 about what shape and utility his or her legs (a better example might be the child's gonads) will have 20 years in the future. Likewise, human planning, communication, work, and play all are directed within the present toward some general directions or purposes of the participants. For example, in planning dialogue for a play, children work with the general theme and aims of the performance as they manage specific wording decisions of the moment (Baker-Sennett, Matusov, & Rogoff, 1992). Ochs (1994) argued that in creating narratives, people move their lives forward in time by mentally and verbally stretching their past life events into the future. Goals or purposes need not be tightly formulated (and certainly need not be subject to reflection) to guide present action.

Thus, we emphasize that planning occurs in the service of endeavors involving prior events and anticipated events and cannot be severed from goals to be accomplished or from the history of the activity. People's history and goals are inherently involved in a unit of analysis focusing on events or, in the term used by sociocultural theorists, an activity, discussed in the next section.

A UNIT OF ANALYSIS FOCUSING ON PROCESS: SOCIOCULTURAL ACTIVITY

Sociocultural theorists employ the *activity* as the unit of analysis, studying a unit that consists of the ongoing processes of interest without dissecting them (Laboratory of Comparative Human Cognition, 1983; Leont'ev, 1981; Vygotsky, 1987; Wertsch, 1985). The activity involves active and dynamic contributions from individuals, their social partners, and historical traditions and materials and their transformations, in mutually defining relations. This differs from the common approach of viewing social and cultural processes as separate factors or influences that affect basic individual factors or characteristics. If individual, social, and cultural processes are treated as inseparable and mutually constituting, it is inappropriate to try to locate them in the individual.[1]

Activity theory posits that in addition to developmental transitions occurring across an individual's life (ontogenetic development), transformations in thinking occur with successive engagements in an activity, even in time spans of minutes (microgenetic development; see Siegler & Crowley, 1991; Wertsch, 1979). These are embedded in and at the same time constitute the developmental processes involved in societal and phylogenetic change. Development within lives proceeds along with cultural and species development occurring over historical time (Scribner, 1985). Even solitary planning operates in social, cultural, and historical institutions.

Developmental processes in each of these time frames can be viewed as involving observation of the whole coherent process in different planes of analysis (Rofoff, in press a). If we regard personal, interpersonal, and community/institutional processes as mutually constituting, it is at times convenient to focus attention on one or another plane of analysis, keeping in mind that each one cannot be separated from the others, since each is defined in terms of the others. In other words, one plane of analysis may be foregrounded for close examination, but the others remain active even while they are not the focus of attention (just as the negative space in a painting is essential to understanding the focal images that constitute the positive space). This notion contrasts with the idea that any one of these planes is prior to the others or can be defined separately to determine the influence of one upon another.

In contrast to interactional views that separate the individual and the environment (to examine planning either without regard to or owing to the effects of the environment), individuals and the environment are seen as inseparable—processes cannot be independently attributed to one or the other (Dewey & Bentley, 1949; Gibson, 1982; Leont'ev, 1981; Rogoff, 1982). The focus is on the transformations involved in an unfolding event or activity in which people participate.

Thus, along with the contributions to planning made by people's efforts, analysis of a planning activity includes investigating the social order

1. Compatible units of analysis also seem to be employed by some researchers studying events in the brain (such as the functioning of neurons or the development of brain matter) and perception-and-action (such as coordination of limbs in the context of action in real circumstances). For example, see Pribram's (1990) discussion of the hologram metaphor, which he attributes to the parallel distributed processing approach: "Each part of the hologram is representative of the whole. . . . The whole becomes enfolded in each portion of the hologram since each portion 'contains' the spread of information over the entire image. . . . The properties of holograms are expressed by the principle that 'the whole is contained or enfolded in its parts,' and the very notion of 'parts' is altered, because parts of a hologram do not have what we think of as boundaries" (pp. 92–93).

of planning with others (e.g., in school or work or family activities) and cultural tools such as maps, pencils, and linguistic and mathematical systems as well as cultural values and situational constraints and resources involved in the means that are valued for solving problems (e.g., planning during action or planning all moves in advance of action). This perspective can be applied to all planning activities—including those occurring in classrooms, backyards, or laboratories, which all constitute sociocultural events. However, few investigations of cognitive development have focused on the sociocultural conditions in which children create and pursue goals, or on how the activities of individuals themselves constitute and transform historical, cultural, and economic institutions and practices.

Because most research on planning occurs in situations that are devised by the researchers themselves, the sociocultural context of the planning is seldom noticed, since it is embedded within research and educational institutions that surround the investigators. Systems one is completely immersed in are difficult even to detect. Such systems are automatic at the cultural level, much as well-practiced moves are automatic for individuals, and this leads us to overlook their existence, to the point that we fall into the assumption that in laboratories (or in tests) we are able to observe "pure" cognition or individuals' true competence independent of situational "confounds." Analysis of the sociocultural context of social and individual activity is difficult for researchers embedded in educational situations or research traditions that are often seen as the way things must be rather than just one way that things happen to be.

In contrived planning research, researchers may fail to notice that they themselves and the other participants are constrained in the problem definition, the appropriate means of solution, and the material supports and constraints provided by the researcher as an agent of academia. The participants cannot redefine the problem or its appropriate solution without going out of the bounds of the social contract between "subject" and "experimenter." Planning in laboratory studies, as much as in other settings, is a sociocultural process. However, the sociocultural aspects of planning may be easier for us to observe in situations that are not of our own making.

To study the sociocultural context of children's planning, Rogoff, Lacasa, Baker-Sennett, and Goldsmith (1994) observed planning processes of individuals, groups, and communities or institutions as Girl Scouts participated in cookie sales. That the arrangement of the planning tasks in this activity was not designed by the researchers made it easy to see how the planning tasks were constituted by individuals, groups, and the communities involved.

Individual scouts in the annual fund-raising cookie sales carried a great deal of responsibility for planning routes, keeping track of sales, cookies, and money, and managing their time, in collaboration with other scouts, siblings, parents, customers, and adult troop leaders. The collective experience of planning cookie sales occurred in the cultural context of institutional supports and constraints provided by traditions and practices of the Girl Scouts organization, which provides training to troop leaders and many organizational tools that the girls used and adapted. For example, the cookie order form requires customers as they order to calculate the amount due at the time of delivery. In this context customers often provided a talk-aloud plan for multiplying the number of units (at $2.50 each) as fourths of $10 rather than by multiplying each column in turn. The girls were thus often given a strategy for handling the money through their customers' own out-loud calculations, sparked by the organization of the institutional tool, the order form.

The tools that people use in planning, and the involvements with other people and cultural institutions, are clearly inseparable from the ways of planning people engage in. However, they have often been overlooked as an aspect of the planning process, when planning is defined narrowly as a process occurring within an individual's head. We regard them as inherent to rather than external to planning processes. "Even when planning occurs out of the context of action, it often relies upon simulations of aspects of the activity, with maps, lists, or simulations of sequences of events using written, spoken, or drawn symbols as in blueprints, thumbnail sketches, or battle plans. And in planning during action, a planner uses the resources and constraints of the environment in the process of generating and carrying out the plan, again using external aids such as lists, reminders, and the assistance of others" (Rogoff, Gauvain, & Gardner, 1987, pp. 306–307). Material and social aspects of planning are not just accidentally available; they are organized in social institutions and practices having to do with economic, academic, political, and other systems and their associated tools and systems of values regarding what is to be done and how it is best achieved. Spoken, written, and signed language, calendars, maps, and many other cultural artifacts inherited from others and further developed by each generation are central to planning by human individuals and groups. They provide affordances for new goals and opportunities for indirect exploration of planning approaches through simulation of various sorts and are themselves developed through people's adaptations.

With activity as the unit of analysis in a sociocultural approach, planning is inherently developmental; it is a process of transformation of possibilities. The metaphor of planning as the acquisition and accumulation of plans stored in the head gets in the way of an approach that focuses directly on the processes of transformation inherent to planning. We consider planning to be a process of flexibly and deliberately devising means to accomplish interpersonal and practical endeavors. The term "deliberate" was chosen to rule out accidental and automatic action and to allow discussion of planning that gives evidence of orientation toward a goal with flexible means to achieve it (without having to be concerned with hoary issues of consciousness or awareness; see Baker-Sennett, Matusov, & Rogoff, 1993). To plan is to develop an approach to an anticipated event; planning requires flexibility of thinking in order to define both the goals and the means in ways that optimize the inherently changing nature of events. Although these ideas are found in other sources as well, we argue that taking a sociocultural approach makes them central.

With any process, the nature of the phenomenon changes as the process develops. The focus of planning itself develops, with some processes becoming nested in others, thereby addressing the classic issue of automatization: any activity can require deliberateness or can be carried out more or less automatically, depending on how it fits with the goal, how complicated the circumstances are, and how facile the planner is. Automatization is a developmental process that allows people to chunk aspects of the activity as they gain facility, and to turn attention to fitting the chunks together (Bjorklund & Jacobs, 1985; Sternberg, 1985). Throughout microgenesis and ontogenesis, the focus of attention and planning moves to the aspects of the process to which the individual needs to devote attention in order to proceed.

Leont'ev (1981) explicated three interrelated levels in the analysis of activity, which we find useful in considering planning as a phenomenon in which actions are nested within goal-oriented activity, which in turn serves other goals. Leont'ev's global level of analysis is the unit of the *activity*. Activity inherently involves motive, or driving force, which is socioculturally structured (e.g., play, schooling, and work activities). Leont'ev's second level of analysis is the unit of *goal-directed action*. Activity and goal-directed action are different levels of analysis because involvement in a particular activity can be independent of specific actions. The same action can serve very different activities, and different actions can serve the same activity. Leont'ev's third level of analysis is the unit of *operations*. Operations are the means by which actions are carried out—specifically how the action is done, which is defined by the circumstances in which the goal is approached. Actions are concerned with goals, and operations are concerned with conditions. Different operations can be substituted to achieve the same goal-directed action, and the same operations can serve different goal-directed actions. Thus the levels of activity, while nested in each other, are not operational definitions of planning. The levels are not hierarchical in a fixed sense, but rather allow for the likelihood that what serves as an activity in one analysis may function as an action in another (e.g., educational play in a classroom), and what is an operation in one situation is an action in another (e.g., shifting gears in driving may be an action while one is learning to drive or an operation to serve the action of driving to work in unproblematic situations for an experienced driver).

A sociocultural approach to planning involves considering the integration of processes occurring at personal, interpersonal, and community planes of analysis that have frequently been seen as working separately. Leont'ev argued that *"systematic* analysis of human activity . . . allows us to overcome the opposition of social, psychological, and physiological phenomena, and the reduction of one to another" (1981, p. 69).

An analysis of mutually constituting developmental processes across personal, interpersonal, and community planes of observation has yielded insights regarding the development of planning that have been underemphasized, we think, in work on planning that employs the metaphor of cranially stored objects. Specifically, such an analysis of processes and a view involving integrated planes of analysis calls attention to the importance of flexibility in planning.

FLEXIBILITY IN DEVELOPMENT OF GOALS AND MEANS DURING PLANNING

We focus here on the importance of flexibility in planning to provide an example of how a focus on planning as process advances our understanding of planning through empirical observations and conceptual perspectives addressing the transformations inherent in planning.

Researchers have generally characterized more mature planning as involving planning in advance of action (Brown & DeLoache, 1978; Forbes & Greenberg, 1982; Klahr, 1978; Magkaev, 1977). However, the importance of development of flexible planning—involving both advance planning and improvisation fitted to the circumstances—has been emphasized by Dewey (1916), Miller, Galanter, and Pribram (1960), Rogoff, Gauvain, and Gardner (1987), and Hayes-Roth and Hayes-Roth (1979). These authors have noted that the search for problem solutions often proceeds by generating best guesses rather than searching systematically and exhaustively for the final solution in advance of acting.

Leont'ev (1981) extended the importance of flexibility to include the development of goals. Planning is not only a process of reaching goals through planful sequences of actions but also a process of forming the goals themselves. Goals need not be preset but may emerge or be modified in the course of an activity. Opportunistic planning involves a flexible combination of advance planning and improvisation, developing skeleton plans to be elaborated to various degrees during action.

There are some advantages to planning in advance of action (Rogoff, Gauvain, & Gardner, 1987)—placing one's emphasis on advance planning may simplify tasks by limiting and organizing options and promoting systematic consideration of the relative advantages of the options—but advance planning is often unnecessary, inefficient, or impossible (Goodnow, 1987; Rosaldo, 1989). Improvisation allows a planner to take advantage of changeable circumstances and to avoid the mental effort and delays required to formulate an advance plan outside of action (Gardner & Rogoff, 1990). Improvisation also has the virtue of emphasizing preparing to be flexible and to take advantage of events that are as yet unknown in developing both means and goals. It involves a flexible attitude involving decision making in action, which takes advantage of as yet undetermined opportunities for creative handling of problems; it does not simply defer decision making in case things go wrong.

The importance of flexibility of planning is especially notable when planning is viewed as a sociocultural activity occurring with other people in particular events that involve cultural organization and the use of cultural tools.[2]

The study of how Girl Scouts planned routes for selling and delivering cookies reveals the necessity of flexibility (Rogoff, Baker-Sennett, Lacasa, & Goldsmith, 1994). Had the girls limited themselves to planning the whole route in advance, their effectiveness in selling and delivering cookies would have suffered. For example, one girl began her delivery by separating out each customer's order and marking it with a Post-It note showing address and amount due, then lining up all the customers' orders according to their addresses, creating an efficient route around her neighborhood. She lined up dozens of groups of orders on the sidewalk in front of her house, asked her mother which addresses would be closest to which others, then stacked the linear array *in reverse order* in a wagon (to have the beginning of the route on top).

This approach looked sophisticated by criteria that focus on advance planning. But when the scout began delivery she soon found the need to change the fixed order because some customers were not home, her companions lost interest, and so on. In subsequent deliveries, this scout (like many others) used a more flexible strategy, choosing a small number of orders to deliver in a small area and adjusting delivery according to what occurred in the process. This plan meant anticipating some

2. It is interesting that the compatible view of planning provided by Hayes-Roth and Hayes-Roth (1979) involves a metaphor of coordination of a social group—specialists who suggest decisions when promising opportunities arise.

backtracking of routes; however, if such flexibility had not been planned, backtracking still would have been necessary because of the impossibility of anticipating all aspects of the delivery.

Another study underlining the importance of flexibility in planning involved the creation of a classroom play (Baker-Sennett, Matusov, & Rogoff, 1992). A group of six second- and third-grade girls spent ten 20- to 30-minute sessions planning and preparing to perform a play based on *Snow White* as a class assignment. Their planning was analyzed at five levels ranging from advance metaplanning in deciding how to plan the planning process and establish decision-making rules to local planning and improvisation of more concrete decisions about specific words and actions. The girls in the early sessions considered many issues that formed the metaplanning and interpersonal foundation for their later concrete planning decisions. They considered alternatives for deciding how to go about planning the play, discussed how to develop strategies and procedures for handling disputes during the planning process, and worked on the main theme and events of the play and how to divide and distribute roles.

The interpersonal process was the same as the creative planning of the play itself, for in the effort to resolve disputes, some of the most creative planning of the play occurred. For example, a major advance in planning the play occurred when the girls, with the help of their teacher, resolved their differences in recall of the "true" story line of *Snow White* by deciding to create a twisted version of the tale. From then on the girls coordinated more easily in their planning as they transformed the story line to their own plan.

Both the interpersonal process and the play-planning process required flexibility in order to coordinate efforts. Some of this flexibility was needed to cope with plans' being derailed by absences of group members, with later lack of agreement or of understanding by those who had been absent, and with running out of time at the end of a session before a process came to conclusion. Although these "inconveniences" are carefully controlled in most laboratory planning sessions, during everyday endeavors they are the occurrences that make the creative planning process a challenge and provide opportunities for breaking to new patterns. In most of life, it is impossible to anticipate all the obstacles and opportunities that will arise during the course of events.

Most of the flexible planning the girls engaged in was not in response to intruding events but was instead the means by which they managed the complexities of creating a play and coordinating their often discrepant ideas. Often the girls elaborated on an idea mentioned by another person, with the collaborative product more than the sum of the individual contributions. Ideas changed over the course of resolution of conflict and germs of ideas appeared, submerged, and resurfaced transformed as the girls worked out the scenes of the play. An example involves use of a fortuitous circumstance in planning a scene:

> During the first session, the girls considered how they could have a talking mirror, and a number of possibilities were discussed, one of which was to have a hole in a mirror with an actor speaking in the hole. All six girls participated in this discussion, which ended without resolution as one girl brought them back to the need to focus on main events. Nothing more was done with the mirror issue until the ninth session, when [during rehearsal] the evil queen went to look in a pretend mirror but was inconvenienced by the student teacher who was right where she wanted the mirror to be. She told him to move. But his being there seemed to have prompted the idea of having a person play the mirror, and she asked a classmate to come over to be the mirror and told her the mirror's line. This feature was replayed in the tenth session, and appeared in the final performance as well. In this example, the creative planning built on an intrusion to develop a creative germ that had been mentioned long before. (p. 104).

The collaborative process necessitated explicit planning and flexibility in order to allow cooperation among group members and to take advantage of creative opportunities offered by the group process. The process was filled with interruptions and topic changes that nevertheless were managed by the group in working together by sharing attention, communicating about ideas, and adjusting individual ideas to facilitate the group process and progress on playcrafting.

Underlying these analyses of planning is the shift in perspective regarding planning as process rather than the acquisition or accumulation of cranially stored objects, with sociocultural activity rather than individual characteristics as the unit of analysis and with analysis of the transformations inherent to the activities rather than a search for mechanisms of acquisition or accumulation of plans conceived as objects. Such an analysis has drawn our attention to the centrality of flexibility as a feature of planning, a feature whose necessity is less noticeable in analyses that focus on planning as the acquisition of cranially stored objects and with the individual as the basic unit of analysis. In the final section of this chapter, we briefly note several changes in the questions to be addressed, given a shift to a focus on planning as process.

CHANGES IN THE QUESTIONS TO BE ADDRESSED

Our suggestion that planning (remembering, feeling, etc.) can be studied and referred to in the active form (as "verbs") rather than in static forms (the possession of plans, memories, affects, etc.—"nouns") that require the postulation of some other entity to make them active (the homunculus or executive) may appear at first to be a semantic distinction between talking in verbs versus in nouns. Indeed, this is how it began for us, upon reading the suggestions of Leont'ev (1981), Gibson (1979), and Pepper (1942) to this effect.

> [The Gibsonian approach] suggests that cognitive processes be cast in active form (e.g., remembering, thinking, perceiving) rather than as objects possessed by a thinker (e.g., memories, cognitions, perceptions) (Bransford et al., 1977; Gibson, 1979; Johnston & Turvey, 1980; Pick, 1979a). As Michaels and Carello (1981) put it, "Ecological psychologists prefer to talk about knowing as something that the organism does rather than knowledge as something the organism has [p. 62]." The thinking person is active in participating in an event, exploring a situation, directing attention, attempting solutions. The person is not merely the receptacle for interacting mental entities that are responsible for selecting information, adding interpretations, and embellishing stimuli in ways consistent with the biases of memory. The *person,* rather than elements contained in the person, is active (Michaels & Carello, 1981; Shotter, 1978). (Rogoff, 1982, p. 136)

If such a shift is made, however, it soon becomes apparent that the consequences are much deeper. They extend to transformations in what questions seem important (or even sensible to address). The most obvious changes in questions include the following:

- A focus on how people re-present prior activities and anticipate events to themselves and each other rather than investigating *where mental representations are stored* in the brain and how they connect.
- A focus on how children's participation in cognitive activities transforms with their continued involvement rather than on *when children first possess* particular cranially stored concepts and skills (the onset question; see Rogoff, in press b).
- A focus on the nature of people's actual involvement in ongoing events, substituting an interest in understanding what children *do* do and think for questions of what children *can* do and think (seeking *competence* assumes an underlying stable "ability" that can in some ideal world be separated from the context to be assessed in "pure" form; see Rogoff, in press a,b; Rogoff, Radziszewska, & Masiello, in press).
- A focus on how individuals and communities construe activities to relate to each other rather than assuming that what is observed on one occasion is *general* (broadly or within domains) or that *transfer* from one situation to another occurs through mechanical similarity of the situation or automatic processes of the brain (see Rogoff et al., in press).
- A focus on how people together transform their responsibility in participation in sociocultural activities rather than on how external mental knowledge and skill is *internalized* or how the social world *influences* the individual (see Rogoff, in press a).

Researchers who use the cranial storage metaphor to organize their way of thinking about psychological processes are often concerned that the alternative eschews the scientific aim of reaching generalities about human functioning. But this is not the case. Instead of looking for generalities by trying to locate psychological processes in the form of knowledge and skills stored in the brains of individuals,[3] the approach we are suggesting attempts to build generalities in terms of patterns of convergence of processes observed across varying activities. The resulting generalities have to do with processes of people engaged in sociocultural activities, not with processes independent of sociocultural activities. For example, in both the Girl Scout cookie study and the playcrafting study, we noted the importance of a flexible approach to planning in circumstances where the contributions of other people and uncontrolled events cannot be foreseen, or in which it is more trouble or less satisfying to attempt to foresee them than to improvise during the process. This generalization emerges from the convergence of patterns of findings in the two studies.

We suggest that the metaphor of brain storage has been reified and has become applied as an axiomatic assumption. Our aim is to draw attention to the metaphor so that researchers can consider whether or when it serves a useful function. We argue that in a sociocultural perspective, treating the metaphor as an assumption is not parsimonious and gets in the way of studying cognitive and sociocultural processes. However, there may be other approaches for which the metaphor is useful; we suggest its utility may be evaluated for such endeavors if it is used in a more self-aware fashion.

SUMMARY

In this chapter our aim was to describe how planning can be studied as an inherent part of human activity rather than as the acquisition and storage of isolated elements in the brain. When activity is the unit of analysis, a conceptual shift in the way we think about such issues as the nature of time, change, and purpose occurs in both theory and methodology. This approach moves us away from traditional developmental perspectives that examine age-based comparisons of individuals and cognitive perspectives that rest with relabeling planning processes in terms of static objects.

3. We are not arguing against the importance of brains; we see our approach as having parallels in the study of brain activity (rather than brain localization). We are intrigued by recent developments suggesting that it is fruitful to examine brain functioning in terms of the activity of communities of neurons. It is interesting to us that the brain researchers with whom we have discussed our ideas are divided into those who find them counterintuitive and those who find them common sense, as with researchers of other topics.

Rather, a sociocultural approach allows us to examine the roles and responsibilities that people take in activities and to see how their participation evolves over time. People take advantage of new aspects of developing events and adjust to unforeseen circumstances to plan in the context of activities occurring in actual material circumstances, with other people, engaged in activities based on and contributing to sociocultural practices, communities, and institutions with associated values and tools relevant to planning. As they participate, they change. Viewing planning as a sociocultural process has led us to question the assumption that planning involves possession of cranially stored objects and to investigate (in a manner we regard as more straightforward and parsimonious for our purposes) how planning involves people's changing their involvement in sociocultural activities in anticipation of future aspects of their endeavors.

REFERENCES

Baker-Sennett, J., Matusov, E., & Rogoff, B. (1992). Sociocultural processes of creative planning in children's playcrafting. In P. Light & G. Butterworth (Eds.), *Context and cognition: Ways of learning and knowing* (pp. 93–114). Hertfordshire, Eng.: Harvester-Wheatsheaf.

Baker-Sennett, J., Matusov, E., & Rogoff, B. (1993). Planning as developmental process. In H. W. Reese (Ed.), *Advances in child development and behavior* (Vol. 24, pp. 253–281). New York: Academic Press.

Bjorklund, D., & Jacobs, J. (1985). Associative and categorical processes in children's memory: The role of automaticity in the development of organization in free recall. *Journal of Experimental Child Psychology, 39,* 599–617.

Brown, A., & DeLoache, J. (1978). Skills, plans, and self-regulation. In R. Siegler (Ed.), *Children's thinking: What develops?* (pp. 3–35). Hillsdale, NJ: Erlbaum.

Dewey, J. (1916). *Democracy and education: An introduction to the philosophy of education.* New York: Macmillan.

Dewey, J., & Bentley, A. F. (1949). *Knowing and the known.* Boston: Beacon Press.

Fabricius, W. V. (1988). The development of forward search planning in preschoolers. *Child Development, 59,* 1473–1488.

Forbes, D. L., & Greenberg, M. T. (1982). *Children's planning strategies: New directions for child development* (Vol. 18). San Francisco: Jossey-Bass.

Gardner, W., & Rogoff, B. (1990). Children's deliberateness of planning according to task circumstances. *Developmental Psychology, 26,* 480–487.

Gellatly, A. (1989). The myth of cognitive diagnostics. In Gellatly, A., Rogers, D., & Sloboda, J. A. (Eds.), *Cognition and social worlds* (pp. 113–131). Oxford: Clarendon Press.

Gibson, E. J. (1982). The concept of affordances in development: The renascence of functionalism. In W. A. Collins (Ed.), *Minnesota Symposium on Child Psychology* (Vol. 1, pp. 55–81). Hillsdale, NJ: Erlbaum.

Gibson, J. J. (1979). *The ecological approach to visual perception.* Boston: Houghton Mifflin.

Goodnow, J. J. (1987). Social aspects of planning. In S. L. Friedman, E. K. Scholnick, & R. R. Cocking (Eds.), *Blueprints for thinking: The role of planning in cognitive development* (pp. 179–201). Cambridge: Cambridge University Press.

Guba, E. G., & Lincoln, Y. S. (1982). Epistemological and methodological bases of naturalistic inquiry. *Educational Communication and Technology Journal, 30,* 233–252.

Hayes-Roth, B., & Hayes-Roth, F. (1979). A cognitive model of planning. *Cognitive Science, 3,* 275–310.

Hoffman, R. R., Cochran, E. L., & Nead, J. M. (1990). Cognitive metaphors in experimental psychology. In D. E. Leary (Ed.), *Metaphors in the history of psychology* (pp. 173–229). Cambridge: Cambridge University Press.

Klahr, D. (1978). Goal formation: Planning and learning by preschool problem solvers, or "My socks are in the dryer." In R. S. Siegler (Ed.), *Children's thinking: What develops?* (pp. 181–212). Hillsdale, NJ: Erlbaum.

Klahr, D., & Robinson, M. (1981). Formal assessment of problem-solving and planning processes in preschool children. *Cognitive Psychology, 13,* 113–147.

Kvale, S. (1977). Dialectics and research on remembering. In N. Datan & H. W. Reese (Eds.), *Life-span developmental psychology: Dialectical perspectives on experimental research* (pp. 165–189). New York: Academic Press.

Laboratory of Comparative Human Cognition. (1983). Culture and cognitive development. In W. Kessen (Vol. ed.), *History, theory, and methods,* Vol. 1 of P. H. Mussen (Ed.), *Handbook of child psychology* (pp. 294–356). New York: Wiley.

Leont'ev, A. (1981). The problem of activity in psychology. In J. V. Wertsch (Ed.), *The concept of activity in Soviet psychology.* Armonk, NY: Sharpe.

Magkaev, V. K. (1977). An experimental study of the planning function of thinking in young schoolchildren. In M. Cole (Ed.), *Soviet developmental psychology: An anthology* (pp. 606–620). White Plains, NY: Sharpe.

Michaels, C. F., & Carello, C. (1981). *Direct perception.* Englewood Cliffs, NJ: Prentice-Hall.

Miller, G. A., Galanter, E., & Pribram, K. H. (1960). *Plans and the structure of behavior.* New York: Holt.

Ochs, E. (1994). Stories that step into the future. In D. Biber & E. Finegan (Eds.), *Sociolinguistic perspectives on register.* New York: Oxford University Press.

Pepper, S. C. (1942). *World hypotheses: A study in evidence.* Berkeley: University of California Press.

Pribram, K. H. (1990). From metaphors to models: The use of analogy in neuropsychology. In D. E. Leary (Ed.), *Metaphors in the history of psychology* (pp. 79–103). Cambridge: Cambridge University Press.

Roediger, H. L., III (1980). Memory metaphors in cognitive psychology. *Memory and Cognition, 8,* 231–246.

Rogoff, B. (1982). Integrating context and cognitive development. In M. E.

Lamb & A. L. Brown (Eds.), *Advances in developmental psychology* (Vol. 2, pp. 125–170). Hillsdale, NJ: Erlbaum.

Rogoff, B. (1990). *Apprenticeship in thinking: Cognitive development in social context.* New York: Oxford University Press.

Rogoff, B. (in press a). Observing sociocultural activity on three planes: Participatory appropriation, guided participation, apprenticeship. In A. Alvarez, P. del Rio, & J. V. Wertsch (Eds.), *Perspectives on sociocultural research.* Cambridge: Cambridge University Press.

Rogoff, B. (in press b). Transitions in children's participation in sociocultural activities. In M. Haith & A. Sameroff (Eds.), *5–7 year transition.*

Rogoff, B., Baker-Sennett, J., Lacasa, P., & Goldsmith, D. (1994). *The sociocultural context of errand planning in Girl Scout cookie sales.* Manuscript in preparation.

Rogoff, B., Gardner, W. P. (1984). Adult guidance of cognitive development. In B. Rogoff & J. Lave (Eds.), *Everyday cognition: Its development in social context* (pp. 95–116). Cambridge: Harvard University Press.

Rogoff, B., Gauvain, M., & Gardner, W. (1987). The development of children's skills in adjusting plans to circumstances. In S. L. Friedman, E. K. Scholnick, & R. R. Cocking (Eds.), *Blueprints for thinking: The role of planning in cognitive development* (pp. 303–320). Cambridge: Cambridge University Press.

Rogoff, B., Radziszewska, B., & Masiello, T. (in press). The analysis of developmental processes in sociocultural activity. In L. Martin, K. Nelson, & E. Tobach (Eds.), *Cultural psychology and activity theory.* Cambridge: Cambridge University Press.

Rosaldo, R. (1989). *Culture and truth: The remaking of social analysis.* Boston: Beacon Press.

Scribner, S. (1985). Vygotsky's uses of history. In J. V. Wertsch (Ed.), *Culture, communication, and cognition: Vygotskian perspectives* (pp. 119–145). Cambridge: Cambridge University Press.

Siegler, R., & Crowley, K. (1991). The microgenetic method: A direct means for studying cognitive development. *American Psychologist, 46,* 606–620.

Sternberg, R. J. (1985). *Beyond IQ: A triarchic framework for intelligence.* Cambridge: Cambridge University Press.

Vygotsky, L. S. (1987). *Thinking and speech.* In R. W. Rieber & A. S. Carton (Eds.), *The collected works of L. S. Vygotsky* (N. Minick, Trans.) (pp. 37–285). New York: Plenum.

Wertsch, J. V. (1979). From social interaction to higher psychological processes. *Human Development, 22,* 1–22.

Wertsch, J. V. (1985). *Culture, communication, and cognition: Vygotskian perspectives.* Cambridge: Cambridge University Press.

Chapter Thirteen

The Origins of Future Orientation in the Everyday Lives of 9- to 36-Month-Old Infants

Janette B. Benson

She has a videotape of *Bambi* that she loves. She says, "Bambi, Bambi" as she beats her hands on the television screen. Then she'll say, "Bambi, Bambi. OK," to mimic us giving her permission to watch it. Then she tries to put the videotape in [the VCR]. She'll hit the buttons on the remote control and on the TV to try to turn it on. When none of that works, she'll just stand in front of the TV and scream.

This scenario illustrates a rather typical event in the life of a young child. In this case a mother is describing the actions of her 15-month-old daughter, who is desperately trying out several approaches to make her beloved *Bambi* video appear on the television screen. Many of us would characterize this little girl's behavior as early planning or problem solving, because it is apparent that she is attempting several different actions that are oriented toward the inferred desired future state of seeing *Bambi*. A key feature of her behavior is that it is clearly future oriented—

This work was supported by the MacArthur Foundation Research Network on Transitions in Early Development and reflects a collaborative effort among Marshall M. Haith, Barbara Rogoff, Janette B. Benson, research assistants Beth Lanthier and Joan Bihun, and University of Denver undergraduates Carrie Herder and Mary Thomas. None of us claim to be experts on self-report techniques, although we accept full responsibility for what worked and what did not. We express our gratitude to Robert Emde for his support of this effort and to the parents who participated in this study.

she is acting in the present to bring about a future goal. Early in development similar future-oriented processes may very well be the foundation for later, more mature behaviors such as planning and problem solving.

INTRODUCTION

Little theoretical work or empirical research exists on the origins of future-oriented processes in infants and young children, and there is even less information about the onset and range of such behavior in the context of everyday life. Future-oriented processes include such themes as planning, goal orientation, anticipation, expectation, preparation, set, and intention. These processes are vital to how we organize our current thoughts and behavior with respect to events that will happen in the future. What is known about future-oriented behaviors is largely based on laboratory studies of how older children perform on planning and problem-solving tasks such as the Tower of Hanoi (see Bidell & Fischer, this volume; Klahr & Robinson, 1981; Welsh, 1991) or errand-running tasks (Hayes-Roth & Hayes-Roth, 1979). Even less work has been conducted with infants and toddlers, and what is known about such future-oriented behaviors in these early years has been based mostly on laboratory studies of manual object search (e.g., Diamond, 1991; Willatts, 1984).

The laboratory research approach has a long, rich tradition in psychology, has obvious advantages, and has provided us with important information, especially with respect to the operationalizing of specific processes that can be systematically examined. In the laboratory, there are well-defined and standardized procedures that focus on a limited set of processes. However, when the domain of interest is relatively new, is less well defined, and enjoys virtually no theoretical underpinnings—such as the case of naturally emerging, everyday future-oriented processes in very young children—research that is confined exclusively to the laboratory may prevent us from appreciating the full range of future-oriented behaviors in these early years.

There are other drawbacks to standard laboratory tasks. One problem is that skills like planning and problem solving may be less likely to be used by young infants and toddlers for laboratory tasks, whose goals may be clear to the experimenter but not to the young child. The unfortunate consequence is that the experimenter may conclude that very young children are incapable of certain future-oriented behaviors when a more familiar task or situation would suggest otherwise. For example, the type of future-oriented behavior described in the opening *"Bambi* video" scenario is less likely to be seen in the context of standardized laboratory tasks. Because standardized laboratory procedures are partly designed to constrain behavior so as to isolate specific underlying processes, these constraints may also reduce our ability to observe the origins of future-oriented behavior and its developmental course. We are then left to acknowledge the presence of cognitive skills only at the point in development when children are old enough to participate in tasks that operationalize such behavior. The future-oriented processes that have been observed in older children's planning and problem-solving behavior must come from somewhere in development; but because what is known about such behaviors is closely tied to standardized laboratory tasks, we have only limited insight into their origins. Instead of assuming that future orientation is present in development only at the age when a child can participate in a specified laboratory task, we need to know when and in what context infants and young toddlers show future orientation and how such processes develop. Thus, by broadening our observations to behaviors that occur outside the laboratory, we are less likely to miss occurrences in the everyday lives of children that are interesting and important for understanding the origins of future orientation. Everyday life experiences are rich in meaning, familiarity, and social support (Rogoff & Lave, 1984), and these factors may scaffold future-oriented processes in very young children better than do most standardized laboratory procedures.

Because of the problems associated with the laboratory approach, we considered alternatives for our initial investigation. Like others in psychology who have found themselves entering uncharted waters, we opted to take a more naturalistic approach. Thus we turned to the reports of those who are most familiar with young children's behavior in the context of everyday life experiences. The parents of young children are in a special position to observe future-oriented behaviors as they naturally occur. This alternative research strategy should yield a broader sense of both the origins of future orientation and the role of context in its development. Furthermore, an initial examination of the emergence of future orientation in everyday life will permit us to ultimately design standardized laboratory tasks that both are meaningful to young children and will avoid or reduce some of the drawbacks inherent in standardized laboratory procedures.

Overview

In this chapter I suggest that future-oriented behavior emerges during the first three years of life in the context of everyday experiences and activities. I argue that early examples of such behavior can inform us about the developmental basis of the future-oriented processes involved in later behaviors like planning and problem solving. I also demonstrate that parents' reports of observations of children in their everyday context are a good beginning source for information about future-oriented processes in young children and a practical first step toward creating a taxonomy of future-oriented processes in early development. It is from this initial database that we hope to sharpen our understanding of the full range of future-oriented processes. Eventually we will use this information to generate ideas for suitable laboratory paradigms that have both psychological and ecological reality because they are grounded in everyday experiences.

With a few exceptions that I will describe next, little empirical research and few normative data exist on the developmental course of future-oriented behaviors within the first three years of life. By normative data, I mean information about such questions as: At what age does a baby understand what is going to happen when a parent says, "OK, we're going to eat breakfast now and then go to the park"? Or at what age does a toddler notice a change or violation of some expected event, such as not going to the park after being told he would go? Or at what age can a baby anticipate what others will do, such as knowing that if she raises her arms she is likely to be picked up? To my knowledge, we have no developmental inventories or milestone schedules for future-oriented behaviors. Moreover, we currently have no taxonomy for describing and distinguishing among different types of future-oriented behaviors. Finally, with the exception of Piaget's (1952, 1954) analysis of means-ends relations in the sensorimotor period, few theoretical analyses exist of the role that future-oriented processes play in cognitive development or in the young child's understanding of the world. Yet it is clear that everyday future-oriented behaviors depend on the temporal and causal understanding of sequences of events and actions, the ability to form expectations and to know when they have been violated, and the ability to organize experience in past, present, and future time—all of which are important processes that are necessary for later, more complex behaviors.

Before I describe our attempts to collect information about everyday future orientation in early development, I will report what we found in the empirical literature. The short answer is not much, except for some interesting studies on language development and young children's understanding of temporal order. A brief review of these studies gives a sense of our starting point.

FUTURE-ORIENTED BEHAVIOR AND PREVIOUS RESEARCH: LANGUAGE DEVELOPMENT AND TEMPORAL ORDER

There is no denying that language may be the single most important acquisition during the first three years of life and that language development is related to future-oriented processes. But language development alone does not tell the full story about the origins of future orientation. We already know that very young infants are capable of forming visual expectations for very near-term future events (see chapters by Haith and Reznick, this volume) long before they are able to produce or understand time words (e.g., "later" or "after") or to use verb tenses. Also, sometimes it is difficult to determine what a child knows about the future from what she says. For example, when a child says, "Tomorrow I went to the zoo." what can be inferred about her understanding of events in time? Nor is there agreement among various language researchers about when young children come to understand the categories of time and to distinguish among events in past, present, and future time from analyses of their linguistic comprehension and constructions. Nevertheless, to gain a better sense of the origins of future orientation, it is important to consider what is known from language studies on when and how children differentiate among events in past, present, and future time.

At the most general level of experience, we divide time into the three categories of past, present, and future. As Harner (1982) points out, this division treats the past and future as mutually exclusive categories with the present serving a dual function as both a reference point and an expandable category of experience (e.g., the present soon becomes the past, but it always precedes the future). Two key questions are: How are these categories of time known by young children? and What is the developmental sequence in which they are acquired (e.g., is the past understood before the future)?

Language Development

In the English language, inflections are added to verb tenses to indicate the time of an action or experience. For example, the inflection -ed indicates the past and -s indicates the present, but there is no inflection for future verb forms, so modal auxiliaries (e.g., may, will, must) are used to denote the occurrence of future experience (Harner, 1982). Does this linguistic structure affect how categories of time are learned and conceptualized by children? Werner (unpublished paper, n.d.) suggested that initially there is only a present that is extended to include both the immediate past and the immediate future. Then a distinction is made between the present and "not present" as evinced by young children's interchangeable use of "yesterday" and "tomorrow" to refer to nonpresent time without distinguishing between past and present. Eventually children correctly use the present and past tense of verbs, modal auxiliaries, and adverbs to differentiate among the past, present, and future. Werner was not specific about the developmental sequence of past and future but did suggest that the present is known before the not present. In addition to verb tenses, children may learn about the categories of time as they acquire word meanings. Clark's (1973, 1983) semantic features theory of word meaning was put forward to explain why children are likely to learn some words before others and why word meanings are often overextended. Accordingly, children learn "yesterday" before "tomorrow" because the past is experienced and understood before the future, and because of the tendency for overextension, children will overextend the meaning of "yesterday" and may often interpret "tomorrow" to mean "yesterday." Together these two views suggest that children are likely first to understand and use words that relate to the present, followed by the past, and then the future.

Harner reviewed the time language literature and concluded that "the evidence does not indicate clearly whether children learn to refer to either past or future events first or to both at the same time" (Harner, 1982, p. 149). This literature represents three views about the developmental order of how children come to know events in time: children come to know the past before the future; children come to know the future before the past; and children come to know the past and the future at the same time in development. These different conclusions often stem from studies that typically examine different types of data.

The Past Is Known before the Future

This position is supported by studies in which a relational word that refers to the past is known before one that refers to the future (i.e., studies of "before" and "after," "now" and "later," or "yesterday" and "tomorrow"). For example, in a language comprehension task, Harner (1975) found that young children learned the terms "yesterday" and "tomorrow" in an asymmetrical manner. "Yesterday" was learned first but initially meant "a time other than this day" and then took on the meaning of past time. Children then learned "tomorrow," but only to refer to any time in the future.

The Future Is Known before the Past

This position is supported by studies that have typically examined children's naturally occurring language usage. For example, in a language production study, Ames (1946) reported an age trend demonstrating that the content of children's spontaneous expressions focuses mainly on the present, then the present and the future, and finally all three categories of time are discussed.

The Past and Future Are Known Simultaneously

This position is supported by studies that have examined both tense and word meaning together. For example, in a language comprehension study, Harner (1980) reported that children learn the past and future as mutually exclusive categories, but the order depends on the linguistic form that is used. For example, children comprehend linguistic forms that indicate time reference in the following order: before (future reference); after (past reference); past tense (past reference); and future tense (future reference).

This last position is further supported by a recent psycholinguistic analysis of temporal systems based on children's acquisition and production of Polish that also cites additional crosslinguistic evidence. Based on his observations of young children's language comprehension and production, Weist (1986, 1989) proposed a four-stage model in which children initially are restricted in their talk to events in the here and now (present), but by 3 to 4½ years of age are able to coordinate and talk about events in the past, present, and future. Weist (1989) argued that references to the future appear very early in language acquisition and often are not readily acknowledged by researchers. The implication is that children make reference to both the past and the future early on in language acquisition, but Weist does not specify if one appears before the other in language development.

In summary, the findings conflict regarding whether the past is understood before the future or vice versa. The disagreement of these data may stem from the asymmetrical structure of time expression across different languages (e.g., in English tense inflections exist for only the present and past but not the future, whereas these relations are more clearly defined in Polish), the different methodologies that have been used (e.g., direct interview versus observation of spontaneous speech), and the type of data that have been examined (e.g., responses based on linguistic comprehension versus production). However, there is agreement that children gradually understand the different categories of time as they are mapped onto different linguistic forms, and can accurately use and refer to the past, present, and future by age 6 or 7 (Friedman, 1990; Harner, 1982). The question about the developmental ordering of the acquisition of time categories and exactly how children understand events in time remains open. (For a detailed discussion of these psycholinguistic issues, see Bates, Elman, and Li, this volume.)

Adult-Child Language Interactions

Despite the conflicting evidence from the language literature about when young children distinguish among categories of time, there are studies on adult-child language interaction that provide very interesting suggestions about how early language experiences with adults may influence future orientation in early development. Note that these language experiences are commonplace for most children and are almost always experienced in everyday life. Based on the analysis of one child's crib speech both when alone and when talking with her parents before sleep, Nelson (1989) observed that parents spend a great deal of time talking to their children about things that will happen in the near future, which could be important for helping the children structure their immediate future. A similar observation has been reported by Savage-Rumbaugh (1990) based on her work with Kanzi, a young bonobo or pygmy chimpanzee, who has acquired the ability to use lexigrams to communicate with her human caregivers. Savage-Rumbaugh (1990) observed that, like the parents of human infants, Kanzi's caregivers talk about things that are going to happen next, especially during shared routines. As Savage-Rumbaugh has pointed out, it may be that these shared routines are important for how both human and bonobo infants (with human parents!) learn about what will happen next, and that an important motivation for future orientation is to gain control over what will happen next by being able to initiate and participate in shared routines. Likewise, Sachs (1983) has suggested that the roots of young children's ability for "displaced reference" in language (i.e., going beyond talking about events in the here and now to talking about nonpresent entities), is likely to emerge from "conversational routines" between children and adults. Sachs describes these conversational routines as having similar topics (e.g., the location of a referent, such as, "Where's Daddy?") and similar conversational structure over time (e.g., child asks a question that the adult answers and perhaps elaborates by asking the child questions), but the exact content and linguistic forms that are used in such conversational routines vary. For example, Sachs (1983) illustrates how the typical conversational routine for "talking about events and plans for the day" provides a natural, everyday context for young children to begin to understand the sequencing of events in time and to learn what will happen next. Thus the language context itself appears to influence the development of future-oriented processes in young children.

These ideas are provocative, but they are based on few children (and even fewer bonobos) and primarily have to do with language skills. It is reasonable also to consider what role action and other nonlanguage skills play in the acquisition of future orientation during the first three years of life.

Action-Based Studies and Knowledge of Temporal Order

Several theorists have suggested that the origins of the understanding of time and temporal order, a correlate of future understanding, may be rooted in early regular experiences (Fraisse, 1963; Friedman, 1990). In early development, regular experiences may first occur in common daily routines and activities that begin with initial biological rhythms (e.g., circadian rhythms, sleep-wake, and feeding cycles) that expand into more idiosyncratic, yet commonplace, regular routines (e.g., wake, bathe, get dressed, eat breakfast, and so on). Initially, common routines may aid the young child in simply knowing that certain activities and events "go together" and "what happens next" without knowing either the causal or enabling relations among events or realizing that regular events are ordered along the dimension of time. For example, a toddler may come to know that one component of the bedtime routine is a bedtime story, and that reading the story "goes together with" putting on pajamas, getting into bed, and going to sleep. But often to the frustration of parents, the young child may not yet understand that a story is read only *after* putting on pajamas.

Piaget's (1954, 1969) position is that infants initially exist in a "continuous present" that includes the immediate past and is known primarily through actions. The acquisition of secondary circular reactions permits the infant to gain a primitive notion of the future as indicated by the differentiation of means and ends when intentional actions can be directed to achieve desired ends. For Piaget, the past is not known until the end of the sensorimotor period, when infants are able to manipulate true mental images or representations in the evocation of memories of past experiences (as opposed to the earlier function of "recognitory assimilation"). Thus Piaget suggests that the developmental ordering is one of present, future, and then past as first acquired through the infant's actions. This sequence is also suggested for the development of temporal order at the conceptual level after the acquisition of mental representation. In a fashion analogous to the seriation of objects along a physical dimension (e.g., seriation of sticks by increasing length), the older child can first seriate events in forward temporal succession, but it is not until children acquire an understanding of reversibility that seriation is possible for both forward and backward temporal order. With the acquisition of reversibility children gain the ability to view each event as occurring *both* before and after other events.

Piaget's basic position has also been extended to include the concept of temporal decentering—the ability to shift one's reference time from one's own immediate present to some other reference time, such as a time in the past or future (Cromer, 1971). Temporal decentering is a logical precursor to a complete understanding of the reversibility and coordination of multiple time references. That is, one must be able to talk about a nonpresent time in the present before multiple time references can be coordinated. The ability to temporally decenter is likely to occur when children can form mutually exclusive categories of past, present, and future but before they can flexibly seriate events in time.

The data that exist are interesting but do not provide conclusive evidence about how children master either time concepts or sequential order, nor is there agreement on the developmental sequence of their acquisition. With respect to sequential order, O'Connell and Gerard (1985) reported that, in an elicited imitation task, 36-month-olds were able to correctly imitate a sequence of three actions when demonstrated in either a canonical (typical), backward, or scrambled order, whereas 24-month-olds were able to imitate only the canonical sequence. A group of 28-month-olds could reproduce the canonical sequence, but they spontaneously "corrected" the backward order by reproducing it in its canonical order. The authors interpret these findings to suggest that, in a highly structured and simplified task, children as young as 3 years have some understanding of the sequential order of activities, but even before this age they can demonstrate that they know something about the experienced order of activities before being able to correctly reproduce alternative sequences. Thus a sensitivity to the regularity of activities, in the sense that they "go together" in a typically experienced order, precedes the ability to sequentially order such activities. These authors speculate that the earliest script representations of an event are not necessarily encoded by children with respect to sequential order, because familiarity with the event components appears to be separate and prior to knowledge of sequential order.

Bauer and Mandler (1990, 1992) present an alternative possibility that even from the earliest ages infants can and do use temporal information to organize their representations of events. They explain that the difference between their position and that of O'Connell and Gerard is based on both methodological and conceptual grounds. For example, the elicited-imitation task used by O'Connell and Gerard required a relatively high level of motoric complexity that produced high rates of subject attrition. Also, the inclusion of familiar modeled sequences that were reversed and scrambled may have violated infants' expectations of these sequences and therefore interfered with their performance. They argue that to determine whether young children understand temporal order, it is important to include sequences of events that are truly novel or arbitrary and, at the same time, to vary the causal and temporal relations among components in a sequence. The familiar scrambled and reversed sequences used by O'Connell and Gerard were not truly novel or arbitrary, because they violated known relations among components that were based on familiar, highly routinized sequences.

Based on a series of several studies using a variation of the elicited-imitation paradigm with familiar, truly novel, and novel arbitrary event sequences (with noncausally related components that could be combined in any fashion), and novel causal sequences including an irrelevant component, Bauer and Mandler (1990) concluded that infants as young as

16 months were able to temporally organize their representations of both familiar and novel events as demonstrated by tests of immediate recall. Moreover, 20-month-old infants could show immediate and delayed recall for both familiar and novel events, and they tended to either displace or leave out the irrelevant component from the novel causal, but not from the arbitrary event sequences. Before the third year of life it appears that children are sensitive to both the temporal and causal ordering relations among components in a sequence. These findings are intriguing and offer both conceptual and methodological refinements for the study of young children's understanding of temporal order. Unfortunately, Bauer and Mandler (1990) did not focus on what happens between 16 and 20 months to produce differences in the understanding of temporal order. Also, questions about the origins of such understanding, their further development, and how young children are able to distinguish between temporal and causal ordering relations remain topics for future research.

Summary

The findings from both language studies and research on temporal knowledge lead to the general conclusion that infants and young children have some understanding of the categories of time, as shown in early language skills and in how young children understand temporal and causal ordering relations among components in a sequence. In certain situations young children correctly refer to and understand statements about events in past, present, and future time. In addition, infants and toddlers appear to be sensitive to the ordering of events, as shown by their ability to imitate modeled forward and backward event sequences. Many of these studies provide evidence for the future-oriented processes discussed earlier. It is difficult to draw more specific conclusions about the development of future-oriented processes, however, because many of these studies use different laboratory procedures, examine different types of data, and as a consequence, lead to contradictory interpretations of the developmental ordering and of how young children acquire an understanding of events in time.

Despite the many valuable contributions these studies make, several important questions about the origins of future-oriented behavior remain: What is the range of future-oriented behaviors that young infants and children naturally engage in? How does the context of everyday life, including family practices and routines, scaffold future orientation? And are there important everyday future-oriented behaviors and experiences we have not yet thought about that exist beyond existing laboratory procedures? With questions like these in mind, we developed a strategy to obtain direct reports from parents to gain a sense of everyday future-oriented behaviors in infants and toddlers. These are difficult questions to address, and very little information exists for guidance.

PARENTAL OBSERVATION OF EVERYDAY FUTURE ORIENTATION

We first turned to parents to tell us about their observations of everyday future orientation in their children. We recognize the obvious problems with self-report methods (e.g., pressure for responses to be socially desirable), but this approach was a necessary first step to obtain a sense of the full range of future-oriented behaviors and of when they occur in early development. Moreover, we hoped that an appreciation of the natural context in which future-oriented behaviors emerge would ultimately lead us to design meaningful laboratory procedures for future study. Thus the interview and questionnaire data I describe next are somewhat preliminary and exploratory, but also very exciting in terms of suggesting future research questions.

Preliminary Interview Study

We began with a pilot interview study based on ten women who each had a child between 9 and 36 months of age. Parents were invited to come to the University of Denver so that we could ask them open-ended questions, to cast as wide a net as possible to capture their thoughts about their children's understanding of the future. One interesting outcome of this initial work was that many parents said *they really had not thought much about their children's understanding of the future,* yet the more they thought about our questions, the more they began to reflect on aspects of future orientation in their children's behavior. Often parents would telephone us several days after their interview at the university to describe additional examples of future-oriented behavior they had observed or remembered. Here are a few examples of responses to the question: What does your child do that suggests to you that he or she knows about the future?

The mother of a 10-month old girl said,

> Her red dog, that is a toy that goes places with us that she doesn't play with at home . . . and when the big red dog comes out she gets a little excited like when I pack the diaper bag, because it means we are going somewhere. It's kind of like, "Oh, I think we are going somewhere."

The mother of a 24-month-old boy told us,

> One day I said to him, "Tomorrow we are going to the zoo." All of a sudden he ran to his room, laid down on his bed and closed his eyes—it

seemed like he was thinking it would be tomorrow and we could go to the zoo when he opened his eyes.

And the mother of a 36-month-old boy said,

J understands a limited future. He understands if you wake up in the morning and say, "Today is a preschool day." We have two different backpacks. One that goes to preschool with the lunch box inside that also goes to preschool. But he doesn't need that for the day care lady. So, he'll understand that if a [certain] backpack comes out, where he's going. But some things he doesn't get. Like if you ask him—sometimes he gets the words mixed up and I think the concepts too. He calls tomorrow, "To-mayo," and a lot of times it means today. It's not real clear for J. At night he'll ask what we're doing "Tomayo," and a lot of times it's either a rehash of what we did today or he's still thinking that we're on today.

These responses and others suggested possible domains of future-oriented behavior and also provided the basis for a questionnaire to obtain more systematic data about the early development of these behaviors. We had several goals for our questionnaire. Most important was to gain a general sense of the landscape of future-oriented processes at this age and how they change. Since parents might be able to provide examples of early future-oriented behaviors that could eventually be examined in the laboratory, they were also asked to provide their own specific examples. During the interviews many parents spontaneously mentioned their beliefs and theories about the origins of future orientation in their children and the role of family practices and daily routines. This information was especially interesting, becuase it provided insight into important contextual factors that are likely to influence the development of future orientation. As a result, several sections of the questionnaire were devoted to these areas of family influence.

THE DEVELOPMENT OF FUTURE-ORIENTED PROCESSES QUESTIONNAIRE

An overview of the organization of the Development of Future-Oriented Processes Questionnaire and sample items are shown in Table 13.1. In addition to a section on standard demographic information, the questionnaire has two parts—one focusing on contextual factors in the family that might influence the development of future-oriented processes, and the other on the child's behavior across several categories, or domains, of future-oriented processes.

Family Context Factors

Part 1 of the Development of Future-Oriented Processes Questionnaire focused on the family context. First, parents were asked about their

TABLE 13.1 Overview of the Development of Future-Oriented Processes Questionnaire (for 9- to 36-Month-Old Infants)

Demographic information
General information was asked about ethnicity, number of siblings, daily care of the target child (e.g., preschool, child care), and maternal and paternal age, education, employment, occupation, and income.

Part 1: Contextual influences
Parental beliefs: What child knows about near- vs. far-term future (4- point scale: understands well—does not understand)
    Sample items—My child:
        understands what "later" means
        understands what "tomorrow" means
Parental theories: How child knows about the future (relative importance rankings)
    Sample items—My child will know about the future by:
        having a regular daily routine
        my talking about things that will happen next
Family practices (4-point scale: almost always—almost never)
    Sample items—In our family we:
        talk about what is going to happen next
        eat dinner around the same time each day
Precedent family practices (4-point scale: almost always—almost never).
    Sample items—Whan I was a child our family:
        emphasized things that would happen in the future and the
            importance of planning for them
        ate dinner around the same time each day

Part 2: Domains (and subdomains) of future orientation (4-point scale: very true—not at all true)
Order
    Sample item—My child understands that some things must happen *before* other
        things (e.g., you must wash before eating)
Routine
    Sample item—My child goes through the same routine every night before bed
        (e.g., first my child puts on pajamas, then puts her doll to bed, says good-
        night, and finally climbs into bed)
Planning
    Sample item—My child does things that show preparation for the future (e.g.,
        My child gets a toy to take to Grandma's)
Expectation—divided into four subdomains
    Cues
    Sample item—My child knows what will happen later from the things that happen earlier (e.g., When the baby sitter arrives, I will leave the house)
    Violations
    Sample item—My child's mood changes when something she or he was told would
        happen does not (e.g., my child has a fit when we do not go to the park)
    Language Comprehension
    Sample item—If an event is familiar and I tell my child it will happen, then my
        child will expect it (e.g., my child clings to me when told we are going to
        the doctor)
    Language Production
    Sample item—My child can talk about things that will happen if they have happened before (e.g., when we go to Grandma's, I can play on the swings)

TABLE 13.1 (*Continued*)

Time—divided into four subdomains
  Terms
    Sample item—My child knows what "later" means (e.g., you can have a cookie *later*, means not right now)
  Duration
    Sample item—My child understands time if I compare it with something familiar (e.g., it will take as long as "Sesame Street" for the cookies to be ready)
  Verbs
    Sample item—My child uses words that refer to the future (e.g., "I wanna," "I will," or "I'm gonna")
  Tools
    Sample item—My child can understand clocks (e.g., when the little hand is on the 6 and the big hand is on the 12, we will eat dinner)
Problem Solving—divided into three subdomains
  Flexibility
    Sample item—My child will try several different ways to solve a problem (e.g., asking the baby-sitter for something both parents have said no to)
  Goal Orientation
    Sample item—My child will try to get a toy she or he wants even if it is way across the room
  Social Agents
    Sample item—My child tries to get help from others to get something done (e.g., putting my hand on the music box to make it play)

beliefs about how much their children understand about events in the near- and far-term future. Parents rated each item along a four-point scale ranging from "My child understands well" to "My child does not understand." For example, parents were asked about the child's understanding of "before, later, tomorrow" and the meaning of different units of time such as "several minutes, an hour, a few days, a week, a month." We included these parental belief items because we thought that what a parent believes about the child's level of understanding is likely to influence the way the parent interacts with the child.

We were also intrigued with the theories that several parents offered about how children acquire knowledge about the future. Therefore we asked parents to rank the relative importance of different statements about how a child comes to know about the future. Several statements were generated that represented the wide range of theoretical orientations parents mentioned in the pilot interview study. These included a nativist position (e.g., "My child will know about the future naturally, because my child was born with this ability"), a maturationist position (e.g., "My child will know about the future simply by getting older"), and several experience- or learning-based items (e.g., "My child will know about the future by having a regular daily routine" and "My child will know about the future by learning that if someone says that something will happen, it really does happen").

Because we thought that parental beliefs and theories about future orientation might affect family practices, we asked parents to rate several items about common family practices and routines on a four-point scale from things they "almost always" do to things they "almost never" do. We thought these ratings would provide insight about the experiences that structure children's daily lives that could also influence the development of future-oriented processes. We generated items modeled after work on family rituals and practices by Fiese (1992; Sameroff & Fiese, 1989). For example, these items included, "In our family we: 'plan for dinner in advance,' 'have a set routine for holidays,' or 'talk about things that will happen next.'"

The last contextual factor we were interested in concerned parents' perceptions of their own family practices when they were growing up. We were interested in how current family practices evolve. The question was whether intergenerational transmission occurs through the precedent family (the parent's own family when he or she was a child) and is a main source of variation in current family practices. Several items were generated, including a subset of questions from the family practices section described above, and these items were rephrased so that the lead-in to each made parents consider their own experiences as children. Sample items included, "When I was a child, our family: 'ate dinner around the same time each day,' 'regularly celebrated special days (e.g., birthdays and Thanksgiving),' or 'had a set routine for holidays so that everyone knew what to expect.'"

Domains and Subdomains of Future-Oriented Processes

The second part of the Development of Future-Oriented Processes Questionnaire included items across six domains of future orientation that emerged from what parents talked about in the pilot interview. A primary goal was to find normative trends for the approximate time in development when children were likely to demonstrate these various behaviors. Parents rated the items in each domain on a four-point scale indicating how true the item was for their children. The scale ranged from "very true" to "not at all true." Since we were interested in a broad age range, items varied with respect to being "not language based" and "language based," and parents were reminded that, since we were covering an age range from 9 to 36 months, some items would not be appropriate for the ages of their children. Items were written in the form of a general statement about things a child could or could not do, followed by an example, often from ones given in the interviews. Parents were provided with an opportunity to write their own unique examples if they desired.

The six domains of future-oriented processes and sample items from each domain are shown in part 2 of Table 13.1. The first domain, Order, included three items that assessed when children understand the relations of "before, after, and sequence" for various events or activities. Order could include temporal, enabling, causal, or arbitrary relations among events or activities in a sequence. A sample item is, "My child understands that some things must happen *before* other things (e.g., you must wash before eating)." The second domain assessed what children know about Routines, and included two items. A sample item is, "My child goes through the same routine every night before bed (e.g., first my child puts on pajamas, then puts her doll to bed, says goodnight, and finally climbs into bed)." The third domain, Planning, assessed the degree to which children prepare for things in the future. Two items were included, one of which was, "My child does things that show preparation for the future (e.g., my child gets a toy to take to Grandma's)."

Each of the remaining three future-oriented processes domains was organized into various subdomains. The fourth domain, Expectation, was divided into four subdomains and included a total of 13 items across subdomains. Since previous research has shown that young infants can form visual expectations in a laboratory setting (e.g., Haith, Hazan, & Goodman, 1988), we were interested in the different types of expectations young children form from their everyday experiences. These expectation items were grouped by subdomain because the parental interview data suggested that young children form different types of expectations—some based on cues and others based on language production and language comprehension. Also, parents suggested that once children form expectations, they are also able to notice violations of formed expectations, and so a subdomain of items was included to examine when children notice and respond to such violations. The first Expectation subdomain included five items that assessed the child's understanding of expectations based on Cues. We were interested in knowing about the types of expectations that infants form based on cues that signal an upcoming event. A sample item is, "My child knows what will happen later from the things that happen earlier (e.g., when the baby sitter arrives, I will leave the house)." The second Expectation subdomain included three items that assessed Violations of expectations. Parents were asked whether children noticed, asked about, or changed their affect to show that an expectation had been violated. A sample item is, "My child's mood changes when something she or he was told would happen does not." The third Expectation subdomain contained two items based on Language Comprehension. We were interested in how well young children were able to form expectations for a future event based on the parent's telling the child something about an upcoming event before it actually happens. A sample item is, "If an event is familiar and I tell my child it will happen, then my child will expect it (e.g., my child clings to me when told we are going to the doctor)." And the last Expectation subdomain explored the formation of expectations based on the child's own Language Production. This subdomain contained three items, including, "My child can talk about things that will happen if they have happened before (e.g., when we go to Grandma's, I can play on the swings)."

The fifth future-oriented processes domain was designed to tap young children's understanding of different aspects of time. The Time domain was composed of eight items across four subdomains. Again, this domain was divided into four subdomains based on the different aspects of time parents indicated their children understood in the pilot interview. The first Time subdomain assessed children's understanding of Time Terms and included three items. A sample item is, "My child knows what 'later' means (e.g., you can have a cookie *later* means not right now)." The second Time subdomain measured children's understanding of Time Duration and contained two items. One of these items is, "My child understands time if I compare it with something familiar (e.g., it will take as long as 'Sesame Street' for the cookies to be ready)." The third Time subdomain tapped children's use of Time Verbs and was composed of one item: "My child uses words that refer to the future (e.g., 'I wanna,' 'I will' or 'I'm gonna')." And the last Time subdomain was designed to measure children's understanding of Time Tools and included one item each about children's understanding of clocks and of calendars.

The last future-oriented processes domain, Problem Solving, contained a total of eight items across three subdomains. These subdomains examined young children's Flexibility, Goal Orientation, and use of Social Agents in problem solving. The first Problem Solving subdomain, Flexibility, is composed of three items. A sample item is, "My child will try several different ways to solve a problem (e.g., asking the baby sitter for something both parents have said no to)." Goal Orientation in problem solving was the second subdomain and included four items. One of these items is, "My child will try to get a toy she or he wants even if it is way across the room." The last Problem Solving subdomain measured young children's use of Social Agents as a means to solve problems. The one item in this subdomain is, "My child tries to get help from others to get something done (e.g., putting my hand on the music box to make it play)."

Parents from the University of Denver volunteer subject pool were

TABLE 13.2 Characteristics of the Sample ($N = 68$)

	% or mean (SD)	Range
Child's age in months		
9 (10)[a] 14.7%		
12 (10) 14.7		
18 (10) 14.7		
24 (12) 17.6		
30 (10) 14.7		
36 (16) 23.5		
Child care		
At home with parent	43.0%	
Mother's age in years	33.1 (4.3)	22–43
Father's age in years	36.2 (4.9)	26–49
Ethnicity		
European-American	94.1%	
Annual income		
Greater than $40,000	62.9%	
Mother's highest education		
Grade school	0%	
High-School graduate	1.5	
Some college	22.1	
College graduate or higher	76.4	
Father's highest education		
Grade school	0%	
High-school graduate	4.4	
Some college	20.6	
College graduate or higher	75.0	

[a] Number of children.

approached by telephone to solicit their participation in a mail out/mail back questionnaire study. Parents who were approached each had a child who was within two weeks of the following target ages: 9, 12, 18, 24, 30, and 36 months. Almost all parents agreed to participate by returning the completed Development of Future-Oriented Processes Questionnaire within two weeks of its receipt.

Sample Characteristics

The demographic characteristics of the sample are summarized in Table 13.2. We received responses from a total of 68 parents, with at least 10 parents in each of six different age groups between 9 and 36 months. During our initial telephone contact we asked the parent who spent the most time with the child to complete the Development of Future-Oriented Processes Questionnaire, and for the most part this was the mother. Parents were instructed to complete and return the questionnaire by mail within 10 days. In general, the parents in this sample were in their early to mid-30s, ethnically homogeneous, and primarily middle to upper-middle class; the majority of both parents were college graduates with some graduate or professional training.

DATA ANALYSES

Internal Consistency of the Future-Oriented Processes Domains

First we examined how well the items in each domain and subdomain hung together as they had been grouped. Internal consistency reliabilities, based on Cronbach's alpha coefficient, were calculated for each future-oriented processes domain and subdomain. We expected that some domains and subdomains contained items that would not be age appropriate for almost all infants in the younger groups, who would therefore receive an item score of 1 ("Not at all true of my child"). Because the alpha coefficients could be inflated by those items that were not age appropriate, separate coefficients were also calculated for these domains and subdomains for restricted age groups. The age groups were restricted by including only those ages where at least three subjects within the group had an item score greater than 1.

The alpha coefficients for each domain and subdomain for all subjects are shown in Table 13.3. The alphas for those domains and subdomains with restricted age groups are also shown in Table 13.3 in parentheses. The alpha coefficients for the six domains of future-oriented processes that were not restricted by age met acceptable levels of reliability above or very near to .70. Alpha coefficients for three non-age-restricted subdomains were not reliable (e.g., Expectations based on Language Comprehension, Time Tools, and Flexibility in Problem Solving). As expected, the age-restricted alpha coefficients were lower, but except for the subdomain of Time Tools, all met acceptable levels of reliability. The unreliable items in these subdomains will be revised in the next version of the Development of Future-Oriented Processes Questionnaire. Almost all parents reported that their children had no understanding of clocks and calendars, and because there was almost no variability for these items, the reliability of the Time Tools subdomain was poor. With the exception of the three unreliable subdomains, it appears that most of the items we generated from what mothers told us in the pilot interview fit together within the domains and subdomains.

We wanted to know how these domains were interrelated independent of age, even though we had already restricted the age range for some domains. Partial correlation coefficients were calculated to control for the influence of age to determine these interrelations. The partial correlations, controlling for age, between the Order domain, the subdomains of Expectations based on Language Comprehension and Lan-

TABLE 13.3 Item Internal Consistency Reliabilities (Cronbach's Alpha) for Future-Orientation Domains and Subdomains

Domain and subdomain (restricted age groups)	n	Alpha	Number of items
Order	66	.85	2
Routine	68	.67	2
Planning	66	.80	2
(24–36 months)	(38)	(.71)[a]	2
Expectation	61	.92	13
Cues	66	.83	5
Violations	63	.90	3
(18–36 months)	(45)	(.82)[a]	3
Language Comprehension	66	.28	2
Language Production	63	.90	3
(24–36 months)	(35)	(.80)[a]	3
Time	63	.86	8
Terms	65	.87	3
(18–36 months)	(47)	(.81)[a]	3
Duration	64	.75	2
(24–36 months)	(36)	(.68)[a]	2
Verbs	—	—	1
Tools	66	−.10	2
(36 months)	(16)	(−.44)[a]	2
Problem solving	66	.79	8
Flexibility	66	.50	3
Goal Orientation	66	.74	4
Social Agents	—	—	1

[a]Alpha coefficients in parentheses were calculated using data from restricted age groups (at least three subjects within an age group had an item score greater than one).

guage Production, and all other domains and subdomains are shown in Table 13.4. There were consistent positive correlations between the Order domain and all others. The Order domain was significantly correlated with every other domain and subdomain except Time Verbs, which was only marginally related ($r = .24$, $n = 34$; $p = .15$). Thus it appears that parents' reports of their children's behavior concerning sequence and the order of events and activities related to their report of the children's performance across a wide range of future-oriented behaviors.

Given the age range of this sample, it is possible that the children's language development could play a role in parents' reports of future orientation. For example, some parents may over- or underreport their children's understanding of the future based on perceptions of their language ability. Unfortunately, an independent language assessment was not included as part of the Development of Future-Oriented Processes Questionnaire. However, there were items in the Expectation domain that asked about expectations based on language comprehension

TABLE 13.4 Partial Correlations among Selected Domains and Subdomains, Controlling for Age

| | Order | | EXPECTATION | | | |
| | | | Language Comprehension | | Language Production | |
	r	n	r	n	r	n
Order	—	—	.29°	(63)	.64°°	(34)
Routine	.32°°	(63)	.22	(63)	.05	(34)
Planning	.54°°	(35)	.34°	(35)	.61°°	(34)
Expectation						
Cues	.56°°	(63)	.24	(63)	.24	(34)
Violation	.28°	(45)	−.13	(45)	.51°°	(34)
Language Comprehension	.29°	(63)	—	—	.02	(34)
Language Production	.64°°	(34)	.02	(34)	—	—
Time						
Terms	.62°°	(45)	.19	(45)	.49°°	(34)
Duration	.40°	(34)	−.03	(34)	.48°°	(33)
Verbs	.24	(34)	.33°	(34)	.59°°	(33)
Tools	—	—	—	—	—	—
Problem Solving						
Flexibility	.53°°	(63)	.19	(63)	−.14	(34)
Goal Orientation	.58°°	(63)	.16	(63)	.30	(34)
Social Agents	.30°	(63)	.23	(63)	−.06	(34)

°$p < .05$; °°$p < .01$

and production. We created a language index score from parental responses to the Language Comprehension and Language Production subdomain scores. These scores serve only as a rough proxy for a real language assessment, but they permit an exploration of the relation between language skills and the other domains. As shown in Table 13.4, compared with the Order domain, the Expectation Language Comprehension subdomain was related to only two other domains besides Order—the Planning, and Time Verbs domains. The Expectation Language Production subdomain was significantly related to these same three domains (Order, Planning, and Time Verbs), in addition to the Expectation Violations, Time Terms, and Time Duration domains. Thus even very crudely constructed language scores correlated with parents' reports of future orientation in their children. However, domains other than language skill, such as the understanding of Order, also tapped an important aspect of future orientation. Again, caution is warranted when making interpretations here, because these speculations are based on a very rough assessment of language skills. Remember that the alpha coefficients were high for the Expectations based on the Language Production subdomain (.90

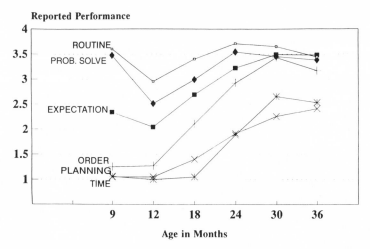

Figure 13.1   Age trends for mean domain scores.

for all subjects and .80 for the restricted ages) but were unreliable for
the Expectations based on the Language Comprehension domain (.28
for all subjects). In the current revision of the Development of Future-
Oriented Processes Questionnaire we plan to assess language skill directly by including a slightly modified version of the short form of the
MacArthur Communicative Development Inventory (Reznick & Goldsmith, 1989) as an independent language assessment.

Age Trends for Future-Oriented Processes Domains

A primary goal in collecting these data was to examine normative age
trends across a wide array of future-oriented behaviors that were represented by our domains. Would rates of change in reported performance
across age differ for different domains? In Figure 13.1 the age trends
for each domain are shown by plotting the mean domain score for each
age group. The parents' report of children's performance ranged from
1 to 4, with higher scores reflecting higher child competence (e.g., "Always true for my child"). A systematic increase in reported level of
child understanding across all six domains was found, with the greatest
developmental increase occurring between 12 and 30 months of age.
The trends between 9 and 12 months of age were less systematic and
showed slight decreases in level of performance for the Routine, Problem Solving, and Expectation domains and almost no change for the
Order, Planning, and Time domains. This pattern of results indicates
that the items in the questionnaire capture changes in future-oriented
processes between 12 and 36 months of age but may not be age appropriate for infants under 12 months.

The data in Figure 13.1 also suggest that the different domains do not change at the same rate across age. For example, across all ages, parents reported relatively high levels of child performance for the items in the Routine domain. In contrast, parents of the youngest infants reported that their children did not perform many of the items in the Order, Planning, and Time domains. However, reported performance in each of these three domains increased across age, with performance of behaviors in the Order domain increasing fastest. By 36 months of age, the six domains appear to form two clusters, separated by an almost one-point mean difference on our four-point scale. Parents reported relatively high levels of child performance for behaviors in the Expectation, Routine, Problem Solving, and Order domains, but only moderate levels for items in the Planning and Time domains. This pattern makes sense because, compared with those items in the other four domains, many of the items in both the Time and Planning domains asked about the child's understanding of objective time units. For example, items in the Time domain asked parents to rate their children's understanding of events occurring "tomorrow, later, days or weeks away." Items in the Planning domain asked parents to rate their children's understanding of events in the longer-term future, such as the ability to "prepare for the future." Thus the age trends across these domains and their clusterings are reasonable, because they support the general finding that, with age, children's understanding of events in time expands from the short-term to the longer-term future (Friedman, 1990). Moreover, these trends provide an initial, best estimate for the upper and lower age bounds for reported child understanding and performance of these future-oriented behaviors. For example, it may make sense to include parents of 42- and 48-month-old children in future research, since reported levels of performance for several domains did not reach ceiling levels for the 36-month-olds. Also, these data suggest that dramatic increases in reported child understanding occur for many of these domains of future orientation between 12 and 30 months of age, a range we will focus on in future laboratory studies.

Would there be similar systematic age trends for the different subdomains? In particular, we were most interested in age trends for the Expectation subdomains. Based on laboratory studies (Haith et al., 1988; Canfield & Haith, 1991), young infants are capable of forming visual expectations for single and multiple predictable events, and they notice a violation of an expected sequence of events as indicated by changes in their visual response patterns. Everyday life is full of both regularities (daily routines) and unexpected violations of regular events.

The mean Expectation subdomain scores are plotted for each age group in Figure 13.2 for the Cues, Language Comprehension, Violations,

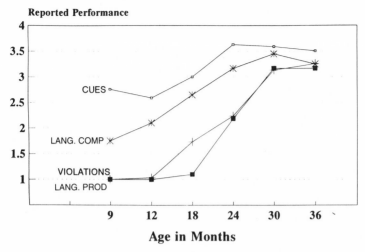

Figure 13.2   Age trends for mean Expectation subdomain scores.

and Language Production subdomains. At all ages, parents reported higher levels of performance for expectation behaviors based on both Cues and Language Comprehension compared with Expectations based on Language Production and Violations. These findings indicate that some time elapses after children are able to form expectations before they can notice when those expectations have been violated.

In summary, the items in our future-oriented processes domains appear to tap everyday examples of future orientation demonstrated by young children. We now have some indication that the items in the different Development of Future-Oriented Processes Questionnaire domains are reliable, that the greatest increases in reported child performance across most of the domains occur between 12 and 30 months of age, and that the developmental ordering of children's understanding across domains is reasonable. Because items in some of the subdomains were not reliable, they will be either dropped or rewritten in the revised questionnaire. Finally, an independent language assessment will be included to gain a better sense of how language development is related to the development of future-oriented processes.

FAMILY CONTEXT FACTORS

Parental Theories

The sections of the Development of Future-Oriented Processes Questionnaire that were designed to assess contextual and family factors re-

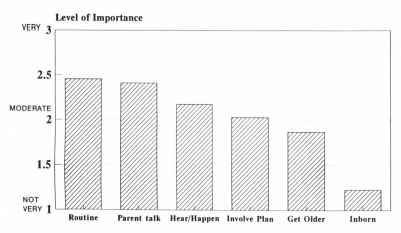

Figure 13.3   Mean relative importance rankings for parental theories about how children learn about the future.

vealed some interesting patterns. Parents had definite ideas about the relevance of different theories for how their children learn about the future. Parents made relative importance rankings along a three-point scale that included the categories of "not very," "moderately," and "very" important. The mean relative importance rankings are shown in Figure 13.3. The two statements that received the highest mean rankings were "by having a regular routine" and "by my talking about things that are going to happen." Parents rated the next two statements as being moderately important for how their child learns about the future: "by hearing people talk about things that will happen in the future," and "by being involved with me and others in planning for future events." Finally, parents ranked two statements as being generally not very important for how their children learn about the future: "simply by getting older" and "naturally, because my child was born with this ability." This pattern suggests that parents gave the highest relative importance rankings to those statements that reflected an experience- or learning-based orientation to their children's acquisition of knowledge about the future, while the two statements suggestive of little intervention from the parent received the lowest rankings. Thus parents believe, at some level, that the things they do with their children (e.g., routines, talking about the future) are likely to be important for how they learn about the future.

This finding fits nicely with the arguments made earlier, based on work by Nelson, Savage-Rumbaugh, and Sachs, about the role that language context and adult-child interaction play for how young children

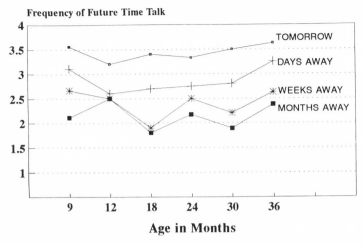

Frequency of Future Time Talk

Figure 13.4   Age trends for mean ratings of frequency of future time talk.

gain an understanding of what will happen next. Even though parents reported that it is important for their children to hear about events in the future as a means of acquiring a sense of future orientation, we looked to the family practice items to determine how frequently parents actually engaged in such interactions (or at least reported that they did).

Family Practices

The items contained within the family practices section of the question-naire included family routines such as dinner and holidays as well as how much parents talk to their children about upcoming events. These items covered a wide range of family practices and met acceptable levels of reliability, alpha $= .75$, $n = 68$, number of items $= 18$.

One aspect of family practices that we wanted to know about focused on parents' future time talk with their children. How frequently do parents report talking to their children about future events? Do parents report talking more to their children about events in the near-term or the far-term future? Also, do parents talk differently about the future depending on the age of the child? To assess parents' future time talk, a series of questions asked parents to report the frequency with which they talk to their children about events that will occur in the short-term future, such as "tomorrow and days away," and in the longer-term future, such as "weeks away" and "months away." The mean ratings, by age, of reported frequency of future time talk are shown in Figure 13.4. Parents reported that they talk most frequently about events occurring in the near-term future—"tomorrow" and "days away"—and less frequently about events in the longer-term future—"weeks away" and "months away." Did this pattern of response differ for children in the different age groups? Much to our surprise, the frequency of reported parent "future time talk" did not change much across the different age groups. This was unexpected given that most parents are generally very good at adjusting their behavior to the changing competence of their children (Dix & Grusec, 1985). When it comes to talking about events in the near-term or far-term future, parents do not seem to adjust their behavior to the age of the child they are talking to.

Precedent Family Practices

The items that assessed precedent family practices also showed acceptable levels of reliability, alpha = .79; n = 68; number of items = 9. These items were more generally about planning for family routines focused on dinner, celebrations, and holidays and were not as specific as the "future time talk" items discussed previously. First, parents' ratings of those items that were directly parallel across the sections on current and precedent family practices were compared. Of these six parallel items, parents rated three to be higher in their current family than in their precedent family. That is, parents rated their current family practices as more planful for weekend activities, $t(62)$ = 6.60, p = .000; having more established holiday routines, $t(65)$ = 2.94, p = .005; and more oriented around planning for the future, $t(63)$ = 2.93, p = .005, compared with the practices of their precedent family. These six parallel items were moderately related, as indicated by an average correlation of .31 (SD = .14; range = .19 to .60). However, when ratings for all current family practices were compared with ratings of precedent family practices (including those items that were not directly parallel), there was little difference between current and precedent family practices, $t(66)$ = 0.20, n.s. If all our current and precedent family practice items are considered together, it appears that parents tend not to deviate in their reports of current family practices from the family practices they reported experiencing in their own childhood. This finding suggests that the frequency of current family practices that may foster the development of future orientation in children may in part be influenced by the parents' perception or memory of their own experiences as children, since there is little reported difference between current and precedent family practices. This is an interesting finding that deserves future attention.

Parental Beliefs

The items included in the parental beliefs section of the questionnaire may also be related to family practices. Like the other family context

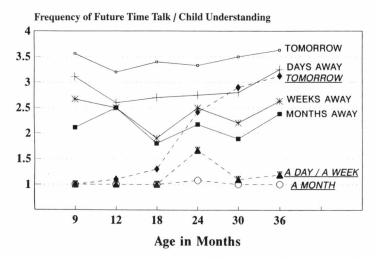

Figure 13.5   Age trends for mean ratings of frequency of future time talk and ratings of children's understanding of time units.

items, these showed high reliability, alpha = .87; n = 68; number of items = 11.

Given that parents report talking a lot to their children about future events and that this future time talk varies little with the child's age, what do parents believe about their children's understanding of the near- and far-term future at different ages? That is, what do they believe their children know about the future, and do these beliefs relate to the frequency of future time talk they report? Parents rated how well their children understand the meaning of events in the near- and far-term future. Because we wanted to relate parental beliefs to practices, parents' mean ratings of their children's understanding of the meaning of "tomorrow, a day, a week, and a month" (as shown in Figure 13.4) were plotted along with parents' reported frequency of future time talk about events "tomorrow, days away, weeks away and months away." These data are shown together in Figure 13.5. Parents' mean ratings of their children's understanding of the meaning of time units in the near- and far-term future are shown by the dotted trend lines, and their labels are under-lined at the right side of the figure. Parents' mean ratings of reported frequency of future time talk about events that will occur in the same time units in the near- and far-term future are shown by the solid trend lines. Relative to how frequently parents report talking about events in these future time frames, parents also report that at most ages their children do not understand much of what they are saying. Although parents' report of the frequency of future time talk remains fairly constant over the age groups, they report that they believe their children's understanding of events in these time frames changes fairly dramatically, at least for "tomorrow."

It is noteworthy that parents report talking to their children a lot about the future when at the same time they believe their children know very little about the future. There are at least three possible explanations for this pattern of findings. First, across age, parents may be less accurate in their reports of how frequently they talk to their children about the future. Even though parents are generally credited with accurately reporting what their children understand with age, it is not clear why they would be less accurate in their reports of how frequently they talk to them about the future. A second possibility is that parents actively structure and scaffold (in the Vygotskyian sense) an understanding of the future for their children, through activities like talking, long before the children have this understanding. Parents may first overregulate their children's understanding of the future through activities like "future time talk," until they become more skilled in understanding the future through their own language and cognitive skills. Third, because of the complications of organizing daily family life, parents may "think aloud" about what they have to do next to ensure that things will run smoothly. Initially, parents may talk about the future with little intent to actually communicate these thoughts to their young children. Parents may maintain a constant rate of "future time talk" despite the age of the child; however, because parents are good at adjusting their behavior to their children's increasing abilities, as the children get older parents may alter the content of their "future time talk" to communicate what will happen next, perhaps intending to recruit the children's cooperation. A dawdling child can unknowingly wreak havoc on a parent's efforts to leave the house early enough to get to the baby-sitter's house and still arrive at work on time. Once parents recognize that their children understand the future consequences of their behavior, they can communicate what will happen if the child does not cooperate to leave the house on time. Thus parents may accurately report a constant rate of "future time talk" across ages that does not reflect changes in *what* they may communicate about the future. Deciding which of these interpretations is best awaits future research.

CONCLUSIONS

Despite the problems inherent in self-report data, we have been able to develop some meaningful categories of everyday future-oriented behaviors that were not obvious from the existing literature and became obvious only once we began talking to parents. These behaviors may provide a basis for some of the future-oriented processes that emerge later, such as more sophisticated planning and problem solving. Six domains of early future-oriented behaviors have been identified that appear distinct yet also seem to be related at a broader level to provide a general picture of future-oriented processes in early development. The creation of these separate domains and subdomains is at least a start toward a taxonomy of future-oriented processes that appear during the first three years of life. Of course we need to get a better handle on some domains, like language skills, but now we at least have a preliminary sense that there are skills other than language that are involved in the early development of future orientation.

The age trends that were revealed are also encouraging, because they appear to be very systematic across a wide range of future-oriented behaviors. This information represents the beginnings of a database for answering questions about normative indexes for when children acquire knowledge about aspects of the future. Of course, there is more work to do before we can have greater confidence in providing precise answers.

The quest for developmental norms in future orientation raises the important question of individual differences in the development of future-oriented processes and their possible source. We have speculated that family context factors may be very telling about such individual differences that are not simply related to rates of child language and cognitive development. To further explore this possibility it will be necessary to collect both self-report data on parents' beliefs and theories about their children's understanding of the future and child measures of language, cognition, and future orientation.

Because the data presented here are from a restricted sample of well-educated, ethnically homogeneous parents, the range of individual differences may be relatively limited. It is important that future studies include subjects from a broader range, including those from varied ethnic and socioeconomic backgrounds who are likely to experience a wider range of family practices and routines. As an initial attempt to explore how such variations might affect future orientation, we conducted a small pilot study to collect data from poor African American parents living in inner-city Chicago. Although the number of subjects in this sample is too small to permit statistical comparisons, we will use the information to explore how family practices and parental beliefs and theories differ with experience, and whether differences in these family context factors influence young children's future-oriented behaviors. Eventually it would also be interesting to collect data from homeless families, those in the midst of divorce, or others in transition, to relate how disruptions to family practices and routines may affect children's development and their current level of future orientation.

Finally, we are optimistic about many of the examples of future-oriented behaviors that we have discovered from our conversations with parents. We now have a better sense of the types of future-oriented behaviors that children exhibit in their everyday lives. This information should help us move closer to our goal of conducting laboratory studies of future-oriented processes that are based on meaningful and real child experiences.

REFERENCES

Ames, L. B. (1946). The development of the sense of time in the young child. *Journal of Genetic Psychology, 68,* 97–125.

Bauer, P. J., & Mandler, J. M. (1990). Remembering what happened next: Very young children's recall of event sequences. In R. Fivush & J. Hudson (Eds.), *What young children remember and why—Emory Symposium in Cognition.* New York: Cambridge University Press.

Bauer, P. J., & Mandler, J. M. (1992). One thing follows another: Effects of temporal structure on 1- to 2-year-olds' recall of events. *Developmental Psychology, 25,* 197–206.

Canfield, R. L., & Haith, M. M. (1991). Active expectations in 2- and 3-month-old infants: Complex event sequences. *Developmental Psychology, 27,* 198–208.

Clark, E. (1973). What's in a word? On the child's acquisition of semantics in his first language. In T. E. Moore (Ed.), *Cognitive development and the acquisition of language.* New York: Academic Press.

Clark, E. (1983). Meanings and concepts. In J. H. Flavell & E. M. Markman (Vol. eds.), *Cognitive development,* Vol. 3 of P. H. Mussen (Ed.), *Handbook of child psychology.* New York: Wiley.

Cromer, R. (1971). The development of the ability to decenter in time. *British Journal of Psychology, 56,* 386–412.

Diamond, A. (1991). Frontal lobe involvement in cognitive changes during the first year of life. In K. Gibson, M. Konner, & A. Patterson (Eds.), *Brain and behavioral development.* Hillsdale, NJ: Erlbaum.

Dix, T., & Grusec, J. E. (1985). Parent attribution processes in the socialization of children. In I. E. Sigel (Ed.), *Parental belief systems* (pp. 201–233). Hillsdale, NJ: Erlbaum.

Fiese, B. H. (1992). Dimensions of family rituals across two generations: Relations to adolescent identity. *Family Process, 31,* 151–162.

Fraisse, P. (1963). *The psychology of time.* New York: Harper and Row.

Friedman, W. J. (1990). *About time: Inventing the fourth dimension.* Cambridge: MIT Press.

Haith, M. M., Hazan, C., & Goodman, G. S. (1988). Expectation and anticipation of dynamic visual events by 3.5-month-old babies. *Child Development, 59,* 467–479.

Harner, L. (1975). Yesterday and tomorrow: Development of early understanding of the terms. *Developmental Psychology, 11,* 864–865.

Harner, L. (1980). Comprehension of past and future reference revisited. *Journal of Experimental Child Psychology, 29,* 170–182.

Harner, L. (1982). Talking about the past and future. In W. J. Friedman (Ed.), *The develomental psychology of time* (pp. 141–169). New York: Academic Press.

Hayes-Roth, B., & Hayes-Roth, F. (1979). A cognitive model of planning. *Cognitive Science, 3,* 275–310.

Klahr, D., & Robinson, M. (1981). Formal assessment of problem solving and planning processes in preschool children. *Cognitive Psychology, 13,* 113–148.

Nelson, K. (1989). *Narratives from the crib.* Cambridge: Harvard University Press.

O'Connell, B. G., & Gerard, A. B. (1985). Scripts and scraps: The development of sequential understanding. *Child Development, 56,* 671–681.

Piaget, J. (1952). *The origins of intelligence in children.* New York: International Universities Press.

Piaget, J. (1954). *The construction of reality in the child.* New York: Basic Books.

Piaget, J. (1969). *The child's conception of time* (A. J. Pomeras, Trans.). New York: Basic Books. (Original work published 1946)

Reznick, J. S., & Goldsmith, L. (1989). A multiple form word production checklist for assessing early language. *Journal of Child Language, 16,* 91–100.

Rogoff, B., & Lave, J. (1984). *Everyday cognition: Its development in social context.* Cambridge: Harvard University Press.

Sachs, J. (1983). Talking about the there and then: The emergence of displaced reference in parent-child discourse. In K. E. Nelson (Ed.), *Children's language* (Vol. 4, pp. 1–28). Hillsdale, NJ: Erlbaum.

Sameroff, A. J., & Fiese, B. H. (1989). Family representations of development. In I. E. Sigel, A. V. McGillicuddy-DeLisi, & J. J. Goodnow (Eds.), *Parental belief systems.* Hillsdale, NJ: Erlbaum.

Savage-Rumbaugh, E. S. (1990). Language as a cause-effect communication system. *Philosophical Psychology, 3,* 55–76.

Weist, R. A. (1986). Tense and aspect: Temporal systems in child language. In P. Fletcher & M. Garman (Eds.), *Language acquisition.* Cambridge: Cambridge University Press.

Weist, R. A. (1989). Time concepts in language and thought: Filling the Piagetian void from two to five years. In I. Levin & D. Zakay (Eds.), *Time and Human Cognition.* Amsterdam: North-Holland.

Welsh, M. C. (1991). Rule guided behavior and self-monitoring on the Tower of Hanoi disk-transfer task. *Cognitive Development, 6,* 59–76.

Werner, H. (n.d.). *On early development of expression of time.* Unpublished manuscript, Clark University.

Willatts, P. (1984). Stages in the development of intentional search by young infants. *Developmental Psychology, 20,* 389–396.

Chapter Fourteen

The Rashomon Phenomenon
Personal Frames and Future-Oriented Appraisals in Memory for Emotional Events

Nancy L. Stein, Tom Trabasso, and Maria D. Liwag

INTRODUCTION

This chapter focuses on children's and parents' memory for emotional events. In particular, we are interested in determining how memory for emotional events can be characterized when one person, such as a child, experiences an emotional reaction and a second person, such as a parent, either observes or participates in that event. How can we best characterize the structure and content of the memories for such an event when viewed from different perspectives? How similar are these memories? What factors predict the degree of their overlap and discordance for the same event? What dimensions predict the veridicality of each of these accounts, given different representations of the original event?[1]

Although the study of event memory has a long history in both devel-

This research was funded in part by grants from the Smart Foundation on Early Learning, the National Institute of Child Health and Human Development (HD25742), and the Spencer Foundation. Maria D. Liwag was supported by an Irving B. Harris Fellowship from the Harris Center for Developmental Studies and the Harris Foundation. We wish to thank all the preschools, parents, and children in Hyde Park, Chicago, who so generously gave their time, memories, collective wisdom, and support throughout this project.

1. The Rashomon phenomenon refers to a situation where two or more people have observed or participated in the same event but have constructed different and often conflicting interpretations of that event.

opmental and cognitive psychology (Bohannon & Symons, 1992; Brewer, 1992; Conway, 1990; Fivush & Hudson, 1990; J. Mandler, 1984, 1990; Nelson, 1993; Winograd & Neisser, 1992), the type of events that elicit emotion and the role the elicited emotion plays in organizing memory are not well understood. The relationships that link emotion, thinking, planning, and memory are yet to be fully determined. For these reasons, we devote this chapter to examining the role emotion plays in organizing memory for everyday events.

Responding emotionally to an event reflects a personal stake in understanding its circumstances and outcomes. Emotional reactions signify that appraisals have been made about the status of personal goals (Lazarus & Folkman, 1984; Stein & Jewett, 1986; Stein & Levine, 1987, 1989, 1990; Stein & Trabasso, 1989, 1992). These appraisals, in combination with current desires, beliefs, and plans of action, are the stuff that defines and constrains memory for emotional events. In this chapter we attempt to unfold emotion episodes and show how components of these episodes might be represented in memory. We also highlight the importance of future-oriented thinking and planning in constructing a representation of an emotional event.

To accomplish these goals, we first present an overview of our theory of emotional understanding. Our model assumes that the appraisal and understanding of incoming information controls the flow of attention and the encoding process during the experience of an emotion(s). Studies on memory for events that precipitate emotional reactions, especially in contexts of eyewitness testimony, child abuse cases, and traumatic events (Ceci & Bruck, 1993; Christianson, 1992; Doris, 1991; Harber & Pennebaker, 1992; Mason, 1991), point to the necessity of documenting the processes that influence the encoding of emotionally laden events. Therefore we begin with a working model that focuses on some of the processes that guide the appraisal and encoding of an emotional event. We then present results from one of our studies on children's and parents' memories for emotional events. In discussing these data, the role of personal frames and the way future-oriented thinking affects memory will be highlighted. One of our main assertions is that personal frames of reference guide the encoding of emotional events. These frames include beliefs, values, and stored knowledge about the conditions that lead to or preclude the attainment of valued goals. Similarities in children's and parents' frames of reference brought to the encoding of an emotional event predict, to a large degree, the similarity in the two representations of a shared event. Disagreements between parents and children about what is remembered occur, in part, because each person brought a different frame of reference to the situation.

The children and parents in our studies have a different stake in the emotional events they talk about in their recollections. Parents are asked to recall events where their children experienced a specific emotion, and children are asked to verify whether these events occurred. The children are also asked to tell us what emotion they felt in response to the event. Thus the children experienced the emotion, and parents were observers of their emotional reactions. The significance of these events, and their corresponding interpretation, may certainly differ for children and their parents. For the children, the importance of the emotional events lies in their impact on their goals and preferences; but these events are important to parents too, because often they have to act in order to facilitate or constrain their children's emotions.

We attempt to describe the differences in these memories and the contents of frames that are available to both children and parents during the appraisal of an emotional event. We then illustrate how a frame of reference influences thinking and memory. Specifically, we contend that beliefs about the success and failure of valued goals are used to frame an emotional event. Inferences made about the causes and consequences of failure and success then act as additional dimensions to help guide the appraisal and encoding process. To the extent that two people have common goals and experience the same emotions, their memory for a situation will be more similar. To the extent that people diverge on these two dimensions, their memories will also differ, even though there may be some overlap.

Finally, we show how memory for emotional events is heavily influenced by future-oriented thinking. Emotions are aroused under conditions where important goals are being blocked, threatened, or attained. Among other things, emotions are indicative of the value and significance attached to the goal being thwarted or achieved, and emotions are also intimately linked to plans of action and future behaviors.

Important goals are often activated during a specific emotional experience, and they are not necessarily deactivated at the end of the emotion episode. If the thwarted or attained goal is highly valued and directly linked to the maintenance, attainment, or blockage of other goals, it will remain operative even after the initial emotion episode has drawn to a close. The focal goal will then be used to organize and understand future emotion episodes until some type of goal resolution allows for its deactivation. The goals are kept active because of their continued importance to the person who experienced the emotion.

When we construct memories of an emotional event, information from the episode where an emotion was originally experienced is often integrated with events that occurred *after* the initial episode. This integration is the result of an effort to build a coherent understanding of all of the operating conditions that preclude or facilitate successful goal attainment. Thus, memories for emotion episodes not only are oriented toward the event that initiated the change in a valued goal's status, but are also influenced by the continued activation of an important goal.

Misconceptions about another person's emotional experience occur, in part, because people have different goals, values, and beliefs during a given situation. They also occur because the observer of another's emotional reaction does not have access to a person's experience *after* the shared emotional event. Subsequent experience can often cause a substantial restructuring of or additions to the memory representation constructed during an emotion episode. Thus, both prior frames of reference and future-oriented thinking become critical in determining memories for an emotional event.

APPRAISAL AND FUTURE-ORIENTED THINKING

Much of what is remembered on an everyday basis is based on the preferences, values, desires, and feelings that motivate and accompany personal and social interaction. These are not new thoughts. Bartlett (1932), for instance, was quite clear in his assumptions about the basis of memory. He believed that current attitudes, desires, and prior knowledge guided and organized the memory for any event. The problem is how to characterize these mental structures and states so that we can measure them and empirically show how they affect the representations that are constructed during encoding and retrieval.

In a series of papers (Stein & Levine, 1987, 1990; Stein & Trabasso, 1992; Stein, Trabasso, & Liwag, 1993), we have begun to describe those processes and mental structures that we believe represent the experience of an emotion episode. According to our current theory of emotional experience (see Stein et al., 1993, for the most recent version), individuals are assumed to continually monitor the status of goals and preferences that are highly valued. These goals and preferences, when attained or maintained, are assumed to lead to states of well-being. People prefer to be in positive states of goal satisfaction (well-being) rather than in states of goal failure (loss or pain).

For an event to elicit an emotional response, the following four characteristics are required. First, the event should be perceived as one that has changed or could change the status of a valued goal. Second, the event should be novel or unexpected in the circumstances. What is novel about the event should violate a prior set of expectations so that people should challenge the truth value of what has happened or what should happen. Third, when the precipitating event is evaluated and found to be discrepant in relation to existing beliefs, an accompanying increase in the level of autonomic nervous system (ANS) arousal and an affect should occur. Although changes in ANS arousal are difficult to detect without the use of precise instrumentation, increases should always accompany the evocation of an emotional response. Indications of ANS involvement are increases in heart rate, mean blood pressure, and galvanic skin response. Fourth, monitoring changes in the status of a valued goal should lead directly to an appraisal of current beliefs about the appropriate plan(s) of action to be taken in the *specific* circumstances surrounding the event. At this point, thinking about the past becomes integrated with predictions about the future as people attempt to adapt and cope with the current situation. When these four sets of conditions are met, we claim that an emotional reaction will be evoked.

That emotional responses occur primarily when changes in the status of valued goals are perceived constrains the mental structures activated to interpret ongoing events. Specifically, any event that has emotional relevance will be appraised with respect to the past in terms of causes and with respect to the future in terms of consequences of the change in a goal's status. The essence of these appraisals is captured by posing and answering the following three questions:

1. What happened?
2. What can be done about it?
3. What are the likely results of undertaking any plan and actions?

These three kinds of appraisal are carried out in a temporal sequence, for without an appraisal of what happened, plans of action cannot be formulated or enacted. Without some plan, future actions and outcomes cannot be appraised and possibly revised. We provide an example of how each component of the appraisal process is activated and carried out, taking into consideration the following limitations.

First, our description of the appraisal and thinking processes is symbolized by a series of questions that might be asked when experiencing an emotion. We use questions in the metaphoric sense only to demonstrate where attention is focused during the experience of an emotion (see Folkman & Lazarus, 1990; Folkman & Stein, 1992a,b; G. Mandler, 1982, 1984; Stein & Levine, 1990; Stein et al., 1993, for similar arguments), to illustrate the types of causal inferences that are made during appraisal, and to show how links are made between the goals, the appraisal of an event, and preparation for action (Stein & Trabasso, 1992). Moreover, it must be remembered that people are continually monitoring changes in the status of other valued goals, even during the appraisal and planning process associated with a specific set of goals. Should the monitoring system signal that events or goals other than the current ones are more important and need attention, then attention will be mobilized toward the new set of goals. Thus, even though temporal and causal constraints are built into the evaluation process, flexibility in the system is also present, owing to the capacity to simultaneously monitor the world with respect to changes in the state of other valued goals.

Barring the necessity of diverting attention to new goals during appraisal and planning, the following series of questions reflect some of the thinking and reasoning that occur throughout an emotional episode. We first consider the initial phase of trying to understand *What happened?*

> *What happened?*
> What event has occurred?
> Have any of my goals been affected?
> Which goals have changed in status?
> How have the goals changed in status?
> What beliefs about the world have been violated by these changes?
> What do I believe now?
> What or who caused the change in the status of the goals?
> What are the consequences of the status change?

In our studies of emotional understanding, we have found that children, even those as young as 3 years, can understand and talk about each of these components of an emotion episode, either freely in a spontaneous narrative, when probed by questions, or when asked directly to generate causal antecedents and consequences of particular emotional events (Liwag & Stein, 1993; Stein & Wade, 1993; Stein & Jewett, 1986; Stein & Levine, 1989; Stein & Trabasso, 1989; Trabasso, Stein, & Johnson, 1981). An instantiation of this process is taken from a conversation with a 5-year-old girl whose emotional experiences we observed during an investigation on children's understanding of changing emotional states (Stein & Trabasso, 1989). Amy, our subject, was trying to understand the implications of what her teacher had just told her kindergarten class. The teacher announced that she had bought a paint set for each child in the class. She told the class she wanted them to paint pictures that could be hung up on the bulletin board in preparation for Parents' Night. The teacher then told the class that each child could take the paint set home.

A short while after the teacher gave the children their paint sets, our research assistant (RA) approached Amy (A). The assistant noticed that Amy was acting apprehensive and was making faces that seemed to signal anxiety. The following conversation took place and is taken to indicate Amy's effort to understand *What happened?*

> RA: Amy, how do you feel about getting to take the paint box home?
> A: I'm jittery. I'm not sure why she wants to give me the paints.
>   So, do I have to paint all of the time at home?
>   I really don't want to do this.

I didn't think teachers made you paint at home.
I don't like painting that much.
Why does she want me to take the paint box home?

For Amy, the event has activated a goal of not wanting to paint. The teacher's request to take the paint set home has threatened this goal. From her conversation, we learned that Amy prefers not to paint. Given that Amy doesn't like to paint, she is concerned by the teacher's gift and the request to use the paints. She fears that she will now have to paint more frequently. Thus the status of Amy's goal has changed from being able to maintain avoidance of a dormant but nonpreferred activity to being requested by someone in authority to increase the frequency with which she has to enact this nonpreferred activity.

Amy's beliefs concerning a teacher's role have also been violated. At the beginning of the interview, Amy stated that she didn't think teachers made you paint at home. She expressed surprise that her teacher gave her a paint set of her own and suggested that she paint at home. Amy now has to contend with these facts. The teacher was the agent who caused a change in the status of Amy's goal of avoiding a nonpreferred activity. We also discover that Amy's attention has become focused on the consequences of the change in the status of her goal. In the initial states of appraisal, however, she is not clear on what the change will be.

In the second phase of appraisal, *What can I do about it?* three questions reflect the thinking and inference processes that occur.

What can I do about it?
What do I want to do about it?
Can (should) the goal be reinstated?
Are plans of action available that might reinstate or modify the original goal?

In our interview with Amy, the following interchange took place between the research assistant and Amy:

RA: Well, given how you feel, what do you want to do, Amy?
A: I don't want to take the paints home. I want to know why I have to do this.
RA: Well, Amy, what are you going to do about this?
A: I'll take the paints home, but when I get home, I'll ask my Mom why I have to do this.

From the initial part of the interview, we knew that Amy did not want to paint at home. However, Amy's conversation focused on a subgoal of not taking the paint set home, partly because she believed that taking the paints home would obligate her to paint. The remainder of the *What can I do about it?* portion of the interview indicated that Amy did not yet know whether her goal—not having to paint at home—could be realized. However, she was determined to carry through a plan of action that would let her ask why she had to take the paints home. Thus, for Amy, a plan of action was available that might allow her to accomplish her primary goal of avoiding a nonpreferred activity.

In the third phase of our interview, the component that focuses on the question *What are the results of my plans and actions?* six more specific questions can be generated that complete the final segment in appraising an emotional event.

> *What are the results of my plans and actions?*
> Were actions carried out in the service of the goal?
> What were the actions that were carried out?
> What were the outcomes of the action, in terms of achieving or maintaining a goal?
> Were there any unintended outcomes of goal achievement or goal failure?
> Did these outcomes cause a reappraisal or reevaluation of the goals at stake?
> How will the outcomes affect other goals?

On Amy's way out of the class, she did not ask the teacher why she had to take the paints home, but she did ask whether she had to paint every day. The teacher's response was the following:

> T: Why no, Amy, not if you don't want to. I gave you the paints so that you and your classmates wouldn't have to fight over the paint sets every time someone wanted to paint. I didn't mean for you to think that you had to paint. Are you really upset about taking the paints home?
> A: Well no, not if I don't have to paint all of the time. I really like to paint but only some of the time.

Two weeks later, our research assistant engaged Amy in a casual conversation and asked her how she felt about being able to paint at home. Amy responded with the following comment:

> A: Well, I used them once, when my mom wouldn't take me out for an ice cream. I played with Allison. But I didn't tell Mrs. T because she'd be mad at me. But she hasn't asked about my painting, so maybe she forgot.

It is clear from the final part of our interview with Amy that she carried out actions in the service of her goal—not having to paint at home—and that she did achieve this goal.

Amy's initial anxious response to the paint box event was highly predictive of her *future* behavior when she took the paints home. The interview with Amy, two weeks later, confirmed that the event was still problematic to her. Not wanting to paint at home was still an active concern of hers, especially with respect to her relationship with her teacher and how it might be affected should her teacher discover that Amy had not been painting at home. This interview example indicates that events and their effects endure well beyond their immediate context and that goals continue to be salient even when people appear to have attained a goal or successfully resolved a dilemma.

MEMORY FOR EMOTIONAL EVENTS

We now turn to the ways these appraisal processes might function during encoding and retrieval. Our aim is to understand how appraisal processes influence what gets incorporated into the memory representation of an emotional event. The roles that thinking and encoding play in planning and decision making are also of interest. Thus we consider the effects that emotional experience has on future-oriented coping processes.

Emotion plays a unique role in the construction of a memory representation. First and foremost, emotional reactions indicate that some aspect of the precipitating event is novel or unexpected. During the encoding of an event, the evocation of an emotion signals a shift of attention to new information present in the precipitating event. The new information is perceived to be incongruous with what was expected (and known), and the discrepancy between the incoming novel information and prior expectations triggers changes in ANS arousal. The main task of the understander at this point is to evaluate how this novel information affects current goals and how it might affect future important goals and states of well-being.

To the extent that information from environmental events leads to an understanding of the significance of the changes that have occurred to present and future valued goals, then information from the input will be processed and retained. Three types of constraints, however, appear to operate during the experience of an emotion episode. The first comes from the changes in ANS arousal. The second comes from a failure to understand the events in the unfolding of an emotion episode. The third comes from rapid decisions made to act in the service of survival.

The monitoring system is oriented toward tracking the survival of the organism. Increases in ANS arousal can facilitate shifts in attention to relevant external information, but these increases can also threaten the organism's survival. Rapid heart rates, rapid increases in endocrine levels, and profuse sweating can literally shut down the entire nervous system. If a person has awareness of and control over these harmful consequences of ANS arousal, then these consequences can be dealt with immediately. During an emotion-provoking episode, attention may then shift quickly from the processing of external information to the processing and control of the internal effects of ANS arousal. If ANS arousal exceeds certain limits, the organism becomes immobilized, and this may shut off any planning or action. Thus, during many emotionally arousing episodes, such as those documented in medical settings, attention may be devoted largely to monitoring and controlling the pain inflicted by an invasive procedure. If pain can be reduced by the active monitoring of sensory stimulation, then attention will be focused on this goal.

The second constraint on the processing of external information is due to the difficulty of understanding or believing the significance of external events as they unfold. If the significance of one event is not understood or not believed, then attention will remain focused on that event. However, when attention is captured by a single event, the rest of the emotion episode may not be encoded. We frequently see this failure to encode events when unexplainable disasters occur. When the first inklings of the disaster are apparent, attention is often diverted from tracking the sequence of events as they unfold to attempting to understand the prior events that caused the disaster. The shift to understanding causes is related to an urge to replay the situation in order to undo, avoid, or prevent the conditions that led to the disaster. Attempts to reinstate in one's mind the conditions that would preclude disaster reflect an effort to understand what caused the disaster in the first place.

A third constraint on processing external information is related to the necessity of taking action in the service of well-being. The need to act is a frequent cause of encoding failures in an emotion episode. If a person makes a rapid inference that an important goal has been threatened, then attention may immediately be diverted to evaluating the consequences of impending goal failure. As soon as the long-range consequences are comprehended, relevant plans of action are activated to avert the threat. The activation of plans, however, captures attention and uses an enormous amount of the mental resources available to the planner. A wide range of conditions must be reviewed to determine if the available plans are appropriate for the current situation. In many contexts, rapid reviewing is critical so that action can be immediately initiated to avert an impending loss. When fast action is required, almost all attentional resources are focused on the monitoring and evaluation of unfolding plans and actions. Information that is unrelated to the plan or the action is simply not processed. And even when information is relevant to the plan of action, it may not be processed because all attentional resources are devoted to monitoring and evaluating whether the current plan is working.

What we have tried to illustrate by enumerating these constraints is that active planning and appraisal are continuous processes that operate throughout the emotion episode. External events are always evaluated with respect to their relevance to the person experiencing the event. Attention is first and foremost geared to the activation and monitoring of plans that protect and preserve well-being. Many times we think that information has been processed by another person because the information holds importance for us. Unless the other person's frame of reference is known, however, there is no guarantee that the information has been understood or processed. Thus our first task is to specify exactly how people frame and organize information from an emotion episode and how different frames and organizations lead to misunderstandings between two people who are party to the same emotional event, one being a witness and the other the experiencer of the emotion.

CONCORDANCE AND DISCORDANCE IN PARENTS' AND CHILDREN'S MEMORIES: THEORY AND HYPOTHESES

To describe the content of personal frames and document their role in the representation of emotional experience, we carried out a study with preschool children and their parents as subjects. Our first goal was to create a situation where subjects varied in the knowledge and frames they brought to the recall of emotional experience. Our second goal was to order our interviews so that subjects could spontaneously narrate portions of their emotional experiences before any structure was imposed on their recollections.

To accomplish these goals, we interviewed 77 parents about recent events where they had witnessed their children experiencing four different types of emotion: happiness, anger, sadness, and fear. The parents were mostly mothers from middle-class backgrounds. All parents focused on their own children, who ranged in age from 3 to 5½ years. Parents were instructed to recall events where they had observed their children experiencing each of the four emotions within the last week. Parents were asked to report situations where they could actually document and describe their children's expressive reactions to a precipitating event.

Requesting parents to recall their children's expression of emotion as well as their children's interpretation of the experience was included to increase the accuracy of parental reports. Although parents display a sensitivity to their children's emotional experiences, children can easily experience an emotion without giving any indication of what they have felt. When emotional reactions are expressed on the face, in the prosody of speech, and in the movement of the body, it is easier to ascertain that a child did in fact experience a particular emotion. Thus, in their reports, parents were asked to recall events within the past week where they could recount their children's expression of emotion as well as their children's interpretation of the emotional experience.

Parents' reports of the events that precipitated their children's emotional responses were then used to elicit narratives from the children. Our experimenters told children they had talked to their parents about different events that had happened to the children in the past week. Children were presented with each of these, such as the following event:

> Brian's family was going to see Grandpa Jack in Seattle.
> Brian asked his mother if he could take his two Bobo dolls on the airplane.
> His mother said no because they had too many gifts to carry on the plane.
> Brian would just have to leave his Bobo dolls at home.

In relating the mother's event report to the child, we preserved as much of the parent's actual language as possible.

After being presented with a specific event, all children were asked the following four questions:

1. How did you feel when this happened?
2. Can you tell me exactly what happened?
3. What did you think about when this happened?
4. What did you do?

After narrating in response to these questions, children were asked a second set of probe questions, two of which were identical to the questions asked in the first set:

1. How did you feel when this happened?
2. Why did you feel [specific emotion elicited] when this happened?
3. What did you want to do when this happened?
4. What did you really do when this happened?

The second set of questions contained a repetition of the feeling question so that children could generate explanations for each emotion. The action question was in tandem with a goal formulation question to provide a direct comparison between desires and actions.

Since our purpose was to document and understand the similarities and differences in children's and parents' representations of an emotion episode, the following questions guided our analyses and theoretical speculations. First we wanted to know how accurate parents were in identifying events that provoked emotion in their children. If we asked parents to constrain their reporting to those events that had expressive elements attached, would children agree that these events did in fact occur and did provoke some type of emotional reaction? Our hypothesis was that widespread agreement would be found on the fact that the event occurred, but less agreement would exist in the assessment of the emotional reaction to the event.

Our second question, therefore, focused on the amount of agreement found between parents' and children's reports of emotional responses experienced by the children. Our predictions about concordance depended on the type of emotion episode being reported. From past research (Trabasso et al., 1981), we know that events eliciting happiness in children are distinct from and have little in common with events eliciting anger, sadness, and fear. Children become happy when they get what they want or when they get out of a situation they do not want to be in. The goal-outcome states associated with happiness have no overlap with the goal-outcome states associated with the three negative emotions, according to both children's and adults' perceptions (Stein & Levine, 1989). Our prediction therefore was that parents would have little difficulty identifying those events that made their children happy versus those events that made their children feel a negative emotion.

Parental memories of the expressive behavior associated with happiness may modify the selection of the particular event, but conceptual knowledge about the type of event that elicits happiness should play the central role in guiding the parent's choice of an appropriate happy event. Thus we expected parents to use their conceptual knowledge of events that evoke happiness in combination with our instructions to choose from the subset of episodes where happiness was actually expressed behaviorally.

The concordance between child and parent reports of events that elicited negative emotions in their children should not be as high as the concordance found in relation to happy events. Although events that elicit negative emotions are highly discriminable from events that elicit positive emotion, it is possible for the same event to elicit fear, anger, and sadness (Stein & Jewett, 1986; Stein & Levine, 1989; Trabasso et al., 1981), with an event more likely to elicit both anger and sadness than both fear and another negative emotion.

Making accurate predictions about children's memories for anger episodes is difficult for the following reasons. For those events where parents observed angry responses in their children, given that we initially accept the veridicality of the parent's report, we might find that children report a negative emotional experience, but the emotion may not be the one the parent observed. Although children may have initially felt anger, this emotion often gives way to sadness. The reason for the change is that anger and sadness both occur in response to conditions where goals have been denied or a loss has been incurred. In these particular goal-outcome situations, the first desire of most people is to seek out the cause of the loss and attempt to rectify the loss. Anger, according to our theoretical framework, is the emotion that accompanies an analysis of the cause of the obstacle, primarily because a belief about an available plan of action is invoked in the service of constructing a viable action plan to remedy the loss. Frequently, however, the initial plan of action is not successful in overcoming the loss or denial. If subsequent attempts lead to failure, the belief that the loss is permanent and that nothing can be done may be activated. In this case, sadness is evoked.

When emotion episodes involve the loss of a valued possession, friend, ability, or such, wishful thinking endures beyond the limits of the original episode observed by the parent. The pain caused by the loss or denial could be an ever-present reminder of the episode and may even serve as a reinstatement cue. Even though children may experience anger in the initial part of an emotion episode, continued thinking about a failed goal may lead to sadness that is more representative of the fact that all attempts have failed to rectify the loss.

A clear example of the concordance and discordance between the memories of Brian and his mother is illustrated in the two narratives presented in Table 14.1. Brian and his mother agreed that Brian wanted to take his Bobo dolls on the airplane and that his mother had refused Brian's request. They also agreed that Brian stated he wasn't going on the airplane if he couldn't take his Bobo dolls and that Brian ended up in his room as a result of being denied his request.

The disagreements come in recalling the events that occurred before and after the central emotion episode. Within the central episode, the two also disagree on Brian's experienced emotion as well as on the events that led to his being in his room. Also, Brian reports feeling sadness, and he reports "going to his room" and crying because he couldn't take his Bobo dolls on the airplane. His mother reports "putting Brian in his room" because he kicked her. Thus, how Brian got to his room is in dispute as well as why he was in his room. Brian's mother also recalls punishing Brian by denying him dessert at the evening meal, and she reports her emotional reaction to this incident.

Brian also reports a subsequent emotional reaction, but the reaction is expressed in conjunction with his visit to his grandfather's house. Moreover, Brian recalls the enduring consequences of not having his Bobo dolls with him. He is entirely focused on how much the Bobo dolls mean to him, both before he starts narrating the denial of his wish and when he has to deal with the consequences of being without his favorite dolls. Thus we can see the importance of these dolls to Brian throughout the reporting of this emotion episode, and we can also see how being denied his wish shapes almost every aspect of his narrative.

We also know that Brian's mother interpreted Brian's behavior in a different way when she stated that Brian felt his own needs were more important than everyone else's. Thus there is a conflict over whose needs get fulfilled first. What we do not know from this account is whether Brian experienced anger in addition to sadness or whether he experi-

TABLE 14.1 Parent-Child Report of an "Anger" Episode:
The Bobo Dolls

Time line for mother's narrative (Parent reports anger)	Time line for child's narrative (Child reports sadness)
Events and states before precipitating event	
He really thought his own needs were more important than everyone else's.	Really loved Bobo dolls, had two. Slept with the little one, and used the big one as a punching bag.
Precipitating event	
Family going to see Grandpa Jack in Seattle	
Brian asked mother if he could take his two Bobo dolls on the airplane	
His mother said no because they had too many gifts to carry on the plane	
Brian would just have to leave his Bobo dolls at home	
Response to precipitating event	
When she told Brian this	When his mom told him this
Anger reaction	*Sad reaction*
He had a fit. He yelled and screamed at her and told her he wasn't going unless he could take his Bobo dolls on the airplane.	He felt very sad. He didn't want to go unless he could take his Bobo dolls with him.
When she tried to reason with him,	
Anger expression	*Sad expression*
He kicked her in the shins,	
And then she put him in his room for the evening.	So he went to his room and cried. He didn't want to go to his grandpa's if he couldn't take his Bobo dolls with him.
He wasn't allowed to have dessert that evening. And she had to pack his stuff very quickly the next morning. This incident really undid her and the rest of the family too.	
Subsequent events, feelings, and expressions	
	When he got to his grandpa's
	Sad reaction
	he was still sad.
	And he cried every time he went to sleep because he didn't have his Bobo dolls with him.
	He hopes he never has to go away again without his Bobo dolls.

enced only sadness, as he recalls in his reports. However, it is clear from these two narratives that Brian's mother is not aware of Brian's intense feeling of sadness, and she is not aware that he does not remember feeling angry.

Similar discrepancies may be found in parent-child reports of fear events. Objectively, fear is highly distinguishable from anger and sadness, both in terms of the type of events that cause fear (Stein & Jewett, 1986; Trabasso et al., 1981) and in terms of the class of goal outcomes associated with the experience of fear (Stein & Jewett, 1986; Stein & Levine, 1987). Therefore parents' memories about events that evoked fear in their children should be as accurate as their reports of happy events. The type of resolution in a fear episode, however, may determine whether children report feeling afraid in response to a precipitating event.

Children's failure to report fear reactions that others have observed may be explained by the role active planning processes play in changing the nature of the memory representation. Preventing a threat from becoming actualized is the first concern in fear situations (Stein & Jewett, 1986; Stein & Levine, 1987). Therefore fear reactions are rarely prolonged or ignored by both children and parents, especially if children's physical well-being is at stake. Children's prototypic responses to fear are to seek out their parents for help and relief (Stein & Jewett, 1986; Trabasso et al., 1981). Parents' prototypic responses are to generate plans of action that will quickly alleviate their children's fear (Stein, Trabasso, & Liwag, 1991). After relieving their children's fear, most parents then attempt to ensure that their children will learn appropriate plans of action in future threatening situations. Therefore a plan of action that will alleviate or avoid fear in the future is often the focus of attention at the end of a fear episode.

When evaluating children's memory for fearful situations, what gets retained in the representation of the emotional event may be biased by the inclusion of and access to a successful plan of action. Once a workable plan of action is linked to a potentially threatening situation, memory for the original emotional reaction may not be retrievable. The components that may be retrievable, however, are the event that caused the original threat and the plans of action for averting the threatening situation.

What we are suggesting is that the final operating conditions relevant to the initial goal are critical in regulating the accuracy and stability of an emotional representation. Children may be able to recall a possible threat to one of their goals, but the fact that they now have access to a plan of action that prevents the threat from being realized may prevent them from remembering all the components of their initial fear reaction.

Another source of difficulty in achieving concordance between parents and children may have to do with the method used to elicit a narrative. Parents were asked to generate narratives by proceeding from the emotion back to a precipitating event. Thus the requirement to use an emotion in the generation of a precipitating event could have made parents include certain actions surrounding precipitating events and exclude others. Parents' reporting of these episodes therefore could be extremely selective because of our instructions.

CONCORDANCE AND DISCORDANCE IN PARENTS' AND CHILDREN'S MEMORIES: EMPIRICAL EVIDENCE

The results of our analyses of the concordance data were as follows. First, of all events reported by parents, children could remember 87% as actually having occurred. If children could remember that the event happened, they could recall their emotional reaction 86% of the time, and they could report the emotion episode 95% of the time. Thus children's willingness to talk about their memories for emotional responses as well as the details of the episode was high, even for the youngest.

The degree of concordance between parent and child reports of emotional reactions varied depending on the emotion being recalled. The proportion of children agreeing with their parents' observations of their emotional responses was: happy = 80%; sad = 72%; fear = 49%; and anger = 22%. As we predicted, episodes identified by parents as eliciting happiness provided the highest rate of agreement, while fear and anger episodes provided the lowest. Surprisingly, sad episodes led to a rate of agreement almost as high as happy episodes. Thus happy and sad emotions were the easiest for parents to identify in terms of establishing criteria for common frames of reference with their children's reports of these emotions.

Table 14.2 contains a matrix of the percentages of concordant and discordant emotion labels children used in talking about the four emotion episodes reported by parents. When children did not agree with their parents' assessment of anger, the most common alternative emotion they reported was sadness. For fear and happiness, the most common alternative was also sadness. Thus sadness was the most frequent alternative emotion children gave for anger, fear, and happiness episodes recalled by their parents. In children's memories of these emotion episodes, the permanent loss of a valued goal was very salient. For sad episodes, on the other hand, the most frequent alternative emotion children reported was happiness. Thus children were remembering the attainment of a goal rather than the loss of a goal in these sad episodes framed by parents. These data clearly speak to the future-oriented nature

TABLE 14.2 Percentage of Concordant and Discordant Emotion Labels between Children and Parents

CHILD'S REPORTED EMOTION	PARENT'S REPORT			
	Angry	Afraid	Happy	Sad
Angry	.22	.05	—	.02
Afraid	—	.49	—	—
Happy	.22	.05	.80	.19
Sad	.39	.19	.07	.72
Multiple emotions without agreement	.08	.09	—	—
Neutral	.02	.02	.03	.02
Other	.06	.10	.10	.04
Total number of children	49	43	59	47

Note. The percentages in italic along the diagonal are for children whose emotion reports were concordant with their parents'. They include children who recalled multiple emotions, when at least one of the emotions agreed with the parents' reports.

of emotional memories and suggest that the initial reaction to a precipitating event may not be the one that is remembered or retrieved. Rather, children's attention is focused on the forward tracking of their goals until a more permanent resolution is reached, be it positive or negative.

The low rate of parent-child concordance in the anger episodes was directly related to the role parents played during their children's emotional experience. When parental reports were analyzed for whether the parent was an observer or a participant in the emotion episode, we found that parents' participation was twice as high in anger episodes as in any other type of emotion episode. Table 14.3 shows the proportion of emotion episodes where parents reported they were either observers or participant-observers. In anger episodes, parents were participants 64% of the time, whereas they were participants approximately 34% of the time in the other three emotion episodes.

Table 14.4 indicates what role parents played as participants in the different emotion episodes. Again, anger episodes were clearly differentiated from the other three emotion episodes in terms of the role the parent carried out during them. Parents in anger episodes were primarily

TABLE 14.3 Proportion of Episodes Where Parents Were either Participant-Observers or Observers Only

	Happy	Angry	Afraid	Sad
Participant-observer	.32	.64	.26	.43
Observer only	.68	.36	.74	.57

TABLE 14.4 Proportion of Parents Participating in Emotion Episodes Where Parent Was the Cause, Object, Facilitator, or Constrainer of Child's Coping Responses

	Happy	Angry	Afraid	Sad
Cause	.20	.64	.10	.28
Object of emotion display	.12	.25	.00	.02
Facilitator	.63	.05	.82	.70
Constrainer	—	.62	—	—

engaged in restraining or constraining their children's actions and desires, whereas parents facilitated their children's actions and desires in the other three emotion episodes.

That parents act as constrainers puts them in direct conflict with their children in terms of the goals children wish to achieve. The presence of this conflict reduces parents' ability to accurately predict their children's felt emotion to the specific ongoing event. Table 14.5 shows how the rates of concordance between parents and children varied as a function of whether the parent was an observer or a participant. Parents participating in anger episodes had a significantly lower concordance rate than those who were not participants. However, participating parents in happy, fearful, and sad situations were not significantly worse in assessing their children's emotional reactions than those who were observers. The significance of the participatory role was critical only for anger episodes.

The importance of participatory roles only in anger episodes suggests that the conflict or concordance between children's and parents' goals lies at the heart of the differences in parent and child reports of emotional reactions and events surrounding the emotion. When parents acted as facilitators of children's actions, their participation did not reduce their ability to report emotional responses similar to their children's. Thus the participant role, by itself, does not hinder the ability to report concordant emotional data or emotional events. Rather, absence of goal concordance and the presence of conflict appear to be the critical variables that determine agreement between children's and parents' reporting of children's emotions.

Table 14.6 contains another example of a parent's and a child's narra-

TABLE 14.5 Proportion of Participating Parents Whose Reports of Emotion Agreed or Disagreed with Their Children's Reports

	Happy	Angry	Afraid	Sad
Agreed	.78	.15	.33	.74
Disagreed	.22	.85	.67	.26

TABLE 14.6 Parent's and Child's Report of an "Anger" Episode:
The Dinner Guest

Time line for parent's narrative	Time line for child's narrative
Events and states before focal episode	
Setting	*Setting*
"Recently we had guests for a meal. This happened two weeks ago. They were people actually that we didn't know that well."	"There were two guests over, then th-they were talking."
Child's expectations	*Child's belief*
"Robert, when we have guests, he's used to getting a lot of attention, and he's very excited, and he sort of expects that, um, they'll want to talk to him."	Child has a belief that guests shouldn't say words that aren't nice. "It wasn't nice words to say to someone."
Goals	
"Robert was vying for attention, he wanted attention very much, and he was hoping for it and expecting it."	Child wanted to join in the adults' conversation. He wanted to talk.
Focal episode	
Precipitating event	
"He [guest] said something to Robert to the effect of 'when you're little . . . you can't talk . . . and sort of only when you grow up and become an adult, then you get to talk.'"	"And then, um, he [guest] said, 'When, when when I was little, I was quiet and I let the parents talk. The older you grow up, the more you can talk.'"
Change in status of goal	
Goal failure: Aversive state	*Goal failure: Aversive state*
"From Robert's perspective, the man was interrupting him, because each of them was trying to get, you know, different attention." "He was excited about whatever it was he had wanted to tell people, he was mad at the lack of attention he was getting."	He wasn't able to participate in the conversation. "And I had to wait a long time [to talk]."
Emotional reaction	
"He was very angry, um, and upset" "And he sulked a bit" "He was very confused . . . he was baffled by it."	"Sad" Child expressed sadness.
Reasons for emotional reaction	
"Robert immediately sensed it [comment] as quite cruel and discriminating." "When he got it, in his own sense, what he said, was really how it struck him that's not fair."	"Because it wasn't nice words to say to someone."

TABLE 14.6 (Continued)

Time line for parent's narrative	Time line for child's narrative
"He was angry because, all his expectations were shot down. He was excited about whatever it was he had wanted to tell people, he was mad at the lack of attention he was getting and he was mad at this man for so clearly telling him, 'You don't matter.' 'I matter!'"	

New goals

Revenge (?)	*Goal reinstatement*
"Maybe part of him wanted to, to tell the man off."	"I wish he would let me talk."
"On the other hand, he was baffled by it. I'm not sure he knew what he wanted to do."	

Possible plan of action

	"I thinked about . . . why don't I stick out my tongue at him."
	This plan seems to correspond to an unstated goal that might be inferred as desire for "revenge," or it could just be a plan to act out his negative feelings toward the guest.

Actions

"But he said something like, 'That isn't fair.' Um, and he came back with it. He said, 'That's not fair. Children can talk too. That isn't fair that you have to wait till you're grown up.'"	"I went into the kitchen."
	"And I stuck my tongue out on him, at him."
"He, he started to cry, Oh, he cried. He cried and he sulked a bit, and he needed a lot of holding from us."	Note that the plan was enacted, though he didn't explicitly state the goal.
"That's why the tears came, in part. Because it was also confusing to him."	

Consequences

Goal success: Attainment	*Not stated*
"I thought he did a good job defending children's rights."	We don't know how sticking out his tongue or going into the kitchen affected the goal of wanting to be allowed to talk, or the inferred goal of "revenge."
In mother's view, Robert was successful in "telling the man off."	
Note that we don't know what effect this had on the guest who made the comment.	

tive of the same event. In this instance Robert's mother reported an incident where the family had two guests for dinner whom the family did not know well. According to his mother, Robert displayed anger toward the male guest when he told Robert not to talk at the table. The man proceeded to tell Robert that only when he grew up could he join in the conversation. Robert's mother recalled that her son was very angry, upset, confused, and baffled by the man's behavior. In her view, Robert was angry because of the lack of attention. He was also mad at the man for telling him "You don't matter. I matter."

In this episode the parent is a participant, but only in dealing with Robert's reaction to the family's dinner guest. Even though Robert and his mother disagree on Robert's emotional response to this episode, Robert himself reports a goal plan that directly corresponds to one of anger as well as sadness. According to Robert, he was feeling sad because he wasn't allowed to talk, and when he did get a chance, he had to wait a long time. He was also "upset" about the guest's condescending comments to him. Robert reports a summary of what the guest said to him, and then he states, "I thought about, 'Why don't I stick my tongue out at him.' So, I went into the kitchen and stuck my tongue out at him."

Two things are evident in Robert's and his mother's accounts of this situation. First, both narratives include evidence that Robert did indeed display anger toward the family's guest, but Robert's report of his anger comes *after* his report of his sad feeling. Moreover, he reports the emotion as an expression of anger rather than as a feeling of anger. Second, the portion of the precipitating event that made Robert sad was not the portion that made him angry. Robert was sad because he was not allowed to talk and interact in the way he expected, and when he did get a chance to talk, it was only after he had endured a long wait. Sadness is central to Robert because he suffered a clear blow to his self-importance by not being allowed to talk. At the time of the event, there was nothing he could do to gain the floor back from the family's dinner guest, even after an attempt to defend his right to talk (according to Robert's mother). Thus, in the circumstances of this event, there was nothing Robert could do to attain his goal of participating in the interaction.

After reporting his interaction with the dinner guest, however, Robert clearly focused on another aspect of the precipitating event: the bad or mean words the guest said to him. In Robert's narrative, he recalls that the guest told him, "When I was little I was quiet and let the parents talk. The older you grow up, the more you can talk." Clearly this was a violation of Robert's beliefs and expectations, based on his own and his mother's accounts. However, Robert does not report the fact that the guest said: "You don't matter, I matter," nor does he report the fact that he actively defended children's participation in dinner conversation by telling the man, "That's not fair. Children can talk, too. That isn't fair that you have to wait until you're grown up." The anger is directed at the social violation of not allowing children to talk and also being told that the dinner guest is more important than Robert. The active plan of action expressed, according to his mother, was one of reinstating his rights at the dinner table, but Robert does not spontaneously report this. He does report, however, seeking revenge by sticking out his tongue at the man.

The method of analysis that we use to describe the concordance and discordance between children's and parents' reporting of emotion episodes follows the categorical unfolding of the episode we laid out at the beginning of this chapter. The narrative content from Robert's and his mother's memories is parsed according to the functional categories outlined in our initial description of the components of the appraisal process in an emotional experience.

CONCLUSION

From our analyses of these narratives, the following patterns characterize parent-child reports of emotional situations. First, the frames that parents and children bring to the recall of emotion episodes are clearly different. Parents are recalling emotions experienced by their children, and their children are doing the same. But one person is reporting the episode as an observer of the emotion, and the other as a result of experiencing the emotion. The observer/experiencer distinction leads to several differences in reporting, independent of parents' reported concordance or conflict with their children's emotions and goals.

Parents frequently give an explicit description of the prior beliefs that are operating at the time of their children's emotional response. That is, parents explicitly state what their children expected before their children experienced the emotion. This is clearly indicated in Table 14.6, when Robert's mother begins her narrative. She overtly states that Robert is used to getting attention, that he gets very excited when visitors come and expects that they will want to talk to him. The same type of explicit statement is made by Brian's mother, in Table 14.1, about Brian's expectations regarding the trip to his grandfather's house: Brian thought his own needs were more important than everyone else's.

Children do not provide as frequent access to their explicit prior beliefs as their parents do. This difference may be caused by the constraints on the task of understanding emotional behavior. Parents are not privy to all their children's feelings and expectations about important goals when attempting to understand their emotional responses. It is through interaction that a deeper understanding of their children's preferences and expectations evolves. As they actively focus on the antecedent conditions leading to the precipitating event and make inferences about their children's expectations, their children's desires and thinking processes may become more available to them.

It would be important to ascertain whether making explicit statements about the prior beliefs or expectations of a person observed to be reacting emotionally is a general phenomenon that is regulated by the participant-observer distinction. Alternatively, differences in reporting this information may be developmentally constrained by knowledge of narrative form, content, and audience. Our hypothesis is that young children put into the role of observing their parents' emotional reactions would also give explicit evidence of making inferences about their parents' expectations. We say this because we have many examples of narratives from children reporting parents' anger expressed toward them. As part of understanding why their parents were angry with them, children almost always recount what their parents had expected them to do.

A second dimension that distinguishes parents' narratives from those of their children is the general time frame parents impose on their reports in comparison with the ones children impose on their narratives. Parents' reports focus primarily on the actions and events most proximally surrounding the emotion episode, whereas children's reports often contain elements of events that have occurred before and after the focal episode. As we pointed out previously, children's focus in an emotion narrative is primarily on the status of a goal. They will continue to think about and encode information relevant to that goal as long as the goal is important, desirable, and relevant to their well-being. Even when parents are sensitive to their children's mental and emotional states, it is often surprising for them to discover just how much their children's thoughts and attention have been devoted to monitoring certain goals. However, self-reports of emotional experience are almost always apt to extend over longer time frames than reports provided by those observing the experience of the emotion.

The length of time covered in an emotion narrative, however, does not necessarily reflect the veridicality of the report. Rather, the uniqueness of the event, the need to remember the original conditions under which an emotion was evoked, the level of physiological arousal, the focus of attention, and the resolution generated in response to the emotion all play critical roles in building and maintaining an accurate representation of the original situation. Our data indicate that in situations of conflict and anger, parent-child narratives become the most discordant in terms of parents' being able to identify their children's emotional responses. The discordance may reflect encoding biases on the part of both parent and child.

When conflict arises between two people, physiological arousal is increased, and the attention of the conflicting persons becomes focused and consequently biased (Stein & Miller, 1990; Stein, Wright, Calicchia, & Bernas, 1993). When people engage in argumentative dialogue where neither intends to negotiate a compromise, the dialogue, and therefore attention, is focused on the weaknesses associated with each of the two positions. Almost all effort is expended in showing the limitations and constraints of the opponent's position. Establishing who is responsible for the current problem or conflict becomes central. The reasons an opponent gives for maintaining a position, the harm that will come from adopting one's own position, and the role the self played in engendering the conflict in the first place all recede into the background. Thus memory biases for a conflictual interaction may occur right during the encoding of an emotion situation. It is not only the tendency to be future oriented that serves as a potential force in updating memories: selectivity operating at the time of encoding may also affect retrieval.

An important goal in our future research will be to document the role of time frames and future-oriented processes at the time of encoding and at the time of retrieval. In the current literature on children's memory for everyday and traumatic events, it is believed that many of the "errors" in memory representations occur because children are extremely suggestible and easily integrate new information into current memory representations. Few studies have been carried out to illustrate the exact nature of the representation at the time of encoding. Thus the claim that the memory representation changes because of the integration of additional information will have to be explored more analytically. First, we need a more accurate description of the originally encoded situation. Although our data indicate that children do integrate information across time boundaries, they do not suggest that children lose the veridicality of their original representations. Rather, our results illustrate where children and parents choose to focus their attention during retrieval. The data also describe the types of information most central to parents and children when they talk about emotion. To understand the veridical nature of these memories, we need to undertake more studies dealing with the on-line experience and representation of an emotional event.

REFERENCES

Bartlett, F. C. (1932). *Remembering*. Cambridge: Cambridge University Press.

Bohannon, J. H., & Symons, V. L. (1992). Flashbulb memories: Confidence, consistency, and quantity. In E. Winograd & U. Neisser (Eds.), *Affect and accuracy in recall: Studies of flashbulb memories* (pp. 65–91). New York: Cambridge University Press.

Brewer, W. (1992). The theoretical and empirical status of the flashbulb memory hypothesis. In E. Winograd & U. Neisser (Eds.), *Affect and accuracy in recall: Studies of flashbulb memories* (pp. 274–305). New York: Cambridge University Press.

Ceci, S. J., & Bruck, M. (1993). Suggestibility of the child witness: A historical review and synthesis. *Psychological Bulletin, 113*(3), 1–36.

Christianson, S. (1992). *Handbook of emotion and memory: Research and theory.* Hillsdale, NJ: Erlbaum.

Conway, M. (1990). Conceptual representation of emotions: The role of autobiographical memories. In K. J. Gihooly, M. T. G. Keane, R. H. Logie, & G. Edros (Eds.), *Lines of thinking* (Vol. 2, pp. 133–143). Chichester: Wiley.

Doris, J. (1991). *The suggestibility of children's recollections.* Washington, DC: American Psychological Association.

Fivush, R., & Hudson, J. (1990). *Knowing and remembering in young children.* Hillsdale, NJ: Erlbaum.

Folkman, S., & Lazarus, R. (1990). Coping and emotion. In N. L. Stein, B. Leventhal, & T. Trabasso (Eds.), *Psychological and biological approaches to emotion* (pp. 313–332). Hillsdale, NJ: Erlbaum.

Folkman, S., & Stein, N. L. (1992a, August). *Missing pieces in the coping puzzle.* Paper presented at annual meeting of the American Psychological Association, Washington, DC.

Folkman, S., & Stein, N. L. (1992b, September). *Formulation and reappraisal of goals in naturally occurring stressful events: Antecedents and consequences.* Paper presented at NICHHD Conference, Bethesda, MD.

Harber, K. D., & Pennebaker, J. W. (1992). Overcoming traumatic memories. In S. Christianson (Ed.), *Handbook of emotion and memory: Research and theory* (pp. 359–387). Hillsdale, NJ: Erlbaum.

Lazarus, R., & Folkman, S. (1984). *Stress, appraisal, and coping.* New York: Springer.

Liwag, M., & Stein, N. L. (1993). *Children's memory for emotional events: The importance of retrieval strategies.* Manuscript submitted for review.

Mandler, G. (1982). The structure of value: Accounting for taste. In M. S. Clark & S. T. Fiske (Eds.), *Affect and cognition: 17th Annual Carnegie Symposium on Cognition* (pp. 3–36). Hillsdale, NJ: Erlbaum.

Mandler, G. (1984). *Mind and body: Psychology of emotion and stress.* New York: Norton.

Mandler, J. (1984). *Stories, scripts, and scenes: Aspects of schema theory.* Hillsdale, NJ: Erlbaum.

Mandler, J. (1990). Recall of events by pre-verbal children. In A. Diamond (Ed.),

The development of neural bases of higher cognitive functions (pp. 485–516). New York: Academy of Sciences.

Mason, M. (1991). A judicial dilemma: Expert witness testimony in child sex abuse cases. *Journal of Psychiatry and Law,* fall–winter, pp. 185–219.

Nelson, K. (1993). The psychological and social origins of autobiographical memory. *Psychological Science, 4*(1), 7–14.

Stein, N. L., & Wade, E. (1993). *Children's understanding of real-life and hypothetical emotional experience.* Manuscript submitted for review.

Stein, N. L., & Jewett, J. (1986). A conceptual analysis of the meaning of basic negative emotions: Implications for a theory of development. In C. E. Izard & P. Read (Eds.), *Measurement of emotions in infants and children* (Vol. 2, pp. 238–267). New York: Cambridge University Press.

Stein, N. L., & Levine, L. (1987). Thinking about feelings: The development and use of emotional knowledge. In R. E. Snow & M. Farr (Eds.), *Aptitude, learning, and instruction: Vol. 3. Cognition, conation, and affect* (pp. 165–197). Hillsdale, NJ: Erlbaum.

Stein, N. L., & Levine, L. (1989). The causal organization of emotion knowledge: A developmental study. *Cognition and Emotion, 3*(4), 343–378.

Stein, N. L., & Levine, L. (1990). Making sense out of emotional experience: The representation and use of goal-directed knowledge. In N. L. Stein, B. Leventhal, & T. Trabasso (Eds.), *Psychological and biological approaches to emotion* (pp. 45–73). Hillsdale, NJ: Erlbaum.

Stein, N. L., & Miller, C. A. (1990). I win–you lose: The development of argumentative thinking. In J. Voss, D. Perkins, & J. Segal (Eds.), *Informal reasoning and instruction* (pp. 265–290). Hillsdale, NJ: Erlbaum.

Stein, N. L., & Trabasso, T. (1989). Children's understanding of changing emotional states. In C. Saarni & P. Harris (Eds.), *The development of emotional understanding* (pp. 50–77). New York: Cambridge University Press.

Stein, N. L., & Trabasso, T. (1992). The organization of emotional experience: Creating links among emotion, thinking, language and intentional action [Special issue]. *Cognition and Emotion, 6*(3/4), 225–244.

Stein, N., Trabasso, T., & Liwag, M. (1991, April). *Children and parents' memory for real life emotional events: Conditions for convergence and polarization.* Paper presented at the biennial conference of the Society for Research in Child Development, Seattle.

Stein, N. L., Trabasso, T., & Liwag, M. (1993). The representation and organization of emotional experience: Unfolding the emotion episode. In M. Lewis & J. Haviland (Eds.), *Handbook of emotion* (pp. 279–300). New York: Guilford.

Stein, N. L., Wright, A., Calicchia, D., & Bernas, R. (1993, March). *Learning to compromise: The effects of initial knowledge states on the resolution of conflict.* Paper presented at the biennial conference of the Society for Research in Child Development, New Orleans.

Trabasso, T., Stein, N. L., & Johnson, L. R. (1981). Children's knowledge of events: A causal analysis of story structure. In G. Bower (Ed.), *Learning and motivation* (Vol. 15, pp. 237–281). New York: Academic Press.

Winograd, E., & Neisser, U. (Eds.). (1992). *Affect and accuracy in recall: Studies of flashbulb memories.* New York: Cambridge University Press.

Epilogue

Further Directions

Variations in the Use of Future-Oriented Processes

Robert N. Emde

This volume provides the groundwork for a new way of thinking about psychological meaning. Future-oriented processes are at least equal in significance to past-oriented processes for guiding our coherent sense of what matters in the present. Future-oriented processes are fundamental aspects of *development,* and we can remind ourselves that "development" is a dynamic construct that in itself has as much to do with looking ahead as with looking behind. Yet, as the editors state in their introduction, there is a profound paradox in our society's attention to the future. Interest in the future is pervasive, yet we have had little conceptual framework for thinking about it. Future-oriented processes have not received anywhere near the same attention in theory or research as have past-oriented and present-oriented processes.

This book attempts to set a new course. Because there is so much that is new in summarizing and connecting formulations about future-oriented processes, it focuses on basic areas. Still, an implicit theme is that future-oriented processes are significant in our lives because of their "use." Future-oriented processes are basic and pervasive human biopsychosocial capacities. They do not suddenly appear as a class of behaviors at a certain time in either ontogeny (Rumbaugh chapter) or development (Benson), nor do they usually require task-specific features for their activation (Bidell and Fischer). Variations in future-oriented processes appear to be more in their "use."

Doors have been opened by the contributions here, and many productive questions remain to be explored. We have seen glimpses of a new field from the developmental perspectives of cognition, neurobiology, language acquisition, and social interactions. The overwhelming impression from reading this volume is that there are many "future directions" for the field of future-oriented processes. I would like to mention two such directions that are not emphasized. Both concern variations in use, one according to life-span issues, the other according to issues of development and psychopathology.

Life-span variations in adult future orientations are well known and are documented in our novels and biographies, but they have been little studied. We might first think of that aspect of life that most directly concerns an orientation to the future—parenting. There are many variations in how adults form expectations about taking on the parental role (Cowan & Cowan, 1992) and in how much pregnant adolescents or middle-aged adults think about the way their lives will change once they become parents. Variations in the future orientations of parenting are reflected in differing beliefs and sets of expectations about children's development and the roles they will assume in adulthood. Variations in parenting expectations of this sort are profound and can be pervasive determinants of behavior beginning in infancy (see discussions in Sameroff & Fiese, 1992). LeVine (1988) has discussed such matters from the point of view of cultural anthropology. Agrarian cultures, for example, can be contrasted with urban-industrial cultures. According to LeVine's observations, agrarian cultures are concerned with survival in the midst of high infant mortality and are oriented toward the child's needed contribution to the economic well-being of the family. They therefore have different sets of observed behaviors in infancy than do urban-industrial cultures. The latter are less concerned with infant survival and have longer-term orientations for the child making a life outside the family; observed parenting behaviors in infancy therefore show more emphasis on the communication of learning skills and on affiliation behaviors (LeVine, 1988). More research is needed to understand the correlates and consequences of variations in child rearing according to parents' beliefs about the child's future. A related set of questions has to do with variations in life-span attitudes about posterity. Major variations exist among individuals, groups, and cultures with respect to planning for one's children after one is dead.

Everyday experience indicates that there is considerable variation among individuals with respect to timetables in life. Timetables differ in adult life as they do during early childhood (see vivid examples of the latter in Benson, this volume). Some adults have children early, some later, some adults retire early, and some later. A recent novel (*Einstein's*

Dreams; Lightman, 1993) portrays how the young wish to speed up time whereas the old wish to slow it down, and how their subjective experiences, correspondingly, are that time moves too slow or too fast. We might ask other questions. How are variations in such future-oriented processes work graded, role graded, age graded, and culture guided? Are there systematic variations that can be understood in the newly emerging field of "cultural psychology" (Shweder, 1991)? What about biological rhythms in future-oriented processes? What about circadian and ultradian rhythms of hunger, sleep/wakefulness, attention, rest/activity and other functions throughout the life span? Does the organizing influence of environment (the influence of environmental time givers or *Zeitgebers* such as light/dark cycles and social routine cycles) tend to change? Does the organizing influence of biology change across the life span?

Imagination and play, although not dealt with in the contributions of this volume, are important aspects of life that have to do with future-oriented processes. As Bruce Pennington has pointed out (personal communication), play is a characteristic of social animals that has been seen as practice for future social roles and is most elaborate in mammals with the largest relative brain sizes. Play involves simulation and scenario spinning, and in fact theories about the future in science, fiction, or philosophy involve playful simulations. We know that the role of play and imagination changes in dramatic ways over the life span. Interestingly, Singer and Singer (1990) refer to the ages of 4 and 5 years as the "high season of play." There are many unstudied questions, however, concerning variations in imagination, fantasy, and creativity across the life span. In a related vein, what about life-span variations in the use of those future-oriented "signal affects" that are part of an individual's psychological coping and defensive operations (Emde, 1980a,b; Freud, 1926; Lazarus, 1991)?

What about individual differences in one's "having a stake" in future-oriented processes? Linkages are now being explored between the early development of future-oriented processes and individual differences in self-reports of parental beliefs and family practices (Benson, this volume). The matter of individual differences reminds us of still another area of investigative opportunity, that of development and psychopathology. Psychodynamic clinical work has neglected thinking about the future. Psychological meaning has often been regarded largely in terms of the present, as guided by a wider context of the past, especially the past of repeated intimate relationships. Important as such considerations are, psychological meaning is necessarily embedded in terms of a present that is guided by the anticipation of what lies ahead. We look ahead in order to guide our steps, and if we look behind us too much we will not travel far and we will stumble. Interestingly, *all psychopathology* has the characteristic effect of constricting the range of one's possibilities for development and of influencing one's sense of the future. Psychopathology reflects rigid patterns of stereotypic functioning that do not allow flexible adaptation to new situations or contexts. Some syndromes of disorder, however, have more specific features that involve future-oriented processes. Depressive disorders involve a weighty sense of the future, and in extremes they involve a sense of hopelessness. Anxiety disorders involve worrying—preoccupations with immediate and later consequences of one's predicament and potential actions. Worrying is a future-oriented process par excellence. Conduct disorders involve impulsiveness, wherein the consequences of transactions are not sufficiently taken into account. Attention deficit disorders could also be mentioned in terms of not being able to attend to what comes next and to organize oneself in the midst of a patterned flow of stimulus activity. One could go on with other disorders throughout the life span, but I believe the point is made about the importance of studying future-oriented processes in psychopathology.

Rogoff and her colleagues, in their contribution, have touched on important cultural contributions to future-oriented processes. This stimulates me, as a clinician interested in early developmental processes, to think about variations in the coconstruction and "socialization" of future-oriented processes in differing environments. What about those environments that generate apathy and alienation? And what about developmental processes and individual differences in these processes in children experiencing continued exposure to chronic community violence and poverty? What about those terribly difficult environments where children and parents do not believe they have a future (Garbarino, 1990; Kotlowitz, 1991)? What kinds of helpful plans can be mobilized on behalf of children, youth, and adults in such horrible circumstances?

These are some of the questions that come into view. Future-oriented processes most certainly can be considered a basic domain of cognitive development, important throughout life, but variations in their use and their consequences for mental health are unknown. The thinking presented in this volume is likely to move us forward and guide us as we tackle these and still other questions that we have yet to envision.

A final coda about questions. I am aware that I have been stimulated to ask a lot of questions in this epilogue. Questioning involves future-oriented processes and can be regarded either as positive (the excitement and the pleasure of being surprised) or as negative (the anticipated discomfort and distress of being disconnected). Both negative and positive emotions can be aroused because questioning challenges the meaning of the past in the practiced present, and questioning often challenges our values. These are matters of no small consequence. Socrates was celebrated by some of his contemporaries and condemned by many others, ultimately taking hemlock as a result of his lifelong devotion to relentless questioning. Questions often challenge what one has a stake in. They are inherently discomforting to some degree, especially when they are without signposts. The authors of the volume have courage, especially if they continue with their questioning in order to provide signposts for the rest of us within the new interdisciplinary field of future-oriented processes.

REFERENCES

Cowan, C. P., & Cowan, P. A. (1992). *When partners become parents: The big life change for couples.* New York: Basic Books.

Emde, R. N. (1980a). Toward a psychoanalytic theory of affect: I. The organizational model and its propositions. In S. Greenspan & G. Pollock (Eds.), *The course of life: Psychoanalytic contributions toward understanding personality development: Vol. 1. Infancy and early childhood* (pp. 63–83). Washington, DC: U.S. Government Printing Office.

Emde, R. N. (1980b). Toward a psychoanalytic theory of affect: II. Emerging models of emotional development in infancy. In S. Greenspan & G. Pollock (Eds.), *The course of life: Psychoanalytic contributions toward understanding personality development: Vol. 1. Infancy and early childhood* (pp. 85–112). Washington, DC: U.S. Government Printing Office.

Freud, S. (1926). Inhibitions, symptoms, and anxiety. In *The standard edition of the complete psychological works of Sigmund Freud* (J. Strachey, Ed. and Trans.) (Vol. 20, pp. 77–175). London: Hogarth Press.

Garbarino, J. (1990, November). *Community violence and child development: Coping and resilience in conditions of chronic danger.* Opening address at conference on Community Violence and Children's Development: Research and Clinical Implications, sponsored by NIMH and Washington School of Psychiatry.

Kotlowitz, A. (1991). *There are no children here: The story of two boys growing up in the other America.* New York: Doubleday.

Lazarus, R. S. (1991). *Emotion and adaptation.* New York: Oxford University Press.

LeVine, R. A. (1988). Human parental care: Universal goals, cultural strategies, individual behavior. In R. A. LeVine, P. M. Miller, & M. M. West (Eds.), *Parental behavior in diverse societies. New Directions in Child Development, 40,* 3–12.

Lightman, A. (1993). *Einstein's dreams.* New York: Pantheon.

Sameroff, A. J., & Fiese, B. H. (1992). Family representations of development. In I. E. Siegel, A. V. McGillicuddy-Delisi, & J. Goodnow (Eds.), *Parental belief systems* (pp. 347–369). Hillsdale, NJ: Erlbaum.

Schweder, R. A. (1991). *Thinking through cultures: Expeditions in cultural psychology.* Cambridge: Harvard University Press.

Singer, D. G., & Singer, J. L. (1990). *The house of make-believe: Children's play and developing imagination.* Cambridge: Harvard University Press.

Contributors

Jacquelyn Baker-Sennett
Department of Educational Psychology and Special Education
2125 Main Mall
University of British Columbia
Vancouver, BC V6T 1Z4

Elizabeth Bates
Center for Research in Language 0526
University of California, San Diego
La Jolla, California 92093-0526

Janette B. Benson
Department of Psychology
University of Denver
2155 South Race Street
Denver, Colorado 80208

Karen F. Berman
National Institute of Mental Health
St. Elizabeth's Hospital
WAW Building
Washington, DC 20032

Thomas Bidell
School of Education
Boston College
Chestnut Hill, Massachusetts 02167

Jeffrey Elman
Center for Research in Language 0526
University of California, San Diego
La Jolla, California 92093-0526

Robert N. Emde
Department of Psychiatry, Box C-269
University of Colorado Health Sciences Center
4200 East Ninth Avenue
Denver, Colorado 80262

Kurt Fischer
Department of Human Development
Harvard Graduate School of Education
Larson Hall 703
Appian Way
Cambridge, Massachusetts 02138

James Gold
National Institute of Mental Health
St. Elizabeth's Hospital
WAW Building
Washington, DC 20032

Terry Goldberg
National Institute of Mental Health
St. Elizabeth's Hospital
WAW Building
Washington, DC 20032

Marshall M. Haith
Department of Psychology
University of Denver
2155 South Race Street
Denver, Colorado 80208

Claes von Hofsten
Department of Psychology
University of Umeå
S-901 87 Umeå
Sweden

David Klahr
Department of Psychology
Carnegie Mellon University
Pittsburgh, Pennsylvania 15213

Ping Li
Department of Psychology
Chinese University of Hong Kong
Shatin, Hong Kong

Maria D. Liwag
Department of Psychology
University of Chicago
5848 South University Avenue
Chicago, Illinois 60637

Eugene Matusov
Department of Psychology
University of California, Santa Cruz
Santa Cruz, California 95064

Michael Ondrejko
Department of Psychology
University of Denver
2155 South Race Street
Denver, Colorado 80208

Bruce F. Pennington
Department of Psychology
University of Denver
2155 South Race Street
Denver, Colorado 80208

J. Steven Reznick
Department of Psychology
Yale University
Box 208205
New Haven, Connecticut 06520-8205

Ralph J. Roberts Jr.
Department of Psychology
University of Denver
2155 South Race Street
Denver, Colorado 80208

Barbara Rogoff
Department of Psychology
University of California, Santa Cruz
Santa Cruz, California 95064

Duane M. Rumbaugh
Language Research Center
Departments of Psychology and Biology
Georgia State University
Atlanta, Georgia 30303

E. Sue Savage-Rumbaugh
Language Research Center
Departments of Biology and Psychology
Georgia State University
Atlanta, Georgia 30303

Nancy L. Stein
Department of Psychology
University of Chicago
5848 South University Avenue
Chicago, Illinois 60637

Tom Trabasso
Department of Psychology
University of Chicago
5848 South University Avenue
Chicago, Illinois 60637

David A. Washburn
Language Research Center
Department of Psychology
Georgia State University
Atlanta, Georgia 30303

Daniel R. Weinberger
National Institute of Mental Health
St. Elizabeth's Hospital
WAW Building
Washington, DC 20032

Author Index

Page numbers in italic indicate figures or tables.

Subject Index

Page numbers in *italic* indicate figures or tables.